Russian
Peasant
Women

Russian Peasant Women

EDITED BY

Beatrice Farnsworth

Lynne Viola

New York   Oxford
OXFORD UNIVERSITY PRESS
1992

Oxford University Press

Oxford   New York   Toronto
Delhi   Bombay   Calcutta   Madras   Karachi
Petaling Jaya   Singapore   Hong Kong   Tokyo
Nairobi   Dar es Salaam   Cape Town
Melbourne   Auckland

and associated companies in
Berlin   Ibadan

Published by Oxford University Press, Inc.,
200 Madison Avenue, New York, New York 10016

Oxford is a registered trademark of Oxford University Press

Library of Congress Cataloging-in-Publication Data
Russian peasant women / edited by Beatrice Farnsworth and Lynne Viola.
p. cm.   ISBN 0-19-506693-6   ISBN 0-19-506694-4 (pbk.)
1. Rural women—Soviet Union—History.
2. Women farmers—Soviet Union—History.
3. Women—Soviet Union—History.
4. Peasantry—Soviet Union—History.
5. Soviet Union—Rural conditions.
I. Farnsworth, Beatrice.   II. Viola, Lynne.
HQ1662.R875   1992
305.5'633'0947—dc20   91-15573

9 8 7 6 5 4 3 2 1

Printed in the United States of America
on acid-free paper

Acknowledgments

The editors would like to acknowledge the assistance and advice provided by the following friends and colleagues: Barbara Clements, Barbara Engel, Sheila Fitzpatrick, Stephen Frank, Wendy Goldman, Tim Mixter, Rochelle Ruthchild, Kira Stevens, and William Wagner. We are especially pleased to acknowledge the many kindnesses and the support provided by Nancy Lane of Oxford University Press. David Roll and Cathy Frierson gave their time to selecting a picture for the cover. We thank them. Finally, a special word of thanks is due to Tracy McDonald, a graduate student in the Department of History at the University of Toronto, for her able assistance in preparing the manuscript.

Contents

I / Peasant Women
   Before the Revolution

There is no full-length history of Russian peasant women in either Russian or English. Aleksandra Efimenko's pioneering, "Krest'ianskaia zhenshchina" (Peasant Woman), in Russian is the closest approximation to a nineteenth-century study.[1] The student seeking information on women has had to find it piecemeal, within larger works on the peasantry and in scattered articles and conference papers. For those who do not read Russian, the subject of rural women is soon exhausted.

Western historians of the Soviet Union are late in coming to the topic of Russian peasant women—half of the key social group that constituted the majority of Russia's population until after World War II. Diplomacy and politics long dominated Western study of Russian history. In the 1970s, in what was then a significant departure from traditional fields, American scholars, influenced in part by the social movements of the 1960s and 1970s, turned to the study of Russian women, beginning their work generally in the area of intellectual history or biography. In the 1980s these scholars, following a path already taken by students of European history, moved to social history, focusing on working-class and peasant women.

The study of Russian peasant women remains at an early and intellectually exciting stage. In a real sense, the essays in this volume are original, encouraging us to look at Russian history in new and different ways and to question assumptions that the Revolution was a unique milestone in women's history.

Revolutions, Fernand Braudel suggests, are never really breaks in a country's civilization; rather, they are "surface flashes of light" that illuminate change already under way.[2] Soviet publicists have offered an opposite view. In a typical statement, I. I. Ansheles implied that until the Bolshevik Revolution rescued her with its liberating legislation, a peasant wife "was a slave to her husband in this [prerevolutionary] wicked time."[3]

Braudel's observation might be taken as the motif for our volume. Together, the essays show clearly the various forces—economic, social, and ideological—that shaped and transformed Russian peasant society, especially the changing position of women within it, from the 1860s onward. The collection demonstrates that while the Revolution affected the pace and direction of change, the process of change had begun well before 1917.

Indeed, a new periodization may be in order. Instead of viewing 1917 as the dramatic turning point in Russian society, we propose to look at the Revolution as part of a continuum.* The point at which we begin to look for incipient changes in the dynamics of the household and thus ultimately in peasant women's lives, might

---

*For purposes of editorial organization and division of labor, however, we have divided this volume at 1917.

be 1861, the time of emancipation, although even that great socioeconomic watershed was but part of a gradual transition in peasant life.[4]

Although the institution of serfdom had begun to erode well before 1861, the act accelerated the development of capitalist relations in the village. The expansion of nonagricultural employment that followed emancipation caused a weakening of the authority of the head of the family, the *bol'shak,* who traditionally presided over a household of married sons. The rate of family divisions increased, with sons establishing their own households. The dynamics of the household began to modify, albeit slowly and with regional variations.

How do we know? The student of peasant society, to be sure, is hampered by the lack of customary written records, diaries, letters, and memoirs. For written sources, the historian must turn primarily to the records of observers. In the case of the peasantry after 1861, such records are fairly abundant: *zemstvo* (district and provincial councils) statistics, the reports of ethnographers and rural doctors, foundling homes, government commissions, newspapers and journals, and, becoming more and more available in the Soviet Union, an enormous supply of archival materials from agricultural estate records and various state and social organizations. In some instances, as in folk songs, we can hear the peasant woman's own voice. Peasant township court records detail family disputes and occasionally reprint verbatim transcripts of cases. The authors of the essays in this collection, then, have a wealth of material on which to base their conclusions.

Implicit throughout the volume is the impact on peasant women of prerevolutionary industrial development, especially in the second half of the nineteenth century. The effects of industrial development varied by region, as Barbara Engel demonstrates in an informative article (which unfortunately was not available for us to reprint). Engel studied two districts of intense seasonal male outmigration in the province of Kostroma—Soligalich and Chukhloma—in which, long before emancipation, in response to declining agricultural opportunities in the village, peasants customarily sent their sons to the cities as early as age twelve, to learn a trade—carpentery, housepainting, barrel-making, coppersmithing, metalworking, joining, blacksmithing, and so on. The vast majority of the migrant workers married village girls, which ensured the maintenance of the family economy since the wife, in accordance with peasant custom, lived with her in-laws and worked in her husband's stead. Female seasonal migration was small scale, limited largely to women who accompanied husbands as cooks for communal apartments or workshops.

The existence of male outmigration significantly affected the nature of female life. On the positive side, wages provided by the absentee husband resulted in a higher level of economic well-being. Women became more literate as increasingly literate husbands, fathers, and brothers taught them to read. Elsewhere in Russia, in areas not marked by intense male outmigration, female literacy was generally low. For example, for the village population of Russia in 1897, the literacy rate was 25.2 percent for men and 9.8 percent for women.[5] In 1867 in Chukhloma, literacy for men was 33.9 percent; for women, 6.3 percent. By 1873, the rates were 63.2 percent for men and 16.6 percent for women. Female literacy in the outmigration area had more than doubled.[6]

Physical violence against women was reported to be relatively rare in comparison with that in other more sedentary regions where men were cruder, more ignorant, and more economically frustrated. Infant mortality for the Russian Empire, the highest in Europe—as Samuel Ramer indicates in his article in this collection—decreased because of better nourished mothers whose standard of living was higher than that of women in sedentary peasant areas. Almost half of the children in the latter regions died before they were five years old. Women ran the farms in the absence of husbands, served in village governments in their stead, and had greater control of their own lives.

On the negative side, outmigration increased a woman's physical burden and deprived her and her family of husband and father. In response presumably to greater stress, female alcoholism, generally absent in sedentary areas, became more common, a not unusual phenomenon in societies in which men were absent for long periods and women bore greater responsibility. A physician–chronicler in the Kostroma area reported, "Even in the inns and taverns these days the shrill, drunken voices of women drown out the hoarse bass notes of men."[7]

Other areas of Russia, though they did not experience the intense male outmigration of the Kostroma district, were also affected by industrialization. By the 1880s, household insufficiency had become common. Exhausted by centuries of primitive cultivation, the land could not provide the surplus necessary for taxes or food for the expanding peasant population. In many areas, wage labor became a necessity. The general consequences of the changing economy between the 1880s and 1914 was that women took increasing responsibility for working the land to free men for outside wage work. Where male wages were insufficient, women too sought wage labor, generally of a variety that could be combined with household and field obligations, such as knitting woolen gloves and stockings or unwinding cotton for factories. Women who lived in proximity to large cities supplied agricultural and dairy products, their wage labor dependent on the availability of urban markets and factory putting-out systems. Over the years as peasant needs went unmet, increasing numbers of women left for the factories. As Rose Glickman points out, most women workers in Russian factories began life as peasants.

Developing industrialization affected peasant women not only by luring peasants to wage labor, but by encouraging family division, the *razdel,* which Cathy Frierson describes. The phenomenon of family division existed before emancipation, but in the decades after 1861 it steadily increased, facilitated by the ability of sons to earn wages on the side. The factor of outside wages created an "individualistic" state of mind as well as the practical means for married sons to separate more easily from the parental household even before the death of the father, the *bol'shak.*

Much still eludes us about the inner dynamics of the extended peasant family, the multigenerational household consisting of two or three married sons and their parents. Historians do not even agree about how long this was the dominant family form in rural Russia or whether, by the time of emancipation, the nuclear family had not, in fact, begun to prevail.[8] We do not know whether the complex family tended to be blended, functioning as a unit, or whether it is better described as several small families coexisting more or less peevishly.

Recent historical research emphasizes the lack of cooperation, the quarrelsome and vituperative nature of peasant society (marked by intergenerational conflict), and the oppression of serf over serf.[9] Women lived no more harmoniously than men. The quarrels of sisters-in-law, mothers-in-law, and daughters-in-law ranked high among the multiple causes of family division. Anecdotes abound regarding the separatist tendencies of rural wives who, according to observers, were more individualistic than men and less inclined to join family activity. One commentator described how women in multifamily households would wash only the section of the table where their own families ate. Women, by the second half of the nineteenth century, reportedly were turning their energies toward convincing husbands to leave the parental household.[10] Certainly women benefited on more than one level from family division. They fared better in regard to inheritance of property in the resultant small nuclear family. Consider, first, the situation of family members in the multiple-family household upon the death of the *bol'shak*. According to the custom of most areas of central Russia, in an extended family, male members at the time of a *bol'shak*'s death received equal shares of the movable and immovable property. The widow of the *bol'shak* usually received about one-tenth or one-seventh of the property, while an unmarried daughter did not inherit if she had brothers. Instead, she received support until her marriage and frequently a dowry—a moral rather than a legal obligation on the part of a brother.[11] The occasional spinster daughter over age thirty might receive a share equal to that of her brother.[12]

A daughter-in-law in an extended family customarily became marginal upon her husband's death. No role was more humiliating than that of a young widow in a multiple-family household. Defenseless without a husband, she might be treated not as a family member but as a *rabotnitsa,* a working woman.[13]

A childless widow who had lived briefly with her husband received no property. She might return to her parents, leave for wage labor, or continue to seek shelter with her in-laws.[14] In some areas, if she had lived with her husband for a long time, she earned a right to her husband's property by her own labor.[15] If she had sons, she received her husband's share of property on their behalf. A widow with only daughters generally got nothing from the family property. Or she might receive a little grain or cattle to support her daughters at the discretion of her father-in-law.[16] With the introduction of township courts in 1861, widows sometimes received a share of their husband's property on behalf of their daughters.[17]

In the nuclear family, however, a widow inherited as her husband's co-worker.[18] Yet her situation could still be complicated by in-laws. A father-in-law, even after his son had separated from the parental family, might claim the property, offering to take in and support the son's widow. A court was likely to deny his request if the widow had lived with her husband in a long marriage. Even if the marriage was short, but the widow had contributed her labor, she would inherit the property.[19]

The small family may have improved a woman's status in nonmaterial ways as well. In a nuclear family, relations between husband and wife reportedly were more equal, the wife achieving new significance as she became her husband's sole partner, whose help was essential to his economic survival.[20] A woman might, in fact, be burdened with more domestic and farm work in a nuclear than a multiple family, but she worked independently, able to determine her own domestic labor, free of a mother-in-law who allocated tasks and a father-in-law who controlled the purse strings.

One observer, writing in the nineteenth century, went so far as to say that the destruction of the extended patrimonial family, whose demise she reported already under way, was the first step in the liberation of peasant women.[21] As evidence that the multiple family was declining, she noted that peasant women did not openly object to their roles except in situations where the large, extended family was already on shaky ground. Female protest in postemancipation township courts may thus have been a sign that the patrimonial family in the countryside was beginning to lose its power, a victim of changing economic forces.[22]

The question of a wife's role in instigating family division is significant because it suggests the degree of her influence within a marriage. On some matters, such as the quality of a peasant woman's life and her actual status in the family, there is no agreement among historians, just as the related question of the degree of economic well-being of the peasantry in the late nineteenth century eludes consensus.[23] Were there a significant number of assertive women? Or were women generally subject, crushed by the misery of family oppression and beaten by husbands and in-laws with the tacit approval of rural society? Two poles of the argument are presented here by Glickman and by Beatrice Farnsworth.[24]

Theoretically, peasants were governed by customary, not imperial, law. But the nature of customary law is difficult to define, since it incorporated imperial law to some unspecified degree.[25] A kind of collective mentality, customary law was particularly elusive because it varied by locality; generalizations about the extent of the influence of imperial law are therefore unreliable. For example, in the first half of the nineteenth century, according to imperial law, husbands were forbidden for the first time to beat their wives. Dorothy Atkinson claims that these provisions did not directly affect the peasantry or the peasant practice of wife-beating, which she, like Glickman, believes was sanctioned by customary law.[26] Farnsworth presents another view, pointing out that although peasants technically were not subject to imperial law, peasant township court decisions, as recorded by scribes after the emancipation, contained occasional references to Volume x in the Code of Civil Law and to the law forbidding the arbitrary beating of one's own wife.

The question of corporal punishment further illustrates the difficulties in determining the extent to which imperial law influenced customary law. A Senate decree of April 17, 1863, forbade corporal punishment of women.[27] In some peasant township courts, the law was upheld; in others, it was not.[28] Although the laws against flogging were not scrupulously observed, some women found the prohibition a means of protection against the arbitrary exercise of family and community power. Consider a case in 1868 in Mitinskii township of Moscow province. After a woman was flogged by the court for leaving her husband three times, the case was investigated. Although the court denied knowledge of the law against flogging women, the investigators established that the edition of the *Moskovskiya Gubernskiya Vedomosti* (Moscow Province Gazette) in which the prohibition was announced had reached the township in 1863. As a result, the former judges and elder were convicted, the three judges for decreeing the flogging in violation of the law and the elder for carrying out the punishment.[29]

The initial reaction of students of the prerevolutionary Russian peasantry to signs of social progress is surprise. Understandably, the tendency is to highlight innovation. It would be a mistake, however, to focus too much on the positive and exaggerate its general significance. We would be wrong to let indicators of change cause us to lose sight of the squalor of peasant women's lives. Examples abound of superstitious peasant women living in illiterate, miserable subordination. As Ramer points out, for most of the rural population diet was insufficient, housing over-crowded, and clothing inadequate. Elemental hygiene and sanitary measures were largely ignored or unknown.

Yet, withal, we still hear of peasant women who exercised rights and personal initiative, who somehow energized themselves to go to court, protesting an in-law's economic exploitation or brutality, a husband's beatings, or the chicanery of a neighbor. Young women sometimes broke engagements, casting doubt on the stereotype that peasant women were invariably forced into economically arranged, loveless marriages. Mothers as heads of families exerted authority, contracting for sons to be apprenticed to learn trades, and women made separation agreements enabling them to leave unhappy marriages.[30]

As we trace the transformation of their status and role from the mid-nineteenth century to the present, we ought not to generalize about the nature of peasant women. Women in prerevolutionary rural Russia, depending in part on region, lived a variety of lives, subordinate and assertive, resistant to and embracing modernity. In the essays that follow, the student will find evidence to support diverse supposi-tions about peasant women. Clearly their lives were not static. The revolutions of 1917 brought legal improvements in a woman's status, but they were in the direction of changes set in motion generations earlier.

Notes

1. Aleksandra Efimenko, "Krest'ianskaia zhenshchina," *Delo* no. 2 (1873): 57–99, 173–207. Also in Russian is Dmitrii N. Zhbankov, *Bab'ia storona* (Kostroma, 1891).

2. Fernand Braudel, "Time, History, and the Social Sciences," in Fritz Stern, ed., *The Varieties of History* (New York, 1972), p. 420.

3. I. I. Ansheles, *Brak, sem'ia i razvod* (Moscow, 1925), p. 16.

4. For the view that a demographic transition was under way well before the emancipa-tion of 1861, see P. Czap, "Marriage and the Peasant Joint Family in the Era of Serfdom," in David Ransel, ed., *The Family in Imperial History* (Urbana, Ill., 1978), p. 122.

5. A. G. Rashin, *Naselenie Rossii za 100 let* (Moscow, 1956), p. 293.

6. Barbara Engel, "The Women's Side: Male Outmigration and the Family Economy in Kostroma Province," *Slavic Review* 45, no. 2 (Summer 1986): 266.

7. Zhbankov, *Bab'ia storona*, p. 2.

8. V. A. Aleksandrov contends that the small family was the predominant form "from the sixteenth right up to the middle of the nineteenth century," suggesting that family divi-sions were a well-established tradition in rural Russia. V. A. Aleksandrov, *Obychnoe pravo krepostnoi derevni Rossii* (XVIII–nachalo XIX v) (Moscow, 1984), p. 68. Steven Hoch, basing his conclusions on research on estates in Tambov province, and Peter Czap, working on estates in Riazan province, contend that the multigenerational, complex, patriarchal household was intact until emancipation. See Steven Hoch, *Serfdom and Social Control. The Village of Petrovskoe* (Chicago, 1986), and Peter Czap, "'A Large Family: The Peasant's

Greatest Wealth': Serf Households in Mishino, Russia, 1814–1858," in Richard Wall, ed., *Family Forms in Historic Europe* (Cambridge, 1983), pp. 105–51.

9. See especially, Hoch, *Serfdom and Social Control,* pp. 128, 135–36, 188–89, and, for analysis of peasant's short temper, Moshe Lewin, *The Making of the Soviet System* (New York, 1985), p. 53.

10. Efimenko, "Krest'ianskaia zhenshchina," p. 66; I. N. Milogolova, "Semeinye razdely v russkoi poreformennoi derevne," *Vestnik Moskovskogo Universiteta,* no. 6 (1987): 40.

11. V. F. Mukhin, *Obychnyi poriadok nasledovaniia u krest'ian* (St. Petersburg, 1888), pp. 134–37.

12. Milogolova, "Semeinye razdely", p. 45.

13. Efimenko, "Krest'ianskaia zhenshchina," p. 72; Mukhin, *Obychnyi poriadok,* pp. 15–16.

14. Efimenko, "Krest'ianskaia zhenshchina," p. 73; Mukhin, *Obychnyi poriadok,* pp. 15–16, 249.

15. Efimenko, "Krest'ianskaia zhenshchina," p. 14.

16. Mukhin, *Obychnyi poriadok,* pp. 145–46.

17. Ibid., p. 266.

18. Ibid., pp. 15–16.

19. In one decision, a childless widow received the home disputed by her father-in-law, since the home was built after the household division and with the help of her dowry. Efimenko, "Krest'ianskaia zhenshchina," pp. 97–98.

20. Ibid., pp. 59, 67–71.

21. Ibid., p. 67.

22. Ibid., pp. 60–61.

23. For controversy over the question of economic well-being, see a review of recent scholarship in Ben Ekloff, "Ways of Seeing: Recent Anglo-American Studies of the Russian Peasant (1861–1914)," *Jahrbucher für Geschichte Osteuropas* 36, no. 1 (1988): 60–61, 68–70.

24. For historiographic debate over the peasant woman's family status, see ibid., pp. 70–72.

25. A sympathetic student of the township courts, S. V. Pakhman, wrote in 1877 about the decisions of the courts: "There undoubtedly lies at the base of every decision some kind of universally recognized rules or opinions," but the application of these rules depended on subjectivity, the concrete particulars of a case, and the people involved. As cited in Peter Czap, "Peasant-Class Courts and Peasant Customary Justice in Russia, 1861–1912," *Journal of Social History* 1 (Winter 1967): 167.

26. Dorothy Atkinson, Alexander Dallin, and Gail W. Lapidus, eds., *Women in Russia* (Stanford, Calif., 1977), p. 33.

27. *Polnoe sobranie zakonov Rossiiskoi imperii* (St. Petersburg, 1866), vol. 38, p. 353.

28. In twenty-six of forty-four townships in the four provinces of Moscow, Iaroslavl, Tambov, and Kostroma, local laws forbade the flogging in court of women, minors, and those over age fifty (sometimes sixty). Peasants did not always obey the law, but flogging of peasant women by the courts was rare even in townships where the practice was not explicitly forbidden. Occasionally in towns where it was forbidden, it did occur despite the law. See *Trudy Komissii po preobrazovaniiu volostnykh sudov,* 7 vols. (St. Petersburg, 1874), 5: 321.

29. Ibid., 2:511–12.

30. For an example of a mother entering into a contract for her son, see Zhbankov, *Bab'ia storona,* p. 111.

1 / The Peasant Way of Life

MARY MATOSSIAN

Mary Matossian, professor of European social history at the University of Maryland, provides an overview of the Russian peasantry on the eve of emancipation. Her article depicts the life of the average peasant family and provides, as well, a wealth of detail concerning regional variations in village and farmstead, peasant houses, allocation of space, utilization of land, and peasant custom regarding food and dress. The fundamental experience for the peasant was family and community. Village life was insular: "Moscow and the Tsar were far away." Every vital event in a family's life—marriage, birth, military draft, death—was a matter not only of common knowledge but of common concern. Much in the traditional way of life of the peasant community had symbolic significance, even the usual division of labor. The man plowing and sowing the fields was regarded as symbolic of the male role in sexual intercourse. Pagan symbols and folk belief mingled with Christianity to provide a curious spiritual amalgam. Without idealizing or romanticizing peasant life—indeed, Matossian points to intergenerational tensions that recent scholars have emphasized—the author shows how deep peasant communal patterns were, and by inference, why they persisted even after peasants left the village.

What follows is not a "realistic" picture of the Russian peasant way of life in the nineteenth century: it has little to say about the brutality and violence of the peasant world. Neither is it an "idealized" picture, in that the things described were rare or uncommon in peasant experience. Rather, this study is intended to provide a description of the peasant way of life under normal conditions around 1860, on the eve of emancipation. It is a time of neither unusual prosperity nor unusual deprivation. The village and family presented are neither unusually rich nor unusually poor, neither "backward" nor "progressive."

The Russian peasant way of life was full and abundant in its own way. Although the peasants were materially poor by our standards, their life was rich in symbols and rituals and in the drama of everyday life. It was a life of sweat and heartbreak, but it had its moments of peace and joy as well.

"The Peasant Way of Life" by Mary Matossian in Wayne S. Vucinich, ed., *The Peasant in Nineteenth-Century Russia* (Stanford, Calif.: Stanford University Press, 1968), pages 1–40, 288–89. Copyright © 1968 The Board of Trustees of the Leland Stanford Junior University. Reprinted by permission of the publishers, Stanford University Press.

Settlement Patterns and Housing

In the nineteenth century, before extensive railroad building, the villages of Russia were generally located near a good natural source of water: at the edge of a lake or river, or—in the south—along a ravine where spring water was available. The Great Russian villages varied in size from a few households in the far north to four hundred or more households in the south. The buildings were almost all built of weathered, unpainted logs, and the narrow, unpaved streets were often rivers of mud and filth in spring, summer, and fall. Trees and gardens around the houses were exceptional. And yet to its inhabitants, for whom it was the center of the universe, the village might be a beautiful place.[1]

> I love my country, but that love is odd:
> My reason has no part in it at all! . . .
> A well-stocked barn, a hut with a thatched roof,
> Carved shutters on a village window: these
> Are simple things in truth,
> But few can see them as my fond eye sees.
> MIKHAIL LERMONTOV (1841)

The layout of the Russian village might be one of several different types. The most ancient types, but relatively rare in the nineteenth century, were the cluster (*gneszovyi, kuchevyi*), free-form (*bezporiadochnyi*), and hollow-form (*krugovoi, zamknutyi*) types of settlement. The cluster type consisted of scattered nuclei, each of which was probably at one time inhabited by a kin group. Free-form villages developed in locations remote from space-defining rivers or roads, such as on the open steppe of the southern Ukraine. The hollow-form village was built around three or four sides of a hollow square or rectangle, in the center of which was a lake, a field, a common pasture, a church, or a marketplace.

The most typical village layout, as ancient as the first millennium A.D., was the linear type, its houses set in one or more lines along the bank of a lake, a river, or (rarely) a road. As the population of the village increased, new structures were added on lines running parallel or perpendicular to the original line.

The gridiron-type layout, with streets between rows of houses and sidestreets between clusters of houses, first appeared in the eighteenth century and became widespread only in the nineteenth. Most such villages were the result of government decrees from 1722 on intended to reduce the danger of devastating fires by the wider spacing of buildings. Frequently a village was reconstructed in this manner after having once burned down.

A Russian farm family normally lived in its own dwelling on a farmstead. The farmstead was usually rectangular in shape, with the living quarters of the family near the street. In the north Great Russian village it was characteristic for the shorter side of the house to run parallel to the street; in the south, the longer side. Besides family living quarters, a farmstead would ordinarily include a barn, a hayshed, and a kitchen garden. The northern and central Great Russian farmstead also had an *ovin* for drying sheaves before threshing, a *riga* (threshing barn), and a *gumno* (threshing floor). In the southern regions, grain was dried in the open air in sheaves and was more likely to be threshed in the open air. The northern Great Russian farmstead usually included a *bania* (steam bathhouse), but in the south the peasants did their bathing outdoors or on the family stove. Sometimes all the barns and sheds of the peasants were located on the edge of the village for greater fire protection, and the bathhouses were built as a separate group near the river. In villages where the population engaged in a great deal of handicraft work, special workshops would be found among the farmstead buildings.

Most peasant farmsteads had their own wells, but wells were communal in those villages with deep-lying subsoil water. Such commune wells became centers of village gossip: according to the Russian proverb, "Had wells but ears and tongues, not all the water they contain would put out the fire." In the streets of the village there were small ponds, and on the edge of the village large ponds for watering cattle, washing clothes, and bathing. In warm weather the peasants could bathe in rivers and lakes, but frequent cases of drowning made them cautious.

Apart from wells and ponds, the size and complexity of communal facilities varied a great deal in peasant settlements. A *derevnia* (small village or hamlet) had few such facilities; it was not administratively, economically, or sacramentally self-sufficient. The inhabitants of the *derevnia* went to a *selo* (large village or market town) to obtain the goods and services not available at home. Each *selo* had a number of satellite *derevni*. A *derevnia* did not have a church with resident clergy. A *selo* usually did, and the clergy periodically made a circuit of the satellite *derevni* to perform rituals.* The communal buildings of a *selo* might include a windmill or watermill, a tavern, a grain supply store, various shops, a dairy, a firehouse, a school, a workshop for extracting resin from coniferous trees, and a *volost'* [township] government office building.[2]

There were three basic types of peasant houses in nineteenth-century Russia: the north Great Russian *izba*, the south Great Russian *izba*, and the Ukrainian *khata*.

The north Great Russian *izba* was made of hewn logs as long as the serviceable part of tree trunks available in the area. In northern Russia the dwelling tended to be relatively large, since timber was plentiful and extended-type families were common there longer than in the south. Because of the severe winter climate the house was built high off the ground, its timber floor raised above ground level over a cellar (*podklet'*) one-and-one-half to three meters deep. The yard, barn, hayshed, *ovin*, *riga*, and other outbuildings were all covered by a single roof. Sometimes a small unheated frame of logs, the *klet*, was built in the yard. In winter it was used for storage; in warm weather a young married couple without an *izba* of their own could sleep there in privacy. The northern *izba* had a saddleback roof (pitched, with two slopes, to shed snow) and was covered with planks or shingles. The peasants cut windows in the facade of the *izba* and often added a balcony encircling the house at the level of the higher windows. They liked to decorate their window frames, shutters, and roofs with animal, bird, and geometric designs. Especially characteristic of this house was a pair of carved horses' heads (*parnye kon'ki*), facing in opposite directions, sticking up at the end of the roof ridge. These horses were

---

*However, a large old village in southern Russia without a church would sometimes be called a *selo*.

probably an ancient symbol of paired contrasting forces (light and dark, life and death) bound together in an ultimate unity. The horse symbol was also found inside the Great Russian peasant house, carved on the sleeping bench (*konik*) of the male head of the house. Since the care of horses, plowing with horses, and fighting on horseback were characteristic male functions in Russian culture, the horse appears to have been a symbol of masculine vitality. Thus if a Russian peasant was suffering a long death agony, someone in the family might go to the roof of the *izba* and break its ridge (*konëk*) to bring death.[3]

The south Great Russian *izba* was also built of hewn logs, but did not rise as high off the ground. It was usually built over a shallow cellar (*podpol'e*), for in this part of Russia there was little danger from floods and deep snows. Some houses had only a floor of beaten earth and no cellar, however. The southern *izba* usually had a hip roof (four slopes) for protection against strong winds. It was less richly decorated than the northern *izba,* and was more apt to be painted than carved. There was no massive roof covering the courtyard and outbuildings. All but the poorest peasants had a *klet* (for storage or summer sleeping) and a *seni* (an anteroom, used for storage or summer sleeping) attached to their *izba.*[4]

The third type of peasant house was the Ukrainian *khata*. It usually had a *seni* and less frequently a *komora*, equivalent to the *klet*. The walls of the *khata* were plastered and whitewashed, but underneath the plaster there were different kinds of construction. In the northern Ukraine the main construction material was wood, but in the southern Ukraine wood was used only for roof supports, and the walls were constructed of clay, stone, or chalk blocks. The *khata* was built without a cellar and had an earthen floor. Its roof had four slopes and was usually covered with straw thatching (less commonly with reeds, tile, or iron). The peasants often painted brightly colored designs on both the inner and outer whitewashed walls of the *khata.*[5]

The allocation of space in the main room of the Russian peasant home was strictly traditional. There were four regional patterns. In all four there were (1) a cooking corner, where the *pech'* (*pechka:* stove, oven) was located; (2) a *perednyi* (*sviati, krasnyi*) corner, where the icons were hung, guests were entertained, and the family dined on a whitewashed table; and (3) a sleeping corner.

The *pech'* occupied one-fourth to one-fifth of the space in the room. It was usually built of clay, but in the latter part of the nineteenth century many prosperous peasants built them of burnt brick. In the more primitive "black" *izba* of the poor, which survived here and there to the end of the nineteenth century, the *pech'* had no chimney: smoke was supposed to escape through the door or through a special opening in the wall, but since it often failed to do so, the interior became blackened. The *pech'* had many functions: not only did it heat the house and cook the food, but it was used for washing, for drying clothes and agricultural products, and for sleeping in cold weather. The placing of the stove determined the placing of the other elements in the room. The icon corner was always on a diagonal line from the stove.

The north and central Great Russian arrangement is shown in Figure 1.1. This layout was characteristic of the *izba* of the non-black-soil *gubernias* of European Russia and of Siberia. The *chulan,* an area to the right of the broken line next to the *pech'*, was considered the women's side of the house and was sometimes separated from the rest of the house by a curtain or wooden partition. (Names used in other regions for the *chulan* include *upech, sereda, kut', sholnush,* and *shomnusha.*) Here women prepared meals and kept their cooking supplies. A long cupboard, the *golbets* (*kazenka, karshina*), was built along the left side of the *pech'*. Under the *golbets* a stairway led down to the cellar.

From the left of the entrance to the side wall was a wide bench, fastened to the wall, on which the master of the house, and sometimes other men of the house, slept. It was often decorated with a carved horse's head and was known as the *konik*. Along the other three walls there were also benches, tightly fastened to the walls. Overhanging the benches, higher up the walls, were shelves (*polavoshniki*) on which small articles were kept.

In the rear of the house (where the stove and entrance were located) there extended a sleeping loft, or *polati,* from the stove to the side wall. The area under the *polati* was regarded as an "anteroom." Livestock were sometimes kept there in the coldest part of the winter. It was considered unmannerly for a stranger to pass beyond the *polati* without an invitation. If invited, he would be entertained in the front left of the house, near the icon corner, which was the "clean" quarter. Between the icon corner and the *polati* there were usually a loom and a spinning wheel facing the long bench on the left side wall. There the women passed the tedious winter days spinning, weaving, knitting, and sewing.[6]

The southeastern Great Russian variant of the interior arrangement is shown in Figure 1.2. The southwestern Great Russian variant is shown in Figure 1.3. The peasants illuminated all three types of *izba* by suspending from the ceiling beam a *svetets* (*luchnik, komin*), in which they could put a burning splinter (*luchina*).* Kerosene lamps were not ordinarily found in peasant homes until the late nineteenth century. The baby's cradle or *liulka* (*zybka, kolushka*) also hung from a ceiling beam.

The *izba* was usually equipped with a water barrel and dipper. The peasant washed not by plunging and rinsing, but by getting another person to pour water on his head and hands. More thorough bathing could be done in the bathhouse (*bania*), a log structure included in most north Russian farmsteads. In one corner of the *bania* was a *pech' kamenka,* a flueless dome made of stone masonry, sealed with clay, under which a fire was built. When the stones were hot, the peasants poured water over them until the *bania* was full of steam. At the sides of the *bania* were tiers of benches for the bathers to lie on. To remove dirt and stimulate circulation they beat each other with birch twigs. When it got too hot inside they ran out into the snow to cool off.

Russian ethnographic sources are discreetly silent about peasant excretory arrangements. Human waste was probably either collected in a bucket in the *izba* or deposited in a hole in the *seni*. Some peasants must have had outhouses. (Incidentally, cockroaches, lice, and bedbugs were standard equipment in an *izba*.)[7]

The fourth variant arrangement—the *khata*—was typical of western Great Russia (e.g., Smolensk *gubernia*), Belorussia, the Ukraine, and the Don and Kuban

---

*Or they might use an earthen saucer (*kazanets, zhirnik*) filled with animal fat and a wick inserted.

Basic plans of peasant houses
in nineteenth-century Russia

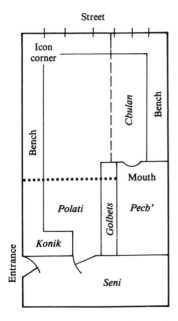

Fig. 1.1. Northern and central
Great Russian *izba*.

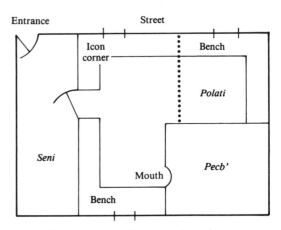

Fig. 1.2. Southeastern Great Russian *izba*.

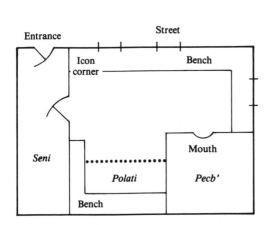

Fig. 1.3. Southwestern Great Russian *izba*.

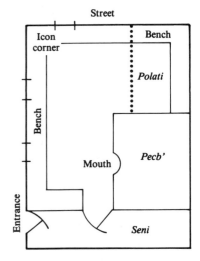

Fig. 1.4. *Khata* of western Great Russia, Belorussia, and the Ukraine.

cossack areas. It was also typical of Poland and much of the eastern Baltic shore. It is shown in Figure 1.4. In the *khata* important dates in family life (birth, marriage, death) were often written or carved in a special roof beam, the *svolok,* and the icon corner was decorated with vigil lights, eggs, dried flowers, or doves made of dough.[8]

The Economic Base

In the nineteenth century the Russian peasant family grew crops with tools and techniques little changed since the Kiev period. The basic technique was plowing with animal power. For milling grain there was wind and water power. In order to survive, the peasant family had to produce each year a minimum of food for its own use, seed for the next year's crop, livestock feed, and a replacement fund for equipment necessary for production and consumption. The surplus production of the family had to cover ceremonial expenses (e.g., weddings, Christmas), its obligations to a landlord, and taxes. In order to meet all these demands the peasant family might resort to any of four supplementary activities: (1) animal husbandry and beekeeping, (2) handicrafting for direct sale, (3) "cottage industry" on a "putting-out" basis, and (4) seasonal labor outside the village. The more fortunate and/or able peasants might be able to hire poor peasants to help with the work; they might obtain additional land to cultivate; they might even invest in improved seed, stock, or tools. But most peasant families felt fortunate if they could simply get enough to eat without falling into debt.

All arable land allotted to peasant families was divided into strips subject to obligatory rotation among families. The peasant commune usually distributed this land among its constituent households according to the number of taxable persons in each household (i.e., all men from seventeen to fifty-five years and all married women up to fifty years of age). Common pastures and meadows were used jointly by peasants and landlords. Forests usually belonged to landlords, who tried to keep peasants from poaching game.[9]

In the first part of the nineteenth century about two-thirds of the Russian peasants cultivated their arable land with the three-field (*parovaia*) system. A given field was alternately left fallow, sown with winter grain (rye, winter wheat), or sown with a spring grain (oats, barley, millet, spring rye, spring wheat). Two other systems were also used. In the *zalezhnaia* system a given piece of land was sown continuously for several years and then served as a pasture or hayfield until it again became fertile. This system was most often found around Ufa, Orenburg, Stavropol, Samara, and Astrakhan. One might find a third system, the slash-and-burn (*lesopolnaia, podsechnoognevaia*), in the northern forest region (Archangel, Olonets, and Vologod regions). Families using this system cleared land of standing trees one spring by cutting them down and leaving them where they fell. Then the following spring they burned the fallen wood, spread the ash around, and at once sowed the soil with barley or turnips in the far north, with rye or wheat a bit farther south. But after 1861 the peasants tended to switch from the latter two systems to the three-field system.[10]

Many of the principal crops cultivated in Russia in the nineteenth century had been cultivated since ancient times. These crops included cereals: rye, wheat, barley, oats, millet, and buckwheat; vegetables: turnips, cabbage, peas, beans, lentils, onions, and cucumbers; fodder: vetch and clover; hops, flax, and hemp. Crops introduced relatively late—between the seventeenth and nineteenth centuries—included corn (maize), tomatoes, potatoes, sugar beets, sunflowers (latter part of nineteenth century), tobacco, and *makhorka* (shag tobacco).[11]

Rye was the basic crop in northern and central Russia; indeed, in the nineteenth century Russia led the world in rye production. Wheat was basic in the south. Oats were the most common spring crop. Barley was used for brewing beer and for fodder. Buckwheat was valued by beekeepers as a nectariferous crop, and cooked buckwheat groats (*kasha*) was a daily dish in the Russian army.

Thread from Russian flax, grown in the northern region, was exported by Novgorod and Pskov between the thirteenth and sixteenth centuries. The Russian peasants made their undergarments of homespun linen until the development of the cotton textile industry in the nineteenth century. They processed hemp fiber into rope and canvas and hemp seeds into cooking oil and cattle fodder.[12]

The basic plowing tool of the north Russian peasant was the *sokha,* a light wheelless wooden plow, usually with an iron share. It was adapted to the stony, shallow topsoil of the forested non-black-soil belt and the north and northeast black-soil belt. The *plug (sabany)* was a wheeled wooden plow with iron share that had to be pulled by up to three pairs of horses or six pairs of oxen. It was used in the steppe and forest-steppe areas of the south for turning up fallow fields and virgin soil. The *ralo* was a heavy plow with many teeth, pulled by one to five pairs of oxen, and used for small-scale plowing in the south. For breaking up clods, the peasants used a harrow (*barona*) pulled by animals. Their other principal tools were hand tools: the scythe (*kosa*) for mowing hay (and, from the eighteenth century on, also for reaping), the sickle (*serp*) for reaping, and the flail (*tsep*) for threshing. They used hand tools in their kitchen gardens, except in the cultivation of potatoes, where the *sokha* was used.[13]

Prior to 1861 the Russian peasant family kept animals mainly for family use, not for the market. These animals were usually horses, cattle, sheep, goats, chickens, and geese. Ducks and pigs were relatively uncommon on peasant farmsteads before the end of the nineteenth century. The peasants usually overworked their horses and fed and maintained them poorly. In winter the horses got straw, with hay and oats if they were doing heavy work (like hauling firewood). In summer they were fed hay, oats, and rye mash when doing heavy plowing; the rest of the time they grazed in pastures. In the north, horses grazed unguarded in meadows and forests; in the central and southern regions, when not working, they were kept in a fenced-in area near the village and guarded at night by the peasants in turn. In cold weather the peasants kept them in stables that were hung with icons representing Floris and Lauris, the patron saints of horses, or with stones of unusual shape with a hole in the center called "horse gods."

The peasants kept cattle mainly as work animals or for milking. They used oxen (bullocks) to pull the heavy plows. The care of cattle was similar to that of horses except that in the south herders tended them in warm weather. The care of horses and bulls was considered a man's job, and only men and boys (usually from poor families) served as herders. Women cared for the remaining domestic livestock: cows, sheep, goats, and poultry. In the fall the peasants might market some of their animals or slaughter them for ceremonial use. Only the richest peasants ate meat regularly.

To guard their domestic animals from harm, the peasants hung their sheds with many kinds of charms: stones with holes in them, multicolored scraps of fabric, sheep's wool, tinsel, crusts of bread, and ancient coins with representations of horses. These offerings were directed to the *domovoi* (family spirit), whom they considered "master" of the family animals. In time of epizootic outbreaks, the Russian peasants resorted to a ritual similar to one practiced by the ancient Greeks and Romans. At night the cattle were shut inside the village, and the men hid. The women of the village, naked or wearing only shifts, and with their hair flowing loose, gathered in a field outside the village. They yoked the oldest woman to a plow, and at midnight plowed a furrow three times around the village, making as much noise as they could with frying pans, iron pots, etc., singing and shouting obscenities. Sometimes they carried an icon of St. Vlasia (*Yegoria*), the patron saint of domestic animals. Thus they tried to drive "death" from the village.[14]

Peasant handicraft work was of four types: (1) for family use, (2) to order for a customer (*remeslo*), (3) for the market directly (*promysel*), and (4) on an order from a capitalist ("putting out"). Women made things mostly for household use, especially textiles of linen, wool, and hemp. They did their spinning on spindles until the end of the eighteenth century, when the spinning wheel was introduced. They used horizontal looms except in the Ukraine, where vertical looms were used in rugmaking.

Men usually made commodities for the market, especially articles of wood and other materials from the forest. Such activity was most common in northern Russia. The men extracted resin, burned charcoal, and constructed barrels, wooden bowls, spoons, toys, bast matting, bast shoes (*lapti*), baskets, wickerwork, and birchbark dishes. Ceramic production was widespread in Russia. Peasant potters shaped dishes on a potter's wheel and fired them in a common kiln. At the river they tanned leather and worked maple and aspen wood into art objects with a simple lathe powered by the river current.[15]

In order to move their firewood from the forest, their crops from the field, and their fishing catch from lake or stream to their homes, the peasants devised carts (two- and four-wheeled), sledges, sleighs, and simple boats (either dugouts or boats made of wooden planks). In the second half of the nineteenth century the richer peasants traveled in carriages of various types. Such carriages usually had springs and a collapsible top, and were pulled by one to three horses.[16]

Food

The peasant toiled in order to eat, but what did he eat? He ate bread, mainly. He treated a loaf of bread reverently, standing it upright on the table and breaking it instead of cutting it. It was bread made by his wife from sourdough leavened with yeast, *kvas,* or beer lees. In hard times she had to adulterate the dough with bran and pigweed.[17] She baked it in the *pech'*, usually on a clean hearthstone. The peasant woman prepared many other dishes based on dough for special occasions (and in richer peasant families, on ordinary days). The most famous were *pirogi*—tarts stuffed with fish, cottage cheese, berries, cabbage, etc., *blini*—thin pancakes, and *knyshi*—puff pastries layered with *kaimak* (cream taken from boiled milk). Another important cereal food in the daily fare of peasants was groats (*krupa*)* prepared from oats, wheat, or buckwheat, and known as *kasha* after simmering.

Vegetables were next in importance in the peasant diet. First came the hardy cabbage, eaten fresh in summer and in the form of sauerkraut in winter. In times of fasting, bread, sauerkraut, and *kvas* were the only food of the poor peasants. Cabbage was the basis of a popular north and central Russian soup—*shchi.*[†] In south Great Russia and the Ukraine the favorite soup was *borshch,* made ideally with meat stock and beets, cabbage, onions, and sometimes tomatoes. In the course of the nineteenth century potatoes became part of the daily diet of even the poor peasants. Other staple vegetables were cucumbers, salted in barrels for winter use, and onions for seasoning. Vegetable oils, from hemp, flax, and sunflower seeds, added vital calories to the diet. For variety there might be peas, horseradish, melons, berries, and other produce from the family garden, as well as mushrooms, nuts, and berries gathered from nearby woods and salted and dried for winter use.

The average peasant associated meat with special celebrations. Late in the fall he killed the livestock and poultry intended for consumption during the winter. (It is interesting that Russian peasants observed a taboo on eating the meat of the bear, the horse, and the hare.) Of greater importance than meat in the peasant diet were fish, especially in villages near lakes and streams, milk and milk products such as cottage cheese (*tvorog*), and eggs.

The most widespread peasant drink around 1861 was probably *kvas,* a near beer made from bran, malt, dried crusts of bread, flour, and water. Another type of home brew was *braga,* usually made from oats, with malt and hops. In some villages it was traditional for the peasants to take a holiday to prepare beer together. Tea was first introduced into Russia from China in the seventeenth century, but it was not a common drink in the villages until the 1880's, when many village homes had samovars. However, these samovars were often used to prepare home-grown "teas" of herbs, carrots, berries, or fruits.

Peasant cooking and eating utensils were of wood, pottery, or metal, with earthenware pots often being used for cooking. Some of the most interesting utensils, from an artistic point of view, were wooden scoops (*kovshi*) and wooden dishes in the shape of a hollowed-out duck.[18]

Dress

The male peasant had his hair parted in the middle and trimmed in the shape of an inverted bowl. His beard, especially before 1861, usually was not trimmed if he was

---

*Groats are hulled grain broken into fragments larger than grits. They can be prepared for eating in about fifteen minutes by simmering.

†In the far north where cabbage did not grow, *shchi* referred to a thick soup of potatoes and groats.

a Great Russian. (Ukrainian males shaved for ceremonial occasions.) In warm weather he wore a cylindrical hat felted from sheepswool* and in winter a fur or lambskin cap, sometimes with earflaps. During the nineteenth century the visor cap (*kartuz*) came into fashion as well.

The basic male garment was the *rubakha,* a long tunic-like shirt with sleeves and a stand-up collar made from homespun linen or a commercial fabric. All peasant garments were fastened by placing the right side of the garment over the left, as American female garments are fastened now. Such a style was typical of peasants in Eastern European valleys as far east as the Volga, and distinguished the peasants from the steppe nomads, who fastened their garments left over right.

There were distinctive regional variations in the decor of the peasant shirt. The more ancient Ukrainian type was fastened in the middle front of the body, had a stand-up collar and was often embroidered. The Great Russian type, which probably diffused from Moscow not earlier than the fifteenth century, fastened at the left side of the neck. It was often decorated with *poliki*—embroidered insets—placed on each shoulder. In north Great Russia, Belorussia, and the Ukraine these insets were "square," and in south Great Russia, "slanted" or trapezoidal.

A peasant's trousers in Great Russia, Belorussia, and right-bank Ukraine were tight-fitting, but in left-bank Ukraine, under Cossack and ultimately nomad influence, men wore loose, full, baggy trousers (*sharovary*). Great Russian and Belorussian men wore their shirts hanging out over their trousers, in the ancient peasant style. Ukrainian peasants, under nomad influence, tucked their shirts in.

The peasant's outer dress was usually the *kaftan,* a long tunic girdled at the waist and fastened on the left side. It was made of coarse brown or grey homespun wool or of some heavy commercial fabric. In severe weather he wore a sheepskin coat, often wool side in, either long and wide (*tulup*) or short (*polushubki*). His legs were wrapped with linen or cotton rags, inside of which he might deposit small precious items, such as coins. These leg wrappings were held in place by ties attached to *lapti*—woven bast shoes—usually of linden (limewood) bark. Sometimes he wore birchbark clogs on his bare feet or (especially in the Ukraine) crude leather moccasins. But what he preferred to wear, if he could afford them, was a pair of high-top boots (*sapogi*). They were expensive and had to be bought in town, so he often wore them only on holidays. In very cold weather he kept his feet warm in high-top all-felt boots (*valenki*), first produced in Russia in the early nineteenth century.[19]

A Russian peasant girl did not cut her hair, but braided it in a single plait, sometimes with ribbons and other decorations entwined on festive occasions. Only on her wedding day did her hair flow loose in public. In warm weather she sometimes wore a circlet with an open crown. In cold weather she might wear a kerchief (*platok*), but this custom was relatively new in the nineteenth century. A married woman always covered her hair, especially in the presence of strange men and older men of her husband's family. When a girl assumed the headdress of a married woman it was an important moment in the wedding ceremonies. Tokarev thinks that these customs are rooted in a primitive belief in the magic power of hair, especially long head hair. An unmarried girl's hair was not considered dangerous to her own family, but a

*At the time of Haxthausen's visit (1843), and in early photographs, this felt hat had a brim, and the cylinder was encircled by a ribbon fastened with a buckle, reminiscent of the English and American Puritan hats of the seventeenth century.

married woman was an "alien" to her husband's family, and her hair was therefore "dangerous" to them. The married woman's headdress in northern Great Russia was usually based on the *kokoshnik,* which resembled a tiara covered with brocade or other valuable material and embroidered with pearls and precious stones (real or imitation). In southern Great Russia the headdress base was the *kichka,* which resembled a pair of horns. The married woman parted her hair in the middle and braided it in two braids that were fastened to the head under the headdress.

The basic female garment, the *rubakha,* was like the male's. In the summer unmarried girls might wear this "shift" without any overgarment, but a married woman always wore an overgarment. The most primitive of these was the south Great Russian *ponëva* (Ukrainian *plakhta*), ritually placed on the bride during the wedding ceremony. It was made of three widths of woolen fabric that were not sewn together, but hung as flaps from the waistband. During the nineteenth century the *ponëva* was gradually replaced by either a true skirt, borrowed by Ukrainian and Belorussian women from the West several centuries earlier, or the north Great Russian *sarafan,* which was given the name *shubka.* The *sarafan,* typical overdress of the north Great Russian woman, resembled a jumper with narrow shoulder supports, or a pinafore without ruffles. It came to Russia from the West in the fifteenth and sixteenth centuries.* The other overgarments and footgear of the peasant women resembled those of the men.

In her holiday attire the peasant woman was colorful: red predominated, followed by yellow and blue. She decorated herself with embroidery, woven strips, ribbons, glass beads, spangles, drake and peacock feathers, and goose down. She especially treasured river pearls. Haxthausen reports that all the women he saw in the Nizhi-Novgorod area had at least three or four strings of pearls.[20]

The Peasant Family

We know relatively little about the Russian peasant family of the nineteenth century, but its general characteristics can be described. The Russian peasant family in the nineteenth century might be a "small family," which included parents, children, and possibly grandparents, or a "large extended family," which included two or more married brothers with their offspring and possibly their parents, the essential characteristic being the presence of collateral lines in a single household. At the beginning of the century the large extended family was the more common of the two types, but families tended to split up after 1861, and the average family had only five to six members in 1897. Small families were most typical in the north Great Russian non-black-soil region and in the Ukraine. The large extended family was most likely to be found (1) in the south Great Russian black-soil zone, (2) among middle peasants who engaged in seasonal work outside the village, (3) in border areas where land allotments were relatively large, such as Cossack areas and Siberia, (4) in the far

---

*The most ancient type of *sarafan* had false sleeves hanging down behind called *shushun* (*sushpan, sukman*). In the nineteenth century these were worn in the Pskov, Novgorod, and Olonets regions, chiefly by old women. Similar false sleeves, vestiges of the medieval gown, were worn in the West from the sixteenth to eighteenth centuries. (See Philippe Ariès, *Centuries of Childhood* [New York, 1965], p. 56.)

northern forest district of Tver *gubernia* and in the Belozersk district of Novgorod *gubernia,* and (5) among the rich peasants generally in north Russia.[21]

The figure of central authority in the family was usually the patriarch (*bol'shak, batiushka, nabol'shii khoziain;* Ukrainian: *starshii;* Belorussian: *bats'ka, dziadz'ka*). He managed the collective family property, making the ultimate decisions on the timing of field work and the buying and selling of alienable property. Normally he was the oldest male member in full possession of his faculties; however, a more competent junior male or senior female might be more influential in actual practice.

Much of the traditional work of the man in the family had symbolic significance. A man plowed and sowed the fields: these actions were regarded as symbolic of the male role in sexual intercourse. A man cared for his horse: the horse was a masculine symbol. A man cut firewood and constructed wooden buildings using an axe, another masculine symbol. A man also harrowed the fields, mowed hay, threshed grain, and carted tools and produce. In the crowded *izba* he kept order through the long winters, which often forced a peasant family to live in a single room, perhaps ten feet by fifteen feet, for seven months of the year.

The strongest member of the family in practice, however, might be *matushka*—mama—a symbol in Russian culture of endurance and healing love. She was often the great binding force in the family.[22] All year long she cooked, cared for children, spun, wove, sewed, washed, milked cows, and cared for domestic cattle and poultry. In summer she would, in addition, rake hay, reap grain, weed, pull flax, and care for the kitchen garden. Although she had no right to inherit a share in the real estate of the family of her birth, she could dispose of her dowry (which might include land and livestock) and the fruits of her *babskoe khoziaistvo* (handicrafts and products of livestock and poultry in her charge). Then her daughters might inherit from her.

The children of the family were expected to assume responsibilities in the work of the family at an early age.[23] They were trained to respect the authority of elders, and were taught the importance of harmonious teamwork and of restraining their aggressive tendencies. They learned to perform routine tasks reliably, since such routine performances might make the difference between survival or catastrophe. As adolescents they did not suffer from the strain of deferring marriage long past puberty, nor did they take on the responsibilities of running an independent household immediately after marriage.

There were two especially difficult roles in the peasant family. One was that of the daughter-in-law (*snokha*). In the early nineteenth century, according to some reports, an underage boy might be married to an older girl for economic reasons, and she would become mistress of her father-in-law (who was then called a *snokhach*).[24] After the abolition of serfdom such arrangements became uncommon. Even when they did not exist, however, there must have been frequent tension arising from the presence of an eighteen-year-old female and a forty-year-old male, no blood kin to each other, living in a tiny room together for many months. In the warm weather a young couple could retire to the *klet,* but in winter they might be forced to move in with the older couple to economize on fuel. Sexual rivalry was probably a factor in the notoriously hostile mother-in-law and daughter-in-law rela-

tionship. The daughter-in-law often felt overworked and unappreciated in her husband's family; the mother-in-law often considered her lazy and irresponsible. Sad
indeed was the fate of a daughter-in-law whose husband was drafted—at least
before the 1874 Reform. Any children they had were cared for by his family, but he
was lamented as if dead, and she might be treated as a family hired hand or sent
away to work in a factory.

The other difficult role was that of son-in-law (*ziat'*). A well-to-do family with
no sons of its own might "adopt" a son-in-law of humble birth and take him into the
household. According to a Russian proverb, "If you have no devil in the house, take
in a son-in-law." One can imagine his discomfort as a dependent of a woman's
family.

The experience of family living was so influential in shaping the Russian peasant's mentality that he tended to people Nature with imaginary families. The *leshii*
(wood spirit) and *vodianoi* (water spirit) were sometimes said to have wives and
children. When there was a storm in the forest or the water churned in the river, it
meant that the spirit therein was "celebrating his marriage." Jack Frost in Russia
was "Grandfather Frost" (*Ded Moroz*). The earth itself was sometimes personified
as "Damp Mother Earth," to whom the peasants addressed prayers in ancient times.

The Russian peasant's home was a place of worship—the worship of the family
itself as an ongoing, living entity. This worship was bifocal. One focus was at the
pech'. When a family moved from one house to another it carried embers from the
fire of the old stove in a jar to start a fire in the new stove. If the distance was too
great, the family merely took the fire shovel and other implements of the old stove.
In the Ukraine, a piece of clay from the stove (*pechyna*) was wrapped in the
swaddling clothes of a newborn infant when it was taken for baptism. The stove was
also involved in wedding rituals (*see below*).

The Eastern Slavs believed that in each home resided an ancestral spirit, or
domovoi (*khoziain, dedushka, susedko, sam*; Ukrainian: *domovik, khovanets, vik-
hovanok, skarbnik*). This family spirit was usually in or behind the *pech'*. When the
family pushed the embers of the old stove into the new stove they repeated the
formula "*Domovoi na tebe sani, poezzhai s nami*" (*Domovoi*, the sleigh is ready for
you, go with us). A *domovoi* was supposed to be warm and soft, like a sheepskin
coat. In general he was a protective spirit, but he might engage in malicious teasing,
such as making noises that kept the family awake at night. They propitiated him by
putting offerings of food, especially eggs, on the stove. In Belorussia the *domovoi*
was called *tsmok* (snake), which suggests the ancient Greek association of house-
snakes and ancestors. A Russian family in a new neighborhood hung in their stable
another animal symbol, a bear's head, to protect them from the house spirits of their
new neighbors.[25]

Diagonally across from the *pech'* was the other sacred place in the room: the
icon corner (*perednii ugol, krasnyi ugol, sviati ugol*). When a stranger entered a
Russian household he was supposed to take off his hat, cross himself facing the icon
corner, and then greet the heads of the household. The jar that a family used to carry
embers from an old stove to a new was broken and buried at night under the icon
corner of the new house. In order to safeguard the family head or the first member of
the family to enter a new home, they killed an animal, usually a rooster, and

sprinkled the foundations of the new house with his blood. Then they buried his head, in private, in the spot where the icon corner was to be located. In the pre-Christian era the icon corner may have been the place where ancestral images were kept. Some Russian peasants believed that after a dead member of the family was buried his soul took up residence behind the family icons.[26]

A Russian family gave special thought to its dead on certain occasions during the year: the eve of *Maslenitsa* (Shrovetide), *Radonitsa* (Tuesday of the second week after Easter), St. Dimitri's Saturday (the eve of October 26), and *Semik* (Thursday before Trinity Sunday). The family celebrated such occasions by visiting the graves of the family dead. There at the cemetery they had a picnic that the dead might attend and "enjoy." They left offerings of food for the dead and asked them to help make the crops grow.[27]

The Life of a Typical Peasant Family

Let us try to imagine an ordinary day in January, 1860, in the life of the Ivanovs, a peasant family living in the *derevnia* of Beryozka just north of Moscow. At daybreak, Marya, the *matushka,* sits up on her pallet of straw on the sleeping bench, throws aside her sheepskin cover, and stirs up the fire in the stove. She has bread for breakfast on hand: dark sourdough rye loaves. All that is needed besides is to draw some *kvas* from the barrel in the cellar. While she is in the cellar she gets some sauerkraut, onions, and buckwheat groats to make into *shchi* and *kasha* for dinner. She does her cooking for the whole day now, and leaves the food in the *pech'* until needed. The rest of the family get up soon after and begin the morning chores. Marya's husband Ivan and her son Andrei cut firewood and care for the horses. Her daughter, Marfa, and Andrei's wife, Anya, fetch water for the water barrel from the family well, take out the straw pallets, care for the cow, sheep, and poultry, sweep the floor, and set the table in the icon corner. Then the family gathers for breakfast. Seated at the table under the icons is Ivan (the *bol'shak*), forty-five years old; next to him is his eldest son, Andrei, who is twenty-five; opposite the men are Marya (forty-three), their unmarried daughter Marfa (sixteen), and Andrei's wife Anya (twenty-three), who is feeding oatmeal porridge to their son Petka (four). One member of the family is missing, namely Sergei (twenty), who is away for the winter working in a textile factory in Ivanovo–Voznesensk. Sergei is unmarried and sends most of his earnings home. So far he has not been taken into the army, and Marya prays each day that the draft will pass him by.

Winter days are short in Beryozka, so the Ivanovs take advantage of the hours of light to make salable articles for the Moscow market. Marya embroiders a blouse, Anya weaves, and Marfa knits on a sweater. Ivan and Andrei carve wooden spoons and toys. In the early afternoon the family gathers for dinner, consisting of *shchi,* bread, and *kvas*. After Ivan says grace, each member of the family dips his wooden spoon in the common soup bowl in the middle of the table. In the afternoon they take their handwork to a neighbor's *izba* for socializing and storytelling. The neighbor offers them a snack of tea with fruit preserves on bread. Then they return home to finish the evening chores before dark. They must care for the animals, prepare firewood for the *pech'*, and lay out straw to sleep on. The last meal of the day consists of buckwheat *kasha* with some flax seed oil and *kvas*. Then Ivan and Andrei go off to drink at the village tavern (*traktir;* Ukraine and Belorussia: *korchma*) and to hear the latest news. Meanwhile Marya sits near the stove and tells Petka the ancient tale (*skazka*) of Maria Morevna. When the light of the last *luchnik* flickers out in the *svetets,* everyone is stretched out asleep on a straw pallet under a sheepskin. They hope that the *domovoi* will not wake them by scratching around in the back of the stove.

Days such as the one described above melt one into the other, making little impression on the memory of the Ivanovs. But every Ivanov remembers, discusses, and is influenced by the vital events of family life, especially birth, marriage, and death.

The Ivanovs want to have a big family and do not practice birth control. Marya Ivanov has three children, but she gave birth to three others who died in infancy. Her daughter-in-law Anya lost a baby last summer. Petka, like most children in the village, was born in the family bathhouse. Anya lay upon a straw pallet with a smooth cover laid on one of the wide shelves usually used by bathers to enjoy the steam. The village midwife (*babka*) delivered Petka easily; in difficult cases she might resort to the magic of untying knots, unlocking locks, etc.—symbolic of the unbinding of vital forces.[28] The peasants believe that childbirth is easier if few are present; single girls are not allowed to attend. Petka's umbilical cord was cut with an axe, symbol of masculinity; a girl's cord would have been cut with a distaff.

About three days after his birth Petka was formally received into the Ivanov family and the Beryozka community. This was done by the Christian ceremony of baptism, at home or in church; not only Ivanov kin, but other villagers attended. During the ceremony Petka's godparents played the most active role, while his parents remained in the background. After the ceremony the Ivanovs entertained kin and friends, who provided refreshments and gifts for Petka. The special dishes served on this occasion were *krestil'naia kasha* (christening pudding) and *kisel'* (a starchy jelly leavened with yeast), which is also served at other major family celebrations. On the day of the christening, or thereabouts, there was an additional, purely family ceremony of purification of mother and midwife (*razmyvki;* Ukrainian: *zlivki;* Belorussian: *zhmurinki*). In the days between delivery and this ceremony Anya was separated from the rest of the family and considered "unclean."* She did no housework and could not eat with the family, milk the cows, or touch an icon. At the *razmyvki* the midwife and Anya mutually washed their hands. The Ivanovs then paid the midwife with some coins, which they dipped in water. Petka settled down in his curtained-around swinging cradle of bast (*liulka, zybka*), and his mother resumed her housework. In a week she might be performing all her normal duties.[29]

Petka was nursed at Anya's breast for fifteen months, but he was given solid foods—thin oatmeal and scrambled eggs—much earlier. When Anya was too busy to rock his cradle she gave him a pacifier (*khlebnaia* or *kashnaia soska*) made of

---

*A curious reverse interpretation of the actual biological situation, since Anya was in greater danger of contamination by the family than vice versa.

flour, bread, or cooked groats tied in a rag. Anya has little time to entertain her boy, but she and all members of the family treat him with great affection. He loves to hear his grandmother tell stories in the evening. As he grows older he will enjoy the outdoors more and more: in summer, finding birds' nests, fishing, and exploring; in winter, playing in the snow. When he is about seven years old he will begin to help his father with "man's work": chopping firewood, caring for the horse, sowing, plowing, etc. He is learning to be honest, obedient, and hardworking, and he is learning early, for as the peasant proverb puts it: "If you don't teach him when he lies across the width of the sleeping bench, then you will not be able to teach him when he stretches out on the whole length of the bench."

Marfa has been helping with housework since she was six, and has learned most domestic skills. At harvest time this year she will no longer baby-sit with Petka but will wield a sickle all day behind Marya. She is looking forward to haymowing time when the whole village will be out mowing together.

There is no school in Beryozka, and all the Ivanovs there are illiterate. But twenty miles away, in the *selo* of Staritsa, there is a three-year parish school that one of their cousins, Alexander Vladimirov, attends. At thirteen he can read a newspaper haltingly. Will the Ivanovs send Petka to school in Staritsa? That will depend upon how much they need his help at home, how prosperous they are, his aptitudes, and the climate of opinion about the value of education. They will probably not hire him out as a herdsboy or apprentice him to an artisan in Staritsa, as poor families must do with their sons.[30]

There is no question of sending Marfa to school. But she doesn't miss it: right now she is having the time of her life. Almost every evening this winter she goes to a *posidelka* (Ukrainian: *bechornitsa;* Belorussian: *becherok*) at an *izba* that Marfa and her girlfriends (aged sixteen to twenty) have rented for the winter from an elderly couple without children. The *podrostki* (girls aged fourteen and fifteen) have their own *posidelki,* as do the *perestarkie* (girls over twenty). The girls work on their spinning, knitting, sewing, and embroidering under their mothers' supervision. At such sessions they often sing lyric songs about the life of women. Later in the evening the young men come: one bringing firewood, another his concertina, and the others refreshments—nuts, seeds, candy, cakes. The girls turn from work to play: games, singing, dancing. Then the boys may escort the girls home.* During

---

*According to one Soviet source, in some villages, especially in the Ukraine, the youths and girls might spend the night together after a *posidelka* (S. A. Tokarev, *Etnografiia narodov SSR* [Moscow, 1958], p. 82). D. S. Shimkin says that young men visited girls sleeping in haylofts in summer and that an illegitimate child might enhance a girl's chances of marriage, since it showed her to be highly fertile. (See his "Culture and World View: A Method of Analysis Applied to Rural Russia," *American Anthropologist,* 55 [1953], p. 331.) However, a recent Soviet enthnographic summary declared that if a girl lost her virginity before marriage the family gate might be tarred and the family might have a hard time finding her a husband (*Narody Mira* [Moscow, 1964], pp. 408–9). The demand for "proof" of virginity after the wedding night in peasant customs tends to support this view.

One may account for such differences in testimony on the grounds that different regions are involved. Also, peasants (and indeed human beings everywhere) have highly ambivalent feelings about the power of sexual attraction: they both fear it and worship it. It makes marriages and breaks them. According to a Russian proverb, "The devil pours a spoonful of honey into someone else's wife." It seems likely that the Russian peasants condoned some premarital sexual experimentation, especially between a couple who

the spring and early summer the same gang will sing, dance *khorovody*, and play games together outdoors. On the threshold of marriage the boys and girls of a village are well acquainted. But if they wish to seek a mate outside the village they will look the prospects over in Staritsa at the holiday fairs. Or they may find a mate on a pilgrimage to some chapel, miraculous spring, or other holy place.

When it is time for a Russian peasant girl to marry, her parents might either discreetly seek out a husband for her or sanction an already blooming romance. They will want the boy to be of a family at least as well-off as themselves, in good physical and mental health, and of good moral reputation. In case either his parents or her parents disapprove of the match, the couple may elope and get married secretly (marriage by *samokhodka, samokrupka, ubeg*). Then they will wait awhile, perhaps until the birth of their first child, after which they will apologize to the reluctant parents, asking their forgiveness.[31]

For over a year Marfa has been flirting with Vladimir Petrov (nineteen) at the holiday fairs in Staritsa. In the fall of 1860 their engagement takes place in the following manner. One evening the Ivanovs have some "surprise" visitors—at least the Ivanovs act surprised. The visitors, dressed in their best clothes, include Anton Petrov, uncle of Vladimir Petrov (Vladimir's *svat*), and Dunia Stepanov, Vladimir's married aunt (the *svakha*). First the visitors chat casually with the Ivanovs, and then make complimentary references to both Marfa and Vladimir. In a little while, the Petrov contingent, sensing a warm response, makes a formal marriage proposal. The Ivanovs refuse gently at first, saying that Marfa is "too young to marry" or "too much needed at home." Both families refuse to commit themselves: since there is a business side to the deal, any undue eagerness on one side can be materially damaging. The only person who has a material interest in agreement per se is the *svakha,* and she pushes the negotiations forward.* The Ivanovs say they will think the matter over and give their answer in a few days. Since the answer is favorable, the Petrov party visits again to make the betrothal agreement. Ivan, speaking for the Ivanovs, bargains with Anton Petrov as to the size of Marfa's dowry (*pridanoe*), which may include bedding, livestock, and even land, as well as the customary linens prepared and embroidered by the bride. They also discuss the *kladka* (the groom's contribution for the bride's wedding apparel and for the wedding expenses). The matchmaker is successful: Ivan finally accepts the proposal, and both parties drink a toast to the union (ritual of the *malyi zapoi*). After this the Ivanovs pay a visit to the Petrov home in Dubrava to see if it is satisfactory. Satisfied, they invite the Petrovs back to their *izba* in Beryozka for the *rukobit'e* (*bol'shoi zapoi, zapivanie, propivan'e*) when, with ceremonial toasts, the two fami-

---

were good candidates for a match. There were surely many opportunities for this in warm weather in the countryside. On the other hand, girls were usually married before they developed a taste for a variety of sexual partners.

However, cases of adultery after marriage appear to have been fairly common. Although the village would gossip about such a case, peasants not directly involved would not intervene unless a married woman of the village paired off with a man from outside the village. Ordinarily it was the husband's duty to punish an errant wife. (See A. N. Engelgardt, *Iz derevni: 12 pisem 1872–1877* [Moscow, 1937], p. 36.)

*Such proceedings are depicted in the Soviet film *And Quiet Flows the Don.*

lies strike the final bargain. After this, neither party can break the agreement without making some compensation to the other "to pay for the dishonor."

Once engaged, Marfa is freed from all housework. With the help of her girlfriends she finishes preparing her needlework dowry. She goes about in a special "sad" dress, covering her head, as she bids her relatives in the village farewell. It is befitting that she at least appear sad, for the Russian proverb declares: "Weeping bride, laughing wife; laughing bride, weeping wife." On the day before the wedding she and her girlfriends go to the bathhouse for a ritual bath. Then Vladimir visits the *izba* bringing her presents. That evening there are two parties. At the Petrov house is a bachelor party (*mal'chishnik, parnëvik*), with drinking, singing, joking. At the Ivanovs is the *devichnik* for Marfa and her girlfriends at which there is a dramatic ceremony of Marfa's farewell to maidenhood. Her maidenhood is symbolized by the *krasnaia krasota,* a wreath of ribbons, flowers, and ornaments Marfa has twined in her single braid of maiden hair. Singing ritual songs, the girls unbraid Marfa's hair and then rebraid it for the last time in a single braid.* One of the young married women of the bride's family or among her friends warns her in a song that she will be ill-treated by her in-laws. Marfa, she says, should go out in the open country and wash away her grief:

> Fall down on the damp earth,
> Upon the burning stones,
> For surely you know, dear sister,
> That our mother, the damp earth, will not betray you,
> That the burning stones will not repeat it.
> But you will go to strange people,
> You will wipe off the burning tears.
> Do not show your feelings to people.[32]

Meanwhile Marya and Anya Ivanov, with all their married female kin and friends, are busy making wedding refreshments. The married women of the Petrov household are doing the same thing.

The next day comes the main event—the church wedding—but there are also rituals of pre-Christian origin. In the morning Marfa's friends help her dress and adorn her with the bridal crown. Her parents and godparents bless her. Vladimir's parents bless him with the family icon in their *izba*. Then Vladimir sets out with his party to fetch Marfa. His suite includes all his available kin and friends, cast in various formal roles. The *druzkha,* or best man, who leads the suite and serves as master of ceremonies at the wedding feast later, has been chosen from among Vladimir's married male kin. The symbols of his office are a piece of linen thrown over his shoulders, a gun, and a lash. There are various companions of the groom (*podruzh'e, druzhki, tiasiatskii*), the *svat* and *svakha,* the groom's parents and godparents, and the groom himself. On the road they meet various obstacles placed by the bride's party, such as barricades and straw bonfires. The best man "buys off" the obstructionists with little gifts. At the Ivanov house the parties of bride and groom have an antiphonal choral contest. Vladimir's party goes into the Ivanov *izba*

---

*If the Ivanovs had been richer, Marfa's hair would have been rebraided with strings of pearls and pieces of gold intertwined.

and there is a joking scene: Vladimir "buys" a seat next to Marfa; the best man "buys" Marfa from Petka (since she has no younger brother); and then one of Marfa's girlfriends steps forward pretending to be Marfa. Following this the two parties have some refreshments together. The bride and groom are led to the middle of the *izba* and placed on a fur coat (in this case a sheepskin) laid with the nap side up. Ivan and Marya Ivanov come forward and bless them. The *svakha*, Dunia Stepanov, unbraids Marfa's hair. Marfa touches the Ivanov *pech'*, pulling off a bit of clay, in a last farewell. Then they are ready to leave for the church in Staritsa.

As the couple departs, there are various magic rituals to ward off evil: the best man shoots his gun into the air and cracks his whip. In Staritsa the wedding party circles the church three times, carrying an icon, and making as much noise as possible to ward of evil spirits. As the Orthodox Christian ceremony goes on, various doors and windows are closed to exclude evil spirits. Just after the church ceremony Marfa's loose flowing hair is braided into two braids, fastened to her head, and crowned with the headdress of the married woman. Then the wedding party sets out for the Petrov house. The bride's movable dowry is transferred there too.

When Vladimir and Marfa arrive, Vladimir's parents are there to meet them with ceremonial bread and salt. They bless the young couple and sprinkle them with hops and kernels of grain. Vladimir's father removes Marfa's bridal veil. Then the newlyweds sit down at the table in the icon corner and are welcomed by the whole family. The guests begin the wedding feast, but Vladimir and Marfa eat separately in the *klet* or in the *chulan* behind a partition. Then they are led to the general feast table. During the feast there is an orgy of singing, dancing, and drinking, led by the best man and the *svakha*. In the wedding songs the bride and groom are compared to a white swan (quail, duck) and a falcon, a duck and drake, a pair of doves, the moon and sun (dawn), a pearl and *iakhoni* (ruby, sapphire, or amethyst), a marten and hunter, a grape vine entwining a post or large tree, an oak (or *iavor,* sycamore) and a *kalina* (snowball tree, guelder rose).[33] Marfa gives her new relatives little sweets, and they give the young couple money (this is the "gilding"—*zolochenie*). Marfa, according to ancient custom, takes off Vladimir's boots as a sign of submission for all the company to see. During the feast she sits wrapped in a scarf, but does not participate in the merrymaking. At the end of the feast the best man and the *svakha* lead Vladimir and Marfa to bed in the Petrov *klet,* while the wedding guests sing bawdy songs.

The following morning Vladimir and Marfa are awakened by the best man and *svakha,* who collect Marfa's shift, now spotted with blood. Then they parade around this "proof" of her premarital virginity, beating earthen pots. Vladimir and Marfa get up and take a ritual steam bath together. Having gathered at the Petrovs, the guests now go back to the Ivanovs for the *chuloba* ritual. The first dish served is an omelette, which Vladimir tastes. Then he puts money in a glass of wine and gives it to Marya Ivanov to make it understood that he regards Marfa as "honorable." After this, the wedding guests return to the Petrovs for a second day of feasting. On the third day Marfa takes off her scarf, dances, and makes merry with the guests. The Petrovs playfully "test" her domestic skills by making her work hemp and then sweep. At first they throw litter under her broom, then money. After the third day of feasting there may be other parties given by relatives invited to the wedding in honor of the newlyweds. Marfa has now officially taken up residence with the Petrovs. But she and Vladimir will try to visit the Ivanovs on Sundays and holidays and especially during *Maslenitsa* (Shrovetide) week.[34] And so Vladimir and Marfa begin married life only after passing through elaborate rituals, richly loaded with symbols from the deep past. And however shabby the *izba* in which they live, their lives together will be symbolically rich.

After Marfa's wedding Ivan Ivanov feels increasingly unwell, and one morning Marya finds him lying in agony on his sleeping bench. She decides that he is dying, and summons Marfa and Sergei and a priest for the Orthodox last rites. In order to end Ivan's suffering they cut an opening in the wall of the *izba* (an old superstition).* When he finally dies, Andrei pulls his body over to the bench in the icon corner, pointing his head in the direction of the icons and his feet toward the outer door of the *izba*. Then he goes out to finish the coffin he had begun earlier. The Ivanovs dress Ivan's body in his best clothes and lay it in the coffin with his axe, a loaf of bread, and a lump of salt. Leaving the top of the coffin off, they carry it out of the *izba* through a window, taking care not to let it touch the house, so that no evil spirit might attach itself to the house or find its way back in through the front door. With Marya, Anya, and Marfa and a few close female relatives lamenting loudly all the way, they carry the coffin to the cemetery, where it is buried with Orthodox rites. The priest performs these just before sunset; thus the sun can show Ivan's soul the way to his future abode in the dark beyond.

Back at home the Ivanovs set to work to purify the *izba*. They take the clothing in which Ivan died and his rag bedding to the henhouse. They burn the straw on which he lay, sweep the floor, and strew it with grain. They discard all the water that had been in the house at the time of his death. When the house is clean, the Ivanovs and a few close kin eat the funeral repast (*pominka*). Ivan's place at the table is left vacant, for the family believes his spirit to be still among them. The meal includes *blini, kisel'*, and *kut'ia* (a cereal dish with honey). The Ivanovs will pray for Ivan's soul on the ninth, twentieth, and fortieth days after his death, and again six months after his death. In addition they will remember him on the various days on the Church calendar set aside for the remembrance of the dead.[35] In these many ways the link between living and dead is strengthened and any negative feelings of the living toward the dead are discharged.

Thus the Russian peasant family endures through the cycle of birth, marriage, and death, each generation joining hands with the next. And though each knows he must die—Ivan, Marya, Andrei, Sergei, Marfa—each believes that the Ivanov family will endure, and he seeks to make it prosper.

---

*In the Ukraine a dying man was laid on a straw pallet on the earthen floor so that he wouldn't "die hard." This suggests a belief in the soothing effect of Mother Earth. To prevent prolonged suffering the ridge (*konëk*) of the roof would be broken. The Ukrainians and Belorussians put a candle in the hands of a dying person, perhaps to light his way into the darkness of the beyond (Tokarev, p. 85, and W. R. S. Ralston, *Songs of the Russian People*, 2d ed. [London, 1872], p. 314).

Village Life

Beryozka, the village in which the Ivanovs live, is too small (eighty households) to have its own church, but large enough to constitute a commune (*mir, obshchina*). Andrei as head of household now represents the Ivanovs at the meeting (*skhod*) of the commune, usually held in the open air near the center of town. The village elder (*starosta*) and his assistants, chosen at the *skhod*, are part-time officials, not professional bureaucrats. Beryozka has its own smithy and tavern, but it is too small to support other commercial ventures. Thus the Ivanovs often make trips to the *selo* of Staritsa, a market town with a church, a resident clergy, parish school, *volost'* government center, fire station, general store, and marketplace, where the local fairs (*iarmarki*) are held.

The various households of Beryozka are largely self-sufficient, but they will cooperate on an ad hoc basis for particular projects and help households in unusual need. Such help (*pomochi*) is given gratis on Sundays or holidays to build a house for a family burned out of its *izba*, to gather crops for widows and orphans, to help families crippled by illness,* and to build a church. In the fall the women will process flax and hemp and mince cabbage cooperatively, and the men will brew beer together.

Another form of peasant cooperation is the *supriaga*, a union of two or more households for joint working of the land. This is particularly common in the south, where a heavy plow pulled by several pairs of work animals is needed: peasant households short of persons of working age or of the needed work animals are attracted to such an arrangement.[36]

Every vital event in the life of the Ivanov family, and every other family, is not only a matter of common knowledge but of common concern in Beryozka. In particular, a wedding is a big event for the village. If both bride and groom are from Beryozka the whole village might participate in the wedding.

When a young peasant is drafted, the whole village mourns him. He is expected to go on a drunken debauch until the date he is to report for duty. The village holds a *pechal'nyi pir* (sorrowful repast) for him at which professional wailers bewail his loss in the name of his mother, wife, sisters, and other dear ones. After being blessed by his parents, the recruit is accompanied by a great crowd of peasants to the outskirts of the village.[37]

The people of Beryozka participate in a seasonal cycle of holidays and work common to Russian Orthodox peasants everywhere. One of the holidays is November 14—St. Philip's Day. The village is still discussing the wedding of the fall, but the splurge of celebrations is over: it is time for Philip's fast, which will end Christmas Eve. The men are threshing the last of the grain, hauling firewood, and making

---

*In time of illness the peasants might call a *koldun* (*koldun'ia*: sorcerer, witch), whose "gift" is regarded as coming from an unclean source; or a *znakhar* (*znakharka*), whose "gift" is regarded as coming from God. These healers use some rational kinds of cure as well as the power of suggestion (*Narody Mira*, p. 411). (Modern medical care did not reach the villages until the *zemstvo* program late in the century.)

agricultural tools for the coming year. The women are finishing the processing of hemp.[38]

The Yuletide season is the first of two major winter holidays. In pre-Christian times it was probably a holiday celebrating the winter solstice, the time of rebirth of the sun. In the nineteenth century it lasted from *Rozhdestvenskii Sochel'nik* (December 24 evening) to *Kreshcheniia* (January 6). This holiday period was a time not only of merrymaking but of ritual activity to further the well-being of the family and insure an abundant harvest in the coming year.

On December 24 the Ivanovs go through their usual holiday preparations and make wax candles. The family will eat no regular meal during the day, but the women are working on a special Christmas Eve feast. Andrei clears away snow from the *izba* door, gets the sleigh ready, and goes to Staritsa to buy a fish for the family's Christmas dinner. Perhaps he will go to the woods and cut a little fir tree (*yolka*) to decorate.

The Christmas Eve meal is a rather serious family affair, joyous and peaceful. Under the tablecloth grains of all kinds of cereals are laid on the table in the shape of a cross. Andrei throws a handful of grain into the air saying, "Health for men, for cows, for sheep." The special dish of the evening is *kresty*—crosses of baked dough.[39]

The Yuletide season usually includes various parties, with characteristic games, caroling, and special dramatic presentations. The amount and complexity of celebration depends on the size and wealth of the community. One year when the harvest was good the well-to-do Vladimirov family, cousins of the Ivanovs in Staritsa, decided to give a big party on New Year's Eve, to which the Ivanovs and other cousins were invited. The Vladimirovs had a large, magnificently decorated *yolka*. The main dish of the evening was roast suckling pig, symbol of abundance and fertility. The other refreshments included fish jellied in aspic, jellied cold cuts, *pirogi,* slices of cold roast meat, *shchi* made with meat stock, chicken and noodles, milk, *kasha, kisel',* dumplings, and fruit compote with vodka, brandy, and beer.[40] The party games included Burial of the Gold. A gold ring was passed from hand to hand, and a girl in the center of the circle had to detect it. While passing the ring, the group sang that the ring had fallen among guelder roses, raspberries, currants (symbols of a nubile girl), that it was hidden in dust, grown over with moss.[41] Fortune-telling was another feature of the party. The tail of the suckling pig was broken into pieces and distributed among the single people present. Then a dog was let into the room. It was foretold that the person whose piece was first devoured by the dog would be married within a year.[42]

In a gay mood the young people decided to go caroling to the homes of their friends. The carols (*koliadki*) included almost no Christian motifs: typically they invoked good harvest, wealth, luck. Singing such songs the carollers went from *izba* to *izba,* asking each master's permission to enter, honoring him with songs, and scattering grain on the listeners. Then they received previously prepared refreshments and sometimes a few coins.[43]

Yuletide ends on January 6. In Staritsa a cross-bearing procession from the church goes to an ice hole in the river, and the priest consecrates the waters. The more pious and hardy souls take a quick dip in the ice hole. During January the Ivanovs are forced to stay indoors much of the time to avoid the bitter sub-zero cold. Andrei finishes threshing grain and transporting hay from the meadow. Marya and Anya skim and store cream for use in the coming holiday cycle. In February the weather is still very severe. The family does handicraft work indoors.[44]

The second winter festival is *Maslenitsa* (Shrovetide, Carnival), which falls in late February or early March, the last week before the beginning of Lent. This celebration is dominated by symbols of the sun, and the festivities are probably pre-Christian ways to "help" the reanimating sun. The traditional dish is *blini*—round pancakes. At a safe distance from the village the peasants light bonfires and wheels of straw on poles. But the greatest diversion is sleighing, with special runs sometimes being constructed. The sleighs and horses (harnessed troika-style preferably) are decorated and driven in a circle around the village. Marfa and Vladimir come to Beryozka for a visit. The Ivanovs take fried eggs to the cemetery as offerings for Ivan and the other departed Ivanovs. The climax comes with the burning of a straw dummy representing "the spirit of Maslenitsa." First the peasants pull it on a sledge to the outskirts of the village, singing bawdy songs* and urging winter to depart. After setting the dummy afire they pull it apart with sticks, chasing each other with firebrands, tossing and scattering them.[45]

After Maslenitsa comes the Great Fast—Lent—which lasts the seven weeks preceding Easter. Lent is a time of preparation for spring work. Andrei repairs his tools and carts. In March the birds begin to come back from the south, and March 9 is the day of welcoming the birds and "calling" spring. Marya bakes some little birds made of dough, and Petka takes them to the field and tosses them into the air, crying "Fly to the field, bring health: first to the cows, second to the sheep, third to man!" The girls of the village form two choral groups and, imitating birds, ask spring to come. The women go out in the meadow, spread out a white linen cloth, place bread on it, and say, "This is for you, Mother Spring."[46]

As the snows thaw in March the ceiling of the Ivanov *izba* begins to leak badly. In April the ice on the rivers breaks up, and the upward roads become mud wallows. This is called the time of *rasputitsa* (roadlessness). The first greenery to be seen is the shoots of wheat or rye sown the previous autumn. Within ten days the scene may change from one of grey ice, snow, and slush, with yellow flattened grass, to one with tender green carpeting all around. The flowers blossom: lily-of-the-valley, cowslips, solomon's seal, the golden globe flower. The most beautiful of the flowering trees is the *cherëmukha* (black alder, bird cherry).[47]

Lent ends at midnight Easter Eve. The Ivanovs go to Staritsa for midnight mass, which culminates in joyous embracing among the people assembled. Christ is risen! Indeed he is risen! There are two distinctive Easter dishes served on Easter night and Easter day: *kulich,* a very rich bread, and *paskha,* a cylindrically shaped mixture of curds, eggs, and sweetening. And of course there are brightly colored Easter eggs, some of which the Ivanovs leave at the cemetery on Easter Sunday. Easter games

---

*Maslenitsa, like Shrovetide and Carnival, has overtones of a sexual orgy. See Y. M. Sokolov, *Russian Folklore* (New York, 1950), p. 187.

include swinging on swings (an ancient rite thought to enhance fertility) and rolling the Easter eggs.

Following Easter are the seven most joyous weeks in the year, especially the seventh week (*Zelenie Sviatki, Russal'naia Nedel'ia*). The nubile boys and girls go outside the village to dance, sing *khorovody,* and play games, many of which are the same as the Yuletide games.[48]

But the Ivanovs are working, as well as celebrating the arrival of spring. In April they thresh the grain which will be used for sowing, and Andrei plows the field for spring crops. Andrei, who is now the *bol'shak,* does the sowing. To prevent the weeds from germinating he wears a clean garment. He carries the seed to the field in unfastened bast bags so that the soil will not "tie up" the seed. Sowing by hand, he puts in the spring wheat first. Then, when the ground is still very moist, he sows the oats. The women manure the kitchen garden and put in all their vegetable crops except garlic (sown in the fall). They sow cabbage in a special patch in a damp low place near the river, and put the potatoes in the spring crop area, as near to the village as possible.[49]

On April 23, the Day of Yegorii (Vlasia), who is the protector of domestic cattle, the Ivanovs join their neighbors for the blessing of the cattle. All the cattle are driven to the common pasture, where public prayers are conducted with consecration of water.[50] In May the women weed and thin the sprouts in the kitchen garden. Andrei sows the remaining oats, then hemp and flax. As soon as the spring floods are over, he works with his neighbors to repair the village bridge, badly damaged by the torrents. He also patches his roof and does other necessary repairs on the *izba.* In early June he sows buckwheat and barley. Then he takes manure to the fallow field and plows it in.[51]

Trinity Week (*Zelenie Sviatki*) is the climax of the spring holiday cycle. Instead of the Yuletide fir, the people of Beryozka honor the birch, symbol of reanimated nature. On Thursday or Saturday before Trinity Sunday the girls of Beryozka go into the woods to choose birch trees and garland each with flowers. They single out one birch and put fried eggs and beer under it. Joining hands in a circle, they sing and dance around it. Then they kiss each other through the garland on the trees, making oaths of friendship and adoption. On Trinity Sunday they will go back and look at the garlands. If a garland is withered, the girl who made it will marry in the coming year or die, they believe. If it is not wilted, the girl will stay a maiden. The garlands are then thrown into the river: if they don't sink, that means good luck.

During Trinity Week the peasants dig up a choice birch from the forest and plant it in the village. The young people of the village do a circle dance and play games around the tree. The peasants decorate their *izbas* and the church with birch, maple, and linden branches, flowers and fragrant herbs. They build bonfires and jump over them, and go bathing in the river.

Shortly after the summer solstice comes the Day of St. John Kupalo—June 24. The oldest person in Beryozka lights a bonfire by rubbing pieces of wood together, and the peasants go leaping over it. They drive their cattle over a bonfire of nettles to protect them from evil spirits, associated with the "waning" power of the sun. Some peasants go bathing in the river and sprinkle others with water. As during

Trinity Week, the girls go through sister adoption rituals and throw garlands in the river to tell fortunes. The children play a game in which a woman called "Kostroma" plays dead, is mourned, and then suddenly jumps up and startles the children. The peasants make another straw dummy, which is buried with lamentations, torn to pieces, burned, or drowned. On the evening of June 24 the peasants look for a special fern in the forest which they think can help them find buried treasure. They also gather medicinal herbs, assuming the vegetation is now at its height and greatest medicinal potency.[52]

The Day of St. John Kupalo falls within the period of St. Peter's Fast, which lasts from Trinity Sunday (the seventh Sunday after Easter) until St. Peter's Day (June 29), three to six weeks in all. On the first Monday of Peter's Fast the peasants make a ceremonial farewell to spring. They construct a straw dummy, and after various rituals tear it apart and throw the straw to the wind.[53] St. Peter's Day, at the end of this period, is the last day of fun before the most grueling work of the year. The youths of Beryozka swing on swings in the woods, dance, and sing *khorovody*. As the sun sets they kneel or bow to it, saying, "Farewell, beautiful Spring, farewell! Come back quickly again." On this day the village presents its herders with oil, cottage cheese, eggs, and bread, as payment for services rendered.[54]

After St. Peter's Day the entire able-bodied population of Beryozka turns out to cut hay in the common meadow. The target for finishing the haymaking is July 8. The men do the cutting with scythes, the women rake the hay into heaps, and whole families work at putting it in shocks. The shocks are then placed on a platform to keep the hay from rotting. Once haymaking is done the men harrow the fallow fields and the women begin to reap cereals, starting with winter rye. Reaping is the hardest of women's work, and this period is called the time of *strada* (toil). Marya, as the senior able-bodied woman in the family, leads her daughter-in-law Anya to the field, bearing bread, salt, and a Christmas candle. As they reap the first sheaf they repeat, "*Stan' moi snop, na tysiachu kop*" ("Stand, my sheaf, for 60,000 sheaves"). The first sheaf, called the *imyaninnik,* they take home and place near the icons. They thresh it separately and either mix it with the seed corn for the next season or use it to fight cattle diseases.[55] The women leave the sheaves in the field to dry in the sun. When they are ready to harvest the hemp and the flax to be used for fiber the women do not cut them, but uproot them. They soak them a little to make them rot, and then crumple, swingle, and comb them.

The peasants take a rest from their toil on July 20, the Day of St. Ilya (Elijah), the protector of cattle. They gather at the church in Staritsa, where cattle are slaughtered and the meat is distributed to the poor and the parish clergy, as well as used for a common dinner of the people. The dinner meat is boiled in parish vats and laid out on long tables for all the adults of the parish. The priest blesses the beer (*kanunnoe pivo*) that the peasants have brewed especially for this day. Then they drink beer and eat *pirogi* at a picnic in the meadow.[56]

The women continue harvesting through August, taking in barley, wheat, oats, and buckwheat. Meanwhile the men thresh grain for family use and sow winter wheat and rye (which will sprout in early spring). On August 18, the day of Floris and Lauris, they drive the horses to an outdoor chapel to be blessed and sprinkled with holy water.[57] On the night of August 31 the people of Beryozka extinguish all their fires; on the morning of September 1, they relight them ritually.* The girls make small coffins of turnips and other vegetables, enclose flies and other insects in them, and bury them with laments.[58]

In late August or early September Marya and Anya, with Andrei's help, finish the reaping. As they approach the end they roll or somersault over the field saying,

> Stubble of the summer grain,
> Give back my strength
> For the long winter.[59]

While this is being said, a pregnant woman or a priest in full vestments is put in a cart and driven across the field. All work together on the last strip of oats. A few stalks are left standing and Marya, the oldest person in the family, twists them tight, saying "*Vot tebe Ilya, boroda, a ty poi i kormy moego dobrogo konia*" ("This is for you, Ilya, the beard, but the feed and mash of my dear horse"). The reference to the beard, possessed by the billy goat as well as men, is probably connected with the primitive Eurasian belief that the spirit of the harvest is a billy goat, or a goatlike creature, that is pursued by the reapers and hides in the last unreaped sheaf. When Marya twists or knots the stalks of this sheaf she is "plaiting the beard of Ilya," and thus protecting the harvest. She leaves bread and salt at the unreaped patch, and it is taboo. Then the Ivanovs take the last sheaf of oats home ceremoniously and put it under the icon of Floris and Lauris until Pokrov Day, October 1, after which they feed it to the livestock.[60]

The grueling work continues in the month of September. The men complete the sowing of winter wheat and rye and begin to thresh the harvested grain. (If the weather has been dry the sheaves have dried in the field and are ready for threshing. But if it has not, in October and November the Ivanovs have to put them in the upper room of their *ovin* [drying shed, or oven]. They start a fire in the lower room, and the heat, rising through an opening, dries the damp sheaves during the night so they are ready for threshing in the morning.) The Ivanovs have a covered threshing floor. Since they have only three threshers in the family, they form a labor pool with their neighbors, the Vasilievs. After threshing comes winnowing, which they do with shovels, and cleaning of the grain by sifting. They then take the threshed grain to the local watermill for processing into flour and groats, after which they store it in their log granary (*zhitnitsa*).[61]

The women meanwhile are doing additional chores. Marya and Anya are processing hemp and flax, harvesting the kitchen garden, shearing the sheep, and slaughtering some geese (September 15) and chickens (November 1). Many peasants brew beer in September and October; Andrei attends a beer bust for men only.[62] In October Andrei collects and chops firewood for the winter, while the women process help. The Ivanovs can now relax and celebrate. Food is abundant, and there are several weddings in Beryozka.

But soon the snows will be upon them. It is time to repair the chinking of the *izba* walls and straighten the shutters. As the roads turn to rivers of mud once again the Ivanovs feel ready for the long winter ahead: the firewood is cut, the granary is

---

*These customs of August 31–September 1 are probably vestiges of the period 1348–1700, when the New Year was celebrated at this time of year.

full, and there is flax, hemp and wool fiber ready for spinning and weaving. The geese have left; it is time to climb up on the *pech'* and wait for spring.

Conclusion

The Russian peasant way of life represents a skillful adaptation to a harsh environment. The peasant family could survive the long, frigid winters of Russia only with great toil and careful management, given the backward technology of 1860. What the family dreaded most was infertility: crop failure, barrenness in livestock, lack of children. What it revered above all was fertility, which meant life and the continuation of the family. The individual Russian peasant sought immortality through the survival of his offspring.

Within the village and in the surrounding fields the peasants felt secure. But as they moved out into the dark forest, the world became increasingly chaotic and menacing. "Out there" were the *leshii* and his companion, the bear, as well as wolves and other carnivores. But the forest also had treasures which could be gathered in summer: berries, nuts, mushrooms, medicinal herbs, flowers. In the forest there were also bark for *lapti* and fuel for the winter. Going into a forest, as well as sailing down a river, meant adventure.

The peasants tended to regard time as cyclical, passing through an endless round of death and rebirth. The cyclical pattern was most evident in the recurrent seasons. They tried to hasten the end of an "old" season and give birth to a new one by various ancient rituals: destroying or burying a dummy representing the spirit of the old season, lighting "new" fires, leaping over bonfires, bathing ritually, staging contests, caroling, and engaging in wild orgies of drinking.

The lifetime of the peasant contained critical moments celebrated in ritual. One was birth, celebrated both by baptism and *razmyvka*. Then there were complicated wedding rituals that were dedicated to fertility. Finally there were funeral rituals that served to purify the home from the "pollution" of death, and to stress the sacred union of living and dead. Life was thus an endless round of birth, death, rebirth. And this round took place in a cosmos of concentric circles with a symbolic sacred axis at the center. This center was the church in the *selo:* Moscow and the tsar were far away.

Notes

1. Wright Miller, *The Russians as People* (New York, 1961), p. 64; A. F. L. M. Haxthausen, *The Russian Empire* (London, 1856), p. 21; and S. A. Tokarev, *Etnografia narodov SSR: Istoricheskie osnovy byta i kul'tury* (Moscow, 1958), p. 51.

2. S. P. Tolstoi et al., eds. for the Akademiia nauk SSSR, Institut etnografii, *Narody Mira: Narody evropeiskoi chasti SSSR,* I (Moscow, 1964), 283–90. Hereafter cited as *Narody Mira.*

3. Ibid., pp. 298–303, and Tokarev, p. 85.

4. *Narody Mira,* pp. 305–10, and Haxthausen, p. 101.

5. Tokarev, pp. 57–59, 69.

6. *Narody Mira,* pp. 309–10, and Haxthausen, p. 101.

7. Harold W. Williams, *Russia and the Russians* (New York, 1914), pp. 336–37; *Narody Mira,* p. 311; Tokarev, p. 65; and Miller, p. 26.

8. Volodymyr Kubijovyc, ed., *Ukraine: A Concise Encyclopedia* (Toronto, 1963), pp. 306–7, and *Narody Mira,* p. 311.

9. *Narody Mira,* pp. 156–57.

10. Ibid., p. 166.

11. Ibid., pp. 106, 170.

12. Ibid., pp. 170–72.

13. Ibid., pp. 167–83.

14. Ibid., pp. 185–89, and W. R. S. Ralston, *Songs of the Russian People, As Illustrative of Slavic Mythology and Russian Social Life,* 2d ed. (London, 1872), p. 396.

15. *Narody Mira,* pp. 222–30, and Tokarev, pp. 48–49.

16. *Narody Mira,* pp. 363–64.

17. John Maynard, *Russia in Flux* (New York, 1962), p. 52.

18. *Narody Mira,* pp. 393–99.

19. Ibid., pp. 371, 376, and Tokarev, pp. 71–72, 76–77.

20. *Narody Mira,* pp. 371–76, and Tokarev, pp. 71–78.

21. *Narody Mira,* pp. 462–64, and Tokarev, p. 28.

22. Vera Sandomirsky Dunham, "The Strong-Woman Motif," in Cyril Black, ed., *Transformation of Russian Society* (Cambridge, Mass., 1960), pp. 459–83.

23. Eric Wolf, *Peasants* (Englewood Cliffs, N.J., 1966), pp. 65–70, and *Narody Mira,* p. 468.

24. Lev A. Tikhomirov, *Russia, Political and Social,* I (London, 1888), 187, and Haxthausen, p. 123.

25. Y. M. Sokolov, *Russian Folklore* (New York, 1950), p. 163; Tokarev, p. 86; and Ralston, pp. 134–38.

26. *Narody Mira,* p. 408, and Ralston, pp. 126–27, 135, 138.

27. Sokolov, pp. 164–66.

28. For descriptions of difficult deliveries see Anton Chekhov, "The Name-Day Party," and John Rickman, "Placenta Praevia," in *The People of Great Russia* (New York, 1962).

29. Tokarev, p. 85, and *Narody Mira,* pp. 467–68.

30. *Narody Mira,* pp. 408–9, 468–69, 187.

31. Ibid., p. 469.

32. Sokolov, p. 216.

33. *Narody Mira,* pp. 497, 879.

34. The foregoing account of the wedding ritual is drawn mainly from *Narody Mira,* pp. 469–72, with contributions from Tokarev, pp. 83–84, and Sokolov, p. 206.

35. *Narody Mira,* pp. 472–73; Tokarev, p. 85; Sokolov, pp. 224–25; Ralston, pp. 309–19; and *Ukraine Encyclopedia,* pp. 345–46.

36. *Narody Mira,* pp. 170, 406–8.

37. Ibid., p. 410.

38. Ibid., pp. 163, 199.

39. Ibid., pp. 394, 413–14.

40. Ibid., p. 399.

41. Ralston, pp. 200–201, 283–84.

42. Angelo S. Rappoport, *Home Life in Russia* (New York, 1913), p. 64, and *Narody Mira,* p. 414.

43. *Narody Mira,* p. 414.

44. Ibid., p. 163.

45. *Ibid.,* pp. 394, 415, and Sokolov, pp. 191–92. Rappoport says that the "spirit of Maslenitsa" was represented by a drunken man in a dirty cart bristling with brooms. The cart was pulled by ten horses, each with a rider dressed in rags, his face blackened with soot, and carrying a whip, broom, or other household tool. The cart went from one *derevnia* to another announcing the end of Maslenitsa (*Home Life in Russia,* p. 38).

46. *Narody Mira,* pp. 394, 415, and Sokolov, pp. 191–92.

47. Miller, pp. 27–29.

48. *Narody Mira,* pp. 394, 415.

49. Ibid., pp. 182–83.

50. Ibid., p. 186.

51. Ibid., p. 163, and Miller, p. 30.

52. Sokolov, pp. 195–96; *Narody Mira,* p. 416; and Ralston, pp. 239–40, 391.

53. Sokolov, p. 195, and Ralston, pp. 143–44, 244–45.

54. Sokolov, p. 196; and *Narody Mira,* p. 186. In the Ukraine this is the day for the "maiden fair." The girls of the *selo* and its satellite *derevni* promenade in the center of town in the hope of catching the eye and heart of a desirable young man (*Ukraine Encyclopedia,* p. 331).

55. *Narody Mira,* pp. 174–77; Sokolov, p. 198; and Ralston, pp. 249–50.

56. *Narody Mira,* p. 186.

57. Ibid., p. 188.

58. Ralston, pp. 254–55.

59. Sokolov, p. 200.

60. Ibid., pp. 198–99; Ralston, p. 251; and *Narody Mira,* p.174.

61. *Narody Mira,* pp. 177–80.

62. Ibid., p. 416, and Ralston, p. 256.

Temptress or Virgin? The Precarious Sexual Position of Women in Postemancipation Ukrainian Peasant Society

CHRISTINE D. WOROBEC

Christine Worobec is assistant professor of history at Kent State University. Her article is an exception in that it concerns Ukrainian, rather than Russian, peasant women. Because her theme, the precarious sexual position of peasant women, has broad applicability, it is included. As in Russia, village society in the Ukraine was male-dominated and operated on a double standard. Ukrainian oral culture and township court cases reveal a belief in woman as "temptress." Together with the folk materials, court cases illustrate male brutality and women's vulnerability. Ukrainian peasant culture justified women's subordination on the grounds that they were unclean and given to uncontrollable sexual urges. Women shared the church's belief that their bodies were polluted. Like men, they mercilessly shamed "fallen women." Yet premarital sex was commonplace, encouraged by courtship practices of bundling. It is significant to note that despite the double standard, township court judges penalized men in cases of seduction and false charges of female promiscuity. Rape was treated as a serious criminal act and punished harshly.

Ukrainian peasant women of the postemancipation Russian Empire, like their Russian counterparts, faced an oppressive patriarchal system in both family and village. Over the ages peasants strictly delineated tasks and functions according to gender and age in order to meet the demands of a predominantly agricultural economy. The precariousness of subsistence agriculture and the peasantry's burdensome obligations to family, community, and state reinforced inflexible and oppressive power relations in the village. Ukrainian peasants feared that any departure from the subordination of woman to man, child to parent, young to old, and weak to strong would threaten the existence of their society and culture. The nobility and state, whose power rested—at least in part—on peasant traditionalism, encouraged such fears. Within the matrix of patriarchalism Ukrainian peasant women were decidedly second-class citizens.

"Temptress or Virgin? The Precarious Sexual Position of Women in Postemancipation Ukrainian Peasant Society" by Christine D. Worobec, *Slavic Review*, Vol. 49, No. 2 (Summer 1990), pages 227–238.

The attitudes and behavior of Ukrainian male-dominated peasant society toward women deserves examination. Ukrainian oral culture and *volost'* [township] court cases reveal a pervasive belief in woman as "temptress," justifying her subordination. To permit woman with her insatiable sexual appetite to govern the village and outside world, Ukrainian peasants believed, would spell chaos and disaster—that is, an overturning of the male status quo. Consequently, woman's sexuality had to be harnessed to a strict moral code and subjected to patriarchal control. In this respect Ukrainian peasants shared common cultural features with European Christian societies. The view of woman as temptress was rooted in ancient times and reinforced in the second through fifth centuries by church fathers who interpreted original sin as a sexual act initiated by Eve.[1]

While the image of woman as temptress was not unique to Ukrainian peasants, the Ukrainian peasant worldview contains nuances worth studying. Ukrainian versions of Creation and the Fall had an originality and beauty of their own. Misogynist attitudes toward women pervaded other folktales, courtship practices, and marital relations, creating heavy burdens for women. Ukrainian peasants expected women to retain sexual purity before marriage and marital fidelity in spite of their natural sexual urges and male pressures for sexual favors. The fact that men could blame their sexual desires on the enticing woman reinforced the double standard characteristic of other European cultures.

The sources for studying nineteenth-century Ukrainian peasant attitudes toward women are varied. Ukrainian peasants possessed a rich oral culture that nineteenth century and early twentieth-century ethnographers recorded. These ethnographers were intent upon preserving the peasant ethos in order to define a Ukrainian national culture distinct from the dominant Russian one. There are, however, problems in using folklore materials. At times ethnographers neglected to note the geographical locations of their sources and at other times paid little attention to variations of songs and tales within the same village, *volost'*, or uezd [district]. Even when they recorded variations, they were unable to capture the spontaneity and improvisatory skills of peasants. Furthermore, the suspicion with which peasants greeted outsiders hampered ethnographers' work. Accustomed to tax collectors and exploitative landlords, peasants were masters of deceit, reinforcing outsiders' contradictory views of them as both stupid and cunning. They sang songs and told stories that ethnographers expected to hear, leaving the bawdy versions for occasions when the village was free of busybody officials and scholars. Only an ethnographer who had earned the peasants' trust would have been introduced to the full panorama of peasant oral culture.[2] Furthermore, imperial Russian censorship laws restricted the publication of Ukrainian language materials. The output of nineteenth-century Ukrainian ethnographers is small, therefore, compared to that of Russian folklorists, who had substantial institutional and, in some cases, government support. Despite these shortcomings, however, the recorded folktales, songs, and courtship and wedding customs of the postemancipation Ukrainian peasantry reveal a rich and complex peasant culture that illuminates popular mentalités.

Ukrainian folktales in which the male voice predominates are an excellent source of misogynist attitudes. They describe woman, on the one hand, as sexual agent and, on the other, as an object of male sexual desires and reveal a fascination with her sexual orifices. Both men's and women's voices can be heard in the folksongs. During courtship festivities and weddings men and women sang to each other in antiphonal recitative, describing their expectations of love and marriage. Women also composed love songs, expressing their fears, frustrations, and loves and painting a picture of the world as they understood it. Through these songs the historian glimpses male peasants' treatment and expectations of woman as "temptress."

Volost' court cases of the 1860s and early 1870s from Kiev and Kharkiv provinces supplement the impressions conveyed by oral sources.[3] They provide examples of premarital pregnancies, broken engagements, and rape that required the arbitration of peasant judges outside village kinship networks. While these legal cases cannot be reliably quantified, they confirm the misogynist attitudes of Ukrainian peasants.[4] Together with the folklore materials, they reveal the brutality of men toward women, double standards of conduct for men and women, and the vulnerability of women in an oppressive patriarchal society. Time and again, the picture of woman as temptress colors the Ukrainian peasant worldview.

This study is based mostly on materials from Kiev and Kharkiv provinces, two areas representative of Ukrainian peasant culture despite differences in historical and economic development as well as in landholding patterns. Serfdom lasted longer and was more widespread in Kiev than in Kharkiv. In the postemancipation period Kiev also had a higher concentration of commercial agricultural estates.[5] While hereditary tenure predominated in Kiev, the repartitional commune characterized many of the state peasant enclaves of Kharkiv. Despite these differences, however, the two provinces exhibited similar property devolution systems, subsistence peasant agriculture, and similar cultural features, including the pervasive negative view of woman as temptress.[6] The claim of Kiev and Kharkiv's representativeness is, nevertheless, not intended to diminish or negate the existence of local cultural variations.

Strict patriarchalism reigned in the nineteenth-century postemancipation Ukrainian village. Men deliberated on important village affairs and represented the village in the outside world. They barred women from village politics (except in those instances when they had to accept, if begrudgingly, a widow as household head) and relegated them to a life of subservience. Even the Mother of God, according to a preemancipation Ukrainian popular tale, could not rule the world upon God's death because she was a woman: "What do you mean, the Mother of God?," a runaway serf asked. "That is not a woman's concern!"[7] Ukrainian peasants confined women's responsibilities to bearing and raising children, the usual burdensome household chores of cleaning, baking, cooking, carrying water, and whitewashing the house, as well as tending the vegetable gardens, hemp and flax fields, feeding domestic animals, and lending a hand in the grain fields during busy agricultural periods. Even in such matters, however, the husband enjoyed full authority over his spouse.[8]

All power relations require cultural reinforcements both to legitimize them and to create a value system shared by oppressor and oppressed alike. Postemancipation Ukrainian peasant culture justified the subordination of women on the grounds that they were unclean and prone to uncontrollable sexual urges inherited from Eve. To maintain male domination and deter women from challenging a patriarchal system that provided some order and regularity in an uncertain world, Ukrainian peasants tried to control woman's body through a restrictive moral code. They demanded that woman overcome her sexuality by remaining a virgin until marriage and subsequently maintaining marital fidelity. At the same time, men subjected women to tests, pressuring them for sexual favors. Only a young girl who overcame her natural self and resisted sexual temptations became worthy of marriage. Men who acted on their sexual impulses in such tests could easily condone their actions by blaming woman the "temptress" for arousing their sexual desires, reinforcing a double standard of morality. Within this complicated world fathers and husbands bore responsibility for maintaining their daughters' and wives' honor, seeking retribution against violations of the women's bodies and reputations. By safeguarding a woman's honor, a man demonstrated his ability to control women and preserved his family's honor within the community.

The interpretation of woman's body as evil was not peculiar to Ukrainian peasants. Rooted in ancient Middle-Eastern religions, it became an integral part of Judeo-Christian beliefs. Woman's body, with its cycles and capacity to bear children, inspires both fear and awe in men "since its power belongs to a sphere which is foreign to [them]."[9] Under the influence of the Old Testament, the Orthodox church reinforced taboos concerning menstruating women, suggesting that they were polluted and in danger of fornicating with the devil.[10] It barred women from the church sanctuary and from approaching the high altar, permitting only postmenopausal women to bake communion bread. Women were also physically separated from men in the church. Men stood in front, while women and young girls were relegated to the vestibule, *"v babnike"*[11] [to the old woman's section].

The pervasiveness of Orthodox teachings influenced Ukrainian peasant women's perceptions of themselves. Women not only acquiesced to church demands, but shared the belief that their bodies were polluted. This view had repercussions outside the church, affecting woman's work and childbirth practices. For example, Ukrainian peasant women avoided working in gardens and orchards during menstruation for fear of adversely affecting the growth of fruits and vegetables.[12] They gave birth in such isolated places as the bathhouse, believing that upon delivery they were both vulnerable to evil spirits and dangerous to others. Forty days later they underwent ritual purification. The ceremony of churching was a prerequisite for their reentry into the House of God and into the larger community, a practice rooted in the Old Testament.[13]

This negative Christian appraisal of woman took its justification from the concept of original sin. Ukrainian peasants had their own versions of Creation and the Fall, embellishing the details of the original biblical stories and reflecting similar prejudices toward women. According to a tale from Kanev *uezd*, Kiev province, God created Adam out of earth and woman out of dough, underscoring the fact that woman was made from a different and nondurable substance. When God placed His creations out in the sun to dry, a dog escaped the watchful eye of St. Michael and ate the woman. God then made a new woman out of Adam's rib and called her Eve. Eve's total dependence on Adam for her existence destined her to a life of subordination. In the Radomysl' (Kiev province) version God, after creating Adam out of clay, fashioned woman from a rose and placed her beside the sleeping Adam. When Adam awoke and expressed his displeasure with the rose woman, God placated him by making Eve out of his ribs. God did not discard the rose woman but kept her as a mother for His son. The belief that Eve and the Mother of God were created from different materials suggested to Ukrainian peasants that the female descendants of Adam and Eve were unable to attain the purity of the Virgin Mary.[14]

The Radomysl' tale goes on to describe the Fall. According to Radomysl' peasants, an angel expelled from heaven fell in love with the beautiful Eve and turned himself into the serpent who enticed her to eat the forbidden fruit. When God banished Adam and Eve from the Garden of Eden, He sent them an angel who taught Adam to plant rye and Eve to seed and prepare hemp for clothing. That same angel answered Eve's query about how to beget children by having sexual intercourse with her. Cain was the result of that union.[15] Another tale was even more explicit in claiming that original sin was a sexual act, noting that after Eve's sexual encounter with the devil, she shamed Adam by teaching him all she knew about sex.[16]

The nineteenth-century Ukrainian popular tales of Creation and the Fall paint Eve as sexually enticing and adulterous, character flaws she bequeathed to her female descendants. Therefore, women were viewed as sexual agents, prone to break the law of chastity. Numerous tales from Kupian *uezd* and Shebekino *volost'* in Kharkiv and Kursk provinces depict women as sexual aggressors, suggesting that females of all ages are preoccupied with sex. Thus we read about a three-year-old sticking her finger in her vagina, girls forcing prepubescent boys to have intercourse with them in order to avoid unwanted pregnancies, and prospective brides choosing suitors on the basis of large penises. These tales also portray the attraction of large male sexual organs for married women, prompting them to engage in extramarital sex. One tale reveals male insecurity by concluding that if "all men had similar cocks, there would be less sin among women, especially married women." Still other stories depict women's untiring sexual energies. A woman in one so exhausted her husband that he was incapable of an erection. Another tale explains that a woman is able to have intercourse ten times a night because all she possesses is a "hole." A third story describes how a woman fell seriously ill because she had not had intercourse with her husband over a long period of time. She was completely cured after tricking her husband into penetrating her three times in one night.[17]

Even in instances of male aggression, tales note the pleasure that female rape victims derived from the sexual act, blurring the line between rape and seduction. According to one story a woman subjected to a gang rape initially resisted her assailants but subsequently yielded to their demands because of the enjoyment she derived from the sexual act. In another, a rape victim exclaimed that at the beginning of the sexual assault "I thought that I would not live, but near the end it became nice for me." In another tale a witness to an alleged rape claimed that the plaintiff had enjoyed sexual intercourse with the defendant so much that when he wanted to take leave of her she grabbed his loins, demanding that he penetrate her again. Finally, an unmarried girl of still another story, not knowing that she was being raped, delighted in her physical sensations and asked that they continue.[18] By

stressing women's preoccupation with and enjoyment of sex, men could convenient-
ly blame women for arousing their sexual desires.

Ukrainian peasants also widely believed that women in imitation of Eve were
prone to fornicate with the devil. Tales about devils appearing before girls in the
guise of their boyfriends and engaging them in sexual acts were common. Other
stories depicted devils visiting maidens and young married women at night and
draining their blood by sucking at their breasts. In some tales sexual intercourse
between a woman and devil resulted in the woman giving birth to a serpent.[19]

While the voice in the above tales is decidedly male, Ukrainian peasant women
subscribed to the negative appraisals of their character, even if at times they felt
victimized by men. They wholeheartedly embraced a strict morality that controlled
their sexuality and guarded their morals, seeking out deviant behavior. To prevent a
woman from straying into sin and awakening the spirit of Eve that lurked within her,
the moral code required her to retain her virginity until marriage and subsequently
become a virtuous wife and mother. Deviants had to be publicly shamed in order to
deter others from similar actions because deviants were guilty of more than sexual
immorality: They challenged patriarchalism and the foundations of peasant life. An
unchaste bride questioned her husband's total possession of her and the paternity of
her first child, while an adulterous wife challenged her husband's sexuality and her
subservience to him.[20]

Women no less than men rigorously punished fallen women. In wedding songs
and customs they celebrated virginity as a prerequisite for a successful marriage and
derisively mocked a disreputable young woman. The responsibility for maintaining
a maiden's virginity rested with the girl and her parents, who were honored or
shamed after their daughter's marriage was consummated, depending upon the
presence or absence of virgin blood on the bride's wedding shirt. Wedding guests
sang songs taunting a bride whose wedding nightshirt was not soiled with virgin
blood, calling her "as good as a bag with holes." One song asks the bride with
whom has she sinned: "with the priest, with the cantor, with the cantor's helper,
or . . . with a dog?" Another accuses an unchaste bride of letting pigs graze on her
vagina.[21] Wedding guests also publicly humiliated the bride's parents for not protecting their daughter's virginity. They placed a worn-out wheel on the roof of their
home, a straw yoke around the father's neck, and drove the mother through the
village in a straw box, shouting obscenities at her.[22]

Ukrainian peasant women mercilessly shamed unmarried girls with tarnished
reputations. In the 1870s, the Russian revolutionary, Praskovaia Ivanovskaia, made
the following assessment of their unenviable position among Ukrainian migrant
laborers on an estate in Kherson province: "Should a girl get pregnant, it was
generally she alone who was censured by those around her, cruelly and cate-
gorically, for her weakness and inability to protect herself. The girl bore all the
consequences of the couple's mutual sin."[23] Calling an unchaste girl a *probroitsia*
or *nakrytka* (the mother of an illegitimate child),[24] female villagers unplaited her
hair, covered her face with a kerchief or head with a headdress commonly worn by
married women, and placed a straw yoke around her neck or covered her head with
the hem of her skirt. Then they paraded the disreputable girl, with the symbolic
representation of her delinquency clearly visible to all community members,

through the village streets to the accompaniment of tin drums and jeers.[25] These shaming practices were meant not only to punish transgressors, but also to deter respectable young girls from falling into the trap of sexual depravity.

To protect their daughters' virginity and maintain the family honor, mothers indoctrinated their daughters from an early age in the strict moral values of the community, pointing out the punishments that awaited them should they act on their natural sexual impulses. Preserving young girls' ignorance of their bodies and sexual practices in general was one way to subvert their sexuality, although not a foolproof one. One tale noted that a young girl, intent upon maintaining her honor, engaged in sexual intercourse with a young man, not realizing that in doing so she jeopardized her honor.[26] In the village Solov'evka, Radomysl' *uezd,* parents also asked for spiritual intervention and prayed to St. Kas'ian to protect their maiden daughters from the temptation of sexual indulgence.[27]

Despite these precautions, however, the extensive courting and bundling young people engaged in made it increasingly difficult for postemancipation Ukrainian girls to retain their virginity until marriage. Bundling was an important component of postemancipation Ukrainian courtship practices and the passing on of community values that frowned upon premarital sex, but celebrated sexuality in marriage.[28] Intimate encounters between members of the opposite sex that did not lead to sexual intercourse initiated young people in carressing and fondling, permitting them to let off pubescent steam. They also provided them with an opportunity to examine a prospective suitor or bride for physical defects that would make a permanent union undesirable. Bundling customs were furthermore the ultimate traditional expression of the double standard. With community approval young men tested their girlfriends' moral strength by making sexual advances. Only a girl who controlled her temptress impulses and refused to give sexual favors was worthy of marriage.

A girl who failed the morality tests risked public humiliation. Both boys and girls greeted her with whistles and pig snorts.[29] Village boys further shamed her by tarring her father's home, drawing obscene pictures on the walls, and stealing the gates to the hut. Such public advertisement of her crime made a sexually victimized girl liable to public censure from the community at large, lessening her chances of finding a lad in the village willing to marry her. Her seducer, on the other hand, escaped public humiliation.[30] The community left the matter up to the discretion of the girl's father whether or not to press legal charges. In the event of a legal inquiry, the onus fell on the father and daughter to prove that she was an exemplary model of a woman capable of controlling her sexual urges.

Courting songs sometimes expressed girls' fears of premarital sex and the consequences they would suffer if their crime became public knowledge. In one song of the village Lozoviki, Skvir *uezd,* Kiev province, a young girl invites her boyfriend to spend the night with her and suggests that he is having an erection by asking, "Why is your jacket inflated?" Nevertheless, she adds that he must love her nicely; anything "dirty" is strictly forbidden. In another song a girl acquiesces to a Cossack's request to let him in for the night, but only on condition that he not break her rue, that is, destroy her virginity. In yet another, a girl mourns the fact that she must bear sole responsibility for loving her fellow and having a son by him.[31]

Illegitimacy rates for Kiev province, although low by west European standards, indicate that premarital sex was a matter of some concern, despite contemporary ethnographers' assertions to the contrary.[32] In 1897 in the rural populations of Kiev and Kharkiv provinces the contribution of unmarried women to overall fertility was 2.7 percent and 1.2 percent, respectively. In comparison to the average of 1.9 percent for the rural population of fifty provinces of European Russia, the figure for Kiev province was significantly higher and was surpassed by only fifteen other European Russian provinces, located mainly in the Baltic (including Lithuania), north, north-west, Urals, and Moscow regions. Early ages at marriage for Ukrainian peasant women and underreporting of illegitimate births mask the frequency of premarital sex by depressing illegitimacy rates.[33] Only access to parish records, which provide dates of marriage and birth of the first child, will resolve the question of how frequently shotgun weddings occurred among Ukrainian peasants.

At the end of the nineteenth century parents and government authorities were aware of the dangers of night courting for young girls and in some areas placed curbs on it. An 1893 song from the village Bilozerki, Kherson province, noted that the *desiatskii* [village officer] would not allow *vechernytsi* [evening gatherings] to take place: "Bilozersk boys are fools!/They want to spend the night with us,/[But] the *desiatskii* won't allow it."[34] In areas of Kupian *uezd,* Kharkiv province, rich families banned their daughters from attending the *vechernytsi,* while giving their sons free access to such gatherings. When a poor peasant of the same *uezd* was asked why he permitted his adolescent children to indulge in bundling, he replied:[35]

> Under the condition of our lives it is impossible to make grown-up children sleep at home, especially in the winter when we all sleep in the house; they would seriously squeeze us [i.e., there would be no room]. As you know, we marry early, at ages 18–19: by age 35 we can already have grown children—a daughter-in-law, married sons. And we live in one small house [and] sleep on the floor in a row; the old father [sleeps] on top of the oven, the old mother on the *lezhanka* [sleeping shelf over the stove], so that a young fellow or girl has to sleep side by side with his or her father and mother . . . That is why we do not keep our grown children at home, but allow them to frequent, even send them to, the *vechernytsi.*

His reply suggests that the peasant was advocating some privacy for himself and his wife in their small hut. Having older children sleep outside the home was also a preventative measure against incest.

Furthermore, songs and court cases concerning seduction and premarital pregnancies from Ukrainian provinces, including Kiev and Kharkiv, abound, confirming the common practice of premarital sex. The nineteenth-century historian and ethnographer N. I. Kostomarov noted that songstresses normally viewed the seduced as victims, portraying men as deceivers. They also depicted the irreversible transformation that maidens underwent because of sexual intercourse, a transformation that could not be kept secret from villagers. In one song a Cossack describes for his sweetheart a paradise on earth and tells her that he would like to take her there. The girl believes him and dismisses a warning from a friendly cuckoo that no such paradise exists. The Cossack subsequently seduces the gullible girl under a maple tree. In another song a Cossack plies a girl with mead and wine at an evening social and then leads her to a white birch where he seduces her. The song poetically depicts the girl's loss of her virginity: "Yesterday she was like a cranberry in the meadow.,/But today she has become like white clay./Yesterday she was like a rose in the garden,/But now she has become like rue in water." In other songs the seducer mocks his lover, telling her that she is neither wife nor maiden, but an object of gossip for the entire village. He tells her that he will marry a maiden, while she must wear the headdress of a married woman. In yet another song a young lad boasts to a girl he has just seduced that he had previously deceived ten girls.[36] Variations of a song in which an unmarried girl committed infanticide and beseeched her mother not to allow her other five daughters to attend *dosvitky* [young people's gatherings], which always ended in bundling, were widespread throughout Ukraine.[37]

Cases of seduction that came before the *volost'* courts in Kiev province demonstrate that young girls who acquiesced to the pressures of males to indulge in sexual intercourse often did so with the understanding that their suitors intended to marry them. In 1872 in a case before the Uman *volost'* court, a father charged a young man with falsely promising to marry his daughter; as a result of this promise the daughter broke her engagement to another and agreed to have sexual intercourse with the defendant. Once the girl became pregnant, the father continued, the defendant refused to have anything to do with her and became engaged to another girl. The defendant justified his actions by saying that when he was courting the plaintiff's daughter, he learned that she was having affairs with other village boys and decided to leave her for his present fiancée. Since the defendant admitted to fathering the child the plaintiff's daughter was carrying, the *volost'* court judges ordered him to pay the unfortunate girl 5 rubles. This trivial sum, intended to aid the mother in looking after her newborn, indicates that the judges believed the defendant's slanderous testimony about the plaintiff's daughter. In another case, this time before the Semenov *volost'* court in Berdichev *uezd,* judges were more sympathetic to a young girl's plight, probably in light of the strong character references she received from fellow villagers. They fined her seducer 18 rubles for promising to marry her if she engaged in sexual intercourse with him and fined four other village inhabitants 6 rubles each for falsely accusing the female victim of having sexual relations with them.[38]

Volost' court judges were sensitive to the plight of a young girl falsely charged with promiscuity. The chances that a maiden declared to be unchaste and publicly shamed would marry were slim. Her family would also unjustly suffer a loss of honor within the village. As in the previous case, the judges severely punished pranksters who cast aspersions on a young girl's character without any basis. In Bogodukhov *volost'*, Kharkiv province, judges fined four men 5 rubles each for irresponsibly charging a girl with having sexual relations with a Cossack and required them to swear in writing that they had not had sex with the plaintiff. In another case, this time in Dergachev *volost'*, Kharkiv province, parents demanded that each of the young men who tarred the gates to their house, thus falsely accusing their daughter of moral impropriety, be given fifty or more lashes.[39]

In addition to treating false accusations with severity, *volost'* court judges treated rape as a serious criminal act, punishing a convicted rapist quite harshly, at least by *volost'* court standards. For example, In Kiev province between 1864 and 1871 judges fined three rapists between 10 and 25 rubles each and sentenced a fourth to twenty lashes, the maximum corporal sentence permitted in the *volost'* court.[40] Rape was recognized as an act of force, not a voluntary act on the part of the victim.

Peasant judges, however, did not necessarily respect women or disavow the view of woman as temptress. In cases with no witnesses, a rape victim had to prove her innocence on the basis of exemplary character references and at times a physical examination. For example, in a case in Kanev *volost'*, Kiev province, the defendant, Hryhorii Shkortenko, admitted to having had sexual relations with Uliana Chuprynova but justified his actions on the grounds that she was not a virgin. His casting aspersions on the plaintiff's moral character was sufficient for the *volost'* court judges to favor the defendant and conclude that the matter was one for God to decide. In a case before the Smelian *volost'* court in Cherkass *uezd*, Kiev province, on 20 December 1871, the peasant I. Denysenko charged eighteen-year-old Rostymyshyn with beating his eighteen-year-old daughter Ekelyna and forcing her to have sexual relations with him. The judges ordered a local doctor to examine Ekelyna to determine whether she was a virgin. The outcome of the humiliating physical examination was not in Ekelyna's favor. The judges acquitted Rostymyshyn of the rape charge, although they punished him for beating the plaintiff's daughter.[41] A case that came before the Gornostai-Pol' *volost'* court, Radomysl' *uezd*, clearly exemplifies the misogynist attitudes of *volost'* court judges, attitudes that they shared with the rest of the Ukrainian rural population. They acquitted an accused rapist on the grounds that his victim was a soldier's wife and, therefore, a loose woman. The judges simply presumed that the plaintiff in this case was responsible for being raped, ruling that if she "did not want to carry shame, then she should be more careful in future, not drink vodka until she is senseless, and not sleep alone away from other women."[42]

The position of the postemancipation Ukrainian peasant woman was an unenviable one. She lived within a misogynist culture that justified her subordination on the grounds that she was a temptress, prone to sexual activity that threatened the patriarchal structure of peasant society. Women had inherited those negative traits of Eve and were accordingly treated as second-class citizens. A variety of tales, songs, and courtship practices illustrates the oppression that women faced in the postemancipation village. Young women were expected to retain their virginity until marriage and then become virtuous wives and mothers. Yet, courtship practices of bundling subjected them to the pressures of men who tantalized them with promises of marriage if they indulged in sexual intercourse. Men could afford to overturn the moral code because the fault of sexual promiscuity lay squarely on women's shoulders. The onus was on the female to prove her innocence when charged with transgressing the moral standards of the village. Girls with tarnished reputations were publicly shamed, while their seducers escaped such censure. The brutality of men toward women, the sexual double standards, and the vulnerable position of women in a patriarchal society underscore the harshness of Ukrainian peasant life in which the struggle for survival in a precarious agricultural economy was constant.

Notes

I am grateful to Barbara Evans Clements, Barbara Alpern Engel, and John-Paul Himka for providing detailed criticisms of an earlier draft of this paper which was presented at the American Historical Association Annual Meeting, 30 December 1987, in Washington, D.C. Research for this paper was accomplished with the generous support of the Research Office, Division of Research and Sponsored Programs, Kent State University.

1. Bonnie Anderson and Judith P. Zinsser, *A History of Their Own: Women in Europe from Prehistory to the Present*, 2 vols. (New York: Harper & Row, 1988) 1:78–79.

2. Fortunately for the purposes of this study, there is an extremely rich collection of 319 bawdy Ukrainian folktales from Kharkiv and Kursk provinces. See Pavlo Tarasevskyi, *Das Geschlectleben des ukrainischen Bauernvolkes folkloristische Erhebungen aus der russichen Ukraina*, vol. 1: *Dreihundertneunzehn Schwänke und novellenartiger Erzählungen, die in der Gegend von Kupjanśk und Šebekyno der Gouvernements Charkiv and Kurśk gesammelt worden* (Leipzig: Deutsche Verlagaktiengesellschaft, 1909).

3. When the Liuboshchinskii Commission for Reforming the Volost' Courts conducted its appraisal of the new court system in the early 1870s, it investigated courts in fifteen provinces, including those of Kiev and Kharkiv. These provinces were selected as representative of all the regional, economic, and ethnic diversities of European Russia. See the *Trudy Kommisii po preobrazovaniiu volostnykh sudov: Slovesnye voprosy krest'ian, pis'mennye otzyvy razlichnykh mest i lits i resheniia: Volostnykh sudov, s"ezdov mirovykh posrednikov i gubernskikh po krest'ianskim delam prisutstvii*, 7 vols. (St. Petersburg, 1873–1874). Hereafter cited as *Trudy Kommisii*. Another source for *volost'* court cases in Ukrainian provinces is P. P. Chubinskii, comp., *Trudy etnografichesko-statisticheskoi ekspeditsii v. zapadno-russkii krai*, 7 vols. (St. Petersburg: Izd. Iugozapadnago otdela Imperatorskago russkago geograficheskago obshchestva, 1872–1874), vol. 6.

4. The *volost'* court commissioners did not collect court cases in a systematic and standardized fashion. The criteria for selection appears to have varied with each commissioner. Furthermore, commissioners did not indicate what percentage of court cases they recorded.

5. For a discussion of the effect of commercial agriculture on peasants in postemancipation Kiev province, see Robert Edelman, *Proletarian Peasants: The Revolution of 1905 in Russia's Southwest* (Ithaca, N.Y.: Cornell University Press, 1987).

6. See Christine D. Worobec, "Patterns of Property Devolution among Ukrainian Peasants in Kiev and Kharkiv Provinces. 1861–1900," *Kennan Institute for Advanced Russian Studies Occasional Papers*, no. 206.

7. Apparently St. Nicholas was not to his liking either because the saint did not mind prayer services. The runaway serf cast his vote for St. George because St. George "would slay all the diabolical lords." Recorded in Mykhailo Drahomanov, comp., *Malorusskiia narodnyia predaniia i razskazy* (Kiev: Izd. Iugozapadnago otdela Imperatorskago russkago geograficheskago obshchestva, 1876), p. 140, no. 33.

8. For an example of a folktale justifying male authority in the domestic sphere on the basis of woman's stupidity, see Ivan Savchenkov, "Narodnaia legenda o prave zhenshchiny v malorusskoi sem'e" (1890), cited in D. K. Zelenin, *Opisanie rukopisei uchenago arkhiva Imperatorskago russkago geograficheskago obshchestva*, 3 vols. (Petrograd: Izd. Imperatorskago russkago geograficheskago obshchestva, 1914–1916) 2:623.

9. Martine Segalen, *Love and Power in the Peasant Family: Rural France in the Nineteenth Century*, trans. Sarah Matthews (Chicago: University of Chicago Press, 1983), p. 125.

10. Anderson and Zinsser, *A History of Their Own*, pp. 22–23.

11. S. A. Khotiaintseva and A. A. Usikova, "Sl. Mostki," in *Materialy dlia etnograficheskago izucheniia Khar'kovskoi gubernii*, in *Khar'kovskii sbornik* 8 (1894) part 2: 76.

12. V. Miloradovich, "Zhit'e-byt'e Lubenskago krest'ianina," *Kievskaia starina* (February 1903): 188, 202.

13. Anderson and Zinsser, *A History of Their Own*, pp. 23, 80.

14. Both versions are recorded in Chubinskii, *Trudy* 1 (part 1): 145–46. For another version, see Drahomanov, *Malorusskiia narodnyia predaniia*, pp. 91–93, no. 2.

15. Chubinskii, *Trudy* 1 (part 1): 146–47.

16. Cited in Tarasevskyi, *Das Geschlectleben des ukrainischen Bauernvolkes*, 219–21, no. 242.

17. Ibid., 98–99, no. 133; 19–20, nos. 34–35; 23, no. 39; 247–48, no. 251; 250–51, no. 252; 282–83, no. 263; 26, no. 43; 219–21, no. 242; 254–55, no. 254.

18. Ibid., 18, no. 33; 61–62, no. 92; 21, no. 37; 216–17, no. 240.

19. V. Miloradovich, "Zametki o malorusskoi demonologii," *Kievskaia starina* (September 1899): 380–400; Linda J. Ivanits, ed., "Russian Folk Narratives about the Supernatural," in *Soviet Anthropology and Archeology* 26, no. 2 (Fall 1987): 72–74; P. M. Shinkarev, "Sl. Belo-Kurakino," *Materialy diia etnograficheskago izucheniia Khar'kovskoi gubernii*, in *Khar'kovskii sbornik* 9, part 2 (1895): 272–73; A. V. Ivanova and P. Marusov, "Materialy diia etnograficheskago izucheniia Khar'kovskoi gubernii: Sl. Kaban'e," *Khar'kovskii sbornik* 7 (1893): 434.

20. Simone de Beauvoir, *The Second Sex*, trans. and ed. H. M. Parshley (New York: Bantam, 1970), p. 143.

21. Quoted by Khvedir Vovk, "Shliubnyi rytual ta obriady na Ukraini," in his *Studii z ukrains'koi etnohrafii ta antropolohii* (Prague: Ukrainskyi hromads'kyi vydavnychnyi fond [1926]), pp. 305–6.

22. Afanasii Aiudkevich', "Malorossiiskraia svad'ba s ee obriadami i pesniami, u krest'ian Letichevskago uezda" (1980), cited in Zelenin, *Opisanie rukopisei* 3: 1081.

23. Translated in *Five Sisters: Women against the Tsar: The Memoirs of Five Young Anarchist Women of the 1870's*, ed. and trans. Barbara Alpern Engel and Clifford N. Rosenthal (Boston: Allen and Unwin, 1987), p. 111.

24. Simeon Lukhanov, "Etnograficheskiia svedeniia" (1851), cited in Zelenin, *Opisanie rukopisei* 3: 1104.

25. *Trudy Kommisii* 5: 2, 8, 16, 161.

26. Tarasevskyi, *Das Geschlectleben des ukrainischen Bauernvolkes*, 213–14, 239.

27. Ivan Prokop'ei Savchenko, "Narodnyi kalendar' Vodotniskoi volosti Radomysl'skago uezda" (1886), cited in Zelenin, *Opisanie rukopisei*, p. 616.

28. Bundling occurred during the autumn and winter socials called *vechernytsi*. When the evening's work and festivities were over, couples spent the night together in a group. In the summer individual couples slept together on their own in the unheated portions of peasant huts and barns, away from the watchful eye of parents and other youths. For descriptions of evening socials, see P. V. Ivanov, *Zhizn' i pover'ia krest'ian Kupianskago uezda, Khar'kovskoi gubernii*, in *Sbornik Khar'kovskago istoriko-filologicheskago obshchestva* 17 (Kharkiv, 1907), pp. 208–16; V. Iastrebov, "Novyia dannyia o soiuzakh nezhenatoi molodezhi na iuge Rossii," *Kievskaia starina* (October 1896): 110–28; Volodymyr Hnatiuk, "Pisnia pro pokrytku, shcbo vtopyla dytynu," *Materiialy po ukrains'koi emol'ogii* 19–20 (1919): 286–93.

29. G. A. Kalashnikov and A. M. Kalashnikov, "S. Nikol'skoe," in *Materialy dlia etnograficheskago izucheniia Khar'kovskoi gubernii*, p. 213.

30. In some areas a boy who was a repeated offender may have been barred from evening socials but was not publicly shamed (Iastrebov, "Novyia dannyia," pp. 122–23).

31. The song from Lozoviki is in A. G. Khatemkin, "Pesni molodezhi v sovremennoi derevni," *Kievskaia starina* (September 1897): 309, no. 55; the next song is in N. I. Kostomarov, "Istoricheskoe znachenie iuzhnorusskago narodnago pesennago tvorchestva," in *Sobranie sochinenii N. I. Kostomarova: Istoricheskiia monografii i izsledovaniia*, 21 vols. in 8 bks. (1906; reprint ed., The Hague: Europe Printing, 1967), 8: 952; and the last in V. Miloradovich, *Narodnye obriady i pesni Lubenskago uezda, Poltavskoi gubernii, zapisannye v 1888–1895 g.*, in *Sbornik Khar'kovskago istoriko-filologicheskago obshchestva* 10 (Kharkiv, 1897), part 2: 73, no. 56.

32. The majority of nineteenth-century observers of courtship practices among Ukrainian village youth reported that premarital pregnancies were rare. See Kostomarov, "Istoricheskoe znachenie," 951; Kalashnikov, "S. Nikol'skoe," 206; Valerian Borzhkovskii, "'Parubotstvo,' kak osobaia gruppa v malorusskom sel'skom obshchestve," *Kievskaia starina* (August 1887): 774; A. Gubnykh, "Sl. Bondarevka," in *Khar'kovskii sbornik* 12 (1898), part 2:233. Laura Engelstein has found the same underreporting of peasant sexual practices among doctors studying syphilis in Russian villages. She claims that doctors avoided attributing the virulence of syphilis to extramarital and homosexual relations among peasants, preferring instead to maintain a myth of a puritanical peasantry. See her "Morality and the Wooden Spoon: Russian Doctors View Syphilis, Social Class, and Sexual Behavior, 1890–1905," *Representations* 14 (Spring 1986): 169–208.

33. Legal ages at first marriage were sixteen for females and eighteen for males. In 1897 the mean age at first marriage for females was 20.8. See Chubinskii, *Trudy* 6: 38; Ansley J. Coale, Barbara A. Anderson, and Erma Härm, *Human Fertility in Russia since the Nineteenth Century* (Princeton, N.J.: Princeton University Press, 1979), pp. 136–38, 251–53.

34. Hnatiuk, "Pisnia pro pokrytku," 252, no. 3.

35. Ivanov, *Zhizn' i pover'ia*, p. 209.

36. Kostomarov, "Istoricheskoe znachenie," 976–81. For other songs which describe the seduction of maidens, see Khatemkin, "Pesni molodezhi," 290–91, 298–301.

37. See Hnatiuk, "Pisnia pro pokrytku," 249–389; Miloradovich, *Narodnye obriady*, p. 120, no. 24; Kostomarov, "Istoricheskoe znachenie," 985n; Khatemkin, "Pesni molodezhi," 315–16, no. 69.

38. *Trudy Kommisii* 5: 317, no. 25; 155 (27 April 1871). Similar cases may be found in ibid., 348, no. 4; Chubinskii, *Trudy*, p. 187.

39. It is unclear whether the judges acquiesced to this unusual request, given the fact that twenty lashes was the maximum penalty for any offense that came before the local courts (*Trudy Kommisii* 4; 13; 79–80).

40. Ibid., 5: 69, no. 2; 286, no. 34; Chubinskii, *Trudy*, pp. 186–87, nos. 204–5.

41. Chubinskii, *Trudy*, p. 187, no. 207; *Trudy Kommisii*, p. 246, no. 20. Russian peasants also subjected maidens suspected of moral impropriety to physical examinations. See M. M. Gromyko, *Traditsionnye normy povedeniia i formy obshcheniia russkikh krest'ian XIX v.* (Moscow: Nauka, 1986), p. 98; Hnatiuk, "Pisnia pro pokrytku," 332–33.

42. *Trudy Kommisii*, p. 125, no. 11. For a discussion of the marginality of soldiers' wives in postemancipation Russia, see Richard Stites, "Prostitute and Society in Pre-Revolutionary Russia," *Jahrbücher für Geschichte Osteuropas* 31, no. 3 (1983): 351; Beatrice Farnsworth, "The Soldatka: Folk Lore and Court Record," paper presented at the Conference on the Peasantry of European Russia, 1800–1917, University of Massachusetts–Boston, August 1986. Farnsworth's paper has been published; see Beatrice Farnsworth, "The Soldatka: Folklore and Court Record," *Slavic Review* 49 (Spring 1990): 58–73.

3 / Peasant Women and Their Work

ROSE L. GLICKMAN

Rose Glickman, adjunct associate professor at the State University of Buffalo, presents a particularly bleak picture of peasant women, "subordinate, not just to one father or one husband, but to the entire male community . . . she was mute and powerless." But as Glickman points out, a peasant woman's contribution to family survival was great. She worked in both household and field. As agricultural production declined and the significance of the market grew, women became more responsible for the land as men left to seek seasonal wages. Peasant women in many instances also sought money, looking to occupations that coincided with their domestic and agricultural work. Glickman surveys peasant women's market crafts: among them lacemaking, knitting, weaving, unwinding cotton, and sewing kid gloves for factories. When they could, peasant women sold their agricultural and dairy products. Invariably, women commanded less money than men. Women earned less even in occupations such as agricultural day labor, which they shared with men. Glickman concludes that the patriarchal mentality was so deeply ingrained that women never questioned a discrimination that must have seemed natural to them.

Most women workers in Russia began life as peasants. They abandoned traditional agrarian life, as did men, because the land would no longer support Russia's burgeoning population in the decades after the emancipation of the serfs. Although the underlying impulse to leave the land was the same for men and women, the woman came to the factory according to a rhythm that was governed by her sex and her role in the peasant household and economy. She came with different life and work experiences, different expectations and aspirations, which tempered her experiences as a factory worker and marked them off in significant ways from those of her male counterpart. We must, therefore, briefly examine the life of the peasant woman, her status in the family and the community, and more specifically, her place in the peasant economy: the work that women had traditionally performed in the countryside and how it changed during the period under consideration.

The core of peasant life from which all relationships radiated and which determined values, obligations, rewards, and behavior was land. And land was a male attribute. Although the land was not the private property of any individual male, the right to the land devolved from father to son or, in the absence of sons, to other male

Rose L. Glickman, *Russian Factory Women: Workplace and Society, 1880–1914* (Berkeley and Los Angeles: University of California Press, 1984), pages 27–58. Copyright © 1984. The Regents of the University of California. Reprinted by permission.

relatives. Similarly, the homestead, kitchen garden, farm implements, and domestic artifacts were the collective property of the household and passed indivisibly from one generation of males to the next. Women had rights only over their dowries, which consisted primarily of clothing and kitchen utensils, occasionally a sheep or a cow. As a student of Russian peasant society put it, "Peasant law did not consider women, strictly speaking, members of a household. . . . Therefore, a woman did not hold property rights over a household if male members of a family lived."[1]

Marriage was virtually universal and patrilocal. The peculiarities of patrilocalism in Russia contributed to the woman's instability and contingency within the household:

> As a girl the essence of her existence is to leave her own family for a strange one, that is, to marry. When she is married—taken [*vziata*], that is—from [her own] family, she is bound to the [new] family only by her husband; should he die, she can return to her kin. She may, of course, remain in her husband's family, but in both cases only to work according to her strength in return for sustenance. In other words, there is no solidity to the woman's position, no organic knots to bind her to the family. This is one of the reasons why the woman is at the bottom of the family. Her entire significance . . . consists of undertaking every task assigned to her in the household economy and providing it with new members—most important, sons, who are its real representatives. Girls are accepted only as a necessary evil.[2]

The multiple-family household, controlled by the male parent, was the most prevalent form of family organization until the revolution. The patriarch's authority over the household's life from the smallest detail to the largest included the right to sexual intercourse with daughters-in-law, a practice sufficiently common to merit a special word in the Russian language—*snokhachestvo*. Adult sons had a consultative voice in common family affairs and dominance over their wives. As for the woman, "She may not participate in the governance of common [household] affairs. Every male has the right to participation once he is of age: she, in the final analysis, is considered lower than any adult male."[3]

The rigid partriarchy of peasant society was hardly unique to Russia. In Russia, however, the peasant woman was subordinate, not just to one father or one husband, but to the entire male community. Peasant households were organized into communes and governed by elders, male heads of households who acted in the name of the entire commune. They conducted all transactions with individuals and with the state on behalf of the commune's members; they redistributed land among member households periodically, collected taxes, allocated military obligations, and adjudicated in a variety of ways. The peasant courts (*volostnoi sud*), which were the courts of original and final jurisdiction over all civil and some criminal disputes between peasants, consisted of judges chosen from among male peasants. Women were represented neither in the commune nor in the courts.[4]

Thus, the peasant woman had neither direct access to land, the most vital component of subsistence, nor a role in the conduct of domestic or communal life. She was mute and powerless, a condition expressed in a pithy peasant proverb: *Kuritsa ne ptitsa, da zhenshchina ne chelovek*—a hen is not a bird, a woman is not a person. Her contribution to family survival was nonetheless great. Commentators on peasant life in the prerevolutionary period sometimes speak of the woman's role in peasant economy as "supportive" or "auxiliary," a formulation that derives from a modern definition of work as an activity rewarded with money.[5] Survival in agrarian society, however, was consequent on the indivisible contribution of the family as a unit. In an economy that was for the most part at subsistence level and that relied on domestic production for many necessities, such a functional distinction of the peasant woman's work is misleading and inappropriate. Let us look then at the peasant woman's work.

The multiple-family household often included as many as four sons and their families and could be as large as twenty-five or thirty people.[6] Domestic obligations were allocated among the unmarried daughters and the daughters-in-law by the wife of the male head of household. The mother-in-law, however, commanded only the activities of the women, for like all other women, she had no power in the male establishment and was herself under the thumb of the patriarch. The mother-in-law's power and abuse of power over the women in the household was notorious, and for good reason. As the popular peasant saying described the daughter-in-law's lot: "And who carries the water? The daughter-in-law. And who is beaten? The daughter-in-law. And why is she beaten? Because she is the daughter-in-law."[7] According to the mother-in-law's dictates, the women took turns doing all the domestic tasks, first and foremost those that served the needs of the entire household: cleaning and maintaining the hut, grinding the grain, baking the bread, preparing the daily food, and preserving food for the future. They looked after the livestock and prepared butter and cheese. Sometimes the patriarch assigned the dairy work to the daughter-in-law lowest in his favor as a punishment, for it was heavy and demanding work. The kitchen garden, which produced the larger part of the household's food, was also the women's responsibility.

After attending to the common needs of the household, each woman worked for her own family. She cared for her children, dressed herself, her husband, and her children from head to foot. In some families she was also obliged to provide clothing for the mother-in-law and her husband's unmarried sisters and brothers. No mean task, it often involved the initial preparation of material from the sheep or communal hemp field. Each woman took complete care of her allotment in the household's hemp field from sowing to harvesting, and then prepared garments from the cloth which she spun and wove.

The peasant woman's responsibilities were not limited to the hut and its environs, for the survival of the household depended on her labor in the fields as well. By tradition field work was strictly divided between men and women. Generally, men kept the bees and sheep and ploughed and sowed the land. Women were responsible for fertilizing and weeding before the harvest. During the harvest they mowed the hay (sometimes jointly with the men), stacked it, turned and bound the sheaves. In some regions of the Empire even the joint obligations, like mowing, were traditionally divided by sex; women mowed the hay with a sickle, and men with the scythe.[8] But the sexual division of field labor was not designed to allocate less work to women, nor were these sexual divisions invulnerable to the influence of changing economic forces.

In our period Russian agriculture was suffering from serious underproduction. The land, exhausted by centuries of primitive cultivation, was unable to support a rapidly growing population. The peasant's impoverishment, already observable in the 1870s, was exacerbated in the last two decades of the century when the state initiated a vigorous program of industrialization, for which the peasant bore the cost. Thus, by the 1880s the peasant household was rarely self-sufficient. The land provided neither the surplus necessary for payment of taxes nor food for the peasants, and they were forced to buy goods that they had once produced themselves. Wage labor became a necessity and directly influenced the position and role of the peasant woman in the household and in the larger economy.[9]

As agricultural production declined and the market intruded into the rural economy, the raison d'être of the multiple-family household was undermined. Although the multiple-family household remained the dominant form of family organization to the end of our period, gradually it became more common for married sons and their wives to disengage from the larger household. The smaller family was probably a welcome relief for both men and women. The literature abounds with attestation to the tyranny of the parental generation. The control and independence that the peasant woman acquired may well have been adequate compensation for the increase in her workload. One of the few nineteenth-century sources that investigated the peasant woman noted that in the multiple-family household "she is simply a machine for the execution of predetermined and preallocated family tasks," while "in the smaller family the woman does not work less—perhaps even more, as peasant women themselves acknowledge, especially if they have small children . . . but she controls and manages her own work."[10] Moreover, in the multiple-family household the individual wife's importance was diluted by the other available work hands. In the small family the husband depended mainly on her labor, and her stature must have been enhanced accordingly. She was no longer only one daughter-in-law among many. To abuse the wife unduly, to kick her out of the family (not uncommon in the multiple-family household), or to lose her labor for other reasons could be a catastrophe for the small family.

But we can only speculate about the nature of these changes. The evidence is rare and impressionistic and our own judgment is clouded by the uncomfortable tensions between present-day romanticization of larger extended families and the acceptance of the nuclear family as the norm. Moreover, traditional attitudes and relationships are fiercely tenacious and capable of withstanding serious alterations in the material and economic bases from which they derive. In important ways, the woman's position in both the family and the peasant community remained as it had been. The small family gave her neither greater rights to land inheritance—or even to land use in her own right—nor the right to the slightest participation in village affairs. Patriarchy may have been of a gentler variety with only one male superior to contend with, but patriarchy it remained, down to the husband's prerogative to beat his wife, fully sanctioned by tradition and customary law. His liberal utilization of this prerogative appears to have been preserved intact: "Beating [the peasant woman] is not [considered] an abuse of power, but completely legal and natural to such an extent that the absence of beating is considered abnormal."[11] That observation, made in 1884, could have easily been made in 1914 as well.

The changing economy led to more obvious and tangible changes in the peasant woman's work obligations. Paradoxically, industrialization and the concomitant decline in peasant agriculture increased her share of field labor. The peasant was enormously reluctant to forsake the land entirely, clinging to it as long as it yielded something, however minimal, to family survival. A 1912 *zemstvo* [district and provincial councils] report stated:

> To cast off agriculture completely, to reduce it to nothing, is a decision very few [peasants] can make. But to leave it in the hands of women to carry on some way or other is a decision the majority come to. . . . Therefore, women not only plough, plant, rake, and gather the hay and grain, but often execute the social obligations of men as well.[12]

From all parts of the Empire, transcending the kaleidoscope of regional variations, came reports of women's growing responsibility for the land as men left to seek outside earnings: "Children and old men who remain at home cannot cope with the field work by themselves. Women must take the most active role even in such purely male work as ploughing and haymaking."[13] In 1891 a colorful example was provided in a report from Kostroma province, a province with relatively poor agriculture and many factories: "The stronger representatives of the local peasantry [men] have been driven from here by need, and we find ourselves in a mythical kingdom of amazons."[14] Here, the report continues, women were fulfilling all the duties reserved for men in earlier times, such as the heavy field work, road repairs, and tax collection: "Even in the inns and taverns these days the shrill, drunken voices of women drown out the hoarse bass notes of men's."[15]

The erosion of traditional divisions of agricultural labor was linked to less flexible sexual divisions in the world of wage labor. Men were more likely to see wage labor that took them from the land than were women—not only because women were responsible for child-rearing and therefore less mobile, and certainly not because peasants considered work to be inappropriate for women. Men left the land first, quite simply, because they could earn more than women. Nonetheless, peasant women were forced to earn money as well. Predictably, they looked first to occupations that could be reconciled with their domestic and agricultural obligations.

The picture of women's remunerative work in the countryside must be pieced together from a jumble of inchoate information. The main sources of information are the voluminous *zemstvo* studies and the works of individuals who were devoted to the preservation of peasant crafts. The data range from sophisticated statistical compilations to communiqués from "volunteer correspondents"—village priests, rural intelligentsia, barely literate peasants. The overriding bias in these studies is the compilers' profound opposition to the changes that were occurring in the countryside. Their populist proclivities frequently led them to exaggerate and romanticize the virtues of occupations that permitted peasants to remain on the land, that kept traditional sex roles intact, and to magnify and distort the negative results of emigration to the cities or of any change in traditional village life. By their own admission, and to their consternation, the state of quantitative information about peasant wage work was a shambles, and estimates varied wildly according to fantasies about what ought to be.[16] Still, a clear if only occasionally quantifiable picture emerges of the kinds of remunerative work that women did, the factors that influenced their choices, and the ways in which both changed.

The varieties of women's work were not distributed uniformly throughout the Empire, and depended on the geographical and economic characteristics of each region. For our purposes the country is best divided into three major areas: the Central Industrial Region, the province of St. Petersburg, and the black earth provinces. While this threefold division does not exhaust the country's geographical, climatic, and socioeconomic regions, it encompasses the kinds of wage-earning alternatives available to peasant women throughout the Russian Empire.

The Central Industrial Region was densely populated, and all arable land had been under the plow for more than a century.[17] Long before the spurt of population growth in the mid-nineteenth century, the land had ceased to support the local population, and by 1900 only 6 percent of peasant families survived by the cultivation of their plots alone.[18] In the Central Industrial Region, one of Russia's most heavily industrialized regions, factories were dispersed throughout the countryside as well as concentrated in the city of Moscow. It also had a long and vigorous tradition of *kustar'* production, that is, independent domestic production of hand-made finished products for an undefined market which, since the growth of industry, included putting-out work from the factories.

Table 3.1 shows the most representative women's crafts in Moscow province in 1882, the number of women engaged in each, and the range of yearly income for each.[19]

Women's *kustar'* production fell into three groups: In Group I the woman worker was completely independent; she bought or made her own materials, owned her tools, and sold to merchants either directly or through an intermediary. In Group II a merchant provided the materials and tools and bought back the finished product. Group III was work that was given out by factories to peasant women "because they [peasant women] could be paid less than women working in large factories where the identical work is done on machines."[20]

In the 1880s the knitting of woolen gloves and stockings occupied the greatest number of women:

> Come autumn or summer early in the morning on a market day. On the roads that lead from the countryside to Moscow you will see a strange spectacle. You will see row upon row of wagons loaded down with grass, hay, wood, potatoes, and other vegetables, and driving or walking beside them women talking loudly among themselves as their hands move and their fingers flash. They are knitting stockings. You will see women carrying sacks with jugs full of milk and cream, knitting as they walk.[21]

Under the best of circumstances women took the wool from their own sheep. But as sheep raising declined, the wool had to be purchased. In both cases, the women were independent of middlemen for materials, tools of production, or access to the market. The knitter was poorly paid for her efforts, and the work was performed "in addition to her customary family contributions: field work, housework, satisfying the demands of custom, dressing herself, her husband and her children. She is an essential member of the family. . . . In times of need [her earnings] even pay for bread or a cow or sheep."[22] Knitting was completely subject to the vagaries of urban demand and therefore occupied mainly women who lived within a 30-verst radius from Moscow city. As urban tastes changed and factory-produced stockings and

Table 3.1. Women's *Kustar'* Production: Moscow Province, 1882

Group	Number of Women	Range of Yearly Earnings (rubles)
Group I		
Making lace	959	37–60
Embroidering crosses and stars		
for vestments	47	40–60
Knitting stockings and gloves	12,240	15–29
Weaving fishnets	373	11–17
Weaving rope sandals	53	41–132
Weaving reins	204	20–56
Plaiting bast sandals	87	37–47
Group II		
Making lace with gilded threads	330	21
Making glass beads	125	17
Sewing kid gloves	3,025	32–45
Knitting fringes	378	30
Gluing cigarette tubes	8,765	32–40
Plaiting belts	574	19
Plaiting straw hats	42	60–70
Weaving nets	25	25–30
Knitting kerchiefs	42	17–34
Group III		
Unwinding cotton	10,000	10–25
Cutting muslin threads	12	30–50
Darning and trimming	29	40–100

Source: Sbornik statisticheskikh svedenii po moskovskoi gubernii, t. 7, *Zhenskie pro-mysly,* vyp. 4. M. K. Gorbunova, compiler (Moscow, 1882), pp. iv–v.

gloves triumphed over the handcrafted articles, the latter slowly dropped from the woman's repertoire. In 1889 knitting was still singled out as a major woman's craft, but by 1898–1900 it was not even mentioned in the *zemstvo* reports.[23]

The second largest occupation, unwinding cotton, was a job put out by the factory; "Despite the existence of machines for this work, most of the cotton used in cotton-weaving factories is unwound by hand by peasant women in the countryside."[24] The work of unwinding cotton thread had several convenient features for the peasant woman. The factories that put out the work were widely distributed throughout the province and easily accessible. This was important because it eliminated the middleman, who could otherwise eat into the woman's earnings. Simple enough for a six-year-old child, unwinding required nothing more than a bobbin and a roller, which could be purchased for a pittance or made at home. The work could be done in the peasant hut without encroaching on living space; it required neither the cleanliness, good vision, nor concentration of the more skilled crafts.[25] Yet unwinding cotton was not considered a desirable occupation, for the work was dirty and poorly paid. Women were driven to it either by the decline of better-paying crafts or by their lack of skill—two factors that increased over the years. It was always the choice of last resort. By 1900 more than twice as many peasant women in Moscow province were unwinding cotton as in 1882.[26] But from then on the craft declined steadily, so that by 1912 it had become a "victim of machinery."[27] Similar victims of mechanization were flax and wool spinning, also putting-out processes. Employing 12,000 women in 1882, flax and wool spinning had been swallowed up by the factory by the turn of the century.[28]

Some crafts followed an interesting trajectory from the factory to the village and back again to the factory. The craft of sewing kid gloves is one example. In the 1780s small glove factories using serf labor had begun to appear around Moscow (and St. Petersburg) in response to urban demand. After the emancipation of the serfs the preparation of leather was so perfected that it became cheaper to put out the prepared leather to peasant women to sew the gloves together. This craft, although not highly skilled, was more demanding than many others. It required a degree of cleanliness not easy to come by in the peasant hut, agile fingers (in wet weather it was not possible to sew the gloves, because the fingers tended to swell), and good vision. Still, it was a desirable occupation because it paid well—until the factories began to reclaim it. In 1882, 3,000 women in Moscow province sewed kid gloves at home.[29] By 1900 only 575 women were thus employed, and in 1904 *zemstvo* statisticians noted that even that vestige of a formerly important village craft had totally vanished.[30]

Another example of the fluctuating relationship between the factory and women's cottage industry was the manufacture of hollow tubes, called *gil'zy,* for cigarettes. Although *gil'zy* had originally been manufactured in tobacco factories, in the 1880s it had become cheaper to put the work out to peasant women. *Gil'zy* could be made at home with a few inexpensive materials after a few weeks of training. A middleman would buy or rent a hut in the village, which became the *"fabrichka,"* or little factory. Here he instructed the women and girls and then sent them back to their homes with paper cut to size for the hollow tube, cardboard to make the mouthpiece, a small copper cylinder (*bolvanchik*) around which the paper was wound, and a small primitive instrument for inserting the mouthpiece into the paper tube. Young boys were hired to pack the finished *gil'zy* into large cartons to be transported to Moscow. If the middleman (occasionally middlewoman) was not a factory representative, the work in the *fabrichka* was more complicated, for the boys had to cut the paper for the hollow tubes and cardboard for the mouthpieces. It was not unusual for women to spend thirteen hours a day at this work for thirty-five weeks a year.[31] In 1889 *zemstvo* correspondents from Moscow province agreed that "all women do it with the exception of the elderly whose fingers are no longer dexterous."[32] By 1904 the reports stated that "the hand gluing of cigarette tubes has been replaced by machines in the factory, and now only a few women insert the mouthpieces into finished tubes that they receive from the factory."[33]

A host of luxury crafts catering to urban taste were brought from the city of Moscow to a small number of women in the village. The crafts of lace-making with gilded threads, embroidering crosses and stars for vestments, and knitting fringes to be sewn onto fashionable garments all had a transient life in Moscow province in the 1880s. Subsequently, other minor crafts appeared and disappeared in rapid succession in response to the ephemeral dictates of fashion.[34] But by 1911 the demand for domestic handwork of every kind had diminished radically as "the machine continues to bear down relentlessly on home industry, primarily for women and child workers."[35]

Male peasant wage earners were rather evenly distributed throughout the provinces of the Central Industrial Region. By contrast, the distribution of women workers was irregular and contingent on a greater variety of local conditions. To illustrate, let us compare three districts (*uezdy*) in Vladimir province which, like Moscow province, had a rich *kustar'* tradition and a heavy concentration of industry.

Shuiskii district was one of the most highly industrialized areas of Russia. It contained within its borders Ivanovo-Voznesensk, known as the "Russian Manchester," as well as the city of Shuia and the industrial villages of Teikovo and Kokhma. Altogether the factories in Shuiskii district employed at least 100,000 workers.[36] Outside earnings, mostly from factory work, predominated heavily over agricultural earnings in the peasant budget, and 26 percent of the peasant women were wage earners. Half of the women who worked for wages were employed in the factories and came mostly from households whose land did not produce crops. The other half, nine-tenths of whom had heavy field-work obligations, engaged in domestic hand-weaving (only three-fourths of male domestic *kustar'* workers simultaneously worked the land).[37] Domestic production was strictly divided between men's and women's work in Shuiskii district. Most men made goods from sheepskin, work that paid very well in comparison with women's primary work, domestic hand-weaving on a putting-out basis.

Vladimir district was less industrialized and agriculturally more prosperous than Shuiskii district. Nonetheless, male emigration for outside work was extremely high even in households with relatively large parcels of land, mainly because of the shortage of livestock. But only 7 percent of the district's peasant women were wage earners. Women could not be spared for wage-earning work, since the burden of working the land fell on their shoulders. Half of the women wage earners worked in factories. The other half were divided between agricultural day labor and domestic service, because Moscow was too far from Shuiskii district to stimulate *kustar'* production.[38]

Pokrovskii district exhibited yet another configuration. Like Shuiskii and Vladimir districts, it was highly industrialized, and less than 7 percent of the men were engaged exclusively in farming. Of the remainder, two-thirds emigrated to the factories, "so that all the field work is the women's obligation when the men go out for summer earnings."[39] In spite of the remarkably heavy burden of field work, 47 percent of the district's women were domestic wage earners. Putting-out work from local cotton factories remained available as late as 1908, and domestic silk weaving occupied many women because "machine weaving cannot yet be applied to silk and . . .the factory is still in competition with *kustar'* production."[40] However, half the silk weavers were men because silk weaving was a skilled craft requiring two years of apprenticeship. Wages were high, 70–90 rubles per year compared with 20 rubles per year for cotton weaving, a woman's craft. Another option for women, found only in this district, was tearing the nap from woven velveteen, a fulling process that could not yet be done by machine. In the 1880s it had been men's work.

But remuneration was very small, and it passed into women's hands when factory work became available to men.[41]

Throughout the Central Industrial Region, then, uniform and growing economic distress forced most men into wage labor. The women stayed on the land as long as something could be scratched from it. Nonetheless, in addition to playing a large and often major role on the land, women worked for money. Whether they did and what they did depended on the local economic landscape—in other words, on whether urban markets or local factories made work available to them.

In the province of St. Petersburg peasant women had a substantially different array of wage-earning alternatives. Here the climate was harsher, the land stingier, and the population sparse compared with the Central Industrial Region. Although the province was highly industrialized, industry did not go out to meet the peasant in the countryside as it did in the Central Industrial Region. Factories were almost entirely concentrated in and near St. Petersburg city, and only peasants who lived close to the city worked in factories. Proximity to the city was, however, instrumental in determining women's contribution to family survival, but *kustar'* production, so prominent in the Central Industrial Region, played a negligible role, a few women here and there making gloves and weaving fishing accoutrements.[42] The great majority of women engaged in and dominated the sale of agricultural and dairy products, mainly to the city of St. Petersburg. Of the 4,110 families in St. Petersburg district who owned cows, 3,507 sold milk products.[43] The sale of produce from kitchen gardens to the city or, in the summer, to the resort population was exclusively women's work, as was the collection and sale of wild berries, mushrooms, and flowers. Women had complete responsibility not only for growing and gathering, but for carrying the produce to the St. Petersburg markets as well.[44] Calculating their earnings is not possible, since in this type of wage-earning activity the contribution was lost in the household total.

The outlying areas of the province were popular holiday places for the inhabitants of St. Petersburg city and also drew a large number of peasant immigrants from other parts of Russia, looking for factory work in the city.[45] Thus, second in importance among the local peasant women's earnings was the renting of summer accommodations to vacationers and to immigrants, as well as the provision of a number of related services such as cleaning and laundering.[46]

These occupations were created by St. Petersburg's rapid growth in the decades after the emancipation of the serfs. The city's growing appetite for food and services was never satisfied by the meager resources and sparse population of St. Petersburg province, but it provided a stable seasonal market for those peasant women with the resources to accommodate it. Like women's work in the Central Industrial Region, it allowed women to remain close to the household. The important difference between the two areas was the absence in St. Petersburg of factory putting-out work and domestic *kustar'* production. St. Petersburg city was a great textile-producing and tobacco-processing city, so it must be assumed that the absence of putting-out work in the province was due to the better organization, more sophisticated machinery, and greater labor productivity that distinguished St. Petersburg from Moscow. Why the city failed to provide a stimulus and a market for other kinds of hand-made items as Moscow did is not clear. It cannot be fully explained by the long tradition of local *kustar'* production in the Central Industrial Region. As we have seen, much of the *kustar'* work there originated not in age-old peasant crafts, but in the city or factories. In principle, the urban demand of St. Petersburg city could have encouraged something similar in the surrounding countryside. Yet, it did not.

In St. Petersburg, as in the Central Industrial Region, women stayed closer to home than men, as a result of their domestic responsibilities and because the responsibility for working the land fell to them as men increasingly sought outside earnings. In the Central Industrial Region, staying close to home was compatible with factory work because of the wide dispersion of factories in the countryside. In St. Petersburg province the factories, clustered in and near St. Petersburg city, were not a sufficiently powerful magnet to pull women away from the land and the hut. Although the percentage of women abandoning the land for some kind of city work increased between 1887 and 1912, the basic pattern did not change.[47]

The more prosperous agricultural areas of Russia, the so-called black earth provinces, had, in some cases, no industry, and in others, relatively little.[48] In these provinces fewer peasants sought outside earnings, since the land yielded, if not abundance, at least reasonable subsistence. Urban markets for *kustar'* products were few and not easily accessible. Consequently, women's work was largely on the land. In 1884 the *zemstvo* report of Saratov province indicated that the "outstanding characteristic of peasant women is the great variety of their occupations. Divisions of agricultural work into men's and women's hardly exist, unless we count mowing and ploughing as men's work and care of the kitchen gardens as women's. But this is not a systematic division, and one can find many places where men and women exchange jobs."[49] Even most remunerative work was related to the land, mainly the selling of various edibles.[50] The major nonagricultural option for women was the knitting of woolen socks and gloves, which in some parts of the province occupied women the year round, interrupted only by the most necessary field work. Women took the wool from their own sheep and were responsible for selling the finished product in the city of Saratov or to itinerant merchants. The average income for knitters was 15–20 rubles per year.[51] As the demand for hand-knit articles declined in competition with cheaper factory-made goods, women found new occupations. In the famine year of 1892, for example, the weaving of goat down for headkerchiefs, a great luxury item, was brought to two of the most agriculturally productive districts of Saratov province and took a firm hold. "The female population of the countryside has joyfully seized on this new auxiliary occupation. Almost all the women and girls spin on hand wheels, while adolescents and children clean and comb the down."[52] But local opportunities for outside earnings were so few in this agricultural province that peasants were forced to emigrate when the land did not provide adequate subsistence. Men and women left the countryside in equal numbers. In 1904 a survey of *kustar'* production in the city of Kuznetsk, the most important *kustar'* center of the province, indicated that the city's working population was equally divided between men and women.[53]

In the black earth province of Khar'kov, there was yet another configuration of opportunities to earn money. As in Saratov, very few of the inhabitants—only 10 percent—sought outside earnings. But here industry was growing, and the city of Khar'kov offered nonindustrial urban work opportunities as well. Between 1897 and 1912, peasant wage-earning work changed in the following way:[54]

	1897	1912
Percentage of population in *kustar'* production	5.3	2.0
Percentage of women *kustar'* workers	55.0	28.0
Percentage of men *kustar'* workers	45.0	67.0
Percentage of population in the factory	0.5	3.8

By 1912 peasants in the factory far exceeded those who stayed behind to work locally in *kustar'* production: 130,000 in the former and 34,389 in the latter; the opportunities for female *kustar'* work had suffered most. Obviously, many women were going to the factory, or at least to the city, as the steady increase in passports given out to women indicates.[55] But for those who remained behind there was a significant shift in available work. In 1891 *zemstvo* statisticians noted that in this basically agricultural province, weaving had always been a very important woman's job:

> Women have guarded this craft as a necessary way to cover their needs by the labor of their own hands, since by custom all clothing which is not made at home must be acquired somehow by the woman alone. Neither husband nor father give a kopek. Therefore, the year round, women have no rest. In every home there are one or two weaving looms. Each woman works for herself; the mother, the bride, the daughter. All winter they prepare wool and hemp. Spring, summer, and autumn they weave woolens, linen, belts, foot-cloths. . . . With this they dress themselves, their husbands, and their children and sell the surplus at an average of twenty-five rubles per year per household.[56]

In 1891, then, all women wove; by 1912 only 76.7 percent did. But as weaving declined a variety of small *kustar'* occupations emerged to take up the slack. The most important was the production of spinning cards and looms, a craft that had not existed at all in 1891. By 1912 it was entirely in women's hands. The second was a significant increase of women tailors, from 4 percent in 1891 to 15.7 percent in 1912, catering to urban demand. Further, women had moved into some traditionally male occupations such as basket making, coal working, and shoemaking, albeit in small numbers.[57] Thus, even in the provinces with more sustaining agriculture where outside earning was a small part of family survival, women had a growing wage-earning role, determined in these provinces, as elsewhere, by land conditions and urban demand.

Despite the diversity of regional conditions that influenced the proportions of peasant women wage earners and the kinds of work they did, we can make some generalizations about the nature of women's work in the countryside. The most ubiquitous consequence of the changing economy between the 1880s and 1914 was that women took increasing responsibility for working the land to free men for outside wage work. Where male earnings could not assuage growing peasant need, women too sought remunerative work. But unlike men, they engaged first in a variety of occupations that could be combined with household and field obligations. The traditional division between men's and women's work on the land, collapsing under the impact of altered economic forces, was transmitted intact to the world of remunerative labor. Women's work invariably required relatively little training and skill. While it enabled women to move easily from one occupation to another, it also invariably commanded less money than men's work—and less respect. Indeed, the more skilled *kustar'* production that men did exclusively, like blacksmithy, metal working, carpentry, and stonecutting, was called by another name, *remeslo*.

Women earned less even in those rare occupations that they shared with men. Agricultural day labor, which employed both sexes throughout European Russia, is a good example. In 1887 a *zemstvo* statistician was astonished to discover a farmstead with "an extremely original organization: here men received two rubles and two poods of flour per month and women receive two rubles and one and one-half poods of flour per month."[58] Such near equality of wages was unusual enough to merit special attention. According to a 1907 survey of agricultural wages, women earned from one-fifth to two-thirds of men's wages, depending on the region.[59] As a *zemstvo* report observed in 1908:

> Women's remunerative labor is not only technically simpler [than men's] and closer to the domestic hearth, but is also very low on the social ladder. As a result, the social position of the woman worker is lower and more difficult than men's. For this reason women's work is considered less valuable and is paid less than male labor. Women do not have equal rights with men in labor as they do not have equal rights in social life.[60]

For some decades expanding urban markets and putting-out work from factories enhanced the opportunities for peasant women to combine household and field work with wage work. But by the turn of the century the factory's tentacles began to choke off the demand for handmade crafts and, concomitantly, encroached on the work that it had itself created, that is, the various putting-out processes. Many factories that closed during the slump of the first years of the twentieth century abolished their putting-out departments when they reopened, and the manual work previously done by peasant women in their homes was absorbed within the factory walls to be performed on mechanized apparatuses.[61] A limited amount of putting-out work remained available, however, for the absolute numbers of peasant women thus employed, province by province, remained stable between 1902 and 1910.[62] Many peasant women—perhaps most—continued to seek work that was compatible with remaining on the land. Whether it was the exchange of one putting-out process for another, whether it was an occupation abandoned by men for better-paying factory work, or whether a new urban taste surfaced, they eagerly accepted whatever came their way. The salient point is that such work no longer accommodated peasant need. Over the years as more peasant women had to, or wished to, earn money, domestic *kustar'* production simply occupied relatively fewer women, and they went to the factory in ever increasing numbers.

Unfortunately, the subjective dimension of the peasant woman's life and work cannot be deduced from quantitative information on agriculture and labor. Nor has she left memoirs or other tangible sources from which we can make direct judgments. We must therefore rely on the perceptions of the observers of rural life, who only infrequently recorded the voices of women themselves, but whose observations, sometimes direct and at other times oblique, evoke an impressionistic picture of how the peasant woman experienced her life.

For the most part, those who observed and reported on rural work were biased in favor of preserving village life intact. It would have violated tradition to suggest that the peasant woman do nothing but care for children and hut, since field work had been an indivisible component of her existence from time immemorial. Nor was the transformation of production for home consumption to market production regarded as a threat to rural stability and the stability of sex roles. New crafts introduced to the village were hailed as a good thing, for they replaced dying crafts and permitted women to continue working in the village. One *zemstvo* reporter even concluded that the peasant woman's work was not only an economic necessity but morally uplifting as well: "Debauchery is a rare exception among the women of more prosperous [peasant] families, but is entirely normal among the poorer families."[63] In other words, the peasant woman's solid economic contribution to family survival was fully accepted and encouraged. The goal of the proponents of *kustar'* production was to train peasants (men as well as women) in those village industries that might weather the onslaught of industrialization and retard the erosion of village life. Therefore, the conditions under which peasant women worked, the extra burden they bore, and the physical effects of various kinds of work were irrelevant. In fairness to the observers, they seldom put forth the kind of saccharine and sentimental stereotypes of the jolly, healthy farm woman which appeared so often in Western European literature. The distortions are rather in the absence of analysis.

Most observers assumed that women's wage work could easily be slotted into the crevices of her daily activities. It is more likely that women worked many hours a day in addition to their normal obligations. Often women themselves were at a loss to calculate how much time they spent on a craft: "We have no hours, we just do not know," they would say and then explain that since candles were expensive, they simply arranged their working hours to fit the available light.[64] Even the paltriest of earnings could cost the woman ten to fourteen hours a day.[65] Some kinds of *kustar'* work, like sewing kid gloves, were harmful to the eyesight and could only be done for a limited number of years. Women's *kustar'* work was rarely skilled, creative, or innovative. Most of it was, as one *zemstvo* observer noted, a "daily, monotonous grind, requiring long, exhausting hours. Such work not only exhausts the body, but dulls the mind as well."[66] Once a process had been assimilated, it was simply repeated mindlessly as long as demand remained—and sometimes, however futile, longer.[67] Given the constraints of their lives, their poverty, illiteracy, and lack of skill, it is not surprising that as eagerly as peasant women seized new opportunities, they were rarely capable of creating them or ferreting them out. For the most part, peasant women were the passive beneficiaries of benevolent chance. It was not uncommon for an entire village to ply a craft that had been introduced fortuitously by a woman from another village who married a local peasant.[68] The following report from the Ministry of Education illustrates the obstacles faced by even the most energetic of peasant women:

The peasant women of Iashchery [a tiny village in St. Petersburg district] appealed to the Zemstvo for help in learning how to make lace. As their households live in extreme poverty, they wish to make some contribution. They invited a teacher, Mrs. Pushkareva . . . , rented a space in the village and began to make lace. In the first year the women were able to sell part of their work. In view of the current winter unemployment this kind of work would be a great advantage to them, but they do not have the means to pay a teacher [for further training] or to rent a space.[69]

Cooperation was rare among peasant women engaged in *kustar'* production. Occasionally they would render one another certain kinds of services. For example, factories issued only one packet of cotton at a time to women who unwound cotton thread, thereby limiting the amount of money they could earn. Sometimes when a woman decided to stop unwinding temporarily she would pass her workbook on to a friend so the latter could have more work.[70] There were many crafts that would have lent themselves to cooperative marketing, especially those that depended on a middleman to fetch materials and return the finished product to the factory. The middleman, who absorbed some of the producer's already meager earnings, could have been circumvented if the women took turns going to the Moscow markets or the factories. But apparently it never occurred to them.[71] Their isolation and illiteracy also left them prey to the calculated errors of merchants and factories; because the women were unable to read what was written in their workbooks, how much material had been given them, and what the prices were, they were easily cheated.[72]

A thin stratum of peasant women became *khoziaiki,* that is, they abandoned production and worked as middlemen between merchant and producer. From all reports, *khoziaiki,* or any kind of intermediaries, were exploitative in many ways. Women workers often had to accept whatever form of payment the middleman chose to hand out. Payment in kind could be in the form of useful goods, like bread or tea, but frequently it was in useless goods which then had to be sold back to the shops at half the market price. The only way to mitigate the exploitation was to work through several middlemen so as not to be dependent on one.[73]

Women were indeed aware of their exploited position, but this was balanced by "their gratitude, even when [the middleman] cheated them all the time. . . . Some women sincerely looked upon the *khoziaiki* as their benefactresses, for they did not know how they would feed themselves without the work."[74] One could also question whether they resented the fact that their earning power was consistently and significantly lower than men's, not only because they were concentrated in lower-paying occupations but even when they did work identical to men's. There is, however, no evidence for this. It can safely be assumed that the patriarchal mentality was so deeply ingrained in peasant women as well as men that they never questioned what must have seemed to them a law of nature. But it is clear that when there was a choice, jobs that paid women directly were more appealing to them than those in which earnings accrued to the family unit, at least among unmarried women. In Moscow province, for example, women lace-makers would help the family make brushes when lace-making was slow. "But they do this reluctantly because they do not get their earnings 'in hand' . . . and have to wait until the father doles out the money."[75]

A few *zemstvo* observers, less intent on preserving the village intact at any price, perceived that the sharp distinction between men's and women's work made women "the victims of extreme exploitation."[76] To be sure, these divisions were sometimes based on relative physical strength, but by no means invariably. More often, the divisions were based on patriarchial definitions of what was appropriate to women. After the turn of the century, then, the more sensitive *zemstvo* observers approved women's increasing choice of factory work over domestic production. For, to the peasant women, long accustomed to contributing to their own and their family's survival, "It is a misfortune not to work. . . . It is painful and distressing to sit without occupation; bread is dear."[77]

Among Russian peasants, qualities attributed to women and prized by other classes, like beauty and grace, were at most of secondary importance. The most desirable wife was one who even as a girl had demonstrated her capacity for work. Work, paid and unpaid, was the focal point of existence for peasant women as well as men. The specific economic niche occupied by peasant women, assigned them by tradition and modified by the exigencies of an industrializing economy, thus provided them with a legacy of expectations quite favorable to the move from farm to factory. To work hard, to contribute to their own survival and that of their families, was in no way a transformation of their destiny.

Peasant women also brought with them to the factory a legacy of subordination: in the family hierarchy, in community governance, in occupational divisions, in remuneration and rewards, and in status. A romantic view of precapitalist and early capitalist society postulates that when the family was the basic unit of production the woman "had a respected role within the family, since the domestic labor of the household was so clearly integral to the family as a whole."[78] The logic in this assumption is belied by historical reality. True, in our discussion of the peasant woman's world we have not speculated on the informal arrangements that may have been negotiated in subtle and unarticulated ways but not reflected in the codifications of law or inheritance relationships. The bonds of love and affection, of loyalty and other emotional commitments, may have palliated the humiliating effects of patriarchal dominance. We have alluded to but not explored the possible enhancement of the woman's position as multiple-family households fragmented into smaller family units, as peasant women took on greater agriculture and wage-earning burdens. These subtleties of her life remain to be investigated, if indeed there is evidence of them in unexplored sources. It is unlikely, however, that either informal familial accord or the influence of the changing economy seriously dented the double legacy of work expectations and subordination that characterized the woman's life as a peasant. It is now our task to examine the interplay between this legacy and the conditions of her new life as a factory worker.

Notes

1. Theodore Shanin, *The Awkward Class* (Oxford, 1972), p. 222.
2. Aleksandra Efimenko, *Izsledovaniia narodnoi zhizni* (Moscow, 1884), pp. 68–69. A married woman's return to her own kin was not welcomed. Her labor was rarely valued, and

her sons were superfluous, since they were not entitled to be counted in land redistribution. See also Peter Czap, "Marriage and the Peasant Joint Family in the Era of Serfdom," in David Ransel, ed., *The Family in Imperial Russia* (Urbana, Ill., 1978).

3. Efimenko, p. 76.

4. Peter Czap, "Peasant Class Courts and Peasant Customary Justice in Russia, 1861–1912." *Journal of Social History* (Winter 1967).

5. Sula Benet, ed. and trans., *The Village of Viriatino* (New York, 1970), p. 18.

6. Ibid., p. 92.

7. Efimenko, p. 79.

8. V. A. Aleksandrov, ed., *Narody evropeiskoi chasti SSSR,* vol. 1 (Moscow, 1964), pp. 174–89; Benet, pp. 14–17, 95; Efimenko, p. 80. The interplay of tradition and relative physical strength in determining men's and women's agricultural tasks in England is discussed in Eve Hostettler, "Gourlay Steell and the Sexual Division of Labour," *History Workshop* (1977), no. 4, and Michael Roberts, "Sickles and Scythes: Women's Work and Men's Work at Harvest Time," *History Workshop* (1979), no. 7.

9. See Lazar Volin, *A Century of Russian Agriculture* (Cambridge, Mass., 1970), pp. 57–76.

10. Efimenko, pp. 91, 94.

11. Ibid., p. 81.

12. *Statisticheskii ezhegodnik kostromskoi gubernii za 1911,* chast' 1 (Kostroma, 1913), p. 78. The *zemstvos* were district and provincial councils in thirty-four of Russia's fifty provinces. Governed by elected boards of peasant and gentry landowners, they were designed to look after local needs, such as education, roads, medical care, agriculture, etc. The *zemstvos* hired appropriate professional personnel and published reports (7,000 between 1864 and 1914) on a great variety of local conditions.

13. *Materialy dlia otsenki zemel' vladimirskoi gubernii,* t. 2, *Vladimirskii uezd,* vyp. 3 (Vladimir na Kliazme, 1912), p. 4.

14. D. N. Zhbankov, *Bab'ia storona (Statistiko-etnograficheskii ocherk)* (Kostroma, 1891), p. 1.

15. Ibid., p. 3.

16. In a summary of estimates of the number of peasants engaged in *kustar'* production, three major proponents of peasant crafts gave the figures 3 million, 7 million, over 15 million, respectively. See A. D. Pogruzov, *Kustarnaia promyshlennost' Rossii, Ee znachenie, nuzhdy i vozmozhnoe budushchee* (St. Petersburg, 1901).

17. The Central Industrial Region consisted of the provinces of Moscow, Vladimir, Kostroma, Tver', Nizhnii Novgorod, and Kaluga.

18. *Moskovskaia guberniia po mestnomu obsledovaniiu 1898–1900,* t. 4, vyp. 2 (Moscow, 1908), pp. 1–3; Jerome Blum, *Lord and Peasant in Russia* (New York, 1964), p. 330: "Data for 1783–1784 for the province of Tver', directly northwest of Moscow, showed that cash income from agriculture of the peasants covered only 40–50 percent of the money they needed to meet expenses."

19. This table, as well as much of the information that follows, is taken from an extraordinary study commissioned by the Moscow provincial *zemstvo.* The author was part of a movement that argued in support of rural industries as a means to mitigate the disruptive effects of industrialization on traditional peasant life. She and her colleagues hoped to influence the government to train peasants in domestic artisanal work sufficient to keep peasants rural and at least partly agricultural. This volume is the result of her exhaustive study of women's occupations in Moscow province, which does not, however, discuss service occupations or "certain others [peasant women] who work as metal craftsmen, blacksmiths, stonediggers [i.e., traditionally male occupations]." *Sbornik statisticheskikh svedenii po*

moskovskoi gubernii, t. 7, *Zhenskie promysly*, vyp. 4 (Moscow, 1882), p. i. M. K. Gorbunova compiler. (Hereafter referred to as Gorbunova.)

20. Ibid., p. iii.

21. Ibid., p. 143.

22. Ibid., p. 146.

23. *Statisticheskii ezhegodnik moskovskoi gubernii za 1889* (Moscow, 1889), p. 4; *Moskovskaia guberniia po mestnomu obsledovaniiu 1898–1900*, pp. 92–94.

24. Gorbunova, p. 279.

25. Ibid., pp. 279–84.

26. A. S. Orlov, *Kustarnaia promyshlennost' moskovskoi gubernii* (Moscow, 1913), p. 7.

27. Ibid., p. 8.

28. Ibid., p. 7.

29. Gorbunova, pp. 174–84.

30. Orlov, p. 7. *Statisticheskii ezhegodnik moskovskoi gubernii za 1904* (Moscow, 1905), p. 15.

31. Gorbunova, pp. 203–30.

32. *Statisticheskii ezhegodnik moskovskoi gubernii za 1889*, p. 19.

33. Orlov, p. 7. *Statisticheskii ezhegodnik moskovskoi gubernii za 1904* (Moscow, 1905), p. 15.

34. Gorbunova, pp. 8–9, 45–56, 89–91.

35. *Statisticheskii ezhegodnik moskovskoi gubernii za 1911*, chast' 2 (Moscow, 1912), p. 17.

36. The information for Shuiskii district comes from *Materialy dlia otsenki zemel' vladimirskoi gubernii*, t. 10, vyp. 3, *Shuiskii uezd* (Vladimir, 1908), pp. 1–25.

37. Ibid.

38. Ibid., t. 2, *Vladimirskii uezd*, pp. 160–65.

39. Ibid., t. 12, *Pokrovskii uezd*, pp. 1, 12.

40. Ibid., p. 17.

41. Ibid., pp. 42–46.

42. *Materialy po statistike narodnogo khoziaistva v s-peterburgskoi gubernii* (St. Petersburg, 1887), p. 270.

43. Ibid., p. 238.

44. Ibid., p. 244.

45. The immigrant (*prishlye*) peasant population had no land and rarely came to St. Petersburg province with children or elderly family members. Therefore, a larger proportion of immigrant women than indigenous women were wage earners and factory workers. Twenty-two percent of immigrant wage-earning women were in the factory, and 14 percent of the indigenous wage-earning women. Ibid., p. 270.

46. Ibid.

47. *Promysly krest'ianskogo naseleniia s-peterburgskoi gubernii. S-Peterburgskii uezd* (St. Petersburg, 1912), p. 51.

48. The black earth provinces in the southern steppe region of Russia stretched from west to east almost the entire width of the European part of the country. They contained Russia's most fertile land and included the following provinces: Kursk, Orel, Riazan', Tula, Tambov, Voronezh, Penza, Khar'kov, Ekaterinoslav, Kiev, Podol', Saratov, Simbirsk, Kazan', Viatka, and Perm.

49. *Sbornik statisticheskikh svedenii po saratovskoi gubernii*, t. 3, chast' 1, *Promysly krest'ianskogo naseleniia saratovskogo i tsaritsynskogo uezdov* (Saratov, 1884), p. 129.

50. Ibid.

51. Ibid.

52. *Issledovanie kustarnykh promyslov saratovskoi gubernii,* vyp. 5, *Balashovskii i serdovskii uezdy* (Saratov, 1913), p. 1.

53. *Issledovanie kustarnykh promyslov saratovskoi gubernii,* vyp. 1, *Gorod Kuznetska* (Saratov, 1904), p. 2.

54. *Kustarnye promysly v khar'kovskoi gubernii po dannym issledovaniia 1912 g.* (Khar'kov, 1913), pp. 1–3.

55. In 1897, 28,149 passports were issued to women. By 1905 that figure had grown at a very steady rate to 37,600. This was a 25 percent increase, while passports issued to men had increased only 19 percent. *Kratkii ocherk mestnykh i otkhozhikh promyslov naseleniia khar'kovskoi gubernii* (Khar'kov, 1905), p. 100.

56. *Doklad v khar'kovskuiu zemskuiu upravu o kustarnykh promyslakh po khar'kovskomu uezdu* (Khar'kov, 1891), pp. 27–28.

57. *Kustarnye promysly v khar'kovskoi gubernii,* p. 6.

58. *Materialy po statistike narodnogo khoziaistva v s-peterburgskoi gubernii,* vyp. 5, chast' 2 (St. Petersburg, 1887), p. 269.

59. "Otsenka zhenskogo i muzhskogo truda na sel'skikh rabotakh," *Zhenskii Vestnik* (1907), no. 2, pp. 48–49.

60. *Materialy dlia otsenki zemel' vladimirskoi gubernii,* t. 10. *Shuiskii uezd,* vyp. 3 (Vladimir, 1908), p. 33.

61. *Svod otchetov fabrichnykh inspektorov za 1906* (St. Petersburg, 1908), p. iv.

62. *Svod 1902,* pp. 34–35; *1906,* pp. 41–42; *1907,* pp. 44–45; *1908,* pp. 44–45; *1909,* pp. 44–45.

63. *Promysly vladimirskoi gubernii,* vyp. 3, *Pokrovskii i Aleksandrovskii uezdy* (Moscow, 1882), p. 113.

64. Gorbunova, p. 42.

65. Ibid., pp. 89–91, 180–84, 209.

66. *Statisticheskii sbornik po iaroslavskoi gubernii,* vyp. 14, *Kustarnye promysly* (Iaroslavl, 194), p. 46.

67. *Statisticheskii ezhegodnik kostromskoi gubernii 1909 g.,* vyp. 1 (Kostroma, 1912), p. 55.

68. Gorbunova, passim.

69. *Tsentralnyi Gosudarstvennyi Istoricheskii Arkhiv* (TsGIA), f. 741, op. 8, d. 11, 1. 2.

70. Gorbunova, p. 280. The author noted that while this kind of service was rare, even rarer was the fact that it was rendered free.

71. Ibid., p. 175.

72. Ibid.

73. Ibid., pp. ix, 97.

74. Ibid., p. 17.

75. Ibid., p. 5.

76. *Materialy dlia otsenki zemel' vladimirskoi gubernii,* t. 10, p. 33.

77. Gorbunova, p. 5.

78. Eli Zaretsky, *Capitalism, the Family and Personal Life* (New York, 1976), p. 29.

4 / *Razdel:* The Peasant Family Divided

CATHY A. FRIERSON

Cathy Frierson, assistant professor of history at Rutgers University, Camden, explores household divisions with the goal of ascertaining how, why, and when they occurred in terms of the internal dynamic of the household. Factors that impelled division were not exclusively economic; in fact, household division often appeared to be economically irrational. Why did such divisions persist in the face of the risks of a smaller labor supply and less property? One must look beyond economics to a young couple's desire for independence and to the personal tensions within the household. The peasant wife played a role, especially the wife of the youngest son, the woman at the bottom of the pecking order, and the wife of the seasonal laborer, who was defenseless within the household. Frierson supports the view that peasant family life, far from being harmonious, was marked by dissension. That household division was a normal, expected element in the life cycle in late Imperial Russia is underscored by the fact that the young family, when it broke away, followed prescribed community norms and rituals.

Семеро воюют, а один горюет
[Seven people fight, but one mourns]

On September 13, 1887, the peasant E. D. M. came before the assembly of Kozlov *Volost'* [canton] in the Sarapul District of Viatka with a request that the members of the assembly formally approve the break-up of his extended family; he and his older son, P., had already carried out the break-up without the permission of the community. The record does not explain why E. D. M. decided to seek the assembly's approval after the fact, although he did take the trouble to present the necessary information for putting the new households on a legal footing. He explained that family quarrels had caused the division and placed the distribution of family property that he and his son had agreed on before the assembly for its approval. From an original household that had included E. D. M., his wife, and their unmarried daughter of 14 years; P., aged 23, his wife of 27, and their son, 1 year old, and daughter, 2 years; and the younger son, I., 19, and his wife, also 19—two new households had formed. In one, E. D. M. remained with his wife, daughter, young-

"Razdel: The Peasant Family Divided" by Cathy A. Frierson, *The Russian Review,* Vol. 46, No. 1 (January 1987) is reprinted by permission. © 1987 by *The Russian Review.* All rights reserved.

73

er son and daughter-in-law, while P. and his wife set up a separate household with their young children. The assembly members found the cause for the division to be well-founded and the distribution of property to be just. They also established that each household would have the means to support itself and to meet its financial obligations. The personal decision of P. and E. D. M. to go their separate ways thus received the stamp of approval from their community.[1] One family contracted, while another started afresh through the process of family fission, an event in village culture in late Imperial Russia that brought individual choices into the community arena and drew attention to the dynamics of rural family life in a period of economic and social transformation. Within these broader processes of modernization, family fission was the product of personal incentives, conflicts and decisions. For the household which took this step, it represented a shift in the cycle of the extended family as a whole and for every one of its members.

This article explores family or household division with the goal of ascertaining how, when, and why divisions occurred in terms of the internal dynamic of the peasant household. By internal dynamic, I mean the relationships between members of the household at various stages of the extended family's cycle and of each individual's life cycle. These relationships shifted according to the composition of the family units that made up the larger extended family. My analysis leads to two conclusions. The first is that family or household divisions were not, in and of themselves, a new, postemancipation occurrence, although their timing and frequency did reflect social and economic developments peculiar to this period. The second is that we should not seek an explanation for the causes of household divisions exclusively among economic factors. When and how and why a household broke up into smaller units depended as much on personal issues and relationships. Simply stated, households divided when someone, usually a junior male, in the extended family decided to move out on his own. Defining the reasons behind that move requires that we discern all that contributed to this decision. I begin by describing the patterns and rituals surrounding fissions and by exploring how these traditions offered guidelines for what a young man could expect from a division. I then discuss the factors from within the household which could motivate him to request a division, as well as the factors from outside the household which enabled him to act on his desire to leave.

For a young Russian peasant coming of age in a patriarchal extended family, there were few realities more pressing than the household in which he lived. There he rose each day; took his daily bread; acted as son, brother, husband, and father; performed the tasks of agricultural labor assigned to him by his elders; and fell to bed each night. This was his immediate universe, the school for the traditions that shaped his first expectations, the source of sustenance, the arena of his productive activity as long as he worked the land, the network of personal relations and power which identified and controlled him. Within this reality, the young peasant man often faced a dilemma as he entered adulthood, a personal dilemma whose resolution had consequences not only for himself and his nuclear and extended families, but also for his local community, and, ultimately, for the whole of the Russian Empire. That dilemma was that, while the extended family offered him security and sustenance within an agricultural economy, it was a setting in which he remained a subordinate long into his adulthood and which fostered frequent and unpleasant dissension. Furthermore, he was aware of the possibilities of working outside the family farm as a seasonal laborer and may have already had some experience living away from his family home and the patriarch's rule. As the young peasant passed from one stage of his life into another, as he left bachelorhood and minority behind to become a husband and father, he saw his home anew and found himself at the intersection of separate, potentially competing concerns. Whereas he had formerly benefitted from the support of the other, senior members of the household and had contributed through his own labor during his adolescence to the general pool, he now had a new focus as husband and father. The questions he faced were where his allegiance lay, whether he considered the share he and his nuclear family received to be adequate and fair, whether he was willing to continue to accept orders as a junior member of the patriarchal hierarchy. Perhaps he and his wife and children might have a better life outside of the extended family, the large household, the houseful of relatives who both contributed to and competed for the contents of the common pot.

During the postemancipation era, and increasingly during the 1880s and 1890s, evidence mounted indicating that more and more sons were resolving to leave the large household rather than to stay through a cycle that included their father's death and their assumption, sometime in their forties or fifties, of the position of head of household. When the Minister of the Interior collected data from governors in the European provinces to find out if the widespread impression that divisions were happening everywhere and with greater frequency had any foundation in fact, the data he received showed that in 43 provinces, the annual average number of divisions had been 116,229 during the first twenty years after emancipation, but that this figure was higher for the second decade alone, 140,355.[2] The annual average was rising. This evidence alarmed state officials and members of educated society; the natural and desirable shape of Russian rural family patterns seemed threatened.

Observers from every position in the social and political spectrum viewed the peasant family division as a signal of change, as a new development in the structure of rural Russia. Populists viewed the phenomenon with alarm because it implied a rise in individualism and the decline of the spirit of collectivism; Marxists found in it a confirmation of the breakdown of traditional structures under the impact of the penetration of capitalism into the Russian village; to conservative bureaucrats, divisions represented the weakening of patriarchy; and zemstvo liberals feared the economic consequences of smaller household economic units as the foundation of the Russian economy.[3] When they turned to the task of gathering information on the frequency, patterns, causes, and impact of the household or family division, members of educated society did so with these concerns in mind. They approached the phenomenon in terms of issues which were largey external to the household itself, seeking rational or logical explanations for this element in the transformation of rural culture, a transformation most of them feared.

The term *razdel* denoted the division of an extended family into separate economic and residential units. It often appeared as *semeinyi razdel,* "family division," although the term "household division" is also appropriate. For a *razdel* brought about the break-up of a larger household, or *dvor,* and in some instances a houseful of extended family members.[4] The division of the *dvor* implied both the fragmenting of the household as a family unit and the distribution of the movable and immovable property that belonged to the household as an economic unit. Division did not occur as part of the periodic repartition (*peredel*) of land within the commune, but upon the initiative of some member or members of the household who demanded the right to set up an independent enterprise. In most areas of Russia, the term *razdel* applied to divisions following the death of the head of the household, the *bol'shak*. In a *razdel*, brothers and sons of the deceased divided the property. In some cases, an elderly *bol'shak* decided to supervise such a division before his death, distributing the property according to his preference; this was also termed a *razdel*.

Two subsets of the *razdel* were *vydel* and *otdel*, in which an adult member of the extended family either left of his own accord with the *bol'shak*'s sanction (*vydel*), or was driven from the household by the *bol'shak,* or left without his permission (*otdel*). When the division occurred during the lifetime of the *bol'shak,* one son usually stayed in the original household to manage its affairs and to care for the *bol'shak* until his death. Similarly, the widow of the *bol'shak* and unmarried daughters lived with the *bol'shak* of the new generation. A division usually involved a physical separation from the original *dvor,* sometimes removal to a newly constructed dwelling (*izba*) on the original household plot (*usad'ba*), sometimes removal to a new plot assigned by the commune. The presence in most peasant families of unattached individuals who were not part of a surviving or soon-to-be-formed conjugal pair meant that not all post-fission family units were nuclear families.

Recording one locality's experience, V. P. Tikhonov described the composition of the households resulting from forty-five divisions in the Sarapul District of Viatka Province between 1887 and 1890. In thirty-six of these forty-five divisions, one of the resulting units included either unattached adults in addition to the central couple or more than one conjugal pair.[5] Even with this number of divisions resulting in families which contained "extra adults" or more than one couple, forty of the forty-five divisions resulted in at least one nuclear household of husband, wife, and dependent children. These were the households that caused concern among students of peasant life, because the presence of only one male of working age seemed to invite collapse of the household in the face of any serious calamity such as ill health, injury, bad weather, loss of livestock, or crop failure. These so-called small families received almost universal criticism from peasants and from educated observers, both of whom viewed the peasant household as the basic, critical unit of the Russian economy.[6]

It seems from scattered reporting to such bodies as the Tenishev Ethnographic Bureau, the Society of Naturalists, Anthropologists, and Ethnographers, the Ethnographic Division of the Russian Geographic Society, zemstvo statistical bureaus, and various journals that household fissions did indeed often lead to "small families" with only one worker, at least for the years immediately following the division. In the Kadnikov District of Vologda Province, for example, S. Dilaktorskii found that in every case but two in sixty-four divisions that occurred between 1893 and 1897, at least one of the postfission households had only one male of working age.[7] Reports such as these from Viatka and Vologda contributed to the general tendency to look to the household division as the culprit in an Empire-wide situation in which the average number of workers per *dvor* was only 1.38 in 1882,[8] and 52% of all households had one or no male workers as early as 1884.[9] Through *razdel, vydel,* or *otdel,* it seemed that the young peasant man was moving to strike out on his own, leaving the relative security of his extended family home.

When he did so, he rarely left without some seed, equipment, clothing, grain, and poultry or livestock to ease his transition. When we examine the procedures of the household division, we find that the community protected both itself and the new householder from disaster by ensuring that he received a fair share from the original *dvor.*

If we were able to peer through the window of an *izba* in the late nineteenth century when a *razdel* or *vydel* was in process within, we would see something close to the description that follows, a composite of accounts from various areas of central Russia. The house would be cleaned in preparation for this public event. In the icon corner a table would stand, covered with a white cloth. On it would sit candles, bread and salt. The room would be crowded, as family members, elders of the commune, neighbors, relatives, and the village priest gathered. The priest would open the proceedings with a prayer. The elders may have reminded the family that, even at this late date, they should reconcile any differences and avoid a division. If the scene were Riazan' District, the family would have been likely to reply, "We are neither the first nor the last to divide." The family would then step up to the table and break the bread into as many pieces as new households would result from the *razdel* or *vydel.* Elders, whom the family had invited to supervise the division, then would review the preliminary allocation of goods and make any adjustments they considered necessary. In the event of disagreement, the participants cast lots to determine the shares. Sometimes an elder or a literate member of the community would prepare a record of the division of the property to submit for the approval to the community assembly, so that the division would be legal according to the emancipation legislation of 1861 and the law of 18 March 1886 restricting divisions. After all was said and done, the family treated the elders to vodka as payment for their services, and the crowd dispersed.[10]

As the elders and the family members negotiated the allocation of goods, equality was their goal, as the proverb, *"Zerno v zerno, krokha v krokhu, vse porovnu razdelit' dolzhny,"* stated.[11]* According to the customs of most areas of central Russia, male members of the family received equal shares of the movable and immovable property. The widow of the *bol'shak* usually received between one tenth and one seventh of the property, while an unmarried daughter received support until her marriage and received her dowry, but depended on the discretion of her uncles and brothers for anything further. In the event of a *vydel,* the *bol'shak* determined the son's share of the whole and gave that to him, along with his portion of the allotment.[12]

A son who left the household against his father's will or was kicked out through an *otdel* usually could depend on receiving his share of the allotment land, if nothing else. Reports varied from region to region on the ability of the head of the

---

*"Grain by grain, crumb by crumb, everything must be divided equally."

household to cut a wayward son off without any property whatsoever. In some areas of Kostroma, Novgorod, Orel and Iaroslavl' provinces, the *bol'shak* continued to exercise this power, while in Kaluga, Viatka, Vladimir, Vologda and Simbirsk, the community intervened to ensure that the young householder received enough land and goods to take up the task of agriculture alone.[13]

In some cases, one party of the division compensated the other or others with cash if he received more immovable property. One example from Tikhonov's record illustrates the extent to which the principle of equal shares for all males could apply. When the two brothers Iv. and F. divided the property in their *dvor,* each received an allotment for 1¾ souls and half of the farm buildings, animals and store of grain. Each took equal responsibility for taxes and other obligations and assumed an equal share of the arrears, and only the share of the *usad'ba* was divided unequally, with Iv. receiving a plot of 20×50 *sazheni* and F. receiving one of 15×30 *sazheni*. The insistence on equality is striking because Iv., aged 38, headed a family of six members, while F. was a bachelor.[14] Such equality did not always prevail in the division of allotment land, as the sixty-four cases from Kadnikov District mentioned earlier indicated. There, in thirty-two divisions, allotment land was assigned according to the number of working males, while the number of mouths to feed established the allotment share in the remaining thirty-two.[15] Adult workers and "eaters" (*edki*) were the most frequent measures for deciding what was an equitable share, as the householders and the community assigned portions with the economic viability of the new family units in mind.

The rituals surrounding the family division and the patterns of property distribution suggest that this was not a new phenomenon that resulted, in some way, from the emancipation. That watershed in the political and social status of the peasantry does not serve as an appropriate marker for patterns of family life. Instead, the break-up of the extended family as a common feature in the cycle of expansion, decline, and expansion existed before 1861 and survived the emancipation, complete with traditions and inheritance patterns. Both Shcherbina and Chernenkov agreed that state peasants often broke into separate households, but continued to report to the authorities as a single *dvor* before the emancipation.[16] V. A. Aleksandrov goes so far as to say that the small peasant family was the predominant form "from the sixteenth right up to the middle of the nineteenth century. . . ."[17] In his study of the Mishino estate, Peter Czap has found clear evidence that family divisions among the serf population were a cause for concern and were regulated by the landlord. He shows that households increased by 45% between 1782 and 1845, while population grew by only 30%. In the decades prior to the abolition of serfdom, there were very few large households or family communes; in 1782, households with fifteen or more members constituted 44% of the total, but in 1858 they had dropped to 13%.[18] In landlords' archives Czap found letters from peasants that suggested that many of them "found these conditions of the large, extended household nearly impossible to bear."[19] On this estate in the preemancipation period, divisions tended to be "piecemeal," that is, divisions in which conjugal units hived off from the main household rather than complete fissions.[20] He concluded that there had been a "modest increase in the rate of household division," even before the emancipation.[21]

On the one hand, the break-up of extended households seems an entirely logical and expected event in the family cycle. Without divisions of some sort, the households would begin to resemble Old Mother Hubbard's shoe, as the younger families brought more and more members to the household. On the other hand, divisions came to be associated in the minds of outside observers with such developments in the countryside as migratory labor, the rise of individualism and the decline of patriarchy. Precisely because divisions tended to occur piecemeal, it was difficult to discern the causes behind their occurrence. The fact that they did not generally happen at any particular point in the family cycle contributed to the perception that they were somehow extraordinary. *Razdely* that took place following the *bol'shak's* death seemed to come at a natural moment, as two or more adult sons with families of their own faced each other and decided whether they were willing to continue in an extended household where only one of them would be the *bol'shak*. *Vydely* at the time of the son's marriage also came at a natural moment, and, in fact, were customary in the Ukrainian provinces.[22] *Razdely* before the *bol'shak's* death, *vydely* in areas where they were not customary, and *otdely* wherever they occurred, were the cause for concern among peasants and outsiders, who viewed these forms of premature fragmentation as a threat to both the economy and the social order of the rural community. Small households were believed to be financially weaker than large ones, and a proliferation of younger heads of households could dilute the authority of the elders and old-style *bol'shaki*. The fundamental characteristics of Russian culture that Haxthausen had described as "family and the common ownership of property"[23] seemed to be at risk. A *razdel* that occurred at the time of the *bol'shak's* death broke up the extended household at a peak in its number of working males, land allotment, accumulation of livestock and equipment, when the dividers could expect fairly healthy portions of a large pie. *Vydely* and *otdely* tore out a piece of the family's holdings before its high point, leaving the original *dvor* weakened and laying a mean foundation for the rise of the new household.

Before we move back into the household to inquire why a son or brother would request a division, we should pause to consider first the relationship between divisions and household size and, second, the relationship between household size and prosperity. Just as the young man who decided to leave the extended family had a fair notion of what he would receive from the original *dvor,* so from his observation of others who had made a similar choice he was familiar with the risks that move entailed.

The prospective new householder knew that he would head a smaller family, a nuclear family if he requested a *vydel* or left through an *otdel*. Unless he had the means to hire another laborer, he could expect to carry the burden of work himself, with only his wife as a partner until any sons they might have reached working age.[24] If he joined with his brothers in a general *razdel,* he could expect to support either an aging parent, an unmarried sister, or younger brothers not yet of working age. The relationship between divisions and family size seemed so clear that the prominent zemstvo statistician F. A. Shcherbina could write in 1897,

the essential fact is generally known, is banal. That families were larger before than now has long been known, of course, without any analysis of statistical data whatsoever. Thus, the comparison of average sizes according to the data on 10th revision and zemstvo population [figures] completely conforms with the conclusion that earlier the peasant family was larger in its composition and that now it is growing smaller and is splintering.[25]

His study of twelve districts in Voronezh Province led to the conclusion that household size had shrunk dramatically between the tenth revision in 1858 and zemstvo surveys in the 1880s and 1890s. This was especially striking in the case of former state peasants whose average household had contained 10.37 members in 1858, but only 7.43 when the zemstvo census was taken. For all peasants in these twelve districts, the average had declined from 9.49 to 6.87 members.[26] Zemstvo statistics gathered between 1892 and 1905 in several districts of the provinces for which Czap found averages in the years surrounding the emancipation also indicate a decline in household size in both the Central Agricultural and the Central Industrial regions. In Orel Province, the average had gone from 9.1 in 1866 to a range of 6.29–6.96 in four districts at the turn of the century. In Kostroma Province, there was a decline from 6.2 in 1877 to a range of between 5.07 and 6.19 in nine districts between 1898 and 1905. In Vladimir Province, the average of 6.9 in 1863 fell to a range of between 5.16 and 6.15 in thirteen districts in the years 1897–1900.[27] In Tambov Province, the average had fallen from 9.94 to 6.91 among former state peasants and from 7.98 to 6.33 for former estate peasants.[28] For the empire as a whole in 1897, the average population per household was 6.3.[29]

On the aggregate level, then, households did seem to be growing smaller. Behind these figures there was variation not only between the Central Agricultural and the Central Industrial regions, or between provinces or districts, but even within districts themselves. Shcherbina attributed the variation in family size in Voronezh to ethnic differences. In his area of study, the districts with a predominantly Ukrainian population had smaller households on the average than those populated by Great Russians.[30] In Orenburg District, S. Ponomarev found that the crucial factor was proximity to town. In the villages close to town, the average population per *dvor* was 4.4, while he found averages as high as 24 per household in remote settlements.[31] In Minsk Province, Dovnar-Zapol'skii observed tremendous variation in family patterns in neighboring districts. In the Dernovich Canton, the *vydel* was virtually unknown. If a son and his family moved out of his father's house, the extended family continued to eat and work together. In Pinsk District, however, divisions had taken off like wildfire to the extent that most large households were moving directly from the very large family-communes to small or nuclear families.[32]

None of the averages tell us what stage in the family cycle each household had reached when the data were recorded. It is likely that families approaching the moment for a division were at the upper end of the cycle and families fresh from a division were at the lower end. Most households traveled from one end to the other in the course of their existence, beginning as small and nuclear and becoming large or extended. Divisions did diminish the size of households in the short run, but most households would expand as children arrived. The phenomenon of the *razdel* before the *bol'shak*'s death, the *vydel,* and the *otdel* in the postemancipation period suggest, however, that the expansion phase of the family was shorter than before as a junior male opted to move out rather than to wait until he could become *bol'shak* in his childhood *dvor*. He did so fully aware that he left security in numbers behind.

He was also undoubtedly aware that his material resources would be slim at the start. The general opinion was that the inevitable outcome of family fission and the consequent diminution of peasant households was poverty caused either by inadequate land or inadequate labor.[33] In his study of Voronezh Province, Shcherbina found that the smaller the household, the fewer livestock, the less the land, and the less the capital for investment—per capita. Also, in these small households the mortality rate for young members of the family was higher.[34] V. Trirogov reported from Saratov Province that, season after season, more small households than large ones collapsed in the face of natural disaster in the commune he studied.[35] P. Semenov's study of the Muraevensk Canton in Riazan' Province also concluded that large, undivided households were prosperous, while small households tended to be needy and financially unstable.[36] Engel'gardt reported as early as 1879 that "everyone knew this . . . and even so they divided."[37]

The question that confounded contemporary observers was why household divisions persisted in the face of the risks that a small labor supply and meager holdings posed. The image of the peasant as essentially an economic actor so pervaded discussion of this and other aspects of rural life that it informed virtually the entire effort to explain why "[t]he evil [*razdely*] is not diminishing, but grows and grows, even in the face of universal opinion among peasants and outsiders that divisions bring financial ruin."[38] By the mid-1880s, the public debate on the peasant question since 1861 had generated an image of the peasant as the product of the agricultural cycle, a specific type which had evolved through generations of struggle with the Russian soil and climate in an effort to master the land rather than be mastered by it.[39] Many bureaucrats, statisticians, and scholars approached every element of village life with the conviction that the answer would lie somehow in the relation of the man to the soil and his effort to produce and provide for himself. The *razdel* was no exception, for family life was one more creation of the primary relationship between man and earth. This relationship shaped the economy of the peasant household, the fundamental element in the peasant's consciousness as he adjusted his behavior to fit the needs of that economy. Tikhonov expressed this conviction when he stated in his explanation of the causes for family divisions that "the chief interest in the peasant's life, which guides all of his actions, is unarguably economic interest."[40]

This predisposition to look for the economic rationale in the peasant's behavior was one reason that much of the discussion of the household division focused on inheritance patterns and the distribution of property in land and goods. These patterns tell us that both the household and the community were careful to preserve financial stability to the fullest extent possible, indicating that economic considerations were clearly at play in the process of the division. But they do not go very far in explaining why a young man would ask for a division in the first place, except insofar as he could be confident he would not be short-changed once he decided to leave. In this sense, inheritance patterns did not discourage him from departure, as long as he did so with the consent of the *bol'shak*.

It was difficult, indeed, to identify obvious economic incentives for departure. This difficulty led many observers to point to a more nebulous set of incentives which usually fell under the phrase "the urge for independence."[41] More than this "urge," however, the tension of personal relations within the extended family headed the list of reported causes for the break-up of the household. From the early 1870s forward, "arguments between women" or "women's quarrels" served as the most popular explanation for the phenomenon.[42] Even Efimenko, a sympathetic student of the peasant woman's life, concurred with the general opinion that the peasant wife was a persistent, nagging strategist who used every means at her disposal to break up the extended family of her husband.[43] She stood at his ear, constantly reminding him of every injustice she suffered, and pointing out to him any disadvantage he experienced in his position as a junior male. She succeeded when she convinced him that, in some way, he and his wife and children got less out of the household than they contributed. Most family members measured their contribution in terms of labor, labor given over the course of a lifetime. Within the structure of an extended family, however, each individual's lifetime was part of at least two cycles—that of his or her nuclear family and that of the larger extended family. Tension in the household was likely to develop when the cycles of the various nuclear units did not interlock smoothly. And, as Chernenkov astutely observed, given the natural inequality in the composition of the separate units, their interests could only rarely coincide.[44] The haggling among the women and the conflict among the men seems not to have focused on the share of goods received so much as on the amount of work each member gave to the household. From the scattered reports to the Tenishev Bureau and in the published accounts of other observers, we find clues to when and why family fights about the distribution of labor would erupt.

The wife of the youngest son was most likely to voice her dissatisfaction with her position. She was at the bottom of the pecking order as a newcomer, as a woman, and as the bride of the most junior male member of the family. Often she had to bear the heaviest burden in child-care, because she was responsible for looking after her in-laws' children in addition to following the orders of all of the other adults in the household. The request for division often came at a moment in the extended family's cycle when one conjugal pair had more children not of working age than the other pairs did. This pattern suggests that not only the wife, but also the husband began to resent working so hard to support his brother's children.[45] Both Tikhonov's forty-five cases in Viatka Province and Dilaktorskii's sixty-four from Voronezh Province point to this as an issue behind the family division. Thus, in Tikhonov's record, we find Ignatii O. (45 years old) requesting to separate from his father's household. He and his wife of 28 had no children, while eight family members, including his brother's four children, remained in the father's *dvor*.[46] A similar *vydel* came at the request of 28-year-old N. and his wife of 27, who had no children, to leave his father's household, leaving eight members, including his brother's four children.[47] Twenty-three of the forty-five divisions fell into this pattern.

In the record of the sixty-four divisions from the Kadnikov District in Vologda Province, thirty-two of the divisions resulted in one household having two or more mouths to feed more than the other new units, indicating that there had been an uneven distribution of dependents in the original *dvor*.[48] T. Rozdin reported from Simbirsk Province that the decision of the *bol'shak*-widower to remarry, bringing a woman of child-bearing age or already with children of her own into the household, could also prompt his sons to request a division.[49] Several students of the household division found that each member's contribution of labor was a bedeviling issue in the extended family. Dovnar-Zapol'skii explained that one characteristic of the large family as opposed to the small was that there was a strict coordination and account-ing of labor to prevent divisive arguments about who was working too much or too little for the general pool.[50] Tikhonov observed that the peasants of Sarapul District avoided the issue of the labor record of each party to a *razdel* when it came time to determine the allotments. Once the question was raised, it would lead to "endless dispute, accusations and recriminations."[51] Bogaevskii reported that peasants point-ed to unequal shares of labor as the source of most divisions, quoting one who opined that, "In the small family . . . everyone works for himself, everyone earns for himself; but if the family is large, then he doesn't end up with anything for himself."[52] Often it was a dispute over this issue that made a young man in the family impatient to set up his own domain. These were the divisions that appeared to be exceptional, coming at various times in the family cycle, and seeming to be independent of such external factors as the relative wealth or poverty of the area.

One external factor, the opportunity to work as a seasonal laborer, did play a role in household divisions, however. Several local observers drew a direct line between seasonal labor and family divisions. Here, too, the issue was often that of carrying one's weight within the household. These reports provide a sense of the dynamic involved in this relationship. They distinguished between the usual *razdel* following the *bol'shak*'s death; and *vydely, otdely,* and *razdely* during his lifetime. One of the most frequent causes for these was the disruption of patriarchal rule caused by one son's departure for seasonal labor. This disruption took essentially three forms. The first was that the son refused to send all or part of his earnings back to the house-hold, and, upon his return to the village, used his earnings between seasons for liquor and generally loose living. The *bol'shak*'s response, supported by the com-munity, was to drive the wayward son out of the extended household, sending his wife and children with him, if he were married. While the *bol'shak* did not neces-sarily have the right to deny such a son his share of the allotment land, he usually did have the right to deny him any share in the other movable and immovable property of the household.[53]

The second form of disruption could result in either *vydel* or *razdel*. In these cases, the son returned from seasonal labor with money in his pocket and a new sense of independence. He was no longer willing to submit to the *bol'shak*'s orders or to contribute his labor to the support of the extended family beyond his own wife and children. Frequently such sons requested a *vydel,* a division with the approval of the *bol'shak,* who decided what share of the household's property the son would receive. In some cases, this request would provide the incentive for a general division and the *bol'shak* would agree to and supervise the division of all of the property among the family members during his lifetime. In this case, the division would be termed a *razdel*.[54]

The disruption could also take a third form in which the desire for the division came from the wife of the seasonal laborer. In her husband's absence, such a woman was often defenseless within the household. Evidence of physical abuse and general persecution of these young wives runs throughout the court cases in the report of the 1872 commission on the cantonal courts, as well as in later reports from the village.[55] Upon her husband's return, the wife would call on him to divide from the household and thus liberate her from the oppression she experienced in his absence. When one member of the household worked as a seasonal laborer, then, his absence could upset the uneasy equilibrium of labor in the household, and his contribution of all or a share of his salary was essential to maintain family cooperation.[56] The opportunity to participate in seasonal labor could also provide the young man who was debating the benefits and risks of departure with a cushion of insurance against financial disaster on his own.

The new householder had another cushion which many outsiders did not take fully into account. That cushion was the wider community, in general, and the members of his former household, in particular, who served as occasional assistants in his farming. When the young household took up residence next door, the larger family sometimes continued to work together and to share such major structures as the barn and kiln.[57] Within the commune, the new family also continued to live according to the agricultural cycle and to join in the cooperative enterprise of their neighbors. These latter considerations probably explain why the communal assembly rarely blocked a household's request to divide. Evidence from state commissions, the survey of the Free Economic Society on the commune in 1880, local accounts, and the responses to the Tenishev Bureau agree that few households took the trouble to seek the assembly's approval, and those that did could be confident of receiving it.[58] Reports to the Ministry of the Interior showed that only 12% of the divisions between 1861 and 1882 had taken place with the approval of the assembly.[59] The governors' survey of 1897 also indicated that, as the report from Samara stated, "The law of 18 March 1886 . .˙. remained a dead letter and had no essential influence on the ordering of family divisions whatsoever."[60] When a family did go through the formality of presenting a request before the assembly, it was usually just that. Contributors to the Free Economic Society's collection on the commune reported from several areas that the assembly rarely blocked a division, but simply worked to make the allocation of property as fair and financially viable as possible.[61] Thus, the elders of the community did not act as a brake on fissions, despite the hope of the government that they would do so by following the law of 1886 restricting divisions.

We do not know, beyond impressionistic reporting and doomsday predictions, how the new households fared. It would be useful to determine, for example, whether the "younger" smaller units did, in fact, have a higher rate of arrears on taxes and other obligations. Also, a demographic study of the relationship between the frequency of household division and the age distribution and marriage rates in various communities for the period 1861–1905 would tell us whether patterns of family formation and fission showed distinct changes during these years.

However much it alarmed contemporaries, household division was a normal element in the cycle of rural family life in late Imperial Russia. At some point the extended family would break up into smaller units. Each male member of the household knew this, and decided whether to step up the date for his separation according to his ability to cooperate in the larger family, to accept his junior status, to ignore his wife's pleading, and to take on his share of the overall burden of work. If he found that he was unable or unwilling to do what was necessary to remain in the extended family, he precipitated a shift in the cycle. He was more likely to take this move if he had opportunities for seasonal labor to supplement the income of a small householder. Further, he could anticipate that the elders of the community would not try to stop him. When he did separate, in most cases, he continued to follow community norms and rituals as he broke away. The final act in the transition from one homestead to another for such a young man in Viatka Province expressed the voice of family and community in this moment of new beginning when his father, uncle or older brother blessed him during the ceremonial departure:

> May God forgive you and bless you. May you always live with bread! May our blessing always be over you! Live in peace! Keep your household in good order. Do not chase after much, and care for all you are given. May you bring praise to our name and be an example to good people.[62]

Notes

The research for this article was made possible by fellowships provided by the Fulbright–Hayes and IREX programs. I would also like to extend thanks to the staff of the Museum of Ethnography of the Peoples of the USSR in Leningrad for their generous and intelligent assistance.

1. V. P. Tikhonov, *Materialy dlia izucheniia obychnogo prava sredi krest'ian Sarapul'skogo uezda Viatskoi gubernii* (Sbornik svedenii dlia izucheniia byta krest'ianskogo naseleniia Rossii, fasc. 3) (Moscow, 1891), pp. 31–31. In voting approval, the assembly agreed that the division met the criteria established by the law of 18 March 1886: that the resulting households would be financially stable; that each new household would receive enough land; and that outstanding debts and taxes were guaranteed. Ministerstvo vnutrennikh del, *Trudy Redaktsionnoi kommisii po peresmotru zakonopolozhenii o krest'ianakh*, 6 vols. (St. Petersburg, 1904), vol. 5, p. 274.

2. Ministerstvo vnutrennikh del, Zemskii otdel, *Zakonodatel'nye materialy po voprosam otnosiashchimsia k ustroistvu sel'skogo sostoianiia*, fasc. 1 (St. Petersburg, 1899), pp. 88–91.

3. A. N. Engel'gardt, *Iz derevni. 11 pisem, 1872–1882* (St. Petersburg, 1882), p. 282; A. Ia. Efimenko, *Issledovaniia narodnoi zhizni*, fasc. 1: *Obychnoe pravo* (Moscow, 1884), pp. 49–63; V. A. Kolesnikov, *Krest'ianskoe khoziaistvo bol'shoi i maloi sem'i*, Iaroslavl' (1903), pp. 9–13; *Doklad Vysochaishe uchrezhdennoi kommissii dlia issledovaniia nyneishogo polozheniia sel'skogo khoziaistva i sel'skoi proizvoditel'nosti v Rossii* (cited hereafter as "Valuev Commission Report"), unnumbered supplementary volumes, Appendix I (St. Petersburg, 1873), p. 253; P. L., *Zemlia i volia* (St. Petersburg, 1868), p. 56.

4. I use the term "houseful" following Peter Laslett in his "Family and Household as Work and Kin Group: Areas of Traditional Europe Compared," in Richard Wall, ed., *Family Forms in Historic Europe* (Cambridge, 1983), p. 514.

5. Tikhonov, *Materialy dlia izucheniia*, pp. 29–58.

6. For two examples of detailed criticism, see Engel'gardt, *Iz derevni*, p. 282, and Kolesnikov, *Krest'ianskoe khoziaistvo*, pp. 9–13. Similar statements can also be found in the

Valuev Commission Report, unnumbered supplementary volumes, Appendix VI, pp. 160, 247; F. L. Barykov, A. V. Polovtsov, and P. A. Sokolovskii, eds., *Sbornik materialov dlia izucheniia sel'skoi pozemel'noi obshchiny* (St. Petersburg, 1880), p. 357; Ministerstvo vnutrennikh del, Zemskii otdel, *Svod zakliuchenii gubernskikh soveshchanii po voprosam otnosiashchimsia k zakonodatel'stvu o krest'ianakh*, 3 vols. (St. Petersburg, 1897), vol. 2, p. 241.

7. Gosudarstvennyi muzei etnografii narodov SSSR, Leningrad, *fond* 7 (The Tenishev Ethnographic Bureau; cited hereafter as "Tenishev Archive"), *opis'* 1, *delo* 244 (Vologda), *ll.* 37–38.

8. MVD, *Zakonodatel'nye materialy,* fasc. 1, p. 8.

9. MVD, *Trudy Redaktsionnoi kommisii,* p. 273.

10. A. A. Titov, *Iuridicheskie obychai sela Nikola-perevoz, Sulotskoi volosti, Rostovskogo uezda* (Iaroslavl', 1888), p. 62; P. M. Bogaevskii, "Zametki o iuridicheskom byte krest'ian Sarapul'skogo uezda, Viatskoi gubernii," in N. Kharuzin, ed., *Sbornik svedenii dlia izucheniia byta krest'ianskogo naseleniia Rossii (Obychnoe pravo, obriady, verovaniia, i pr.)* (Trudy Etnograficheskogo otdela Imperatorskogo Obshchestva liubitelei estestvoznanii, antropologii i etnografii, bk. 9), fasc. 1 (Moscow, 1889), p. 23; P. I. Astrov, "Ob uchastii sverkhestestvennoi sily v narodnom sudoproizvodstve krest'ian Elatomskogo uezda, Tambovskoi gubernii," in *Sbornik svedenii,* 1889, fasc. 1, p. 147; Barykov, *Sbornik materialov,* p. 173; Tenishev Archive, *op.* 1, *d.* 516 (Kaluga), *ll.* 1–6, and *d.* 644 (Nizhnii Novgorod), *l.* 10; Tikhonov, *Materialy dlia izucheniia,* pp. 68–69.

11. Tikhonov, *Materialy dlia izucheniia,* p. 77.

12. The materials of the Tenishev Archive show these patterns to be characteristic. See V. A. Fedorov, "Semeinye razdely v russkoi poreformennoi derevne," in A. A. Kondrashenkov, ed., *Sel'skoe khoziaistvo i krest'ianstvo Severo-zapada RSFSR v dorevoliutsionnyi period* (Smolensk, 1979), pp. 29–52, for a clear review of these materials as they pertain to fission and separation.

13. Tenishev Archive, *op.* 1, *d.* 579 (Kostroma), *l.* 2; *d.* 810 (Novgorod), *l.* 37; *d.* 914 (Orel), *l.* 17; *d.* 1812 (Iaroslavl'), *ll.* 15–17; *d.* 516 (Kaluga), *l.* 5; *d.* 427 (Viatka), *l.* 18; *d.* 6 (Vladimir), *l.* 12; *d.* 35 (Vladimir), *l.* 15; *d.* 136 (Vologda), *l.* 19; *d.* 257 (Vologda), *l.* 11; and *d.* 1513 (Simbirsk), *ll.* 54–55.

14. Tikhonov, *Materialy dlia izucheniia,* p. 51.

15. Tenishev Archive, *op.* 1, *d.* 244 (Vologda), *ll.* 37–38.

16. F. A. Shcherbina, *Svodnyi sbornik po 12 uezdam Voronezhskoi gubernii* (Voronezh, 1897), p. 314; N. N. Chernenkov, *K kharakteristike krest'ianskogo khoziaistva,* 2nd ed., (Moscow, 1918), fasc. 1, pp. 44–46.

17. V. A. Aleksandrov, *Obychnoe pravo krepostnoi derevni Rossii XVII–nachalo XIX v* (Moscow, 1984), p. 68.

18. Peter Czap, Jr., "The Perennial Multiple Family Household, Russia, 1782–1858," *Journal of Family History* 7 (1982): 14–15.

19. Czap, "The Perennial . . . ," p. 25.

20. Peter Czap, Jr., "'A Large Family: The Peasant's Greatest Wealth': Serf Households in Mishino, Russia, 1814–1858," in Wall, *Family Forms,* pp. 137–38.

21. Peter Czap, Jr., "Marriage and the Peasant Joint Family in the Era of Serfdom," in David L. Ransel, ed., *The Family in Imperial Russia* (Urbana, Ill., 1978), p. 119.

22. Valuev Commission Report, unnumbered supplementary volumes, Appendix VI, pp. 5, 104.

23. August von Haxthausen, *Studies on the Interior of Russia,* trans. Eleanore L. M. Schmidt (Chicago, 1972), p. 277.

24. Aleksandra Efimenko was one of the first to describe how relations between hus-

band and wife changed as she became his sole partner. Other scholars later remarked on this transformation. Efimenko, *Issledovaniia*, p. 92; M. Dovnar-Zapol'skii, "Ocherki semeistvennogo obychnogo prava krest'ian Minskoi gubernii," *Etnograficheskoe obozrenie*, no. 1 (1897): 97; Igor Tiutriumov, "Krest'ianskoe nasledstvennoe pravo (Ocherk narodno-obychnogo prava), II," *Slovo*, February 1881, p. 61.

25. Shcherbina, *Svodnyi sbornik*, p. 13.

26. Shcherbina, *Svodnyi sbornik*, p. 315.

27. Czap, "A Large Family," pp. 146–48; I would like to thank Daniel Field for providing me with the averages from the latter period calculated from Z. M. Svavitskaia and N. A. Svavitskii, *Zemskie podvornye perepisi, 1880–1913; Pouezdnye itogi* (Moscow, 1926), pp. 70–145.

28. Chernenkov, *K kharakteristike*, pp. 47–48.

29. Michael Confino, "Russian Customary Law and the Study of Peasant Mentalities," *Russian Review* 44 (1985): 41.

30. Shcherbina, *Svodnyi sbornik*, p. 317.

31. S. Ponomarev, "Semeinaia obshchina na Urale," *Severnyi vestnik*, no. 1, pt. 2., January 1887, pp. 5–6.

32. Dovnar-Zapol'skii, "Ocherki," pp. 85–86.

33. Valuev Commission Report, unnumbered supplementary volumes, Appendix I, p. 253; MVD, *Svod zakliuchenii* (1897), vol. 2, p. 241; D. I., "Zametki sem'i v Novgorodskoi gubernii," *Sbornik narodnykh iuridicheskikh obychaev*, vol. 2 (St. Petersburg, 1900), pp. 51–96; S. V. Pakhman, "Ocherk narodnykh iuridicheskikh obychaev Smolenskoi gubernii," in *Sbornik narodnykh . . .* , vol. 2, p. 71; Kolesnikov, *Krest'ianskoe khoziaistvo*, pp. 9–24.

34. Shcherbina, *Svodnyi sbornik*, pp. 33–34, 354, 407; F. A. Shcherbina, *Krest'ianskie biudzhety* (Voronezh, 1900), p. 112.

35. V. Tririgov, *Obshchina i podat'* (St. Petersburg, 1882), p. 28.

36. Barykov, *Sbornik materialov*, pp. 139–49.

37. Engel'gardt, *Iz derevni*, p. 286.

38. MVD, *Svod zakliuchenii*, p. 241.

39. Cathy A. Frierson, "From *Narod* to *Kulak:* Peasant Images in Russia, 1870–1885" (Ph.D. dissertation, Harvard University, 1985), pp. 125–66.

40. Tikhonov, *Materialy dlia izucheniia*, p. 67.

41. Tenishev Archive, *op.* 1, *d.* 644 (Nizhnii Novgorod), *l.* 2; *d.* 1725 (Tver'), *l.* 42; *d.* 244 (Vologda), *l.* 19; *d.* 1513 (Simbirsk), *l.* 10; Igor Tiutriumov, "Krest'ianskoe nasledstvennoe . . . , I," *Slovo*, January 1881, p. 66.

42. Valuev Commission Report, unnumbered supplementary volumes, Appendix I, p. 253; Engel'gardt, *Iz derevni*, pp. 282–88; Efimenko, *Issledovaniia*, pp. 74–92; Dovnar-Zapol'skii, "Ocherki," chapter 3; *Etnograficheskoe obozrenie*, no. 2 (1897): 1–2; Tenishev Archive, *op.* 1, *d.* 704 (Novgorod), *l.* 5; *d.* 810 (Novgorod), *l.* 26; *d.* 914 (Orel), *l.* 3; *d.* 6 (Vladimir), *l.* 10; *d.* 427 (Viatka), *l.* 9; *d.* 35 (Vladimir), *l.* 9; Barykov, *Sbornik materialov*, p. 253; Andrei Isaev, "Znachenie semeinykh razdelov krest'ian. Po lichnym nabliudeniiam," *Vestnik Evropy*, July 1883, p. 338.

43. Efimenko, *Issledovaniia*, p. 89. Beatrice Farnsworth describes how in the early 1870s the daughter-in-law had already won her reputation as the most troublesome member of the household. See her "The Litigious Daughter-in-Law: Family Relations in Rural Russia in the Second Half of the Nineteenth Century," *Slavic Review* (Spring 1986): 49–65.

44. Chernenkov, *K kharakteristike*, p. 73.

45. Tenishev Archive, *op.* 1, *d.* 810 (Novgorod), *l.* 26; *d.* 914 (Orel), *l.* 5; *d.* 244 (Vologda), *l.* 12; *d.* 1180 (Orel), *l.* 12.

46. Tikhonov, *Materialy dlia izucheniia*, p. 32.

47. Tikhonov, *Materialy dlia izucheniia,* pp. 34–35.

48. Tenishev Archive, *op.* 1, *d.* 244 (Vologda), *ll.* 37–38.

49. Tenishev Archive, op. 1, *d.* 1513 (Simbirsk), *l.* 10; V. Antipov reported the same pattern in Cherepovetsk District of Novgorod Province (*d.* 786, *l.* 22).

50. Dovnar-Zapol'skii, "Ocherki," p. 97.

51. Tikhonov, *Materialy dlia izucheniia,* p. 80.

52. Bogaevskii, "Zametki . . . ," pp. 5–6.

53. Tenishev Archive, *op.* 1, *d.* 136 (Vologda), *l.* 19; *d.* 257 (Vologda), *l.* 11; *d.* 374 (Vologda), *l.* 16; *d.* 1587 (Smolensk), *ll.* 2–4.

54. Tenishev Archive, *op.* 1, *d.* 644 (Novgorod), *l.* 2.

55. Ia. Lud'mer, "Bab'i stony (Iz zametok mirovogo sud'i)," *Iuridicheskii vestnik,* no. 11 (1894): 446–67; Farnsworth, "Litigious Daughter-in-Law," passim.

56. Tenishev Archive, *op.* 1, *d.* 1714 (Smolensk), *l.* 24; *d.* 1587 (Smolensk), *ll.* 2–4; *d.* 1725 (Tver'), *l.* 42; *d.* 43 (Vladimir), *l.* 6.

57. Tenishev Archive, *op.* 1, *d.* 244 (Vologda), *l.* 34; *d.* 214 (Vologda), *ll.* 84–88; *d.* 1714 (Smolensk), *l.* 26; *d.* 786 (Novgorod), *l.* 28.

58. Cathy A. Frierson, "The Peasant Family Division and the Commune," paper presented at the Conference on the Commune and Communal Forms in Russia, University of London, 7–11 July 1986.

59. MVD, *Zakonodatel'nye materialy,* fasc. 1, p. 6

60. MVD, *Svod zakliuchenii,* pp. 233–34.

61. Barykov, *Sbornik materialov,* pp. 136, 106–7, 174, 203, 221, 237, 253, 296, 328–29, 377.

62. Tikhonov, *Materialy dlia izucheniia,* p. 143.

5 / The Litigious Daughter-in-Law: Family Relations in Rural Russia in the Second Half of the Nineteenth Century

BEATRICE FARNSWORTH

Beatrice Farnsworth, professor of history at Wells College, focuses on the peasant daughter-in-law to illuminate family tensions. Historically, the daughter-in-law has been presented as either troublemaker or victim. Basing her study on peasant township court records, Farnsworth depicts the daughter-in-law as the object of familial abuse from in-laws who might steal her clothing, beat, or rape her. But daughters-in-law fought back, using the postemancipation township courts as their vehicles. Farnsworth questions whether the courts necessarily sanctioned either the unwanted sexual advances of a father-in-law or the beatings of a husband, showing both actions being punished. In her view, court cases that record women's protests against beatings discredit the myth that women regarded a husband's beatings as "natural" and legal. Farnsworth concludes that peasant women asserted and exercised rights to a degree not hitherto recognized.

Russian folk wisdom regarded the daughter-in-law, the *snokha* (a word that also meant sister-in-law), as a source of family friction. Unable to coexist in the cramped quarters of the peasant hut, or *izba,* where a mother-in-law ruled over the stove and a father-in-law kept watch on the family purse, the daughter-in-law supposedly made evident her discontent. A host of proverbs and folk sayings attest to the idea of the *snokha* as troublemaker: the saying that the daughter-in-law "likes the family hands but resents the family pot" summed up this resentment.[1] According to this view, the daughter-in-law took but did not give.

Twentieth-century historians, influenced perhaps by Soviet interpretations as well as by literary impressions, see the peasant daughter-in-law in the prerevolutionary era not as a source of friction but rather as a helpless victim of family hostility: a husband's beatings, a mother-in-law's tyranny, a father-in-law's sexual harassment.[2] Neither of these images of the *snokha*—dissatisfied troublemaker or invariable victim—has been subjected to investigation.

"The Litigious Daughter-in-Law: Family Relations in Rural Russia in the Second Half of the Nineteenth Century" by Beatrice Farnsworth, *Slavic Review,* Vol. 45, No. 1 (Spring 1986), pages 49–64.

In fact, we know very little about the dynamics of the large peasant family in the nineteenth century or about the lives of its women. We have hints in estate correspondence before emancipation, according to Peter Czap, that many peasants found conditions within the patriarchal family "nearly impossible to bear."[3] An inquiry that takes us into the peasant household should provide not only a picture of peasant women's lives but also information about the individual and social tensions within the multiple family system. What was the actual situation of Russian peasant women? What were some of the problems between parents-in-law and daughters-in-law, brothers-in-law and sisters-in-law, husbands and wives? While much of the picture of family oppression is undoubtedly true, it is much less certain that peasant women after emancipation lacked recourse and passively accepted their fate. This essay will focus on the family position of the daughter-in-law and the possibility of redress of grievance in the peasant courts established after emancipation.

Insight into family acrimony may be gained from the potentially revealing record books of the township or peasant courts, institutions set up after the Emancipation of 1861 to adjudicate the civil disputes of peasants. The mission of these township courts, each presided over by some four to twelve elected peasant judges, was to administer justice in conflicts between peasants based on the "traditional peasant way of life," on so-called customary rather than imperial law.[4] The basic means to study the records of the township court is the *Trudy Komissii po preobrazovaniiu volostnykh sudov,* a massive work, providing reports of courts cases.[5] Although of enormous value to the student of peasant society, the seven-volume study is not without its limitations. The work of a special government commission carried out between 1871 and 1874 under the direction of Senator M. N. Liuboshchinskii, the commission proposed "to collect such materials and information as would make it possible to obtain an accurate conception of the contemporary state of the peasant court."[6] Investigators for the commission, unable to examine each of the 11,786 townships into which European Russia was divided, selected townships that reflected the widest possible diversity of geographic, economic, and ethnic factors.

The nature of the court system and the inconsistencies of its record-keeping present the greatest problem to the student wishing to quantify rural social relations. Peasants did not bring all their legal disputes to court. Family quarrels, especially problems of division and inheritance, were sometimes handled locally by the village elder or assembly (*skhod*). Indeed in some locales all problems went first to the elder of the village commune, going to the township court only if there were an impasse.[7] The record is further blurred by the practice in some townships of not recording cases—especially family disputes—that the court resolved amicably. It is impossible, therefore, to know how many peasants actually appealed to the courts and with what kinds of cases. Obscuring matters further, the record varies in detail, not always indicating the relationship of the plaintiff to the head of household or making clear the structure of the family (nuclear, multiple, and so on).

Because the investigators for the commission chiefly wanted to obtain representative answers rather than to investigate the most active courts, they sometimes questioned elders and judges about their communities and court procedures in townships that recorded no cases at all.[8] Nor was there any balance in the total number of townships covered in each province: for Kostroma province the *Trudy* reported cases from sixteen townships, about half the total; for Tambov province from eighty-two, all of the townships in the province.

We have then a fascinating mosaic, huge (volume 1 alone runs to more than 800 pages), frustratingly incomplete, and based on the vagaries of local record keeping but providing a rich, if random, picture of peasant life.

This unwieldy panorama cannot tell us in how many instances in central Russia daughters-in-law were, in fact, involved in law suits, but it does indicate in its range of cases the variety of experiences of daughters-in-law in the township courts. If we assume that the cases recorded represent the most intractable conflicts, those that resisted solution at the local level, and if we pay close attention to disputes with a daughter-in-law as a party, either as plaintiff or defendant, we may arrive at a sense of her position within the family.

With this purpose in mind, I have focused on court cases in four provinces of central Russia: three in the Central Industrial Region—Moscow, Kostroma, and Iaroslavl'—and one in the Central Agricultural Region—Tambov. I selected provinces that represented different regions (hence both Iaroslavl' and Tambov), but I was guided also by the practical need to choose provinces with an abundant number of recorded cases. Since for Kostroma province cases were reported for sixteen townships, the fewest among the four, from each of the other three provinces I selected at random sixteen to nineteen townships. From each of these four groups, I next selected eleven townships, each made up of several peasant *mirs* or communes (see Table 5.1). In order to examine as wide a spectrum as possible of family cases involving women, I chose townships that had the largest number of cases featuring women. These townships tended, with a few exceptions, to be the same townships within the sample groups that had the largest number of recorded cases.

The resulting figures are not statistically rigorous; rigor is not possible given the incomplete nature of the *Trudy*. As we will see, however, they are suggestive in a comparative sense. For the years 1866 to 1872 the courts in these forty-four townships recorded 2,108 cases.[9] Of these, women were involved in roughly 685 (or 32 percent) of the cases. The majority of these disputes involved small-scale financial transactions usually centering on failure to pay wages for work completed, to fulfill contracts for which monetary advances had been given, or to make payments in the sale of livestock, firewood, or, sometimes, a hut. Other leading areas of litigation involved petty theft, perhaps of a goose, a load of hay, or clothing, and cases of physical assault or verbal insult. A man charged a woman with biting him, a woman charged a man with hitting her, another woman was accused of calling a villager a thief. Women also figured in cases of property damage: One woman charged that a man's horse had trampled her sown field. Another woman demanded compensation for her pig run over by a horse. Disputes over use of land, broken engagements, even dog bites brought women to court.

Family litigation was at issue in 51 percent of the 685 cases (347 cases), a figure which, we can assume, represents only a portion of the actual number. Despite the patriarchal organization of the family, in a significant number of recorded family

Table 5.1. Court Cases Involving Women, by Township

Township	Years	Primary Activity	Total Cases*	Cases Involving Women (percentage of total)
		Moscow province		
Nagatinskii	1871–1872	Vegetable marketing	9	4 (44)
Pekhorskii	1870–1872	Factory work	5	2 (40)
Shalovskii	1863, 1868, 1869, 1871	Factory work	14	4 (28)
Bun'kovskii†	1867, 1868, 1869 1870–1871	Factory work	18	11 (61)
Iamkinskii†	1868–1872	Factory work	15	9 (60)
Kiiasovskii†	1869–1872	Not indicated	44	21 (47)
Khatunskii†	1869–1871	Primarily trade	127	37 (29)
Vysotskii†	1867–1872	Factory work	47	19 (40)
Pushchinskii†	1867, 1869, 1871–1872	Factory work	39	10 (25)
Glazovskii†	1871	Agriculture	136	34 (25)
Bogoslovskii†	1871	Seasonal work away from village (*otkhod*)	31	11 (35)
Ziuzinskii†	1866, 1868, 1870–1872	Vegetable marketing	80	25 (31)
Vokhrinskii†	1869–1871	Mostly agriculture; Peasants hired out in winter	14	2 (14)
Spasskii†	1871	Mostly weavers	82	16 (19)
Chaplyzhenskii	1866–1871	Trades	29	8 (27)
Dovydkovskii†	1868, 1871–1872	Partly *otkhod*	<u>58</u>	<u>36 (62)</u>
			748	249 (33)
		Iaroslavl' province		
Pleshcheevskii	1868–1871	Partly factory work and *otkhod*	36	8 (22)
Norskii†	1861–1872		68	19 (28)
Krestobogorodskii†	1870–1872	Agriculture, carrier's trade	80	23 (28)
Koz'modem'ianskii†	1867–1869 1870–1872	*Otkhod*, joiners Weavers	29	14 (48)
Kurbskii†	1871–1872	*Otkhod*	46	13 (28)
Shopshinskii	1868, 1871–1872	Agriculture	29	7 (24)
Serenovskii	1871	*Otkhod*	17	3 (17)
Tolgobol'skii†	1871	*Otkhod*	24	9 (37)
Putiatinskii†	1863–1865 1868–1872	*Otkhod* Local trades	44	20 (45)
Dievo-gorodishchenskii†	1869–1872	*Otkhod*	50	16 (32)
Velikosel'skii†	1869–1872	*Otkhod*	40	12 (30)
Boronishinskii	1871	*Otkhod*	44	8 (18)
Mar'inskii†	1869, 1871–1872	*Otkhod*	111	40 (36)
Kriukovskii	1871–1872	Partly *otkhod*	33	10 (30)
Povodnevskii†	1868–1871	*Otkhod*	30	14 (46)

Table 5.1. (*Continued*)

Township	Years	Primary Activity	Total Cases*	Cases Involving Women (percentage of total)
Pokrovskii†	1870–1872	*Otkhod*	54	12 (22)
Bol'shesel'skii	1869–1871	Partly *otkhod*	30	7 (23)
Khopylevskii	1871	*Otokhod*	16	8 (50)
Ivanovskii	1871	*Otkhod*	30	8 (26)
			811	251 (31)
		Kostroma province		
Zavrazhnii†	1870–1872	*Otkhod*	52	9 (17)
Sobolevskii†	1869–1872	Agriculture	15	9 (60)
Noginskii	1867–1869	Agriculture	8	1 (12)
Krasnosel'skii	1867, 1871–1872	Small scale manufacture	13	3 (23)
Bashutinskii†	1868, 1870–1871	Agriculture, some factory work	18	12 (66)
Odelevskii	1869	Agriculture, some factory work	9	4 (44)
Ostrotovskii	1870	Weaving and some factory work	13	2 (15)
Mordvinovskii†	1870–1872	Agriculture, work on Volga	95	35 (36)
Gor'kovskii†	1861, 1863, 1865, 1866, 1871, 1872	Weaving trades	46	9 (19)
Diupinskii†	1868, 1869, 1871–1872	Agriculture, textile production	33	10 (30)
Vozdvizhenskii†	1864, 1868, 1869–1872	Partly *otkhod*	29	14 (48)
Esiplevskii	1861–1864, 1866, 1867, 1871	Primarily agriculture	38	22 (57)
Molvitinskii†	1871–1872	*Otkhod*	31	4 (12)
Borovskii†	1869–1872	Partly *otkhod*	20	4 (20)
Troitskii†	1871–1872	*Otkhod*	27	12 (44)
Gorkinskii	1870	Factory work	6	0 (0)‡
			453	150 (33)
		Tambov province		
Chernianovskii	1870–1871	Agriculture	17	4 (23)
Gorel'skii†	1871–1872	Agriculture	24	11 (46)
Kulevatovskii†	1871–1872	Agriculture	29	5 (17)
Perkinskii†	1870–1872	Agriculture	62	16 (25)
Ot'iasovskii	1870–1872	Agriculture	22	4 (18)
Piterskii	1871	Agriculture, *otkhod* in winter	32	4 (12)
Cherkinskii†	1871	Agriculture, shoe-making in winter	23	10 (43)
Kazachinskii†	1871	Agriculture	47	19 (40)
Taradevskii†	1871–1972	Agriculture, in winter work on Don	44	20 (45)

(*continued*)

Table 5.1. (Continued)

Township	Years	Primary Activity	Total Cases*	Cases Involving Women (percentage of total)
Algasovskii†	1870–1871	Agriculture	62	14 (22)
Rybinskii	1869–1872	Agriculture	13	3 (23)
Nesterskii†	1862, 1871, 1872	Agriculture	25	5 (20)
Kargashinskii	1871–1872	Agriculture	11	1 (9)
Mokrinskii†	1870–1871	Agriculture	31	6 (19)
Barkovskii†	1871		36	4 (11)
Bol'shekhomutetskii	1871	Agriculture	22	4 (18)
Vanovskii†	1870–1871	Little agriculture, wheel and carpenter trades	62	14 (22)
			562	144 (25)

*Numbers are low because courts did not record reconciled cases.

†Township used in compiling statistics.

‡This township's incomplete records make it impossible to determine if women were involved.

disputes, 28 percent (97 cases), the daughter-in-law brought charges against her in-laws (including her brothers-in-law as well as her parents-in-law). Let us look at her grievances.

Perhaps because peasant life was closely monitored by the *mir* and, thus, eroded the concept of privacy, perhaps because privacy could mean little to people crowded together in a small hut, or perhaps simply because they felt terribly threatened, women did not appear reluctant to reveal details of their personal lives in these courts. The daughter-in-law described beatings by her mother-in-law, father-in-law, and brother-in-law or requested the right to live separately or with her own parents while her husband was away at wage work.

If she was widowed, a daughter-in-law frequently appealed to the court for part of her husband's share of the communal property. If her in-laws banished her, she might demand to be taken back into their home.

What help could a woman expect from the court? Much depended on the subjective opinion of the judges. Peasant justice was not blind. Ad hominem, or, in Russian, *po cheloveku*, was a guiding principle. What were the reputations of the plaintiff and the defendants? Was the father-in-law or brother-in-law known to be a drunkard? Was the daughter-in-law a hard worker with a reputation as a good woman? Did she have children? How long had she lived in the family? Could she be expected to support herself? Balancing such considerations with the principles that parents and elders deserved respect and homesteads needed to be preserved at full working strength, the judges, often illiterate, tried to render equity. They could be inconsistent.

A daughter-in-law in Ziuzinskii township in Moscow province charged her in-laws with beating her but was informed that sons and daughters did not have the right to complain against parents. The court advised her to live in obedience to her

elders.[10] Yet in Vysotskii township, in the same province, a father-in-law accused
by his daughter-in-law of abuse was arrested.[11] Similarly, in Bol'shesel'skii township, in Iaroslavl' province, when a father-in-law contended that he beat his
daughter-in-law because she was insubordinate, the court fined him 2 rubles and
warned him that if it happened again the penalty would be greater.[12] The differing
decisions may be explained not only by the subjective reactions of the judges to the
litigants but by the makeup of the three communities. All three townships appeared
to be relatively prosperous—this assumption is based on the facts that each paid its
judges 40 rubles or more a year and that in each people derived a living from sources
other than subsistence agriculture.[33] The townships in which the fathers-in-law
were punished for abusing their daughters-in-law, however, were more economically diversified and therefore, perhaps, more open communities. In Vysotskii
township men worked primarily in factories rather then in agriculture. In
Bol'shesel'skii industry and trade predominated and two-thirds of the males were at
otkhod. In Vysotskii and Bol'shesel'skii townships, moreover, girls attended school
along with boys, a phenomenon not frequently found in rural Russia in the 1870s.[14]

The majority of cases brought by a daughter-in-law against her in-laws involved
property. A woman customarily arrived in her husband's home with her dowry
(*pridanoe*), clothing, and such household items as towels and bedding. A daughter,
if she had brothers, did not inherit within her own family. Her dowry, then, which
might include money and some livestock, was in a sense her share of her family's
property.[15] A daughter-in-law's personal property, over which she had exclusive
control, might need to be protected from the avarice of her new relatives. We find
seven such cases. In each the courts cooperated. Thus, a woman in Mokrinskii
township in Tambov province charged her brother-in-law with breaking into her
dowry trunk. He was given twenty blows. In a similar case in Khatunskii township
in Moscow province a brother-in-law was ordered to provide compensation. A
daughter-in-law in Khatunskii township, presumably preparing to return to her
parents, charged that her in-laws refused to surrender her property and they were
ordered to do so.[16]

The more complex cases involved the demands of the widowed daughter-in-law
against the jointly held property of the husband's family. In dealing with the peasant
household it is important to distinguish between two kinds of property: land and
household. A peasant family did not actually own the land it farmed. Before and
after the emancipation of the serfs in 1861 the commune guaranteed each member
household the right to farm an allotment comprising scattered strips of land. Allotments were periodically redistributed among members of the commune according to
family size, that is by available mouths—*po edokam*—or by available labor. Tools,
livestock, and the hut were, however, the common property of the family. The elder
who headed the household, usually the father, was only its representative not its
owner (although he may have acted as if he were). He had no right to dispose of the
family possessions without the unanimous consent of all the adult members of the
family, women as well as men.[17]

Although a son shared ownership in the household, if he were to die, his widow,
if she were childless, might be left destitute, receiving nothing of her husband's
share of the communal property in accord with peasant tradition that widows did not

inherit.[18] Yet, if she were known to be industrious, and especially if she had lived with her husband's family many years and if she appealed to the court, its judges might award a childless widow one-fourth or one-seventh of her husband's share.[19] If she had sons the daughter-in-law generally received for them that portion of the communal property that would have gone to her husband had there been a family division.[20] A widow with daughters was less secure and more dependent on the generosity of her male in-laws than a widow with sons. In some localities, if she had daughters, a widow might receive at the discretion of her relatives a portion of the moveable property, for example, some grain and cattle.[21]

Among daughters-in-law the plight of the soldier's wife, the *soldatka,* resembled that of the widow. In twenty-three instances an in-law banished the *soldatka* or withheld property from her after her husband left for service. In one such case in Khatunskii township a *soldatka* charged her brother-in-law with ejecting her after refusing to permit her to use a horse that he and her husband owned in common.[22] The court gave her the right to use the horse and to remain in the house. In a similar case, in the same township, the court ordered a brother-in-law to permit a *soldatka* to remain at home and to share the use of the cow.[23] Another court in Krestobogorodskii township defended a *soldatka* against a father-in-law who denied her her husband's share of grain.[24] In other cases the *soldatka* charged her in-laws with petty theft—perhaps of a dress or a coat—and the court ordered that the items be returned.[25]

The plight of the *soldatka* must have reminded many a daughter-in-law that security did not necessarily lie within her husband's family. The problem was not new. Before emancipation, widows with minor children sought the protection of the *mir* governments when threatened with expulsion from their husband's households. The *mir* obliged a father-in-law to provide for his son's family.[26] After emancipation, the widow could appeal to the township court. Evidently, a significant number of daughters-in-law felt the need thus to protect themselves. In fifty of the ninety-seven cases in which a *snokha* brought charges against her in-laws, she protested "unlawful" withholding by her husband's family of property due her or she appealed against banishment. Unfortunately, it is not always clear whether a daughter-in-law seeking property could have remained in her in-law's house had she wished to do so or whether she was, indeed, banished. In all but five instances, the widow or *soldatka* received a court-ordered settlement from her in-laws. If the sums involved exceeded the court's jurisdiction of 100 rubles or if, in the court's view, the plaintiff did not have a valid claim her suit was denied.

The daughter-in-law's plight was due in part to the implicit assumption that she deserved nothing because she was an outsider. This conclusion is reinforced when we look at the tenuous position of a son-in-law (called a *primak*) taken into his wife's household because her family lacked sons of its own. Reportedly treated with little respect by his wife's family, in popular parlance referred to as a henpecked wimp, he is said to have been "cruelly exploited."[27] Even after the death of his father-in-law, when he could formally become head of household, the *primak* might find that the real power in the family simply shifted to his wife and mother-in-law: one *primak* recalled that his opinion was never sought when household problems were discussed.[28] Like the *snokha,* the *primak* could be in a particularly weak position if his spouse died—even rejected without any property from the household in which he had worked. A resourceful *primak* protected himself, when he could, by a written agreement guaranteeing him property rights in the event of his wife's death.[29] Quarrels with in-laws brought the *primak* to court as they did the *snokha*.

Although in the patriarchal peasant family a father-in-law customarily wielded control, sometimes he did not succeed in enforcing his will and he too resorted to the courts. In 5 percent of the recorded family litigations involving women, fathers-in-law and mothers-in-law initiated cases against their daughters-in-law. (This percentage increased to 6 percent when cases brought by brothers-in-law against sisters-in-law are included.) If most of the cases brought by the daughter-in-law involved violation of what she perceived to be her property rights, a father-in-law (in court as plaintiff more frequently than a mother-in-law) was most likely to charge his daughter-in-law with disrespect, going home to her own parents, or simply wanting to work away from his home while her husband was in the city at seasonal labor.

The father-in-law did not always win. If his daughter-in-law could convince the court that oppression from her husband's family was extreme she might be permitted to live separately while her spouse was gone.[30] If a father-in-law, on the other hand, could demonstrate that his daughter-in-law's absence hurt his household economy, his case was strengthened. Consider the peasant in Moscow province who, four days after his daughter-in-law left his home to return to her parents, charged in court that because of her absence he had to hire a working woman at 15 kopeks a day to take her place. Demanding that her parents compensate him the 60 kopeks since she was working for them rather than for him, he insisted she return. The court arrested the daughter-in-law for two days, ordering her back to her husband's family.[31]

Friction between families was exacerbated by the efforts of a daughter-in-law's parents to protect her. In a young woman's relationship with her own family we find a familial closeness that continued after marriage. A father charges a son-in-law with beating his daughter.[32] A mother tries to ease the burden on her daughter by taking in her laundry.[33] The image of the peasant woman giving birth in the fields is familiar, but, in fact, a woman might return to her mother two or three weeks before delivery.[34]

Parental interference in behalf of a married daughter might bring punishment. In one case a mother was arrested for five days for encouraging her daughter to oppose her husband's family. A father was ordered not to invite his daughter home without her husband's permission.[35] In another instance a father was arrested for taking his daughter home.[36]

Given the situation with which a young wife had to cope, her parents' attempts to protect her seem reasonable. A father-in-law or mother-in-law, bringing a complaint against a daughter-in-law for insult, disobedience, or arbitrarily leaving home, inadvertently provided glimpses of sexual tensions created by the close proximity of unrelated men and women in the small peasant household. A mother-in-law asks that her daughter-in-law be punished for constant insult and disobedience. The daughter-in-law, denying the charges, argued that her mother-in-law and husband continually called her insulting names and beat her and that it all started when her brother-in-law raped her. Since then her husband and her mother-in-law had hated her, claiming that she had a sexual relationship with her brother-in-law. The court decided that the family discord did in fact stem from the rape but, declaring that rape belonged in a criminal court, rejected the mother-in-law's case.[37]

Fathers-in-law were particularly susceptible to the sexual pressure resulting from the presence of the young daughter-in-law. A father-in-law charged his daughter-in-law with abandoning his home. The daughter-in-law countercharged that she left because her father-in-law made sexual advances to her and then beat her for refusing him. The family denied the sexual advances and the daughter-in-law, unable to provide evidence, was arrested for seven days for slander. That the elder was charged by the court to watch the family suggests that the judges suspected the young woman was probably telling the truth.[38]

Although in these cases the court seemed reluctant to grapple with sexual conflicts, in other townships, courts reacted differently.[39] One of the most unpleasant features of life in the complex family was, as we have seen, the unwanted sexual approaches of a father-in-law, a practice known as *snokhachestvo*. Once this transgression was brought to its attention, the courts did not take it lightly. A court might consider *snokhachestvo* sufficient cause to justify a family division.[40] In a few recorded instances, a husband successfully intervened and received court permission to move out of his parents' house.[41] According to custom, *snokhachestvo* was punished by fifteen to twenty blows.[42]

A daughter-in-law, unless widowed, was also a wife. It is impossible to appreciate a woman's position as *snokha* fully without considering also her situation as spouse. The catalogue of grievances not only against in-laws but also against husbands was extensive. Over half (66 percent) of fifty-three cases brought by wives against husbands arose from beating. In others she charged nonsupport, failure to send money when working away from the village, or banishment from her home. In twelve instances a woman was motivated by a desire to obtain her passport and go away to work for wages or to recover her dowry and separate from her husband.

Most often (in thirty-five cases) a wife came to court to protest being beaten. In eight of these cases, a daughter-in-law charged her husband and his family with collaboration in her ill-treatment. One woman, accusing her husband of beating her, charged his mother with encouraging him. His mother claimed that her daughter-in-law had been rude to her. The court punished the husband with twenty blows for beating his wife and jailed his mother for three days for joining with him.[43] Another woman, charging her husband with oppressing and beating her, accused her father-in-law of instigating his son's actions. Her husband was flogged twenty times for beating his wife, and his father was jailed for three days for permitting his son's bad behavior.

The problem of wife-beating, endemic in Russian villages, defies easy explanation. We have seen that a man's family might abet him in beating his wife, but was such behavior sanctioned by the community and court? The popular assumption, endorsed by some historians, holds that Russian peasants had the right to beat their wives, that such behavior was sanctioned by customary law, which, looking back to the sixteenth-century *Domostroi* [treatise on household management], asserted its beneficial effect.[44] Indeed, in certain localities, for example in the township of Dymer in Kiev, peasants claimed that disputes between husbands and wives never came to the court, that township courts would not hear a wife's complaints against her husband. If he beat her, she deserved it.[45] According to a leading student of the township courts, Semen V. Pakhman, the localities in which such attitudes prevailed were few.[46] In fact, it was not unusual for neighbors to report peasants guilty of physical cruelty to their wives. In Kriukovsksii township in Iaroslavl' province an elder called such interference essential, since wives of abusive husbands might be too fearful themselves to go to court.[47] The assumption implicit in the elder's observation is borne out by court records. Customary law in the 1870s evidently did not assume a man's absolute power over his wife. (Whether it ever unequivocally did is an open question. Nina A. Minenko gives examples of eighteenth-century women in western Siberia going to local authorities for protection from cruel husbands.)[48] The township court was made up, after all, of ordinary male peasants who would not have defended the interests of women if there existed an unambiguous belief in the rights of husbands to exercise their physical will. The positive influence of the scribe was also a factor in undermining wife-beating. Sometimes the only literate member of the court, he read and explained the law to the judges. Although peasants did not come under the uniform code of law, in court decisions written by scribes we find occasional references to volume 10 in the code of civil law and to a law forbidding the arbitrary beating of one's wife.[49] Thus, one guilty husband told the court that he had not known "the law" that he could not beat his wife.[50] In fact, rural judges legally had no right to draw on the uniform code of law. That they occasionally did so demonstrated the essentially local and ad hoc character of so-called customary law, which makes it difficult to generalize about its properties. Nevertheless, we may conclude that in both the Central Industrial Region to the north and the Central Agricultural Region to the south, from Iaroslavl' to Tambov, the courts, while reminding a woman of her obligation to obey her husband or even chastising her for disobedience, might punish a perpetual wife-beater, on his wife's complaint, with a three-day or five-day sentence or, more commonly, with a criminal penalty of flogging.[51] In seventeen of the thirty-five cases in which wives charged husbands with beating them, husbands were punished; ten were flogged ten to twenty blows. If the court reconciled the couple or if the wife was unbruised and could not produce witnesses, the husband was not penalized.

Wife-beating was punishable, then, throughout rural Russia but in certain areas it may have been more common for abused women to turn to the courts. Indeed, in areas of economic change where men seeking outside wages were less involved in agriculture and where women played a greater role in the community, the number of women involved in court disputes of any sort—wife-beating or otherwise—may have tended to be higher.[52] To make the point negatively, in the township of Dymer in Kiev province the courts did not accept complaints from wives against husbands. Dymer was an agricultural area marked by extreme poverty, backwardness, and the persistence of tradition.[53] By contrast, in Taganchevskii, a more economically diversified township in Kiev, where people worked in factories and both boys and girls studied together in school, women received the court's protection.

It may be superfluous, in light of the above examples, to consider another popular assumption: that peasant women themselves accepted their husband's beatings not as an abuse of power but as natural and legal. This is an appropriate point, however, at which finally to lay that notion to rest. Romantics have long explained that to women beating was a sign of love, an indication of masculine strength. If a husband could be brutal, so the argument went, he could also show mercy; his display of power was proof that he could defend his wife from harm.[55] While here and there one can find reports of Russian women who supposedly held this view, the many court cases recording women's angry protests against beating effectively discredit such a myth.[56]

Along with protests against beating, wives went to court in nine instances to charge their husbands with banishing them or refusing to provide support. In such cases, parents-in-law might have been the instigators of the husband's action. Unfortunately, since court records do not always indicate family structure, it is impossible to determine how many wives who appeared in court against their husbands in banishment cases lived in multiple families. According to one authority, however, banishment usually occurred at the initiative of the in-laws and within a multiple family.[57] Women were rarely banished from the small nuclear family if only because a husband living alone with his wife could not afford to lose the labor of his adult partner.[58]

Although a husband and wife were legally obliged to live together and courts were not supposed to approve acts tending toward separation,[59] in practice township courts varied in the way they handled cases of husbands banishing wives. A husband might be ordered to take his wife back.[60] Thus when a husband and his parents banished a wife, charging her with "ignorance and laziness," the court ordered the in-laws to compensate their *snokha* for her summer's work, to buy back her clothing they had pawned, and to take her again into their home.[61]

If a husband refused to live with his wife he was obliged at least to support her. When a pregnant wife appealed to the court because her husband and his parents had banished her, the court ordered the husband to take his wife back or pay her 3 rubles a month in support.[62] Invariably, if a wife charged nonsupport, the court ordered the husband to provide support. Whether he was required also to live with his wife was not clear.

Just as the daughter-in-law tended to be the initiator in bringing charges against her in-laws, so too in recorded marital disputes, the wife was usually the plaintiff: fifty-three cases were brought by wives; twenty-eight cases were initiated by husbands. Husbands appealed to the court most often (sixteen recorded cases) charging desertion (see Table 5.2).[63] In cases of desertion a husband's family might be a contributing cause. In one instance, a peasant appeared in court complaining that his wife refused to live with him. His wife contended that he and his family oppressed her. The court, calling in the mother-in-law and brother-in-law, ordered them to treat the daughter-in-law decently, and told the young woman to return.[64] In other instances, the wife might be punished—usually by a brief jail sentence—for leaving. Or her husband might be punished with flogging or arrest if the court determined that she left because he beat her or was a drunkard or failed to support his wife and children adequately.

A woman might appeal to the court for release from an intolerable family situation. If she and her husband could agree on separation through mutual consent, she generally won her freedom. Of twelve requests by wives for separations, eight were granted. One means for a woman to escape from her husband and his family—

Table 5.2. Nature of Disputes by Family Relationship

Relationship	Inheritance or Property Division	Desertion by Wife or Daughter-in-Law	Dowry	Beating, Banishment, or Oppression	Insubordination of Wife or Daughter-in-Law	Dissolute Life of Wife	Sexual Advance by Male Family Member
Daughter-in-law and mother-in-law	20			5	2		
Daughter-in-law and father-in-law	33	4	1	7	3		3
Daughter-in-law and both parents-in-law	2			6			
Wife and husband	2	16	7	51	6	5	
Daughter-in-law and brother-in-law	28		3	12	1		1
Sisters-in-law	4						

Note: The predominant disputes are property disagreements between the daughter-in-law and her in-laws (87) and suits involving oppressive treatment of the wife by the husband (51). Since the purpose of this table is to show the varieties of family litigation, a case in which, for example, a daughter-in-law appealed against her father-in-law and brother-in-law will appear twice, once under the category of father-in-law and again under the category of brother-in-law.

particularly if she had no children—was to agree in court that in return for her passport she would pay her husband a sum of money that would enable him to engage someone in her place.[65] In one case, in Kostroma, the wife paid her husband 5 rubles a year so that he could hire a worker in the summer.[66] Another woman in Moscow province paid 20 rubles for a replacement.[67] Here is a separation agreement concluded in Moscow province in 1871:[68]

> 1. I, "I," willingly, in aversion to our family discord, permit my wife to receive from the township government a yearly passport to live where she wishes with the proviso that she pay me in the course of a year 12 rubles in the following way: June 6, 3 rubles, July 20, 3 rubles, October 1, 3 rubles and at Easter, 1872, 3 rubles.
> 2. And I, "H," will pay my husband 12 rubles at the aforesaid times with the understanding that my husband ask nothing more of me.

As the above contract suggests, de facto separations were legally countenanced, although both in law and in popular opinion spouses had an obligation to live together.[69] Divorces were rare, but peasant courts, not bound by a rigid civil law, sometimes dealt more mildly with women than even customary law required.[70] Despite the law that spouses must live together, peasant courts appeared rather accepting of separation by mutual consent.[71] In seven of the eight separations countenanced by the court, husbands appeared to acquiesce. The historian Maksim Kovalevsky attributes this laxity on the part of the courts "in direct contradiction to the law" to the influence of rural tradition. Up to the mid-eighteenth century Russian clergy dissolved marriage bonds often for no other reason than incompatibility.[72]

In this article I have examined the place of the daughter-in-law in the peasant family through the records of township courts and have shown that the daughter-in-law appealed nearly five times more frequently against her in-laws than they did against her. Similarly, wives brought nearly twice as many cases against husbands as husbands did against wives. These statistics are significant, even though they do not necessarily mean that peasant women brought more suits than other members of the family. A father-in-law, mother-in-law, brother-in-law, or husband may have obtained satisfaction in one of the village's unofficial courts, or their disputes, if reconciled in the township court, may have gone unrecorded. Statistics suggesting that the daughter-in-law was the most litigious member of the family tell us only that the cases she brought against family members defied easy solutions, that women who used the courts were determined to resist family despotism, and that their suits, not amicably resolved, were more often entered into the record.

We may conclude that peasant women in general, *snokhi* in particular, asserted and exercised rights, and instigated family and community change to a degree not hitherto recognized. Yet a problem remains. Is it valid to conclude also that *snokhi* were generally discontented within the large family? Given the modest numbers with which I have dealt, the question is whether the cases in the *Trudy Komissii* represent the tip of an iceberg of dissatisfaction or simply the exceptional incidents in a society relying heavily on the extended family. Was there, in fact, a "silent majority" of satisfied or obedient daughters-in-law treated decently by their in-laws?[73] The question needs to be raised but, unfortunately, cannot be definitively answered. We can point only to the absence of evidence. If a contented population of daughters-in-law existed, it eluded folk wisdom, ethnographic investigators, and nineteenth-century historians. In the absence of documentation for the existence of this silent majority of satisfied daughters-in-law and in the presence of ethnographic and historical studies that suggest the contrary,[74] I tentatively conclude that the family conflicts of the forty-four townships in four provinces of European Russia represent the tip of the iceberg of discontent.

Notes

1. For proverbs, M. I. Zarudnyi, *Zakony i zhizn'. Itogi izsledovaniia krest'ianskikh sudov* (St. Petersburg, 1874), p. 157. Aleksandra Efimenko, "Krest'ianskaia zhenshchina," *Delo* (1873): 65–66.

2. A major contributor to the literary image of peasant women was Nikolai A. Nekrasov. See "Frost, the Red Nose," in N. A. Nekrasov, *Polnoe sobranie stikhotvorenii v trekh tomakh,* ed. K. I. Chukovskii (3 vols.; Leningrad, 1967), 2:109. For historians on peasant women, see Barbara Engel, *Mothers and Daughters* (Cambridge: Cambridge University Press, 1983), p. 8; Dorothy Atkinson et al., *Women in Russia* (Stanford, Calif.: Stanford University Press, 1977), p. 33; L. A. Anokhina and M. N. Shmeleva, *Kul'tura i byt kolkhoznikov Kalininskoi Oblasti* (Moscow, 1964), p. 174.

3. Peter Czap, "The Perennial Multiple Family Household, Mishino, Russia 1782–1858," *Journal of Family History* (Spring 1982): 25.

4. For the courts, see Peter Czap, "Peasant-Class Courts and Peasant Customary Justice in Russia, 1861–1912," *Journal of Social History* 1 (Winter 1967): 149–79. Jurisdiction was limited to cases not involving property worth more than 100 rubles, arson, or murder. A township (*volost'*) was made up of several village communities.

5. *Trudy Komissii po preobrazovaniiu volostnykh sudov* (7 vols.; St. Petersburg, 1874).

6. Ibid., 1:ii.

7. Ibid., 3:57–58, 102; in Iaroslavl' province.

8. See Shungunskii township in Kostroma in ibid., 3:306–8, and Arapovskii township in Tambov, also in ibid., 1:10.

9. There are a few entries for 1861–1863; see Table 5.1.

10. *Trudy Komissii*, 2:106.

11. Ibid., 2:206–7.

12. Ibid., 3:179.

13. For this standard of judgment, see Peter Czap, "The Influence of Slavophile Ideology on the Formation of the Volost Court of 1861 and the Practice of Peasant Self-Justice between 1861 and 1889" (Ph.D. diss., Cornell University, 1959), pp. 79–82.

14. In Bol'shesel'skii township, Iaroslavl' province, up to thirty girls attended school and all four judges were literate with salaries of 40 rubles a year. *Trudy Komissii*, 3:176. For Vysotskii township, see ibid., 2:203. Two of the judges were literate; judges were paid 40 rubles a year.

15. Money and cattle were called *nadelok*. The money might go to her husband and the cattle might become part of the general property. Efimenko, "Krest'ianskaia zhenshchina," p. 93.

16. *Trudy Komissii,* 2:185, 190 (Moscow); 1:136 (Tambov).

17. Maksim M. Kovalevsky, *Modern Customs and Ancient Laws of Russia* (London: D. Nutt, 1891), p. 55. Only males were, in fact, consulted. Donald M. Wallace, *Russia* (1905 ed.; reprint, New York: Praeger, 1970), p. 89.

18. S. V. Pakhman, *Obychnoe grazhdanskoe pravo v Rossii* (2 vols.; St. Petersburg, 1877–1879), 2:261; V. F. Mukhin, *Obychnyi poriadok nasledovaniia u krest'ian* (St. Petersburg, 1888), pp. 252–53, 261; *Trudy Komissii,* 1:15 (Tambov).

19. *Trudy Komissii,* 3:75, 85 (Iaroslavl'), and 3:388 (Kostroma); Pakhman, *Obychnoe grazhdanskoe pravo,* 2:270; Czap, "Peasant-Class Courts," p. 165.

20. Mukhin, *Obychnyi poriadok,* pp. 263–64. She could demand in court the right to run her husband's portion of the land allotment if she paid the taxes; ibid. She could also insist that her father-in-law not sell his farmstead since it was the future inheritance of her son. Ibid., p. 65; Pakhman, *Obychnoe grazhdanskoe pravo,* 2:273; *Trudy Komissii,* 1:686, 688 (Tambov); 5:78 (Kiev).

21. *Trudy Komissii,* 2:324, 363, 370 (Moscow); 3:394 (Kostroma); Mukhin, *Obychnyi poriadok,* p. 266.

22. *Trudy Komissii,* 2:182 (Moscow).

23. Ibid., 2:195 (Moscow).

24. Ibid., 3:43 (Iaroslavl').

25. Ibid., 2:212 (Moscow); F. Pokrovskii, "O semeinom polozhenii krest'ianskoi zhenshchiny v Kostromskoi gubernii po dannym volostnogo suda," *Zhivaia starina* 3–4 (1896): 464.

26. See V. A. Aleksandrov, "Semeino-imushchestvennye otnosheniia po obychnomu pravu v russkoi krepostnoi derevne XVIII-nachala XIX veka," *Istoriia SSSR,* no. 6 (1979): 48.

27. *Opyt istoriko-sotsiologicheskogo izucheniia sela "Moldino"* (Moscow, 1968), p. 108 (hereafter cited as *"Moldino"*); Anokhina and Shmeleva, *Kul'tura i byt kolkhoznikov Kalininskoi Oblasti,* p. 173.

28. *"Moldino,"* p. 109; Anokhina and Shmeleva, *Kul'tura i byt kolkhoznikov Kalininskoi Oblasti,* p. 174.

29. Mukhin, *Obychnyi poriadok,* p. 299.

30. Pakhman, *Obychnoe grazhdanskoe pravo,* 2:185; *Trudy Komissii,* 3:289 (Iaroslavl'); 3:393 (Kostroma).

31. *Trudy Komissii,* 2:170 (Moscow).

32. Ibid., 3:165 (Iaroslavl'); 5:132 (Kiev); 1:137 (Tambov).

33. *"Moldino,"* p. 108.

34. A. O. Afinogenova, *Zhizn' zhenskago naseleniia Riazanskago uezda* (St. Petersburg, 1903), p. 76.

35. Pakhman, *Obychnoe grazhdanskoe pravo,* 2:89.

36. Ibid., 2:88; *Trudy Komissii,* 3:16 (Iaroslavl'); 5:91 (Kiev); 3:354 (Kostroma); 3:407 (Kostroma).

37. *Trudy Komissii,* 2:569 (Moscow).

38. Ibid., p. 577.

39. For cases in which both parties were flogged for fornication, see ibid., 3:377, 379; a woman charged a man with rape; he countered that they had lived together lovingly. The court sentenced her to socially useful work and him to twenty floggings. Ibid., p. 142 (Iaroslavl'). A widow who charged a man with fathering her child was awarded support. Ibid., 1:138 (Tambov). See ibid., 3:379 (Kostroma), for a man fined 5 rubles for beating a woman who refused sexual intercourse. For other fornication cases, P. P. Chubinskii, *Trudy etnograficheskoi statisticheskoi ekspeditsii v Zapadno-Russkii Kraii* (St. Petersburg, 1872), pp. 18–19, 186–88.

40. I. Tiutriumov, "Krest'ianskaia sem'ia," *Russkaia rech* (St. Petersburg, 1879), vol. 4, part 1:292.

41. *Trudy Komissii*, 3:394 (Kostroma); also ibid., p. 158 (Iaroslavl'); A. Smirnov, *Ocherki semeinykh otnoshenii po obychnomu pravu russkago naroda* (Moscow, 1877), pp. 46–47.

42. A. A. Leont'ev, *Volostnoi sud i iuridicheskie obychai krest'ian* (St. Petersburg, 1895), p. 15; see *Trudy Komissii*, 6:100–101, for three-day jail sentence.

43. *Trudy Komissii*, 2:208 (Moscow).

44. Atkinson et al., *Women in Russia*, p. 33; Anokhina and Shmeleva, *Kul'tura i byt kolkhoznikov Kalininskoi Oblasti*, p. 174; Kovalevsky, *Modern Customs and Ancient Laws of Russia*, p. 45.

45. *Trudy Komissii*, 5:3, 33, 141 (Kiev).

46. Pakhman, *Obychnoe grazhdanskoe pravo*, 2:112.

47. *Trudy Komissii*, 3:144 (Iaroslavl'); for neighbor's report, see ibid., p. 354.

48. N. A. Minenko, *Russkaia krest'ianskaia sem'ia v zapadnoi Sibiri* (Novosibirsk, 1979), pp. 127–30, 135. Also see N. A. Kostrov, *Iuridicheskie obychai krest'ian starozhilov tomskoi gubernii* (Tomsk, 1876), pp. 20, 26, for relations between husband and wife.

49. Pakhman, *Obychnoe grazhdanskoe pravo*, 2:112–13; *Trudy Komissii*, 2:10 (Moscow). Judge refers to articles 106, 107, vol. 10, chap. 1, in *Svod zakonov grazhdanskikh*. See *Trudy Komissii*, 3:20, for judges guiding themselves by vol. 10 and by *Sel'skii ustav*. In the first half of the nineteenth century, husbands were forbidden in imperial law to beat their wives. Atkinson et al., *Women in Russia*, p. 33.

50. Pakhman, *Obychnoe grazhdanskoe pravo*, 2:105–6; *Trudy Komissii*, 6:279–80 (Samara).

51. For punishment of wife-beaters, see *Trudy Komissii*, 1:32, 39, 295, 440, 443 (Tambov); 2:10, 66, 72, 100, 108, 140, 239, 274, 275, 360, 418, 425, 545 (Moscow); 3:72, 101, 183, 185, 208, 225, 236, 237, 263, 264, 272 (Iaroslavl'); 3:354, 383, 389, 413–15 (Kostroma); 3:444 (Nizhog); 4:109 (Kharkov); 4:260 (Poltava); 5:91, 132, 191 (Kiev); Astyrev, *V volostnykh pisariakh* (Moscow, 1896), p. 266; Tiutriumov, "Krest'ianskaia sem'ia," pp. 142–43. In one case, a wife was dealt fifteen blows for deserting her husband, but he received twenty blows for beating her.

52. See Table 5.1; also wife-beating cases recorded in forty-four townships: Moscow, seventeen; Iaroslavl', eight; Kostroma, seven; Tambov (agricultural) three; and see Pokrovskii, "O semeinom polozhenii krest'ianskoi zhenshchiny v kostromskoi gubernii po dannym volostnogo suda," p. 459.

53. In Dymer with its 1,800 souls the elder received 40 rubles a year; the judges were unpaid. By comparison, in Ivanovskii township in Iaroslavl' with 1,479 souls the elder received 450 rubles a year; the judges 30 rubles.

54. *Trudy Komissii*, 5:161 (Kiev). Taganchevskii township had 2,505 souls; the elder received 210 rubles a year.

55. Efimenko, "Krest'ianskaia zhenshchina," p. 57; Kovalevsky, *Modern Customs and Ancient Laws of Russia*, p. 45.

56. For transcripts in which women protest beatings, see Astyrev, *V volostnykh pisariakh*, pp. 270–71; *Trudy Komissii*, 1:443 (Tambov).

57. Efimenko, "Krest'ianskaia zhenshchina," pp. 86, 88–89.

58. Ibid., pp. 86–87.

59. Ibid., pp. 83, 87.

60. *Trudy Komissii*, 2:168 (Moscow); Pakhman, *Obychnoe grazhdanskoe pravo*, 2:95–97.

61. Efimenko, "Krest'ianskaia zhenshchina," p. 89.

62. Ibid.

63. Four husbands also charged debauchery, one disobedience, two theft, one physical

abuse, and one demanded (successfully) the wages his wife earned working away from home because he had to hire her replacement. *Trudy Komissii*, 3:139 (Iaroslavl'). A judge noted that husbands frequently charged wives with insubordination and wives charged ill-treatment. Ibid., 2:93 (Moscow).

64. Ibid., 3:378 (Kostroma).

65. Pakhman, *Obychnoe grazhdanskoe pravo*, 2:91.

66. *Trudy Komissii*, 3:384 (Kostroma).

67. Ibid., 2:555 (Moscow).

68. Ibid., p. 563. See pp. 555, 557, for other such agreements. Also Astyrev, *V volostnykh pisariakh*, pp. 224–25. Peasants expected wives to pay compensation for the loss of labor their desertion involved. Wallace, *Russia*, p. 545.

69. Pakhman, *Obychnoe grazhdanskoe pravo*, 2:86–87. See *Svod zakonov grazhdanskikh*, vol. 10, chap. 1, art. 103, for spouses' obligation to live together.

70. Efimenko, "Krest'ianskaia zhenshchina," p. 92, claims that township courts treated women with more sympathy than civil courts that were obliged to obey written law rigidly.

71. *Trudy Komissii*, 3:62 (Iaroslavl').

72. Kovalevsky, *Modern Customs and Ancient Laws of Russia*, p. 43.

73. I am indebted to Neil Weissman of Dickinson College for the contrasting image.

74. [V. U. Krupianskaia], *The Village of Viriatino*, trans. Sula Benet (New York: Anchor, 1970), p. 102; Pakhman, *Obychnoe grazhdanskoe pravo*, 2:23–24, 161–62, 185–86; M. I. Zarudnyi, *Zakony i zhizn'* (St. Petersburg, 1874), p. 118; Tiutriumov, "Krest'ianskaia sem'ia," 4, part 1:291–93; Mukhin, *Obychnyi poriadok*, pp. 223–77; Efimenko, "Krest'ianskaia zhenshchina," pp. 65, 72–73, 86.

6 / Childbirth and Culture: Midwifery in the Nineteenth-Century Russian Countryside

SAMUEL C. RAMER

Samuel Ramer, associate professor of history at Tulane University, describes what might be called "slow history," the investigation of resistance to change, in this instance in the area of obstetric reform. The Russian Empire, during the late nineteenth century, had the highest infant mortality rate in Europe. The absence of proper obstetrical care made childbirth potentially hazardous. Older peasant women (called povitukhi), *experienced in delivering babies, customarily officiated. Reformers envisioned training rural midwives, but by the turn of the century, such women assisted only 2 percent of rural births. For peasant girls trained as midwives, training meant emancipation from the countryside and they were reluctant to return. Perhaps more significant, peasant women preferred the local* povitukhi, *who understood their traditions, rituals, and prayers, and who customarily remained in the household for a few days to take over chores for recuperating mothers. Ramer sees obstetric reform as but a chapter in the conflict between rational, secular Western culture, which had taken root in the cities, and the tradition-bound world of the Russian village.*

> We must see to it that children are born properly.
> This is real revolution—of this I am quite sure.
> ISAAC BABEL, "The Palace of Motherhood" (1918)

Almost half of the children born in rural Russia during the late nineteenth century died before they were five years old.[1] The Empire as a whole, with a population over four-fifths rural, had the highest infant mortality rate in Europe. The reasons are to be found primarily in Russia's economic and cultural backwardness. For most of the rural population, diet was unbalanced and insufficient, housing overcrowded, and clothing inadequate. The most elementary hygienic and sanitary measures were for the most part ignored, and there was little popular understanding of their signifi-

"Childbirth and Culture: Midwifery in the Nineteenth Century Russian Countryside" by Samuel C. Ramer, in David L. Ransel, ed., *The Family in Imperial Russia: New Lines of Historical Research* (Urbana: University of Illinois Press, 1978), pages 218–235. Copyright © 1978 The Board of Trustees of the University of Illinois. Reprinted by permission.

cance. Disease flourished in such an environment, taking a disproportionately large toll among infants and young children. Medical care, when it could be obtained at all, was often poor in quality, and in many cases the limitations of contemporary medical knowledge rendered even the best physicians powerless to do more than supervise the inevitable.

Although childbirth itself was not the primary occasion for infant death, it did involve considerable danger for mother and child alike. The absence of adequate obstetric care made these dangers particularly acute during complicated deliveries and contributed to a high rate of infection during the postnatal period. In the middle of the nineteenth century there were virtually no rural midwives with any sort of modern medical training.[2] Peasant women usually gave birth either alone or with the assistance of a *povitukha,* an older peasant woman without formal medical education who was experienced in delivering babies. The infant and maternal deaths which resulted from the *povitukhi's* incompetence were especially intolerable to physicians and medical reformers because they seemed unnecessary. The reduction of such deaths through the improvement of obstetric care seemed a practical possibility which could gradually be realized, despite the expected persistence of Russia's more general backwardness. The task as reformers of the 1860s and 1870s envisioned it was to train a competent corps of rural midwives (*sel'skie povival'nye babki*) to replace the older *povitukhi.* If nothing else, it was argued, such trained midwives could reduce the instances of infection and eliminate the "barbaric" practices for which *povitukhi* were renowned in cases of difficult delivery. It was hoped that rural midwives, together with the physicians with whom they were expected to cooperate, would be able to provide modern obstetric care for the Russian peasantry.[3]

These arguments received a practical implementation. Whereas until the 1860s the only institutions in the Empire which trained a significant number of midwives had been the Imperial Foundling Homes in St. Petersburg and Moscow, by the late 1870s there were over twenty schools in provincial cities especially devoted to the training of such women.[4] By 1905 the total number of schools for midwives had grown to over fifty, with an enrollment of nearly 4,000. The majority, located in the larger cities and sponsored by either charitable organizations or city governments, had no particular commitment to the countryside and trained midwives legally qualified for urban practice. But a number of provincial governments (*zemstva*) and some private organizations continued to support over twenty provincial schools for midwives whose primary orientation was to the countryside.[5]

The same survey of 1905 records over 10,000 trained midwives already in practice, as contrasted to 15,000 physicians and 20,000 *fel'dshers,* or paramedics.[6] The numbers in all these cases are small, considering that the population was over 125 million, but significant progress had been made in the training of midwives. Nevertheless, available statistics indicate that as late as the turn of the century only 2 percent of rural births were attended by trained midwives.[7] The local governments' attempts to provide trained obstetric care for the peasantry would thus appear to have failed almost entirely. How can this be explained?

The central problem, predictably, was not simply a shortage but an uneven distribution of trained midwives. On the whole, these midwives tended to settle in urban areas, despite the fact that many of them had been recruited from the peasantry and trained with the peasantry in mind. This had a positive result in that by the turn of the century access to a trained midwife, and if necessary to a physician, was as readily available in the major cities of European Russia as it was in the capitals of western Europe. But this achievement had come at the expense of the rural population, and as of the turn of the century no dramatic change in this urban concentration seemed imminent.

Trained midwives preferred the city to the countryside for obvious reasons. There were, in the first place, comparatively few salaried positions in the countryside. If local governments failed, it was less in the training than in the support of midwives for rural areas. In 1905, for example, the *zemstva*, which were the chief rural employers, provided only 2,200 positions for the more than 10,000 midwives in practice.[8] The situation in the non-*zemstvo* provinces was even worse.[9] There were a number of reasons why the *zemstva* and other local governments did not provide more salaried positions for midwives. Funds were limited, and the need for physicians and *fel'dshers* (who could be pressed into service as midwives)[10] seemed more compelling. Equally important was the fact that the rural population itself did not share the physicians' perception that trained midwives were needed, and those actually trained were only infrequently called upon. The cost per birth of providing trained midwives was thus relatively high, and the *zemstva* generally acquiesced in this peasant indifference. Local governments devoted little planning or funding to the organization of obstetric care per se until the 1890s.[11]

The majority of trained midwives (over 6,000 in 1905) were in private practice, and most of them worked in cities.[12] There was a demand for their services there, and the proximity of large numbers of reasonably affluent clients allowed at least some of them to support themselves by practicing—something almost impossible in the countryside, for a midwife without a salary, because of infrequent demand and peasant poverty. The competition among urban midwives was fierce, and many were in fact unemployed, but the possibilities for supplemental income either as hospital aides or in non-medical jobs were greater. However difficult life was in the city, private practice in the countryside did not appear as a practical alternative to most trained midwives.

For those able to maintain a practice, the city also provided more attractive working conditions. An urban midwife did not have to travel far to practice her trade, as her rural counterpart frequently did, and it was easier to call upon a physician in unusually difficult cases. While a rural midwife was supposed to refer all complicated deliveries (anything involving the active interference of the midwife) to a physician, and was in fact required by law to do so,[13] distances and poor communication in the countryside often rendered this a practical impossibility, placing upon the rural midwife's shoulders a medical responsibility which exceeded her training and skills.

The concentration of midwives (indeed, of all trained medical personnel) in cities was an old story, and the first sustained efforts to alter the balance coincide with the Great Reforms of the 1860s. During this era the Ministry of Internal Affairs, along with the local governments which it prodded, began for the first time to consider seriously how better obstetric care could be provided for the peasantry.[14]

The solution advocated by the ministry involved establishing schools for rural midwives in conjunction with the maternity wards of provincial hospitals. These schools, at least ideally, would train girls in the hospital for one or two years before sending them to work in rural areas. In its circulars the ministry asked local physicians in its service to poll their peasant communities to determine the viability of such schools, and then to render their own opinions. Public awareness of the ministry's initiatives elicited a number of projects from physicians and concerned laymen on the question of how rural midwives should be trained and how their success as practitioners could be best assured.[15] The projects differed in many ways, but they shared a number of ideas which are of interest because they shed light not only on the problems involved in improving obstetric care, but also on the attitudes of contemporary physicians toward those problems.

The first (and most unequivocal) attitude was that rural midwives should be recruited from the peasantry and, insofar as possible, sent back to work in the areas from which they had come. (This emphasis on the importance of peasant origin should be noted, since by the turn of the century most medical professionals would cease to regard the social origin of medical personnel as a matter of primary importance.) The physicians of the 1860s recognized that peasant girls were not ideal students. Most were not literate when they began their studies, and their way of life in the village had not prepared them for study focused on the written word. Hence, most reformers recommended that schooling for rural midwives be practical, not theoretical, with emphasis on oral instruction and demonstration. Such training demanded an adequate supply of pregnant and parturient women who could be used as teaching material. Even in provincial hospitals it was difficult to maintain this supply at the low level considered sufficient (100 births per year) because of the novelty of maternity wards,[16] the understandable suspicion with which both urban dwellers and peasants viewed the hospital, and the very process of teaching, which violated the privacy in which most women preferred to give birth.

Almost all physicians consulted were in agreement that it was important not only to recruit peasant girls, but to structure life in the school so that they should remain peasants, culturally undifferentiated from the population they were to serve. Thus we find arguments for the maintenance of an austere regime, for the retention of peasant dress, for a ban on any luxuries which urban existence might provide, and for the use of students as service personnel in the hospital during non-school hours so that they "would not grow unused to being peasants."[17] The justification for these arguments was twofold. Reformers wanted to make sure girls returned to the countryside and feared that any pampering would cause them to reject their rural calling. Moreover, they argued that only women who had retained the outward manifestations of peasant culture could win the confidence of the people they would serve. To be effective with peasants, reformers insisted, midwives would have to be "their people" (*svoi liudi*). Insofar as possible, they should be peasants from the local area who were familiar with its customs and known to its people. It was even more important that they not see themselves as superior to the peasantry, that they appear "neither as privileged persons nor as some kind of reformers."[18]

While arguments that students should retain a peasant way of life made sense on one level, they were incompatible with the other mission of midwifery schools—

namely, to transform young peasant girls into capable representatives of modern medicine who would alter, rather than conform to, obstetric practices which prevailed in rural areas. The authors of the projects involved were to an extent aware of this contradiction but resolved it only weakly by implying that trained midwives in the countryside would essentially have to serve as cultural emissaries in disguise.[19] This resolution rested on the common assumption that medical authority among the peasantry was primarily personal in nature and that peasants, if not confronted with an open attack on their whole way of life, would ultimately believe in results. To suppose, however, that a significant number of peasant girls could maintain this sort of dual identity was clearly unrealistic, as experience would show.

If the physicians of the 1860s had no other solutions, it was partly because their imaginations were restrained by the funds available for rural obstetric care. The question of how midwifery schools should be financed was one to which they all directed their attention, and there was a considerable amount of agreement on several basic questions. Almost all the physicians polled by the Ministry of Internal Affairs in 1863 and 1864 agreed that no schools for rural midwives could succeed if the costs of training were put directly on the peasantry.[20] According to the physicians, the peasantry saw no need for such schools; given a choice, the local peasant community would refuse to pay tuition for one of its members to study, and the community could not provide her with a salaried position after graduation. (Several physicians reported no volunteers for study in a midwifery school, even with the guarantee of tuition and room and board).[21] Because of this peasant indifference, most physicians recommended that provincial governments support students and hire trained midwives out of funds not specifically designated for midwifery.

There were some exceptions, the most noteworthy being that of Nikolai Mandel'shtam, the chief obstetrician in Mogilev Province. Ignoring the arguments of other provincial physicians, Mandel'shtam accepted the ministry's original recommendation that local communities (*sel'skie obshchestva* or *mirovye uchastki*) should select and support their own candidates as students and later provide jobs for them. Arguing on the basis of his own efforts in Mogilev, he emphasized both the feasibility of such an approach and the extent to which expense could be minimized by more thorough utilization of existing facilities.[22] The ministry ultimately accepted Mandel'shtam's project as a model for other provinces. It seemed more likely than others to achieve the desired goal, and it "did not demand any special expenditures."[23] The central government's decision to rely on peasant support of midwifery schools, a decision reached in the face of evidence that it would be disastrous for the schools, meant from the outset that the role of such schools would be limited.

The graduates of these early provincial schools did not fare well as rural midwives. Many went to the countryside for a year or two and then, unless supported by a fixed salary, either gave up their profession or retreated permanently to the city. By the turn of the century, according to one account, 90 percent of the graduates with the title of "trained village midwife" quickly passed examinations entitling them to an urban practice and moved to the city.[24] A year in school evidently did alter the expectations of graduates, and even peasant girls often experienced loneliness and social isolation upon returning to the countryside. The culture of the city—and, perhaps more important, its higher material standard of living—were difficult to forget. As one inspector critical of Mandel'shtam's school in Mogilev reported, its graduates "no longer like to live in the countryside, and don't remove their city clothes. They go very unwillingly to visit peasants in their simple carts, and sometimes even refuse. They are so alienated from the peasants, and the latter from them, that the peasants almost never turn to them for help, continuing as before to use simple, untrained women."[25]

The problem was not only that peasant girls trained as rural midwives were attracted to the city because of their training or their difficult experiences. The fact was that, despite initial efforts to recruit midwives among the peasantry, an increasing proportion of the girls trained as rural midwives came from the city to begin with. At the Nadezhdin Obstetric Institute in St. Petersburg, all but three of the 419 girls in training as rural midwives in 1861 were peasants. In the same school during the decade 1881–90 peasants made up only 16.3 percent of all students. Of the others, 27.8 percent were from the nobility, 27.7 percent were children of townsmen (*meshchane*), 15 percent were from clergy backgrounds, and 14 percent were from various lower ranks of society (*raznochintsy*).[26] By virtue of its location in St. Petersburg, the Nadezhdin Institute cannot be regarded as typical of schools specializing in the training of rural midwives, but the trend is representative. Table 6.1 indicates the 1910 enrollments in centers of midwife training in the Empire.[27] Of all midwives in training, less than a quarter were of peasant origin. Even in the schools for rural midwives, students of peasant background constituted only 38 percent of the total. Thus by the eve of World War I (and, by all indications, much earlier) the city had become the main source of Russia's trained midwives, even of those preparing for rural practice. This was occasioned in part by the limited success that peasant midwives had achieved, which invalidated earlier claims made on their behalf. Furthermore, as we shall see, most Russian physicians had by then abandoned the almost exclusive earlier emphasis on social origin in favor of developing the best possible system of medical care.

Perhaps more important in explaining the increasing dominance of the city is the general testimony that most of the girls who were eager to become midwives were urban, and were better prepared to enter a course of medical training than their rural contemporaries. It should be recalled that for many girls, rural as well as urban, training as a midwife was a way of escaping the confines of a traditional way of life. For Jews, and a highly disproportionate number of midwives were Jews (25 percent of those in training in 1910),[28] it meant freedom to live outside the Pale of Settlement. For peasant girls, however they happened to be chosen, midwifery meant emancipation from the patriarchal structure of the village. For the idealistic and politically committed among the educated youth, it offered a skill with which they could serve the people.[29] For all women it was a profession which offered at least the possibility of an autonomous life.

The urban preferences of most midwives, like the failure of efforts to provide trained midwives for the peasantry, cannot be understood without some reference to the peasants themselves. The fundamental and unpleasant fact facing physicians and medical reformers alike was the peasantry's reluctance to call upon the midwives who had been trained for them. The rural midwives themselves, of course, found

Table 6.1. Enrollments at Centers of Midwife Training, 1910, by Social Origin of Students

	Peasants	Townsmen (meshchane)	Nobility	Children of Bureacrats, Teachers, Doctors	Clergy	Military	Merchant	Honored Citizens	Foreign	Misc.
Women's schools for fel'dshers with midwife training	652	1,575	270	215	268	120	94	111	19	215
Schools for fel'dshers with midwife training (coed)[a]	209	604	92	67	37	15	29	26	—	57
Obstetric institutes (urban midwives)	185	569	108	73	36	27	15	23	12	15
Schools for rural midwives	735	948	137	56	53	25	22	32	2	44
Total	1,781	3,696	607	411	394	187	160	192	33	331
Percentage of total	22.8	47.4	7.7	5.2	0.5	2.3	0.2	2.4	0.4	4.2

[a]As of 1910 there were only 210 men studying to become fel'dshers with midwife training.

113

this reluctance not only economically ruinous but also detrimental to their professional skills. How can the rural population's persistent preference for local *povitukhi* be explained?

In answering this question, it is necessary to consider the broader problem of childbirth in Russian peasant society. Customs differed from area to area, and no absolute rules can be offered; however, a number of generalizations seem both valid and germane. First, for the peasant woman parturition was a private, almost secret act surrounded with a great deal of custom and superstition.[30] Pregnancy itself was considered a particularly vulnerable time for a woman, and parturition even more so. One of the great fears was that a stranger would "give her the evil eye" (*sglazit' ee*), causing harm to her child. In many cases peasant women gave birth without any assistance at all. Birth could occur in a number of places, but ideally it did not take place inside the peasant house (*izba*) itself. The *bania* or peasant sauna was preferred, where one existed, and birth frequently took place in the cattle shed or grain storehouse. Since peasant women usually worked right up until delivery, childbirth in the fields was not unusual during the summer months.[31]

Most women gave birth with the help of a *povitukha*. This *povitukha* (or in some cases *znakharka*, or medicine woman) was generally an older peasant woman known in the local area. Often she was a widow, and in most cases she had borne children herself. For her, as for most peasants, birth was not simply a medical phenomenon but the beginning of a life, a mystical event to be accompanied and eased by the appropriate rituals, prayers, and sayings (*zagovory*). There seems little reason to doubt that such *povitukhi* were also capable assistants in cases where birth was normal. In addition to providing the practical and religious support just described, the *povitukha* generally took over household chores for the family for two or three days, allowing the mother to recuperate. This service was highly valued by the peasantry and was more important in accounting for the *povitukha's* popularity than adherence to tradition, if we are to judge by physicians' reports. Someone had to continue the operation of the house—cutting wood, bringing water indoors, firing the stove, preparing meals, caring for other children, feeding and watering the livestock, milking the cow, and so on. The father or relatives might assume some of these tasks, but frequently their own work did not allow them to do everything. For the mother, the performance of arduous tasks immediately after giving birth, particularly in inclement weather, could bring great harm, causing postnatal complications which could maim and even kill.[32]

Because of the need to relieve the mother, the *povitukha* was often a necessity even in cases where a trained midwife was invited to assist at birth. To invite both was usually more expensive, so peasants contented themselves with the *povitukha*, resorting to trained midwives only in emergencies. In reform proposals, physicians repeatedly insisted that trained midwives should be willing to assume the chores which the *povitukhi* saw as an integral part of their work. In all likelihood the peasants themselves were not willing to accept the performance of chores by urban women, even those who did not see themselves as being above it. Lack of skills in rural tasks is another possible problem which should be kept in mind.

The cultural proximity of the *povitukhi*, the practical services they performed, and their relative cheapness were important reasons for their popularity among the peasantry, but there were other reasons as well. The *povitukhi* had the advantages of age, experience, and tradition over the younger, newly trained midwives of the 1860s and 1870s. It does not seem unreasonable, or even unenlightened, that the peasantry should have valued these traits. It is also clear that the *povitukhi* themselves were not disinterested bystanders, indifferent to the appearance of professional competitors. They ridiculed their rivals, sensing correctly that the midwives' youth (some were not mothers themselves) and their neglect of religious custom were serious disadvantages before a traditional audience. And there is no reason to doubt that they believed their own arguments.[33]

The most important single reason for the *povitukhi*'s sustained popularity is that midwives trained for the countryside were rarely able to demonstrate their purely medical superiority and win confidence through results. Doubtless the stories of the *povitukhi*'s barbaric, even grotesque, efforts in cases involving difficult births have some basis in fact. But the trained midwife, confronted with the same cases, could do no better. She could of course take no action at all, summoning a physician instead (a procedure which both her training and the law required). But the condition of the expectant mother and the remoteness of the nearest physician did not always make this alternative practical. Her efforts to proceed on her own might be no more successful than those of a *povitukha,* but her inability or refusal to act was, in the peasant's eyes, an admission of incompetence greater than the *povitukha*'s failure, and it controverted any claims she might have to superior knowledge. In cases where birth occurred without complications, the *povitukha* seems to have been as competent as a trained midwife.

The trained midwives' inability to demonstrate their medical superiority, and the peasantry's coincidental inability to perceive that superiority, was grounded in the fact that such superiority was marginal where it existed at all. Physicians' low assessments of rural midwives' abilities tend to confirm this. Surveying the state of midwife training in Russia in 1870, Dr. I. M. Tarnovskii reported to the Ministry of Internal Affairs that "midwives with their present education satisfy neither the demands of society nor those of physicians."[34] This view would be echoed throughout the rest of the century. The local and provincial governments' refusal to create more positions for trained midwives and to pay them better was directly connected with this generally shared view of their limited abilities. Such governments found it more rational to invest what funds there were in the hiring of physicians, *fel'dshers,* and female *fel'dshers* with training as midwives.

When turn-of-the-century physicians contemplated the failure of efforts to provide modern obstetric care for the countryside,[35] several alternative solutions were offered. The first was the possibility of training the *povitukhi,* since these women already enjoyed popular confidence. Actually, this frequently occurred in an informal way, with either physicians or trained midwives giving *povitukhi* advice on techniques of delivery, and particularly on the need for antiseptic precautions.[36] There had also been at least one formal attempt to recruit *povitukhi* for a one-month crash course in modern obstetrics. The results of that training session, conducted in Saratov Province in 1888, had not been promising, although physicians there did not exclude the possibility of renewed attempts. Ironically, formal study tended to undermine rather than enhance the authority of the *povitukhi* who participated. The physician in charge, A. I. Sukhodeeva, reported that on their return to the village the population faulted them because, "having studied a whole month, they still couldn't cure diseases, and tended to call for a physician at births more frequently than their untrained counterparts."[37]

Because of its author's prominence and the nature of the debate it generated, the most significant proposal was one made in 1899 by Professor Dmitrii Ott, the director of the Imperial Clinical Obstetric Institute in St. Petersburg.[38] Chairman of a special Pirogov Society committee charged with making recommendations on rural midwifery, Ott essentially reiterated the basic positions advocated by reformers during the 1860s. He urged a renewed effort to recruit peasant girls to study obstetrics for eight months in a provincial hospital, after which they would be returned to the countryside. He recognized that this suggestion was not new, but insisted that earlier attempts had failed not because they were wrong in principle, but because they had not been properly implemented.

Ott argued that the existing state of rural obstetric care in Russia demanded some departure from the medical ideals which he assumed all physicians shared. "At the present time," he wrote, "we have a choice. We can either leave things in the sad condition which obtains everywhere, making our peace with the horrible mortality rate among parturient women. Or, without rejecting the ideals we all have in our minds, we can seek through a temporary measure to decrease popular suffering."[39] The reaction of most physicians to Ott's project was negative, indicating that a change had taken place since the 1860s in their attitude toward the importance of recruiting rural midwives from among the peasantry. Most thought it impossible to train a competent midwife in only eight months, pointing to the unsatisfactory qualifications even of those who had been trained for two years.[40] To accept Ott's proposals, they argued, would only serve to legitimate and entrench dangerously incompetent personnel. Moved by these arguments, the Seventh Congress of the Pirogov Society rejected Ott's proposal as "one which contradicts the basic tasks of *zemstvo* medical organization."[41] Underlying this rejection was not only a different estimate of the extent to which certain ideal standards would have to be placed temporarily in abeyance because of Russia's backwardness, but also a clear emphasis on expertise as the exclusive legitimate criterion in the choice of medical personnel. Not all physicians shared this view, of course, and the argument that only peasants would be able to penetrate the countryside was one that retained many proponents. Nevertheless, at the turn of the century the problem, as it was conceived by most physicians working in local governments, involved not the recruitment of peasant girls but the placement in the village of the increasing numbers of talented urban girls who were already studying midwifery. Their commitment to their profession and their overall intellectual superiority made a return to the programs of the 1860s an unacceptable solution for most physicians.

An increasing number of *zemstva* sought to place such urban women in the countryside by training them not only as midwives, but as *fel'dshers* as well, giving them the title of *fel'dsher*–midwife (*fel'dsheritsa–akusherka*).[42] The *fel'dsher* had a broader general preparation in medicine than the midwife, generally four years and sometimes five. Prior to their medical educations, all *fel'dshers* had completed at least four years of gymnasium or its equivalent. Female *fel'dshers* tended to have more general education than their male counterparts, and physicians considered them to be the best-trained auxiliary medical personnel in prerevolutionary Russia.

Combining *fel'dsher* and midwife in one person had several practical advantages. For the rural employer, whether *zemstvo* or otherwise, hiring a *fel'dsher*–midwife served two purposes at the same time. Moreover, experience showed that the combination also tended to promote the obstetric practice of the female *fel'dsher*, thus making real inroads on the territory of the *povitukhi*. The midwife's limited obstetric practice had, in a sense, been self-reinforcing. Called only periodically to assist at peasant births (often to those which were already beyond any medical help), they had little opportunity to win popular confidence by exercising their trade. The female *fel'dsher*–midwife, in her first role, was able to ingratiate herself with the peasantry through the successful treatment of minor illnesses and injuries. Having established herself as a healer in a large number of cases, her reputation grew more rapidly, and the personal relationship and confidence important to peasants at childbirth were created. There were arguments against the growing emphasis on the training of *fel'dsher*–midwives, primarily that the all-consuming nature of the *fel'dsher*'s general medical practice would not allow her the time to function effectively as a midwife. These arguments were not validated by experience, however, and the growing tendency was to provide all medical personnel, male as well as female, with courses in obstetrics and gynecology. In critical cases, the peasantry understandably turned to whatever medical care was at hand, so most *fel'dshers*, whatever their training, assisted at births from time to time.

The problems which beset medical reformers interested in rural obstetric care were much the same as those in other areas of development. As in the more obvious fields of education, or even political reform, obstetric reform was but a chapter in the conflict between the rational and secular culture of the West, which had taken root in the city, and the more tradition-bound world of the Russian village. The central question of Russian development—that is, the extent to which Russia was different from the countries of western Europe, and the extent to which solutions adopted there were applicable to Russia—was mirrored in almost all discussions of rural obstetric care. It was posed exactly in Professor Ott's terms: To what extent should the highest possible medical standards be sacrificed temporarily in order to meet the peculiar and desperate needs of the Russian countryside?

There is no reason to expect a country's general approach to its medical problems (in this case, those of obstetric care) to differ radically from its attempts to solve other problems. In the case of medicine, of course, there is a body of specialized scientific knowledge which differentiates it from other areas of public life; however, the social and economic difficulties encountered in applying that knowledge are, not surprisingly, similar to those encountered by others interested in development. The interrelated character of such problems as education and health care suggests that any major change in one area would affect and be dependent upon changes in others. In the case of obstetric care, it was impossible to alter customs concerning something as intimate as childbirth until the cultural assumptions of the society being affected had themselves been changed. Physicians of the 1860s were aware of this, despite their understandable efforts to isolate the problem of obstetric care from the broader problems of cultural backwardness. As one of their number put it, "As long as the idea of having rural midwives is not a popular one, attempts to introduce them will be unsuccessful."[43] The midwife herself was not a passive observer in this drama, and if she was to be anything but a *povitukha,* she had to become a cultural missionary as well as a medical practitioner. The number of midwives who were able to perform such a role was small, and regular access to qualified obstetric care became a reality only well into the Soviet period.

Notes

The present article is part of a larger study of *fel'dshers* and midwives in prerevolutionary Russia. I thank the Tulane Research Council, the National Endowment for the Humanities, the International Research and Exchanges Board, and the Fulbright Faculty Fellowship Program for their assistance in making the research for this paper possible.

1. The infant mortality rate varied significantly from province to province. For figures and a discussion of regional variations, see V. I. Grebenshchikov and D. A. Sokolov, *Smertnost' v Rossii i bor'ba s neiu* (St. Petersburg, 1901), pp. 20–24.

2. For the Ministry of Internal Affairs' recognition of this, see *Tsentral'nyi Gosudarstvennyi Istoricheskii Arkhiv (TsGIA),* f. 1297, op. 142, d. 292, pp. 6–6 ob.

3. Ibid., p. 6 ob. According to nineteenth-century Russian law there were three titles for obstetric personnel: *povival'nye babki, sel'skie* or rural *povival'nye babki,* and *povitukhi.* The first were distinguished by having completed training in an urban midwife institute. The second had graduated from a school for rural midwives, and were not entitled to practice in urban areas without passing a special examination. The third had no formal training at all, but were required to pass qualifying examinations. They were allowed to practice only when there were no trained midwives available. In practice, so many rural midwives qualified for urban practice that it is useful here to speak of midwives as a single group. Their skills varied enormously, but in the countryside the principal dichotomy was between the *povitukhi* and any midwife with training. Despite the law, many *povitukhi* had no license whatsoever and most practiced in competition with trained midwives. The term *akusherka* "midwife," from the French *accoucheur),* while frequently used in general discussions, did not exist in Russian legislation except when appended to the term *fel'dsheritsa*—i.e., *fel'dsheritsa-akusherka* (*fel'dsher*-midwife). *Spisok statei Svoda Zakonov i pravitel'stvennykh rasporiazhenii o povival'nykh babkakh, sel'skikh povival'nykh babkakh i povitukakh* (St. Petersburg, 1885), pp. 2–3. In 1900 the titles of *povival'naia babka* and *sel'skaia povival'naia babka* were replaced by those of *povival'naia babka* of the first and second order, with no appreciable effect on the problem of obstetric care. *Sobranie uzakonenii i rasporiazhenii pravitel'stva* (St. Petersburg, 1900), p. 1160.

4. *Otchet meditsinskogo departamenta ministerstva vnutrennykh del za 1876 god* (St. Petersburg, 1877), pp. 162–63. These first schools were established in Astrakhan, Vologda, Voronezh, Viatka, Kamenets-Podol'skii, Kishinev, Mitau, Mogilev, Moscow, Penza, Samara, Saratov, Simbirsk, Tambov, Tula, Khar'kov, Kherson, Chernigov and Iaroslavl'.

5. *Otchet o sostoianii narodnogo zdraviia i organizatsii vrachebnoi pomoshchi v Rossii za 1905 god* (St. Petersburg, 1907), pp. 176–87.

6. Ibid.

7. D. A. Paryshev, *Rodovspomozhenie v Rossii po dannym vserossiiskoi gigienicheskoi*

vystavki 1913 g. v S.-Peterburge (St. Petersburg, 1914), p. 1. An absolutely accurate figure is impossible here, and the extent of effective obstetric care varied from province to province. Scattered checks of provincial physicians' reports tend to confirm the general statistic.

8. *Otchet o sostoianii narodnogo zdraviia,* p. 180.

9. For most of its history, the *zemstvo* existed only in the provinces of European Russia. The western borderlands, Siberia, Central Asia and the Caucasus continued to be governed through institutions of the central administration.

10. Those concerned with obstetric care were disturbed by the casual (and common) notion that a *fel'dsher,* or even a physician, was an adequate substitute for a trained obstetrician. Until late in the century *fel'dshers* were not given any obstetric training at all, and there is abundant testimony that a large proportion of physicians was incompetent in assisting at birth.

11. B. B. Veselovskii, *Istoriia zemstva za sorok let* (St. Petersburg, 1909–11), vol. 1, pp. 412–13.

12. *Otchet o sostoianii narodnogo zdraviia,* p. 181.

13. *Spisok statei svoda zakonov i pravitel'stvennykh rasporiazhenii o povival'nykh babkakh, sel'skikh povival'nykh babkakh i povitukakh,* pp. 2–3.

14. The ministry's first circular "Ob uchrezhdenii pri bol'nitsakh Prikaza Povival'nykh uchilishch" is dated November 3, 1863. *TsGIA,* f. 1297, op. 142, d. 292, pp. 6–6 ob. For responses, see pp. 11–361.

15. Many of these projects are bound together with other answers to the Ministry's circular in *TsGIA,* f. 1297, op. 142, d. 292. See also the important project for the improvement of standards for midwives written in 1870 by N. I. Kozlov, N. F. Zdekauer, and A. Ia. Krassovskii, a project which quickly abandoned the exclusive consideration of midwives and in fact used the issue of midwifery as a means of opening up the discussion of women's medical education before the Medical Soviet. *TsGIA,* f. 1294, op. 6, d. 54, pp. 11–23 ob.

16. The estimate of the minimum number of births sufficient to support a midwifery school is that of Nikolai Mandel'shtam. *TsGIA,* f. 1297, op. 142, d. 292, p. 137.

17. Ibid., p. 335 ob.

18. Ibid., p. 326 ob.

19. Ibid., pp. 330–31.

20. Ibid., passim.

21. Ibid., p. 258.

22. Ibid., pp. 136–36 ob.

23. Ibid., pp. 239–39 ob.

24. Dmitrii Ott. *Proekt organizatsii akusherskoi pomoshchi sredi sel'skogo naseleniia (Doklad sektsii akusherstva i zhenskikh boleznei VII s"ezda russkikh vrachei v pamiat' N. I. Pirogova)* (St. Petersburg, 1899), p. 15.

25. *TsGIA,* f. 1297, op. 142, d. 292, pp. 427–27 ob.

26. V. Zhuk, "Shkola sel'skikh povival'nykh babok," *Zhurnal akusherstva i zhenskikh boleznei* 4, nos. 7–8 (July–August 1890): 507.

27. *TsGIA,* f. 1298, op. 1, d. 1754, pp. 3–9.

28. Ibid., p. 8 ob, 9.

29. For an excellent memoir recording the experiences of such a woman, see Anna A., "Na zemskoi sluzhbe. Iz zapisok fel'dsheritsy," *Vestnik Evropy* 25, no. 12 (December 1890): 549–93.

30. For a more detailed discussion of peasant attitudes toward childbirth, see Antonina Martynova, "Life of the Pre-Revolutionary Village as Reflected in Popular Lullabies," in David L. Ransel, ed., *The Family in Imperial Russia: New Lines of Historical Research* (Urbana, Ill., 1978), pp. 171–85.

31. G. E. Rein, *O russkom narodnom akusherstve* (St. Petersburg, 1889).

32. Zhuk, *Shkola sel'skikh povival'nykh babok,* p. 511. See also A. G. Arkhangel'skaia, "K istorii razvitiia rodovspomozheniia v zemskikh guberniiakh," *Zhurnal akusherstva i zhenskikh boleznei* 12 (April 1898): 456.

33. For a good description of this conflict, see I. A. Larin, "Narodnaia meditsina Astrakhanskoi gubernii," *Russkii meditsinskii vestnik* 6, no. 17 (September 1904): 583–86.

34. Tarnovskii did go on to state that "in spite of the extremely limited nature of their knowledge and a very inadequate system of instruction there can still not be the slightest doubt that trained midwives render society a much greater service than rural *povitukhi* who have studied nothing." *TsGIA,* f. 1294, op. 6, d. 54, pp. 2–3.

35. The most significant meeting devoted to this subject was held at the ninth congress of the Pirogov Society in 1906. For papers delivered and discussion as well, see volume 6 of the *Trudy IX-go Pirogovskogo s"ezda* (St. Petersburg, 1906). This was also published separately by G. E. Rein as *Rodovspomozhenie v Rossii* (*Sbornik dokladov na IX Pirogovskom s"ezde*) (St. Petersburg, 1906).

36. Arkhangel'skaia, "K istorii razvitiia rodovspomozheniia," pp. 461–68.

37. *Gubernskie s"ezdy i soveshchaniia zemskikh vrachei i predstavitelei zemskikh uprav Saratovskoi gubernii s 1876 po 1894 god. (Svod postanovlenii),* ed. P. A. Kalinin and N. I. Teziakov (Saratov, 1894), p. 53.

38. Ott, *Proekt organizatsii.*

39. Ibid., p. 6.

40. For a local response, see *Vrachebnaia khronika Khar'kovskoi gub.* 3, no. 5 (Khar'kov, 1899): 315.

41. A. P. Artem'ev, "Kak trudno byt' sostavitelem proekta organizatsii akusherskoi pomoshchi v Rossii," *Zhurnal akusherstva i zhenskikh boleznei* 14 (February 1900): 1.

42. The Medical Soviet had recognized the superiority of schools which combined *fel'dsher* and midwife training as early as the 1880s. A combined course was allowed for the first time in 1879 in a school in Kishinev. I. V. Bertenson, "Vrachebno-professional'noe obrazovanie zhenshchin v Rossii," *Vestnik Evropy* 25, no. 11 (November 1890): 224–25.

43. *TsGIA,* f. 1297, op. 142, d. 292, p. 337.

7/ To Save Oneself: Russian Peasant Women and the Development of Women's Religious Communities in Prerevolutionary Russia

BRENDA MEEHAN-WATERS

Brenda Meehan-Waters, professor of history and associate dean at the University of Rochester, describes women to whom Christianity was so singular a source of strength that they chose to "leave the world" and take up solely religious lives. Russian peasant culture, being a religious culture, generally accommodated their needs. Some women were simply set up in huts on the outskirts of villages where they lived with small groups of like-minded women. Other devoutly religious women, wishing to dedicate their lives to God, played crucial roles in the development of female religious communities. The communities offered peasant women an opportunity for basic education, a means of spiritual and intellectual development, and— most important—promise of eternal salvation. That their own salvation was of paramount importance, more so than the claims of family or village, may suggest that these pious women held a concept of personal autonomy.

Russian Orthodoxy, like Christianity in general, has long emphasized the gift of divine grace, the equality of believers, the dignity of each individual soul, and the supreme importance of eternal salvation. In addition, Orthodoxy—unlike Protestantism or post-Reformation Catholicism—has continued to privilege the monastic or "angelic" path to salvation. Yet the institutional church has been historically hierarchical, and the social and material circumstances of the poorer classes can adversely affect their chances of living a fully dedicated religious or monastic life. The well-to-do, having greater control over their lives and property, can more easily and dramatically renounce wealth and worldly life than the poor, and men have greater control over their life options than do women.[1]

Given these general considerations as well as the specific religious and social structures of prerevolutionary Russia, which included, up until 1861, the institution of serfdom, what were the options for a nineteenth-century peasant woman who wished to dedicate her life to God?

Her chances of entering a convent, or women's monastery (*zhenskii monastyr'*) as it was called in Russia, were problematical both because monasteries traditionally required an entrance donation and because their numbers and size had been severely curtailed by the Church Reform of 1764, which confiscated ecclesiastical property, cut in half the number of monasteries, and created a stipendiary clergy.[2] Now that the state had to pay clerical salaries and fund ecclesiastical institutions, the government vigorously eliminated "superfluous" clergy, churches, and monasteries. In 1762, 881 monasteries had existed in Russia (678 men's and 203 women's); the reform of 1764 reduced the number by more than half, collapsing the total to 385, with 318 men's monasteries and 67 women's.[3] Smaller monasteries were closed, and monks and nuns, many old and ailing, and many of whom had lived and worshipped for decades in monasteries that were now closed, were arbitrarily transferred to larger, funded monasteries in their diocese to rationalize resources. In the process, many former residents of dissolved monasteries found themselves without an assigned, stipendiary slot in the new budget. Hence these surviving monasteries, now called *shtatnye* monasteries because of their place in the official government budget and table of organization, offered little hope of entry for new aspirants. And since the stipend alloted for the support of the monks and nuns was inadequate, the problem would still remain for poorer women of how to support themselves within a monastery if accepted.

Under these circumstances, pious peasant women who wished to live a life of prayer and dedicated celibacy had to take up such a life on their own, within the interstices of village life, and we find that Russian peasant culture, being a religious culture, generally made room for them. Such women were called variously *keleinitsy* (cell or hut dwellers because they or their parents often built them a separate hut on the outskirts of the village) or *chernichki* (probably because they dressed in black, and frequently supported themselves through the reading of the Psalter for the dead) or *spasennitsy* (those wishing to save themselves). Some *chernichki* continued to live with their families, as pious spinsters; others lived alone or in small clusters and were more commonly called *keleinitsy* or *spasennitsy*.[4] As one late-nineteenth-century ethnographer reported:

> Frequently girls reject marriage and express the wish to "*spasat'sia*" (to save themselves), "to leave the world." No matter how unpleasant for the parents, in most cases they do not feel they have the right to refuse her. In earlier times such *spasennitsy* went into monasteries; now since state monasteries have seriously diminished and entering a monastery requires a "sacrifice" (*zhertva*), often very large (100 rubles and more, for example, for the Sviatozerskii women's monastery in Gorokhovetskii district), these *spasennitsy* rarely enter monasteries. More often, they set themselves up in their own village or in the nearest village to be close to the church. Parents are obliged to build her a hut on the outskirts of the village. Sometimes she moves there with 3–5 *spasennitsy*.[5]

Spasennitsy, chernichki, and *keleinitsy,* by whichever name they were called, typically supported themselves through spinning, weaving, knitting, or day labor for prosperous peasants. Their numbers included not only single women but also pious widows without children. Devoutly attentive in church and eager to read liturgical service books, they were often literate, and frequently helped to support themselves through the reading of the Psalter for the dead. According to L. A. Tul'tseva, *chernichestvo* was a "distinctive monasticism" and "a widespread phenomenon among peasant women in pre-revolutionary Russia."[6] Although village culture was generally supportive of these women, such a life did not offer the rich liturgical, spiritual, and institutional support that a monastery provided. In addition, the written lives (*zhitiia*) of renowned peasant holy women of the nineteenth century suggest that women were sometimes constrained by family responsibilities, including the care of elderly parents, to this village-based, semimonastic way of life, rather than the more radical life of a hermit or a complete "fleeing of the world."[7]

In the course of the nineteenth century, a third alternative began to develop—unofficial women's religious communities, called *zhenskie obshchiny*. Developed as a response to the restrictive measures of the Church Reform of 1764, the earliest such communities were formed by displaced nuns of closed monasteries who clung tenaciously to a religious way of life, often hiding in their former cells. Over time, the founders of these initially unofficial women's religious communities were more typically pious gentry or merchant widows who, wishing to live a religious life, founded on their estates religious communities that attracted women of all social classes.[8] Such communities were communally organized and self-supporting, primarily deriving their income from the agricultural labor of the sisters. Because they were communally organized (*obshchezhitel'nye*) and supported themselves from their own labor, they could support more women and women of lower social origins than the traditional women's monasteries, which were noncommunal, idiorrhythmic,* dependent on a government budget and *shtat,* and assumed that each nun would maintain herself partly out of her own resources.[9]

Although women's religious communities began as a grass-roots, autonomous response to the government's curtailment and regulation of official, *shtatnye'* monasteries, they soon came under the wary eye of government and church authorities. Beginning with the nervous reign of Nicholas I (1825–1855), women's religious communities were brought under the "protection and supervision" of ecclesiastical and government authorities.[10] To be officially "established" as a *zhenskaia obshchina* (hereafter referred to as women's religious community) now required sponsorship by the local hierarchy and approval of the Holy Synod.[11] Charters were regularized, and the Chancellery of the Synod scrutinized the financial resources of a community to make certain that it was capable of supporting itself rather than hoping for support from a pecunious treasury.[12] Particular care was taken that every member of a community have a valid passport or internal documentation from the legal authority under whose jurisdiction she fell, indicating permission to enter the community. Peasants needed the permission of their landlord before the Emancipation of 1861, and that of the *volost'* authority after that. Thus women's religious communities became approved institutions of the church, and in the course of the nineteenth century, 67 percent of them eventually became official monasteries, all following communal rather than idiorrhythmic rule.[13] In all, approximately 220 women's religious communities were formed between 1764 and 1917.[14] The average size of a women's religious community, according to 1907 data, was 74 sisters, ranging from small, fledgling communities such as the Neopalimovskaia Mother of

---

*"Idiorrhythmic" is a term used in the Orthodox Church to describe monasteries in which the monastics live separately, hold property, work individually in supporting themselves, and, though members of a monastery supervised by an elected council, are not under daily direct supervision.

God community in Novgorod diocese, with a mother superior and 12 sisters, to a robust community such as Holy Trinity in Kaluga diocese, which numbered 412.[15]

This chapter explores the role of peasant women in the development of women's religious communities and the role of the communities in the development of peasant women, through a case study of one such community, that of Holy Trinity Tvorozhkovo in St. Petersburg diocese. I have chosen this particular community because it is representative of women's religious communities in its founding, organizational structure, religious life, and eventual elevation from a women's religious community to an official women's monastery, and because there are rich archival materials on this community, including lists of the members of the community, their social origins, literacy, and assigned duties.

Although peasant women constituted the overwhelminging majority of sisters in women's religious communities, in only a few known cases did they found them.[16] In this respect, Trinity Tvorozhkovo was no exception. Its founder, Aleksandra Filippovna Fon-Roze, née Shmakova, was born into a noble family in St. Petersburg, educated at the elite Smol'nyi Institute, and married in 1824 to Karl Andreevich Fon-Roze, a wealthy Lutheran nobleman.[17] Her parents were unusually pious, and she developed an early distaste for the vanities of aristocratic social life, preferring the serenity of a chapel to the whirl of a ballroom. After the death of their only daughter, she and her husband became increasingly devout. After his conversion to Orthodoxy, they bought a secluded, undeveloped estate, Tvorozhkovo, in St. Petersburg province, about forty miles from the district town of Gdov.[18] Realizing that with its woods, lake, and distance from other estates it would be an ideal spot for a monastery, they promised each other that if she died first, he would attempt to build a men's monastery there and retire to it, and if he died first, she would build a women's religious community and retire to it. When Karl Andreevich died in 1858, Aleksandra Filippovna sought to establish a women's religious community at Tvorozhkovo at her own expense, but was refused permission by the local metropolitan, who felt it would be too close to the local parish church.[19] In the meantime, she lived quietly and ascetically at Tvorozhkovo, earning a reputation for charity among the local poor. With the appointment of a new metropolitan in 1861, permission was given, and plans began in earnest for a women's community, which necessitated the building of a wooden house and chapel for the sisters. Aleksandra Filippovna pledged the money from the sale of her St. Petersburg town house, and prayed that pious, hardworking women would begin to gather. Believing that the monastic life enhanced one's opportunity for eternal salvation, she was particularly anxious to offer poor women a means of dedicating themselves to God.[20] All the women of the community were expected to lead celibate lives while in the community, although they did not have to take permanent vows.

Various membership lists indicate that this indeed happened. At the time of the official establishment of the community in 1865, there were about fifteen sisters; by 1872, the number had grown to twenty-six, including Aleksandra Filippovna (who, mindful of the angelic model of the monastic life, had been tonsured and taken the religious name Angelina), two widows of government officials, a woman from the merchantry, one from the clerical estate, eight from the artisanal or trading class (*meshchanstvo*), and thirteen from the peasantry.[21] In 1887 the community was elevated to a monastery.[22] (The elevation from community status to a monastery meant that some women would take permanent vows and become professed nuns.)

A decade later, Trinity Tvorozhkovo monastery had grown to fifty-nine: of the thirteen nuns, ten were peasants and three were from the lower bureaucracy; the one novice was from artisanal origins, and the forty-five sisters included thirty-six peasants, four tradespeople, and five from families of the lower bureaucracy. In addition, the monastery ran an almshouse that cared for five peasant women and an orphanage that sheltered and taught nine peasant girls, two merchant girls, and one artisanal girl.[23] Finally, in 1907, the monastery had grown again, to seventy-nine, with an abbess, seventeen nuns, ten novices, and fifty-one sisters; of these, sixteen of the nuns, all ten of the novices, and forty-five of the fifty-one sisters were peasants.[24] As these figures repetitiously but clearly demonstrate, the women's religious community at Tvorozhkovo was overwhelmingly a peasant phenomenon.

The narrative history of Tvorozhkovo also shows peasant women playing a crucial role from the beginning. Peasant women, including Aleksandra Filippovna's former serf-housekeeper, helped with the construction of the wooden dormitory and chapel, both essential to the opening of the community.[25] And the story is told that in 1866, when the community was beginning to develop and the chapel had just been completed, Aleksandra Filippovna, realizing the centrality of a choir to the elaborate Orthodox liturgy, and realizing that there were no singers for the choir, prayed to God to send her some so that a religious community could begin in earnest. At just that moment, a local young peasant woman named Marfa, who was familiar with the struggling new community at Tvorzhkovo, experienced a sudden urge to go on a pilgrimage to Cheremenetskii monastery, where she providentially overheard four peasant maidens with beautiful voices singing. The women had been on their way to the diocese of Novgorod to enter the Korotskaia women's community, but Marfa, extolling the praises of Aleksandra Filippovna, persuaded them to join the Tvorozhkovo community. They were particularly impressed that Aleksandra Filippovna, a gentry woman, had given away all her property for the community and "labored alongside of the sisters."[26] After initial training in liturgical singing from a local deacon, the women formed a much-needed and much-praised choir,[27] a contrast to traditional monasteries where the choir sisters were usually well-born.

Archival sources confirm the role of these women in establishing the choir. The youngest of the four women, Iustina Mikhneeva, a peasant from Luzhskii district, St. Petersburg province, was sixteen at the time she entered the community. Like many of the other sisters, she was taught to read and write in the community. Various service records of the community tell us that in 1877 she was serving in the choir; in 1888 she was director of the choir and in charge of the order of the day (*ustavshchitsa*); in 1897 she was still serving in these positions and, following her tonsure the previous year, had taken the monastic name Angelina in honor of the founder of the community.[28] A 1907 service list indicates that she was still director of the choir but had also served as steward (*ekonomika*) of the monastery.[29]

The economic resources of the community were typical of Russian women's religious communities, combining income from agricultural work, the religious services of the sisters, and donations from benefactors. According to an 1888 report, the main resources for the support of the community included income from land, of up to 2,000 rubles per year; rental income from the St. Petersburg home of a benefactress, 1,000 rubles per year; interest from the 10,000 rubles in fixed capital donated by the founder of the community and interest from capital of 3,000 rubles from various benefactors (amount of interest not given in source); 1,000 rubles per year from collections on behalf of the community; 300 rubles per year from the perpetual reading of the Psalter for the deceased; up to 1,000 rubles per year from the cattle yard; and up to 1,000 rubles per year from church and candle income.[30]

The community owned 1,730 acres of land, including plow land, hay land, forest, and three lakes. Rye, oats, hay, flax, and all garden vegetables were grown on the land and in good harvests were sufficient for the needs of the community for the whole year; in bad harvests, grain had to be purchased. The land was worked by the sisters with the help of five workers (*rabotniki*).[31] One observer of the community, in the course of arguing for the inspiring effect of the sisters' life of work and prayer on the neighboring peasants, gives an interesting, albeit glowing, insight into the communal nature of their agricultural work:

> The people see how from year to year from the first days of spring, the sisters, under the direction of their mother superior, rush to work, clear the fields . . . [at harvest] they gather in the mown hay and bring it to the barn, and for this all the elderly women from the almshouse and all the orphans from the orphanage gather; then these same sisters begin the harvesting of grain, they themselves reap and grind it, and then in the evenings, contented but extremely tired, they return home, singing Psalms—the people, seeing this, are touched by the spirit, and involuntarily cross themselves and utter with all their heart, "May God help you, holy workers."[32]

In addition to their agricultural work, the sisters made their own clothes and shoes, and prepared communion bread. They ran and supported a small almshouse and orphanage, prepared food for their common meals, maintained the library and the sacristy, undertook the perpetual reading of the Psalter for the dead, and maintained a monastic prayer life and liturgy.[33]

Thus the sisters of the community had tasks shared by all (such as the harvest) and particular responsibilities or "obediences" (*poslushaniia*). The reports sent by the head of the community to the diocesan chancellery in 1877, 1897, and 1907 give us a rare chance to find out what kind of duties and roles peasant women were filling within the community.

In 1877, the community consisted of its founder, Mother Superior Angelina, and thirty-one sisters. The treasurer of the community, the second-in-command, was a forty-eight-year-old maiden (*devitsa*) from the merchantry, who had entered the community in 1866. The three women from the artisanal class included a forty-nine-year-old maiden who was serving as sacristan and *prosfornia* (supervisor of the communion bread), a forty-two-year-old widow who was engaged in the reading of the Psalter, and a thirty-three-year-old maiden who was engaged in "various duties." The fifty-nine-year-old widow of a court footman was serving as tutor and preceptor of the orphanage. The duties of the peasant women, ranging in age from thirty-one to fifteen, are for the most part described in a frustratingly general way as "various duties." But we are told that two of them were in the choir (including Iustina Mikhneeva, one of the original four peasant singers who joined the community in 1866), one was collecting money for the building of a church, one was doing a general collection, and one, a nineteen-year-old, was assistant to the *prosfornia*. [34]

By 1897, the community had become a monastery, headed by Abbess Arseniia, daughter of a bureaucrat, who had been transferred there from the Voskresenskii monastery in St. Petersburg in 1887 upon the elevation of the Trinity Tvorozhkovo community to a monastery. The monastery consisted of twelve nuns, a novice, and forty-four sisters. The treasurer, second-in-command, was the nun Estoliia, a peasant who had also transferred to Trinity Tvorozhkovo in 1887. Nine of the remaining eleven nuns were peasants; their responsibilities included gardener, St. Petersburg collectioner, director of the choir, steward, sacristan, and sexton. The sole novice, of artisanal origins, taught in the orphanage and was in charge of the monastery's correspondence. Thirty-six of the forty-four sisters were peasants, whose jobs included cattle farm worker, milk maid, shoemaker, baker, cook, supervisor of the orphanage, and seven choir singers. [35]

In 1907 Abbess Valeriia, from a St. Petersburg trading family, headed the Tvorozhskovo monastery, after transferring to Trinity Tvorozhkovo in 1904 from another monastery. [36] Since the position of treasurer is often the stepping-stone to abbess, it is interesting that Estoliia, who still served as treasurer, had been passed over for the position of abbess in 1904. Estoliia, a peasant, was literate and had been described in the 1897 report as being of "excellent character and exceptionally capable"; [37] but in 1904 she was seventy-two, and perhaps too old to take on the position of abbess.

The 1907 list shows us peasant women in charge of a range of responsibilities such as ringing the wake-up bell, sewing altar cloths, making clothing or shoes for the sisters and orphans, managing the garden, supervising the preserving of vegetables, running the housekeeping, managing the cattle yard and the dairy, running the bakery, running the orphanage, and serving as steward. It also reveals that literacy is associated with top administrative jobs such as abbess, treasurer, and steward, but at the same time almost all the nuns, novices, and sisters did some form of manual or handicraft work and the monastery provided many of them areas of responsibility and management as well as development of individual talents. [38] As one scholar has argued after studying several women's religious communities and monasteries that grew out of them:

> In these monasteries each nun had the opportunity to develop her own talent, whether in the household, in field work, in marketing or selling, in administration, in a handicraft or a skilled craft where icon painting and the embellishment of the church stood in the forefront. Architectural talent was likewise valued, even if it was rarely found. [39]

Women's religious communities also encouraged the development of women's abilities by creating an atmosphere supportive of women's literacy. The lists of 1877, 1897, and 1907 all provide data on the literacy of the members of the community. The 1877 list provides the simple information of whether a sister was

Table 7.1. Literacy of Peasant Women in Trinity
Tvorozhkovo Community

1877	46.2%	(literate)	
	53.8%	(illiterate)	(*n*= 26)
1897	84.8%	(literate: reading)	
	34.8%	(literate: reading and writing)	
	15.2%	(illiterate)	(*n* = 46)
1907	55.7%	(literate)	
	18.6%	(semiliterate)	
	25.7%	(illiterate)	(*n* = 70)

literate (*gramotnaia*) or illiterate (*negramotnaia*). The 1897 list gives information on whether a nun, novice, or sister was illiterate, able to read, or able to read and write. The 1907 list specifies whether the latter were literate, semiliterate (*malogramotnaia*), or illiterate, and where those who were literate learned to read. On the basis of this, we find the literacy rates shown in Table 7.1.

These are remarkably high rates of literacy for peasant women of the time. According to the census of 1897, only 21 percent of the entire population of the Russian Empire was literate.[40] According to one analysis of the census material, in 1897 only 35 percent of all males aged twenty to twenty-nine in European Russia were literate;[41] if we look at the comparable literacy rates of the women aged twenty to twenty-nine in Trinity Tvorozhkovo monastery in 1897, we find that 88.9 percent (16/18) of them could read, and 33.3 percent (6/18) of them could read and write. If we use only the stricter measure of reading and writing as a mark of literacy, these are still high rates of literacy for rural women. To further place these literacy rates in a context of comparability, let us consider the figures of a Soviet source which indicate that in 1897, in the territory of what is now the Russian Republic of the Soviet Union, the average literacy rate of persons aged nine to forty-nine was 29.6 percent. Among men the rate was 44.4 percent, and among women 15.4 percent; in rural areas, these figures were 24.6 percent, 39.5 percent, and 11 percent, respectively.[42] If we return to the list of the Tvorozhkovo community in 1897, and focus on those between the ages of nine and forty-nine (adding into our previous figures the nine peasant girls of appropriate age in the monastery orphanage, and one peasant woman aged twenty-nine in the almshouse), we have a group of fifty peasant women between the ages of nine and forty-nine, of whom 88 percent could read and 46 percent could read and write. Their literacy rates are, then, depending on the looser or stricter definition of literacy, either eight times as high or more than four times as high as the general average for rural women of this age—11 percent.

The women's monastery at Tvorozhkovo, and the less official *zhenskaia obshchina* that had preceded it, encouraged women entering the community to learn to read, if they had not already been taught to do so. Reading was important for the liturgy, for the observance of canonical hours, for the recitation of the Psalter, for the absorption of edificatory readings (particularly from the church fathers and the lives of the saints), and for work in running the community and the orphanage.

Table 7.2. Schooling of Literate Peasant Women in Tvorozhkovo Monastery, 1907

Where they learned to read			Mean age in 1907
In the monastery	16	41.0%	39
In a parish school	14	35.9%	30
At home	3	7.7%	56
In a zemstvo school	3	7.7%	27
Other*	3	7.7%	46
N =	39	100%	

*Chastnaia shkola, 1; shkola gramoty, 1; patrioticheskaia shkola, 1.[44]

The hierarchy of the church also stressed the importance of literacy and education, and increasingly sought information on the schooling and literacy of its clergy. Thus at the request of the Holy Synod, the 1907 list submitted by the abbess of the Trinity Tvorozhkovo monastery to the St. Petersburg consistory contained information on not only which members of the community where literate, but also where they had learned to read.[43] The compilation of these data yields a statistical profile of the peasant women in the monastery in 1907 (Table 7.2).

These data show that more than 40 percent of the literate nuns and sisters had learned to read in the monastery. Many of them had entered the community in the 1870s and 1880s, before the expansion of the parish and zemstvo school system, and in particular before the increased enrollments of peasant girls in these schools.[45] The community thus provided, ahead of its time, an opportunity for basic education for peasant women. Later, as the figures for the numbers who attended parish schools indicate, it attracted women who had received "formal" schooling, a distinct minority within the rural population. One wonders if monastic life, with its particular form of autonomy and self-development, may have had a special attraction to young peasant women with some education, even if rudimentary.

As the case of Trinity Tvorozhkovo community indicates, peasant women played a crucial role in the development, expansion, and operation of women's religious communities. In turn, women's religious communities offered peasant women a means of spiritual and intellectual development. Unencumbered by the responsibilities of marriage and family, the women of religious communities enjoyed areas of autonomy and opportunities to hold positions of considerable authority and power. Rather than being restricted to being lay sisters, they served in the choir and could become professed nuns, positions usually reserved for the upper classes in medieval times. Although no woman of peasant origin served as mother superior or abbess of Trinity Tvorozhkovo, peasant women did serve in important positions such as treasurer and steward and as managers of central aspects of the community's economy. And an analysis of the social origins of those holding the position of mother superior or abbess in the dioceses of Nizhegorod, Novgorod, Moscow, and Tambov in 1903, indicates that 17 percent (12/72) were of peasant origin.[46]

Unfortunately, we have no sources in which the peasant women of Tvorozhkovo tell us why they entered the community. They would hardly have used the term "social mobility," and would probably not have liked the concept. They might have been more sympathetic to explanations of security, conceding that "homeless" and "familyless" women often sought shelter in women's religious communities, as the Synod records hint.[47] If a modern social historian asked them if they had entered because of an excess of single women in the population, resulting from the dislocation due to Russia's modernization and urbanization and the attendant male out-migration from rural areas, they might have responded thoughtfully, after the obscuring language had been translated into the changes they and their fellow villagers were experiencing. But on their own, they would probably have spoken in timeless Christian terms of the overriding importance of eternal salvation and expressed gratitude to their founder, who had been particularly concerned to give poor women like themselves a chance to dedicate their lives to God and to "save themselves." Although they would have disclaimed any feminist goals, in their own way they did make considerable claims to autonomy by the simple insistence that their own salvation was of paramount importance—more important than the claims of family, marriage, or village. Religious communities gave them the opportunity for a contemplative, religiously disciplined life in a supportive community of like-minded women. Religious communities helped them shape their lives as they believed best, and they, in their turn, helped shape the lives of the communities, making them more democratic, self-supporting, and communal than traditional women's monasteries.[48]

Notes

The author wishes to thank the Academy of Sciences of the U.S.S.R., the International Research and Exchanges Board, the National Endowment for the Humanities, the National Humanities Center, and the University of Rochester for support in the research for this essay. She is also indebted to Morris Pierce of the history department of the University of Rochester for assistance in the statistical analysis of the data.

1. For a discussion of how questions of class have affected both the chances of living a saintly life and the chances of being perceived as saintly, see Donald Weinstein and Rudolph M. Bell, *Saints and Society: The Two World of Western Christendom, 1000–1700* (Chicago: University of Chicago Press, 1982), pp. 194–214. For a discussion of the impact of gender, see also Weinstein and Bell, pp. 220–38, and Caroline Walker Bynum, "Women's Stories, Women's Symbols: A Critique of Victor Turner's Theory of Liminality," in Robert L. Moore and Frank E. Reynolds, eds., *Anthropology and the Study of Religion* (Chicago: Center for the Study of Scientific Religion, 1984), 105–25, and *Holy Feast and Holy Fast. The Religious Significance of Food to Medieval Women* (Berkeley: University of California Press, 1987), pp. 23–30.

2. *Polnoe sobranie postanovlenii i rasporiazhenii po vedomstvu pravoslavnogo ispovedaniia. Tsarstvovanie imperatritsy Ekateriny Alekseevny*, no. 167, 28 February 1764; Brenda Meehan-Waters, "Russian Convents and the Secularization of Monastic Property," in R. P. Bartlett, A. G. Cross, and Karen Rasmussen, eds., *Russia and the World of the Eighteenth Century* (Columbus, Ohio: Slavica Publishers, 1988), pp. 112–24.

3. V. V. Zverinskii, *Material dlia istoriko-topograficheskogo issledovaniia o pravoslavnykh monastyriakh v rossiiskoi imperii* (St. Petersburg, 1890), vol. 1, p. xi.

4. M. M. Gromyko, *Traditsionnye normy povedeniia i formy obshcheniia russkikh krest'ian XIX v* (Moscow, 1986), pp. 103–5.

5. N. Dobrotvortskii, "Krest'ianskie iuridicheskie obychai: Po materialam, sobrannym v vostochnoi chasti Vladimirskoi gubernii (uezdy Viaznikovskii, Gorokhovestskii, Shuiskii i Korovskii)," *Iuridicheskii vestnik,* May 1889, p. 270. I wish to thank Rose Glickman for this reference.

6. A. Tul'tseva, "Chernichki," *Nauka i religiia* 11 (1970): 80–81.

7. Compare, in particular, the constraints of the life of the hermit Anastasiia, who lived as a *chernichka* for twenty years while caring for her elderly parents, with that of her spiritual model and guide, St. Serafim of Sarov. See A. Priklonskii, *Zhizn' pustynnitsy Anastasii (Semenovny Logachevoi), vposledstvii monakhinia Afanasii, i voznikovenie na meste eia podvigov zhenskoi obshchiny* (Moscow, 1902), and Brenda Meehan-Waters, "The Authority of Holiness: Women Ascetics and Spiritual Elders in Nineteenth-Century Russia," in Geoffrey A. Hosking, ed., *God's Servants: Church, Nation and State in Russia and Ukraine* (London: Macmillan, 1990), pp. 38–51. For the lives of nineteenth-century Russian holy women, see *Zhizneopisaniia otechestvennykh podvizhnikov blagochestiia 18 i 19 vekov,* 12 vols. (Moscow, 1906–1910), and *Dopolnenie,* 2 vols. (Moscow, 1912).

8. For an analysis of the founders, see Brenda Meehan-Waters, "Popular Piety, Local Initiative and the Founding of Women's Religious Communities in Russia, 1764–1907," *St. Vladimir's Theological Quarterly* 30, no. 2 (1986): 117–42.

9. *Zhensie obshchiny,* and the monasteries that derived from them, were organized according to communal (cenobitic) rule and were called *obshchezhitel'nye,* in contrast to traditional men's and women's monasteries, which were noncommunal (*neobshchezhitel'nye*) and followed an idiorrhythmic pattern. Rather than living in communal dormitories, nuns and novices in traditional monasteries lived in private cells that they considered their own property. Upon entering the monastery, they would buy a cell from a previous occupant or build one of their own; upon transferring to another monastery, they could sell their cell or dismantle it. In addition, each nun had responsibility for her own housekeeping tasks, food purchase, and preparation. When a refectory (*trapeza*) existed, it was most often frequented by the poorer nuns and novices, with the more well-to-do preferring to eat in their own cells. In this situation, there was little communal life or discipline, cloistering was impossible because of the need to shop in markets (and to sell one's handicrafts for self-support), and energy that could have been expended on spiritual edification, communal work, or charitable activity was dissipated on individual housekeeping tasks. Marie Thomas, "Muscovite Convents in the 17th Century," *Russian History,* pt. 2 (1982): 234–35; Sophia Senyk, *Women's Monasteries in Ukraine and Belorussia to the Period of Suppressions,* vol. 222 of *Orientalia Christiana Analecta* (Rome, 1983), pp. 156–64; I. F. Tokmakov, *Istoricheskoe opisanie moskovskogo novodeviich'iago monastyria* (Moscow, 1885), pp. 119–20.

10. For a general discussion of church–state relations under Nicholas I, see David W. Edwards, "The System of Nicholas I in Church–State Relations," in Robert L. Nichols and Theofanis Stavrou, eds., *Russian Orthodoxy Under the Old Regime* (Minneapolis: University of Minnesota Press, 1978), pp. 154–69.

11. The archives of the Synod Chancellery and the Chancellery of the Over-Procurator of the Synod are replete with records documenting the process by which a *zhenskaia obshchina* could be officially established and approved by the Synod. See, for example, Tsentral'nyi gosudarstvennyi istoricheskii arkhiv (hereafter TsGIA), f. 796 (Kantseliariia Sinoda), op. 144, d. 980, "Ob uchrezhdenii v g. Kineshme zhenskoi obshchiny. 17 iunia 1863–8 maia 1869 gg.," and f. 797 (Kantseliariia ober-prokurora Sinoda), op. 24, d. 40, "Po opred. Sv. Sinoda ob uchrezhdenii v sele Kollezhe-Assesora Aristova, Dal'nem-Davydove, Nizhegorod. gub. zhenskoi obshchiny v vospitatel'skim pri nei zavedeniem dliia sirot duk-

hov. zvanii. 14 dek. 1854—a avg. 1857 gg." Synopses of these cases were occasionally published in the *Pol'noe sobranie zakonov* and, later in the century, in *Tserkovny vedomosti.* See, for example, *PSZ*, 2, v. 22, pt. 1, no. 21472, 13 avg. 1847, "O priniatii sushchestvuiushchei v g. Buzuluke zhenskoi obshchiny pod pokrovitel'stvo dukhovnogo i grazhdanskogo nachal'stva."

12. As examples of the regularization of charters, see TsGIA, f. 796, op. 96, d. 16, "Pravilia dliia zhenskikh pravoslavnykh obshchin Nizhegorodskoi ep., 1845 g.," and f. 797, op. 87, d. 94, "Proekt pravil bogorodnykh zhenskikh obshchin" (undated).

13. "Monashestvo," *Entsiklopedicheskii slovar'* (St. Petersburg, 1898), vol. 38, p. 730.

14. Meehan-Waters, "Popular Piety," p. 123.

15. *N* = 31. (My calculations, based on data in Denisov, which contains figures on the size of 31 of the 62 *zhenskie obshchiny* existing in 1907.) L. I. Denisov, *Pravoslavnye monastyri rossiiskoi imperii. Polnyi spisok vsekh 1105 nyne suchestvuiushchikh v 75 guberniiakh oblastiakh Rossii i 2 inostrannykh gosudarstvakh muzhiskikh, zhenskikh monastyrei, arkhiereiskikh domov i zhenskikh obshchin* (Moscow, 1908).

16. Communities founded by peasant women included Spasskaia-Zelengorskaia, Tikhvinskaia-Bogoroditskaia Buzulukskaia, Bogoroditskii Malo-Pitskii, and Spaso-Preobrazhenskaia (Denisov, *Pravoslavnye monastyri rossiikoi imperii,* pp. 542, 735, 530, and 939).

17. For this and the following biographical information, see S. Snessoreva, *Monakhinia Angelina (v mire Aleksandra Filippovna Fon-Roze) osnovatel'nitsa i stroitel'nitsa sviatotroitskoi tvorozhkovskoi zhenskoi obshchiny vozvedennoi v monastyr' s naimenovaniem SviatoTroitskim obshchezhitel'nym zhenskim monastyrem* (St. Petersburg, 1888).

18. Denisov, *Pravoslavnye monastyri rossiikoi imperii,* pp. 751–52.

19. Snessoreva, *Monakhinia Angelina,* p. 17.

20. Ibid., p. 103.

21. Ibid., pp. 151–52.

22. Ibid., p. 163.

23. Leningradskii gosudarstvennyi istoricheskii arkhiv (hereafter LGIA), f. 19 (St. Petersburgskaia dukhovnaia konsistoriia), op. 113, d. 3828, "Vedomosti o nakhodiashchikhsia sestrakh v Sviato-Troitskom Tvorozhkovskom obshchezhitel'nom zhenskom monastyre za 1897," 11, pp. 139–48.

24. LGIA, f. 19, op. 113, d. 4150, "Vedomosti i posluzhnye spiski monashestvuiushchikh za 1907 god," 11, pp. 71–94. Denisov gives figures for 1907 of one abbess, thirteen nuns, one novice, and fifty-five *prozhivaiushchie na ispytanii;* he has no data on social origins (*Pravoslavnye monastyri rossiikoi imperii,* p. 752).

25. Snessoreva, *Monakhinia Angelina,* pp. 18, 24.

26. Ibid., pp. 24–27.

27. Ibid., p. 28.

28. LGIA, f. 19, op. 113, d. 2947, "Vedomosti o nakhodiashchikhsia sestrakh v Sviato-Troitskoi Tvorozhkovskoi zhenskoi obshchin za 1877 god," 1. 3 ob.; Snessoreva, *Monakhinia Angelina,* pp. 26–27; LGIA, f. 19, op. 113, d. 3828, 11. 139 ob. −140.

29. LGIA, f. 19, op. 113, d. 4150, 11. 74 ob. −75.

30. Snessoreva, *Monakhinia Angelina,* p. 102.

31. Ibid., p. 103.

32. Ibid., p. 106.

33. Ibid., pp. 100–102. For the increased development of charitable activity in Russian women's religious communities in the second half of the nineteenth century, see Brenda Meehan-Waters, "From Contemplative Practice to Charitable Activity: Russian Women's Religious Communities and the Development of Charitable Work, 1861–1917," in Kathleen

McCarthy, ed., *Lady Bountiful Revisited: Women, Philanthropy and Power* (New Brunswick, N.J.: Rutgers University Press, 1990), pp. 142–56.

34. LGIA, f. 19, op. 113, d. 2947, 11. 1 ob. −6.

35. LGIA, f. 19, op. 113, d. 3828, 11. 139 ob. −148.

36. LGIA, f. 19, op. 113, d. 4150, 11. 71 ob. −72.

37. LGIA, f. 19, op. 113, 11. 139 ob. −140.

38. LGIA, f. 19, op. 113, d. 4150, 11. 71 ob. −94.

39. Claire Louise Claus, "Die russischen Frauenklöster um die Wende des 18. Jahrhunderts: Ihre karitative Tätigkeit und religiöse Bedeutung," *Kirche im Osten,* Band 4-1961 (Amsterdam, 1969), p. 47.

40. A. G. Rashin, *Naselenie Rossii za 100 let* (Moscow, 1956), p. 284; Rose Glickman, *Russian Factory Women. Workplace and Society, 1880–1914* (Berkeley: University of California Press, 1984), p. 16.

41. Robert Johnson, *Peasant and Proletarian: The Working Class of Moscow in the Late Nineteenth Century* (New Brunswick, N.J.: Rutgers University Press, 1979), p. 184.

42. *Bol'shaia sovetskaia entsiklopediia,* 3rd ed. (Moscow, 1975), vol. 22, p. 246; *The Great Soviet Encyclopedia. A Translation of the Third Edition* (New York: Macmillan, 1979), vol. 22, p. 424.

43. LGIA, f. 19, op. 113, d. 4150, 11. 71 ob. −93.

44. On the origins of the *shkoly gramoty,* which after 1891 came under the control of the Synod, see Ben Eklof, *Russian Peasant Schools: Officialdom, Village Culture, and Popular Pedagogy, 1861–1914* (Berkeley: University of California Press, 1986), p. 165.

45. The proportion of all school-age girls in Russia who had gained some schooling increased from 3.2 percent in 1880, to 6.1 percent in 1894, to 15.2 percent in 1911 (Eklof, *Russian Peasant Schools,* p. 311).

46. This is my compilation based on data from Synod archives. In Novgorod diocese, 4/14 mothers superior and abbesses were of peasant origin; in Nizhegorod diocese, 6/19; in Tambov diocese 0/15; in Moscow diocese, 2/24. Hence 12/72, or 16.6 percent, of mothers superior and abbesses in these sample dioceses were of peasant origin. TsGIA, f. 797, op. 33, II-3, d. 207, "So svedeniami o vsekh, nakhodiavshikhsia v imperii monastyriakh, obshchinakh i pustyniakh, 29 ianv. 20 okt. 1903 (Nizhegorod, 11. 2–5; Tambov, 11. 18–18 ob.; Novgorod, 11. 94 ob.–97; Moscow, 11. 206 ob.–256).

47. *Zhenskie obshchiny* often had attached to them almhouses for women, and so were often associated with the care of homeless, elderly, widowed, and "familyless" women. Some of these women, particularly younger widowed women, may have become members of the communities. See, for example, *Tserkovnye vedomosti,* no. 42 (1888): 207. Earlier in the century, soldiers' wives (*soldatki*) may have been attracted to the communities. "Zhenskie obshchiny v nizhegorodskoi gubernii," *Zhurnal ministerstva vnutrennikh del* 19 (1847): 275.

48. For the role of women's religious communities in the transformation of monastic life in nineteenth-century Russia, see Brenda Meehan-Waters, "Metropolitan Filaret (Drozdov) and the Reform of Russian Women's Monastic Communities," *Russian Review* 50 (1991): 310–23.

II / Peasant Women
After the Revolution

The study of Soviet social history is at an early stage of development in both the West and the Soviet Union. Most scholars have concentrated on the early years of Soviet history (up to World War II), limiting their attention to the urban sector. Until very recently, the role of women in Soviet historical developments was either dismissed or ignored, and very few works explored the rural population.

Social historians are only now beginning to examine gender and the role of women as important historical variables in the Soviet period. Although research in this area is still fairly limited, much of it has focused on peasant women. Several of the pioneers of prerevolutionary Russian women's history—notably Barbara Evans Clements, Beatrice Farnsworth, and Rose L. Glickman—have carried their research into the Soviet period. They are joined by a younger generation of scholars, well versed in the comparative literature on women's history, whose focus from the start has been on the postrevolutionary period. The essays that follow are examples of some of the early work on Soviet women's history—focusing on the peasantry— and to a great extent they represent the first steps in a new direction in postrevolutionary social history. The main contributions of these works are to bring women back into the historical record and to challenge traditional conceptions and periodizations of Soviet history. It was suggested earlier (in the introduction to Part I) that the 1917 Revolution appears less significant a break in history if we explore the life and work of peasant women. How does the traditional picture change if we turn our attention to the history of peasant women in the Soviet period?

Revolution and Civil War

In February 1917, the 300-year-old Romanov dynasty was toppled in what was to be the first act of the Russian Revolution. The political revolution of February was rapidly transformed into a radical social revolution in the course of 1917. This "deepening of the revolution," as William Henry Chamberlin titled it in his classic account of the Russian Revolution,[1] represented a revolt of all social groups against the established authority of long-entrenched political, social, and economic structures.

Among the radical ideas of 1917 were plans to emancipate women and to radically transform the family.[2] Women were granted formal equality before the law,[3] equal rights to education, paid maternity leave, relatively easy access to divorce, and (in 1920) the right to abortion.[4] Women were encouraged to become equal citizens at the workplace and in politics. It was expected that all traces of exploitation of women would soon vanish as collectivist principles of child rearing, housework, and food preparation were introduced in the young Communist state.

137

Theory and legislation, however, were soon undermined by the harsh realities of the times and the entrenched values of a supposedly bygone era.

The prerevolutionary radical intelligentsia, especially V. I. Lenin and his party of Bolsheviks (renamed the Communist Party in 1918), had long assumed that the bases for the exploitation of women were the socioeconomic system of capitalism and the political regime of tsarism. As a consequence, the "woman question" was subordinated to the Revolution, to the seemingly paramount issues of political and class struggle. Once the Revolution overturned the old order, it was expected that the woman question, with the aid of enabling legislation, would be solved.

The prerevolutionary neglect of the woman question—or, more accurately, the failure to consider the question fully and apart from materialist preconceptions, even by such a notable figure as Aleksandra Kollontai—and the general disdain for so-called bourgeois feminism made it highly unlikely that the Communist Party would be able to address the question once it became clear that the Revolution in and of itself did not solve the woman question and that legislation, however progressive, was foundering on entrenched patriarchal attitudes. Given the Marxist doctrinaire emphasis on the materialist underpinnings of human behavior, it is not surprising that the Bolsheviks failed to consider the importance of traditional values and attitudes as variables independent of socioeconomic structures and more enduring than the *ancien régime* itself. Moreover, virtually no attention was given to an exploration of traditional gender roles and their importance in the foundations of a patriarchal system. Consequently, the Revolution served to underscore the problems of women's emancipation rather than to offer an ultimate solution. Further, the civil war that followed the Revolution resulted in a radical reordering of priorities. The mobilization of all resources for the war in the context of an already shattered economy meant that the implementation of social and cultural projects—most importantly those aimed at improving women's conditions—was deferred to the future.

In the countryside, peasant women experienced the Revolution in many different ways, but for all but a very few, the Revolution did not spell emancipation from either the daily drudgery of women's agricultural labor or the patriarchal family. Revolution in the countryside toppled the old tsarist estate system, led to a redivision of much of the land, and brought home the soldiers of World War I. Peasant women were granted formal equality in the household and received the right to be head of household and to participate in meetings of the *skhod,* or village council. However, only a very small percentage of peasant women became actively involved either in village politics or in the new Soviet state through participation in the Communist Party, in the party's *zhenotdely* (women's sections), or as *delegatki* (participants in women's meetings).[5] The majority of peasant women, far from benefiting directly from the Revolution, experienced untold hardships during the years of Revolution and civil war.

According to the work of Barbara Evans Clements, which we were unable to include in this volume, the Revolution and civil war not only caused immense suffering for the peasant women of Russia, but also produced a conservative reaction. Many peasant women viewed Communists and *zhenotdel* representatives as a threat to their way of life and very survival, and consequently fiercely resisted

Communist attempts to transform traditional ways of life. Clements argues that the civil war reinforced for women the importance of marriage and the family to her economic survival.[6] In a time of virtual subsistence farming and constant struggle to survive physically, the family as an economic unit was basic to survival. The Revolution and civil war also hastened the trend toward the nuclear family—a trend that, according to Clements, was already under way from the late nineteenth century.[7] Although this development doubtless benefited many women now free of the domination of in-laws, the smaller family unit remained male-centered and patriarchal.

What Clements and others suggest, then, is that revolution and civil war in the countryside were less than revolutionary for peasant women. Peasant women reacted in ways that could be categorized as conservative or backward but perhaps are better understood as part of a specifically peasant cultural response to the threat of survival in this desperate time of war, famine, and disease. As peasants in general are apt to do in times of crisis, Russian peasant women fell back on that which was familiar and customary—in this case, key aspects of traditional peasant culture, such as the patriarchal family and the commune—as a survival mechanism. This response, moreover, was antithetical to urban, Communist ideas and ideals of emancipation and revolution.

The situation of peasant women in a sense represents in microcosm the Revolution in the countryside. In answer to our earlier question—What does the study of peasant women tell us about the Revolution?—the study of peasant women during these years offers a paradigm of peasant culture and behavior, illuminating the dual nature of the Russian Revolution as a socialist revolution in the city and a peasant war in the countryside. The peasant's revolution, moreover, was one that, far from creating a new socialist order, either reinforced preexisting peasant culture or brought changes that were part of a peasant, not Bolshevik, dream of revolution.

The New Economic Policy and Stalinism

The New Economic Policy (NEP), introduced in 1921 at the Tenth Congress of the Communist Party, represented a retreat from the harsh wartime policies of the civil war. The retreat was dictated by a series of crises that followed the cessation of civil war: peasant rebellions, working-class strikes, and a sailors' mutiny at the Kronstadt naval base. By introducing a partial market economy and more relaxed policies in other social and economic spheres, NEP brought about a period of relative social and cultural pluralism under the conditions of a one-party dictatorship.

Traditional Western scholars view NEP as a tactical, if not opportunistic, retreat intended to allow the party time to regroup its forces for the next revolutionary assault.[8] In the late 1960s and early 1970s, this view was challenged by revisionist scholars who saw NEP as a legitimate alternative policy to Stalin's First Five-Year Plan. In the revisionist view, NEP was a golden age before Stalinism, a period when culture blossomed, class peace and harmony existed in society, and workers and peasants alike experienced relative prosperity.[9]

Both of these views are open to question if we bring women into the historical picture. For women, NEP was not quite the golden age depicted in the revisionist literature. In the cities, prostitution returned, women workers suffered from high rates of unemployment, and funding for all kinds of social programs declined drastically.[10] The so-called sexual revolution of the Revolution and civil war years left in its wake liberated men and an army of abandoned and economically destitute single mothers.

The social problems of NEP, some caused by NEP itself, others by the dislocation of the war years, brought about a conservative reaction in women's issues. The reaction coalesced at the time of the 1926 marriage law debate, when the issue of unregistered marriages was debated. In the debates, it soon became clear that many women—especially but not only peasant women—were opposed to the irresponsible behavior of males that had been unleashed by war and revolution and assumed the form of serial unregistered marriages, male promiscuity, and neglect of male parental duties. Most party officials agreed. Repeatedly, women and officials concluded that stability in the family was a necessary and even a positive goal.[11]

The conservatism surrounding family and women's issues already in the 1920s received final confirmation in the 1930s under Stalin. Although women entered the labor force in record numbers in the 1930s and 1940s, the last dim echos of the revolutionary-era calls for women's emancipation, while officially enshrined, were trampled. In 1936, strict divorce laws were passed, making divorce almost impossible, and these laws were further tightened in 1944.[12] Also in 1936, abortion became illegal except in cases when the mother's life was in danger or in the presence of a serious inheritable disease.[13] A cult of motherhood and domesticity flowered, albeit to be practiced only after a woman completed her eight-hour shift at work outside the home.

Although the retreat from the revolution in women's issues is most often viewed as an integral part of Stalin's thermidorian reaction, it was actually a most likely outcome of the Bolshevik Revolution and, as we have seen, predated Stalin's rise to power. Given the failure of the party to address gender issues outside a materialist conception of history and the prevailing conservatism of the party, it is no surprise that the Revolution ultimately stopped far short of its emancipatory goals. Moreover, it occurred in a peasant nation whose culture was antithetical to the values of the Revolution.

This is not to say that there was no advancement for women in the years after the Revolution. Women benefited greatly from education and employment opportunities and participated in the general social mobility afforded by Stalinist industrialization. Nonetheless, revolutionary ideas of emancipation withered away as women struggled to feed themselves and their families in the context of a backward and conservative new order.

The countryside during NEP was, for the most part, left to its own devices. The interference of party and Soviet officials was limited to their involvement in village affairs during tax time, soviet elections, and land reform.[14] The values and ideals of the urban Communist Party represented an alien force to most peasants and had a minimal impact on peasant women. *Zhenotdel* representatives were often ignored or harassed, and relatively few peasant women took advantage of their new rights as equal citizens in the village council, local soviet, or elsewhere. Peasant women had little understanding of or sympathy for the sexual revolution taking place in the cities. Traditional gender relations and the patriarchal family (perhaps in a less extended form) continued to hold sway during the 1920s, when, as one Soviet historian described it, the peasant economy in its most natural form had its renaissance.[15]

The real revolution for peasant women came at the end of the 1920s during the First Five-Year Plan, when the Communist Party implemented the policy of wholesale collectivization of agriculture, forcing peasants to give up communal agriculture and join collective farms. The collectivization campaign was carried out by outside forces in a brutal and bloody fashion, which led to mass arrests and deportations. For peasant women, collectivization represented an assault on traditional values and economic interests. As the state and its activists attempted to impose their versions of collectivism, the peasant woman witnessed the destruction of the domestic economy—her economic domain—with the socialization of household livestock and, in some cases, the private plot. Many women feared greater upheavals in their personal lives as rumors of wife-sharing and other outrages spread through the villages.[16] The church also came under attack at this time as village churches were closed and priests arrested. Peasant women's reaction to this violent upheaval was anything but conservative. Peasant women led the resistance to collectivization in riots and protest throughout the land.

The outcome of collectivization may have been less revolutionary than the actual process portended.[17] Although communal land tenure was replaced by collective ownership of land and collective labor and the violence wrought by the campaign left the villages in a state resembling wartime occupation, the party was forced to accommodate certain aspects of peasant economy and culture to the new system. Once the initial violence had receded, by the mid-1930s, private plots, domestic livestock, and the household had become fixtures in the collective farm. While women found a new economic independence from the household through the institution of collective-farm-labor day-salary payments and, at least theoretically, had the option to engage in nontraditional types of occupation, peasant men and local officials (many peasants themselves) continued to operate within the traditional culture and to block women's advancement and, in some areas, even pay women less than men for the same work or deny them their voting rights in the collective farms.[18] The state, however, attempted to "emancipate" peasant women—in the interests less of equality than of production— by encouraging employment in nontraditional occupations, educational opportunities, and advancement to positions in the party and soviets. Moreover, peasant women appear to have been less affected by the harsh 1930s legislation on divorce and abortion than their urban counterparts. According to scholars such as Sheila Fitzpatrick and Roberta T. Manning, the retreat in women's emancipation that occurred for working-class and professional women was actually less significant for peasant women.[19] Yet the all-powerful state still ran up against a solid wall of silent opposition from local officialdom and peasants who sabotaged official policies aimed at peasant women's advancement and whose actions and attitudes testified to the staying power of traditional peasant culture and patriarchalism.

War and Postwar

Little research has been done on the experience of peasant women, or Soviet women in general, during World War II. As in the wartime economy of other nations, women came to the fore in production and in some areas of administration, as the state conscripted men into the military. In the Soviet countryside, peasant women led labor brigades, chaired collective farms and local party organs, and fought with the partisan resistance. The advancement of women in these years continued to be less a function of "emancipation" than of production and wartime necessity. After the war, the surviving men came home, displacing many women who had risen to positions of responsibility.

The situation of peasant women in postwar society, like that of the war years, has not been studied sufficiently to make any but a few generalizations. Two basic demographic trends emerged after the war. The first—continuing a 1930s pattern—was the depletion of male labor in the village as working-age men continued to leave the countryside for a better life in the cities. This out-migration of males left the villages overpopulated by the old, the young, and women. In the last several decades, however, a second trend has emerged wherein record numbers of young women have begun leaving the countryside and, as Susan Bridger shows, voicing their opposition to horrendous work conditions and burdensome and unequal family responsibilities with their feet.[20] It is clear that women in postwar rural society continue to perform most of the back-breaking physical labor in the agricultural economy, while men tend to predominate in administrative and mechanized work.[21] As Soviet agriculture "modernized" unevenly and partially, women's agricultural labor remained intensive peasant labor, keenly illustrating the imbalances between the industrial and agricultural sectors in the Soviet economy and the colonylike status of the countryside under the Soviets.

By the post-Stalin era, the Revolution's legacy in the countryside had become primarily one of cultural destruction and economic failure in the form of the collective-farm system. Peasant women generally benefited from the Revolution only insofar as they were willing either to take the enormous risk of nonconformity in the village setting through nontraditional occupations or to leave for educational and employment opportunities in the cities. It is not an exaggeration to conclude that peasant women paid much of the long-term costs of the Revolution in the countryside.

Conclusion

The chapters in this part of the book expand on many of the themes and issues articulated in the preceding pages. They demonstrate how bringing women into the history of the times can revise our understanding of such important topics as the 1917 Revolution, collectivization, and Stalin's conservative policies of the 1930s. Most important, these chapters offer us a new road into the social history of Soviet Russia by showing how the experience of peasant women can illuminate our understanding of peasant culture. In the pages that follow, we see how peasant women lived and worked, interacted with families and formal authority structures, and, most of all and in a multitude of ways, maintained a tradition of peasant resistance from 1917 virtually to the present.

Notes

1. William Henry Chamberlin, *The Russian Revolution,* 2 vols. (New York: Grosset and Dunlap, 1965).

2. For further information, see Richard Stites, *The Women's Liberation Movement in Russia* (Princeton, N.J.: Princeton University Press, 1978), which is the best general history of Russian women. Also of general interest for the Soviet period is Mary Buckley, *Women and Ideology in the Soviet Union* (Ann Arbor: University of Michigan Press, 1989).

3. Women belonging to the prerevolutionary nobility and other formerly privileged social groups were excluded from citizenship after the Bolshevik Revolution (as were their male counterparts).

4. The right to abortion was never considered to be an absolute right or a part of women's equality, but a temporary response to unwanted pregnancy in conditions of poverty and to the harmful effects of illegal backstreet abortions.

5. For more information, see Buckley, *Women and Ideology,* chap. 2.

6. Barbara Evans Clements, "Working-Class and Peasant Women in the Russian Revolution," *Signs* 8, no. 2 (1982): 215–35; Clements, "The Effects of the Civil War on Women and Family Relations," in Diane P. Koenker, William G. Rosenberg, and Ronald Grigor Suny, eds., *Party, State, and Society in the Russian Civil War* (Bloomington: Indiana University Press, 1989).

7. Clements, "Effects of the Civil War," pp. 106–9.

8. For a clear (and recent) example of this orientation, see Richard Pipes, *The Russian Revolution* (New York: Knopf, 1990), p. 713.

9. See especially the important works by Stephen F. Cohen, *Bukharin and the Bolshevik Revolution* (New York: Knopf, 1974), and Moshe Lewin, *Lenin's Last Struggle* (New York: Random House, 1968).

10. Stites, *Women's Liberation Movement,* pp. 366–74, 394–95.

11. Beatrice Farnsworth, "Bolshevik Alternatives and the Soviet Family: The 1926 Marriage Law Debate," in Dorothy Atkinson, Alexander Dallin, and Gail Warshofsky Lapidus, eds., *Women in Russia* (Stanford: Stanford University Press, 1977); Wendy Z. Goldman, "Freedom and Its Consequences: The Debate on the Soviet Family Code of 1926," *Russian History* 11, no. 4 (1984).

12. Buckley, *Women and Ideology,* pp. 128–36.

13. Ibid.

14. For a general history of the relations between the peasantry and the state in the 1920s, see M. Lewin, *Russian Peasants and Soviet Power: A Study of Collectivization,* trans. Irene Nove (New York: Norton, 1975).

15. V. P. Danilov, *Rural Russia Under the New Regime,* trans. Orlando Figes (Bloomington: Indiana University Press, 1988), pp. 33–34, 304.

16. Lynne Viola, "The Peasant Nightmare: Visions of Apocalypse in the Soviet Countryside," *Journal of Modern History* 62 (December 1990): 747–70.

17. R. W. Davies, *The Soviet Collective Farm, 1929–1930* (Cambridge, Mass.: Harvard University Press, 1980), chaps. 3–5, 7; Sheila Fitzpatrick, *The Collectivized Village* (New York: Oxford University Press, forthcoming); Lynne Viola, *The Best Sons of the Fatherland: Workers in the Vanguard of Soviet Collectivization* (New York: Oxford University Press, 1987), chap. 6.

18. For further discussion of these attitudes, see Chapter 11. For information on pay discrimination and/or lack of voting rights for women on collective farms, see *Kollektivizatsiia sel'skogo khoziaistva Tsentral'nogo promyshlennogo raiona* (Riazan, 1971), pp. 321, 804–5; *Saratovskaia partiinaia organizatsiia v period nastupleniia sotsializma po vsemu frontu. Sozdanie kolkhoznogo stroia, 1929–32 gg.* (Saratov, 1961), p. 42; and *Sotsialisticheskoe pereustroistvo sel'skogo khoziaistva Moldavskoi ASSR* (Kishinev, 1964), p. 176.

19. See Chapter 11 as well as Sheila Fitzpatrick, " 'Middle-class Values' and Soviet Life in the 1930s," in Terry L. Thompson and Richard Sheldon, eds., *Soviet Society and Culture: Essays in Honor of Vera S. Dunham* (Boulder, Colo.: Westview Press, 1988), pp. 34–35, and Fitzpatrick, *The Russian Revolution* (New York: Oxford University Press, 1982), pp. 150–51. On the issue of retreat in women's issues in general, see the important article by Janet Evans, "The Communist Party of the Soviet Union and the Woman's Question: The Case of the 1936 Decree 'In Defense of Mother and Child,' " *Journal of Contemporary History* 16, no. 4 (1981): 757–75.

20. See Chapters 13 and 14 as well as Susan Bridger's important monograph, *Women in the Soviet Countryside* (Cambridge: Cambridge University Press, 1987).

21. See Chapters 12, 13, and 14.

8 / Village Women Experience the Revolution

BEATRICE FARNSWORTH

Beatrice Farnsworth explores the interactions of Communists and peasant women in the first decade of Soviet power. Although the Communist image of the peasant woman was that of an ignorant and superstitious baba *(a pejorative for "woman," most often applied to peasant women), Farnsworth demonstrates that the reality of the peasant woman was quite different from the dominant image. Peasant women responded selectively to Communist attempts at socialist transformation on the basis of a quite rational self-interest, accepting what was useful from the new Soviet system while retaining those "cultural symbols" from the past that continued to serve their needs. Relatively few peasant women accepted Communist doctrine completely and joined in the party's work; those who did tended to be women who were traditionally on the margins of village life (e.g., widows and single house-holders). The basic culture of most women, however, was antithetical to Communist culture. The culture of peasant women, according to Farnsworth, was based on a well-developed sense of private property centered on the domestic economy (the woman's traditional domain). In demonstrating this important aspect of the peasant woman's world, Farnsworth anticipates the clash of cultures that was to occur during the collectivization of Soviet agriculture, when the urban-based, collectivist principles of the state came into deadly conflict with the individualistic, small-holding practices of the Russian peasantry.*

Communists regarded peasant women as the "darkest," most backward layer of the Russian population, a dead weight and a potential source of counterrevolution. If women, who constituted the majority in the countryside, were to be drawn into the Soviet sphere, it would require a fundamental change in their outlook and values. From a "correct" Marxist standpoint, such an alteration in attitude could result only from deep economic changes in rural Russia. That such changes were occurring in the early years of the Revolution seemed questionable. The former landlord's land went to the peasants, but they continued to farm in traditional, inefficient, small-scale ways. Women carried on with their accustomed drudgery. Nevertheless, even before the end of the Civil War in 1921, Communists were attempting to a limited

"Village Women Experience the Revolution" by Beatrice Farnsworth, in Abbott Gleason, Peter Kenez, and Richard Stites, eds., *Bolshevik Culture: Experiment and Order in the Russian Revolution* (Bloomington Indiana University Press, 1985), pages 238–260. Copyright © 1985 by Indiana University Press. Reprinted by permission.

extent to induce a transformation in peasant outlook by introducing Soviet mores to women in the countryside. This essay looks at the interaction that resulted: how did the Bolsheviks attempt to reach women in the villages of Central Russia? How did peasant women respond to the new cultural values set before them?

Who was the Russian peasant? The answer has defied consensus. One commentator recently remarked of the peasantry that "no class or group in society has ever received such strikingly mixed notices from anthropologists, sociologists, and historians."[1] The self-governing communes in peasant villages have been idealized as exemplifying the principles of primitive communism, where, in contrast to the wickedness of the towns, the fruits of the social product went to all. The "peasant mind" has been depicted as "childlike" and "uncontaminated." At the other extreme were those who found such images deeply unrealistic. Lenin and Plekhanov attacked the nineteenth-century narodniki for believing in sentimental myths about the *mir* [commune]. Maxim Gorky tried to find the good-natured, thoughtful Russian peasant, the indefatigable searcher after truth and justice so movingly depicted in nineteenth-century Russian literature, but could only discover a person "half-savage, stupid, heavy. . . ."[2]

Oscar Lewis, Edward Banfield, and other social scientists have challenged many of the assumptions of Robert Redfield and his followers who found peasant societies to be smoothly functioning and well-integrated, made up of contented and well-adjusted people.[3] The critics came away from peasant communities with impressions of peasants as often fatalistic and supine, ignorant, dishonest, sunk in apathy and meanness.

The tenor of village life in Russia with its fist-fighting organized as entertainment, its fortune-telling, and its superstition suggests this latter view. The beauty of peasant folk art, its stories and songs tended to be obscured by the squalor of daily existence. By the turn of the century, moreover, urban tastes had penetrated those villages close to markets with well-developed patterns of peasants (mainly men) departing seasonally to earn money. One could find there cheap colored prints on the walls, card playing, city dancing and singing, and consulting of horoscopes. For a village to have few or no books was not unusual. Most of the peasants in Tver province were illiterate, although in some families old people did read aloud from prayer books. In villages in Voronezh province prior to the Revolution there were no libraries, the sole books there being gospels and prayer books.[4]

One should not, however, exaggerate village illiteracy. Viriatino, a village 200 miles southeast of Moscow in Tambov province, had a library in the local school with 153 books. According to teachers, young peasants who used the school library especially liked stories about peasant life and fairy tales. Literate adults more frequently read *The Lives of the Saints* or the Bible.[5]

The Bolsheviks, assuming with Marx and Engels a "rural idiocy," aimed at breaking down the old *byt'*—the complex of customs, beliefs, and manners that determined the peasants' daily life. From the outset, Bolshevik culture was didactic, moralistic, and atheistic, trying to rid the peasant not only of religiosity but of the ancient practices of lying, thieving, bribery, and swearing. Whenever a peasant was brought to court for stealing, making homebrew, or beating his wife or child, some official would launch into a lecture on why a Soviet citizen should abstain from such "bourgeois practices."[6]

At the simplest level Soviet culture meant hygiene and health care, and knives and forks rather than a wooden spoon dipping into a common bowl, a remarkable message to a peasant who may customarily have left human excrement to pile up around the hut.[7] Peasants began to accustom themselves to posters proclaiming: "Syphilitics, do not use alcohol," and "The louse is a carrier of Typhus."[8]

Knives, forks, and public health injunctions could be regarded as a minor affront to traditional ways. Atheism and the new iconography—Karl Marx flanked by Lenin and Trotsky on the walls of the village Soviet in place of St. Nicholas—were a graver threat.[9] Women, traditionally close to Christianity, saw their old faith attacked and slipping away and they feared that their husbands who ate meat on fast days and ceased going to church were damned. Ikons hanging in the corner of the hut, frequently side by side with lurid atheist posters, testified to the clash of cultures.[10]

The very organization of government within the village was alien. The *sel'sovet*, its basic element, was both imported and imposed. The number of peasants taking part in elections after the Civil War remained small (22.3 percent in 1922), and in many villages no more than 10 to 15 percent of the peasants would turn out to vote. Peasant lack of interest is understandable, since the *sel'sovet* was controlled by the authorities and its membership was decided upon by the Party in the district, in consultation with the local Party cell, if there was one. The peasants regarded the ancient *mir*, which had revived during and after the Revolution, as the actual village government.[11]

The Party staffed the *sel'sovet* with the village poor, the *batraki* and the *bedniaki*, or even workers sent out from the towns to strengthen the proletarian element.[12] Thus, this alien import, the *sel'sovet*, elevated those whom the more solid peasants regarded as riffraff.

An aspect of the new culture, then, was the sudden prominence within the village of its poorer inhabitants. Previously, the peasants regarded the village as a unity—the *mir*. Now they were told that it really consisted of three parts—the rich peasants, the middle, and the landless poor. Soviet culture from the outset forced on the peasant a model of class conflict.[13] The famous "Committees of Poor Peasants," backed up by detachments of the proletariat, who came from the towns in 1918 to requisition grain, reinforced the image.

With the infusion of Soviet politics into the village, language itself began to change. Peasants heard about People's Courts, "enemies of the working class," *kombedy, smychka, kommuna, delegatki, komsomol,* and *Commissar.*[14] The Party told the peasant woman that she was no longer a *baba.** An equal citizen now, she should forgo the old term and call herself *krest'ianka.*[15]†

The Communists gave a woman the right to seek a divorce.[16] Activists arriving in the village urged her to learn to read. But above all, Soviet culture was collectivist.

---

*Pejorative for "peasant woman."
†Peasant woman.

The Bolsheviks would attempt to inculcate the religion of "we" and to break down the belief in "I." For women, this may have been the most alien message of all.

To understand how Soviet culture was perceived initially by the *baba* one must first know the values of peasant women, how they related to the values of the peasant community, and how they related to the values of men. A sexual division had to some extent always existed in the village. One need only recall the frequent references in literature to "the women," with the assumption that they were a group apart, to understand that women had their separate sphere in both the community and the household.

What were their values? The peasant woman was a housewife and she wanted to remain one. In a society in which marriage was the norm, most women lived with their husband's family after the age of 20.[17] The Revolution awarded woman full equality within the joint household. She was confirmed in her right to be designated as head of the family which might be large and complex (grandparents and married sons), or small and complex (parents, children, and perhaps a married brother), or more rarely, the small nuclear family common in Russia today.[18] Theoretically no longer subordinate to a patriarchal male, women might legally attend the village assembly (*skhod*) and participate in running the community,[19] but reports suggest that such female participation was uncommon. When one woman attended a village assembly in Smolensk province in 1922 she was greeted with abuse. In areas of Penza province in the mid-twenties, women lived as they had twenty years earlier, unaware of their legal rights.[20] Most married women continued to live in a household headed by a man and to focus narrowly on family, farm, and economic survival.

The household functioned according to a traditional division of labor. Men sowed, plowed, cut hay, prepared fuel, and tended the horses. In many families— especially in Northern areas where men were away for long periods earning wages—women also plowed and harrowed and cut hay, but generally they tended the cattle, worked in the house, and did a certain amount of field work.[21] In poorer families, girls and women might hire out as servants or agricultural day laborers.[22]

In a sense, peasant women also lived as hired laborers within their own extended households, with a mother-in-law distributing the tasks.[23] One authority on peasant life, commenting on the awesome mother-in-law and the quarrelsome sisters-in-law, concluded that it was good to marry an only son and best of all one whose father was a widower.[24] But *snokhachestvo* (sexual advances of the father-in-law) was another feature of the peasant milieu.

Given the harshness of women's lives, the female solidarity of which we have abundant evidence is scarcely surprising: rural women organizing as a group in times of stress; women plundering a local store in protest against high wartime prices; women day laborers refusing to work for a particular landlord who reduced the daily wage from 50 to 45 kopeks; soldiers' wives rioting and resisting separate consolidation of communal lands undertaken in accord with the Stolypin land reform.[25] But that such female cohesion persisted in the routines of daily life seems doubtful. Despite women's tendency to organize against perceived threats to their economic interests and despite their mutual dependence in matters of childbirth, relations among women forced by tradition and economics to live together were predominantly unpleasant. Within the household, tensions built not only over whether mother-in-law or daughter-in-law would predominate at the stove but between younger women who might resent the obligation to care for a sister-in-law's children.[26] In the larger community, malice and competition smoldered over the possession of a man and the birth—or lack thereof—of children.

Although Leo Tolstoy has described a young peasant woman who frankly expressed a sense of release at the death of a child,[27] such an example is probably far less common than that of another nineteenth-century Russian writer: "Peasants . . . view the birth of children as a sign of God's blessing on the parents, whereas not having children is considered a misfortune."[28] Beyond the question of the mother's relationship to the child was the fact that childlessness for the peasant woman was a painful situation which often constituted a source of moral humiliation. In the novel *Brusski,* the young peasant wife longs for a child and release from the mockery of the women at the spring who called her barren.[29] To be barren meant to be deprived of children through whom alone a woman could implant herself firmly in the family of her husband and be guaranteed comfort in her old age.[30]

Before turning to the peasant woman's relationship to property, it is important to understand how peasant property was held within the joint households of Central Russia. Traditionally, the male peasant, owning nothing privately beyond his personal possessions (clothing, harmonica), shared as co-owner in the property of the household: hut, livestock, and tools. His earnings, even when he went away to work, generally went into the general holdings. The peasant's role as a joint owner, living in a commune that periodically redistributed the land, gave rise to considerable disagreement among scholars. Because the peasant's land was not truly his own, because his livestock, tools, and hut were held in common, because his outside earnings went into a common fund and he farmed in accord with decisions arrived at democratically by a village assembly within each commune, it has been suggested that the peasant was a natural socialist. Opponents of this view countered that far from being natural socialists, the peasants required the repartitional mechanism to reconcile their extreme competitiveness and self-interestedness. They pointed out that commune members were not equal either in income or resources, that the poorer peasant envied the better-off, on whom he might be dependent for loans, and that the more prosperous were able to manipulate the decision-making process in the assembly.

What needs to be emphasized here is that this controversy is relevant primarily to the male segment of peasant society. Women certainly did not live as socialists. They were not members of the decision-making village assembly and their earnings were considered private property. This last point needs explanation. Although the Land Code of 1922 accorded women equality as joint owners in the household,[31] their earnings—cash from specifically "female activities" such as selling eggs, mushrooms, and handcrafts, and from weaving and dyeing—were generally separate from common household funds, as had been the case before the Revolution.[32] A woman's dowry, frequently including some livestock, technically remained under her own control, to be passed on to her daughters. Consequently a woman's sense of private property was more developed than that of her husband. Unlike men who worked communally, many women lived, at least part of each day, by the capitalist ethic. The business of linen bleaching is an example: in certain areas women attending fairs solicited orders from other villages, thus developing a home industry.[33] The nineteenth-century historian Kovalevsky, speaking of the joint household, observed that if a movement in favor of private property could be detected it was only in the private earnings of women and girls.[34]

The need to earn and control money of her own is understandable, since it was the custom of the household that no family money was to be spent on the daughter-in-law. The family budget entitled her only to food, an overcoat, and shoes, and she was dealt a ration from the family supply of wool and hemp. What money the woman earned went for petty expenses such as soap, salt, matches, and kerosene. Any necessities for herself and her children had to be bought with her own money.[35]

The daughter-in-law protected what was hers. In the large, joint families of Tver province, small sheds were often built around the vegetable garden, one for each daughter-in-law. Here she could keep her personal property. If her husband brought her a gift upon his return from seasonal work, the wife might not use it as long as she lived together with her husband's relatives. Instead she would hide the item or give it to people whom she could trust until she and her husband separated from the joint family.[36]

Thus it was no surprise that the Bolsheviks met resistance when they called on the peasant woman accustomed to protecting her individual interests to act collectively for the general good. It was hard for the Russian peasants, who traditionally worked hardest on their own strips of land and who were sometimes said to altogether lack a social conscience,[37] to understand the concept of mutuality between city and village. Now the peasant must give grain to the towns because the factory worker could not produce implements for the farms if he had no food. Peasants were exhorted to enter the Soviets, where they would work to help the widows and families of Red Army men. They were to construct shelters and nurseries for orphans and children of the village poor and they were somehow to absorb the uncongenial idea of work without pay.[38] This last injunction proved to be particularly awkward. When the question of wages for the delegates (women elected to receive elementary political training) came up in Kaluga province, the majority of them, not receiving any pay, simply refused to work.[39]

The absence of any general will to collectivity on the part of women is illustrated by their opposition to the early Soviet communes. Women reacted negatively, although they were promised more than their husbands. In 1919 the Communist Party newspaper *Pravda* reported that female antipathy was the chief obstacle to the formation of communes.[40] If they did go into the communes they usually held back from active participation.[41] Although the commune freed women from certain chores it required of them much more readjustment than it did of their husbands, who for the most part went about their accustomed agricultural work. Quarrels arose in the community kitchen and dining halls. Women did not like cooking for those outside their family, doing impersonal, menial jobs, or caring for the children of others. According to one source, the women engaged in all manner of recriminations and dodged the work. One reporter, sympathetic to the commune, found that women disliked the communal nursery as much as the kitchen and had to be rotated very often. Bickering and gossip were the rule.[42] But when they needed to, women did act collectively. Widows, especially, sometimes formed communes in order to support each other. The "Fortress of Communism" was started in the lower Volga region by seven women, some of them widows. Husbands joined upon release from service.[43]

The primary mediator between peasant women and the new political milieu was the Communist Women's Section, the *Zhenotdel,* founded at the end of 1919. Although the zeal of its leaders was impressive, it would be a mistake to assume that rural Russia was saturated with female agitators working to create "new women." Even by the end of the 1920s three-fourths of the villages had no organized Party activity,[44] and in the RSFSR alone there were 150,000 villages. Although Communists in principle favored bringing politically backward peasant women into public life, work among women in the war-ravaged countryside received low priority in the Party at large. The *Zhenotdel's* female leadership constantly protested insufficient funding and shortages of qualified personnel,[45] and usually only part of a province experienced the Women's Section at all.[46] Activity might mean merely a poorly paid district organizer, knapsack on her back, going by foot 20 to 30 versts,* from district to district.[47]

In general, it was the peasant woman who lived in semi-industrial areas like Iaroslavl and Gomel provinces who received the greater cultural impact, since *Zhenotdel* workers from the industrial areas of the province could be sent into the villages to spread the Party message. The purely peasant provinces had a less developed Party apparatus.[48]

Communist women appealed to self-pity, quoting Nekrasov's famous lines: "Oh Russian fate / Oh miserable women's fate / Is it really possible to find anything worse!"[49] Peasant women did work hard and for a longer day than men, as Figure 8.1 suggests.

According to a local doctor in Voronezh province at the turn of the century, women became ill and sought medical treatment at the zemstvo [district and provincial councils] facility more frequently than did men. That this report came from an area of extreme misery and low female literacy should serve to correct the popular image of backward *babas* relying solely on "wise men" and old women.[50] The death rate of women from the ages of 15 to 60 in these same Voronezh villages exceeded that of men.[51] Indeed, throughout European Russia, according to statistics for the period 1867–1881, women's death rate was higher than that of men. Statistics for 1896–1897 show women's death rate higher between the ages 10–39, 55–59, and 65–74. In 1908–1910, the death rate for women was higher up to age 40 and from age 60 to beyond 80. The higher male death rate from 40 to 60 reflected in statistics for 1908–1910 is presumably explained by the increasing hazards of factory work and migrant labor.[52]

Communists, responding to these gloomy statistics, offered rural women an image of a brighter, collectivist future: communal nurseries, kitchens, and laundries, to say nothing of equal access with men to positions in public life. These

---

*One verst is about seven-tenths of a mile.

Fig. 8.1. Labor distribution by sex and age in Volokolamsk Uezd (county).

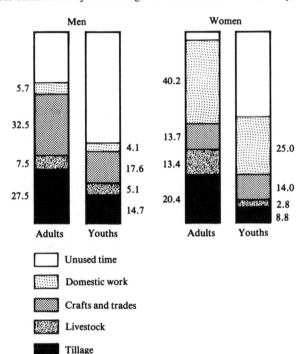

Men   Women

Adults   Youths   Adults   Youths

☐ Unused time

▨ Domestic work

▨ Crafts and trades

▨ Livestock

■ Tillage

Source: A. V. Chayanov, *The Theory of Peasant Economy,* ed. Daniel Thorner, Basile Kerblay, and R. E. F. Smith (Homewood, Ill., 1966, originally published Moscow, 1925), p. 180. Data were presumably collected between 1907 and 1913.

utopian and uniquely Communist promises and expectations were the ones the regime would most conspicuously fail to fulfill. Be that as it may, rural women reacted with suspicion to the phenomenon of zealous, urban females trying to change their lives. In villages where the Women's Section established summer nurseries they were perceived as a threat. Rumors circulated that once in them children were enrolled as Communists and taken from their mothers.[53] Upon occasion, women spoke with particular force against nurseries as indicated by the following resolution taken at a meeting of peasant women in Penza province: "The women's meeting . . . under the chairmanship of Evgeniia Romanovka, unanimously refuses to open and organize a kindergarten and nursery since in our community we don't have mothers who would refuse to bring up their children."[54]

Paradoxically, women complained that Communist investigators were interfering with traditional childraising, threatening to lock them up if they whipped their children. In order for peasants to understand urban concepts in child care, agitators resorted to dramatic devices which were occasionally effective: one was a symbolic "belt burying." Peasant women in Tver province would report that children were not being beaten because the family had "buried the belt."[55]

Communist rural activity included labor conscription, which was decreed in

1920. It was seen as a harsh intrusion by women who worked hard but at their own tempo and who resented regimentation. Although labor mobilization did not require change of location for peasant women with children under twelve, it did mean coerced and arduous work such as clearing snow from railway tracks.[56] Peasant attitudes toward work discipline were unequivocal and reflected work habits alien to modern, industrial efficiency. An American visitor approaching a group of women day laborers working in a *sovkhoz* [state farm] was told very frankly that no, life was not better for them than in the old Tsarist days. "We worked then from dawn to dark—but we didn't have to keep it up all the time. We could even stop to sing, and lie down in the sun and sleep when we wanted to and the foreman didn't mind—he did the same himself. But now they make us stick to our work."[57]

Another cultural change was the introduction of literacy classes for adults.[58] While education might be perceived by a minority of peasant women as an opportunity, literacy centers were irrelevant for many. Occasionally peasant women projected their own cultural values in opposition to those being imposed. One school teacher in Tver province tried to teach some peasant women to read and write. After the third lesson, they asked her for a printed cotton shirt apiece, as compensation for their loss of time.[59]

A certain number of women did become literate, often braving male disapproval. Since the literacy campaign was closely connected with the campaign against religion, orthodox priests took the lead in conducting agitation against literacy centers.[60] Men forbade their womenfolk to participate. Enthusiastic "liquidators of illiteracy" conducted covert propaganda in the villages against male tyranny and persuaded women to visit the centers by stealth.[61]

The Bolshevik idea that girls should attend school was also alien. In a village in Penza province peasants complained that in the old days girls did not go to school. Now a teacher agitates for their attendance and eighteen girls immediately enter.[62] Yet, the number of girls in school there between 1922 and 1924 declined significantly. In some schools there were no girls at all. Traditionally, if a family were to make a sacrifice, it would be for the son. He would be going into the Army and it was inconvenient for a man to be illiterate. But for the girl to remain illiterate seemed no great misfortune. Frequently mothers prevented their daughters from going to school, arguing that the family could not afford it.[63] Those girls who did go to school often left before completing the course of study. On the other hand, girls in Penza province were attracted to the literacy center although they felt shy about attending. Reportedly they wanted a separate women's group.[64]

The same peasant woman who objected to her daughter going to school was encouraged, if she lived in a village where the Party was active, to achieve a different self-image—that of an effective and literate citizen, a member, it is worth noting, of a participatory democracy. She was told that if she learned to read, speculators would not be able to cheat her; if she were to take part in elections to district and village Soviets, they would not be dominated by kulaks and former shop and tavern keepers; if she used her right to vote, the Soviet would be made up of honest people who would defend the village poor; if she participated in the Soviets and in the district executive committees, the Soviets would care more about improving the life of women and children.[65]

Occasionally women were persuaded to enter the Soviet. More frequently they responded negatively:

> "I have small children at home and a farm. Therefore I have no time to work in the Soviet."
> "I am illiterate—what would I do in the Soviet and how will I be of use to the village?"
> "My husband is opposed."[66]

For the married peasant woman of average means living with her husband's family in a village that had experienced little or no organized Party activity, Soviet culture probably meant little besides the resented "tax in kind" that in 1921 replaced the forced requisition of grain. Or, if she traveled into the large towns, there was the "Agitation Point" (perhaps only a kiosk in a station), disseminating Bolshevik propaganda.

The new culture was experienced more intensely by the poor, especially single women householders, Red Army wives, and widows. More vulnerable and generally older, they were the women most receptive to rural activists[67] and the most likely to attend their meetings. Of 134 delegates (63 of whom were peasants and 71 urban women) at a non-Party Conference in Orel province in 1923, the majority (70) were in the 25 to 45 age group. Forty-nine were between 17 and 25 and 18 were older than 45.[68] The Party worker reporting on the Conference was gratified that there were also some young women present who left farm and children to attend. At a similar women's conference in the province of Nizhni-Novgorod that same year a large number of delegates, surprisingly, were under 30.

In general, young peasant women burdened with children were less responsive to the Party, while the young, unmarried woman was the least likely of all to participate.[69] Reports deplored the scarcity of girls in the rural komsomols.[70] In some there were no women at all, or at most, simply one in a cell of thirty—a result, in part, of parental disapproval of a Communist youth group perceived as immoral.[71]

The single woman householder—often a widow—had the most reason to react positively to the Communists. Her life was extraordinarily difficult. She was expected alone to raise children, to maintain the cattle, and to farm. A small percentage of these women moved into the category of the landless peasant—the *bobylok*. The majority of them farmed with varying degrees of success.

Party workers sought out the more outspoken among them. Occasionally a peasant woman would be persuaded to make public demands; A. Volkova from Smolensk province was probably one such recruit. In a letter to the journal *Kommunistka*, she called on the urban working women, the seemingly favored element in the Revolution, to "remember the peasant women." She read in the women's pages in *Rabochi put'* about meetings for city women. She requested similar meetings for peasant women where questions could be answered about problems like the tax-in-kind.[72]

Volkova was typical of the minority of rural women who tended to become the "troublemakers," organizing other village women, attending Women's Section courses, and participating in meetings that today we would recognize as consciousness-raising and that in China would be called "speaking bitterness." At non-Party conferences, peasant delegates would be encouraged to talk about their own lives, not only about the hardship of their past, but also about their current exploitation both by kulaks and by male members of the Soviet power structure in the villages.

Women complained about the conditions of daily life which in some instances were made worse by the Revolution. Drunkenness, well known in the Russian village, continued to plague the countryside, even becoming a feature of local Soviet organs, which in the view of some peasants resembled taverns more than government institutions.[73] Drinking at home seemed to the women to have increased. In the old days there was a formal liquor monopoly. Now each muzhik distilled his own and life had become impossible for the woman.[74]

A 22-year-old peasant woman in the province of Nizhni-Novgorod told of her experiences the previous year as a member of the Soviet. The kulaks proposed that she chair a work committee with the idea—as she now realized—of manipulating her. When she called them to task for their tax irregularities, they threatened to kill her. I don't go to the Soviet anymore, she told the conference. I am 22 and I still want to live.[75]

An older woman in the same area protested that the working woman in the city got four months' maternity leave, while she had borne sixteen children (five of them buried) working continuously. Why weren't the peasant women given the same benefits as the city woman?[76] Distrust of the urban working woman was common among the peasant women, who complained about their exhausting work over a long summer day while the factory woman worked, in their view, not twenty-four hours but simply eight.[77]

At a meeting in Nizhni-Novgorod, women protested against the painful tax-in-kind and the cruelty of sadistic Soviet agents, who, instead of sympathizing with the difficulties of a Red Army man's wife and perhaps letting her off more easily, taunted the woman with outlandish requests, such as that she produce sixty identical black cats so that he could make a fur coat.[78] The Party worker noted that this was only one episode of humiliating injustice occurring locally at the hands of brutal collectors of the tax-in-kind. Indeed the hated tax appears occasionally as the hallmark of Soviet culture in the villages.

But not everyone felt this way. A peasant woman in Orel province recalled that in the past she had no land and the village called her a tramp. "Why? I was not a thief." Now she had 12 desiatins (1 desiatina = 2.7 acres) of land and the kulak who formerly had 40 had 8. She sold her son's miner's clothing and even managed to buy a horse. She lived well. It was warm inside in the winter. Still, she did not want to identify too closely with the Revolution. "They call me a Communist. But I am not a Communist."[79] Another woman explained that she had never before been at a conference. Nor had she known where the city was. But now it seemed to her that Orel was sitting right in her vegetable patch. She summed up the cultural impact of the Revolution on her life by noting that it had taken her out of the village.[80]

Bringing women together to express personal grievances and triumphs was a dramatic way of drawing them into the Soviet orbit. There were other ways: organizations among single women to purchase glass, firewood, and various supplies; and groups to develop summer nurseries which would work together to obtain local funds from committees of mutual aid, district executive committees, and local cooperatives.[81]

The peasants did not always accept the cooperation urged upon them by the authorities, although cooperatives were well known in pre-revolutionary Russia. They made excuses: the *baba* could not live without her daily trip to the city to sell milk and eggs from her own farm; or, peasants were not the kind of people to work together harmoniously.[82] Yet frequently cooperation succeeded.

Work artels brought change to the lives of those relatively few women involved.[83] A member of the *Zhenotdel* reported in 1920 a conversation with a woman who recalled that at first no one in the village wanted to hear about organizing an artel (a peasant association for the common cultivation of land). They told her to get rid of her Bolshevik ideas. But she persuaded other peasant women, especially Red Army wives who farmed alone, to join with her. Together they obtained seed in the city. Their two horses became the common property of the artel. Going beyond joint agricultural work, they organized a children's dining room with the help of the Soviet network. The *Zhenotdel* worker marveled that the artel was begun by the peasant women themselves, despite the mockery of the men. Yet we may assume an ongoing degree of *Zhenotdel* help in the form of encouragement, literature for the reading hut, and evidently the very sheets of paper (unavailable in the village) that the women needed to record the protocol of their meetings.[84]

Peasant women—again in the relatively few villages with energetic Party organizers—might experience the Bolshevik message at any level of daily life. Even allowing for the likelihood that Party workers exaggerated the degree of their actual accomplishments, the scope of agitation was broad.[85] On Sundays women were recruited, ostensibly to gather mushrooms and medicinal herbs, but in fact for political indoctrination. Dramatic and choral circles were created in the villages.[86] Dramatizations and concerts became an integral part of non-Party conferences. Indeed, in some instances, women would attend meetings only if a "spectacle" was on the program.[87] In reading huts, teachers read from scarce copies of the new Party journal, *Krest'ianka*.[88] In Leningrad there were excursions of peasant women to museums, and in Moscow to children's institutions, the museum of the People's Commissariat of Health, to lectures, and to movies.[89] Cultural innovation came to the village in the form of "magic lantern" (slide) exhibits and model vegetable gardens.[90] In the summer of 1920 on the steamship *Red Star* peasant women of the Volga region reportedly marveled at an exhibition of the uses of electricity in the countryside—how in several minutes it was possible from milk to make butter.[91]

The use of street theater was particularly effective in attracting large numbers of peasants, especially the dramatization of people's courts. In Saratov, the *Zhenotdel* presented a staged court on work deserters, gangsterism, sabotage, and "new women." In Ekaterinburg a performance of "the people's court" investigated the morality of "outrages" against women.[92]

In the semi-industrial areas, female Party workers were conscious of the need to develop ties between city and country women. Thus in Kiev, Kostroma, and Penza provinces, delegates' meetings were organized together with city working women.[93] With the same idea in mind, the Kiev all-city delegate meeting decided to take under its wing a district delegate meeting in Budaevka. For local women, the result was an increased urban presence in the village.[94] The Kiev *Zhenotdel* sought further to develop linkages by bringing groups of peasant women into the city to meet in conferences with urban working women. Despite the optimistic conclusions from Party workers that a tie was being forged between rural and urban women, the opposite may have occurred. Peasant women, as we know, resented the urban working woman as the dominant and favored class.[95]

A sampling of rural participation in the *Zhenotdel* network provides a sense of the scope of Communist activity among peasant women. Each woman drawn, however briefly, into the female political orbit was herself something of a cultural phenomenon when she returned to her village.

One report published in 1920 relates that non-Party district conferences of peasant women were conducted in approximately 60 provinces during the previous half year. In all 853 conferences took place,[96] each conference attended by around 200 people.[97]

Delegates' meetings among peasant women were usually conducted in areas having Communist Party cells (the Ukraine, Samara, and Riazan provinces were given as examples). Besides district delegate meetings, there were also village delegate meetings in those villages having large enough populations.[98]

The most important issues discussed at district delegate meetings concerned land and taxes. The tax-in-kind and the Land Code were laws about which the women were most troubled. Other topics of interest were the significance of the committees of mutual aid, the struggle against home-brew, the new rights of the peasant woman in Soviet Russia, hygiene, and the protection of mothers and infants.[99] Questions of antireligious propaganda were rarely put forth at delegate meetings in view, we are told, of the lack of skillful agitators available to propagate antireligious views.[100] Reports indicated that some delegate meetings were poorly conducted, touching not on issues of daily concern to women but on such matters as the international organization of women and Soviet industrialization. Delegates in these instances lost interest.[101]

In Kaluga province a Party worker reported that organizational activity was well developed in 89 districts (out of 176). Delegates worked in all sections of the District Executive Committees. The Kaluga province *Zhenotdel* in 1920–1921 conducted 85 meetings at which a total of 4,500 women participated. Delegates' meetings of peasant women were created in 87 districts, drawing in around 5,000 peasant women.[102] In Siberia, there were 272 district organizers working among peasant women in 1921. In Ufa, Samara, Perm, Astrakhan, and Ekaterinburg provinces and in the Don area, the *Zhenotdel* assigned district organizers, conducted delegate meetings, and apportioned delegates to district executive committees.[103] In Saratov province in 1921 there were up to 1,000 peasant women serving as *praktikants*, receiving political indoctrination from the *Zhenotdel* and working in Soviet institutions, usually for three months.[104]

The concrete results of this spotty but frenzied activity, as measured by actual political participation, were small. In one area in Penza province a peasant woman was chosen as chair of the Soviet. At an *uezd* Congress of Soviets in Penza province out of 110 delegates there were 11 peasant women.[105] Occasionally one met a peasant woman who was a member of a District Executive Committee, a director of one or another section of the District Soviet, or a member of the board of the District cooperative. In 1923 it was estimated that peasant women made up 1.5 percent of the village Soviets. In about 36 provinces there were 1,022 women serving in the village Soviets.[106] A Communist reporter noted frankly that it was difficult even to draw peasant delegates into the Party.[107] According to statistics for 1920 there were 428 peasant women Communists in the 15 provinces surveyed.[108]

In comparative terms the number of peasant women touched by the political culture of the Revolution in its first years was no more than a few thousand, when the countryside of the USSR consisted of 18.5 million scattered small farms.[109] If only a portion of women became activists, we would like to know how many among the thousands attending meetings became sympathetic to Communism. The evidence, admittedly impressionistic, suggests relationships of a personal rather than an ideological nature. We are told that peasant women in Tver province were drawn to meetings because of a particularly charismatic female leader, but that when she left the area, participation fell.[110] We know that peasant women occasionally turned to the *Zhenotdel* as their advocate. In a village in Smolensk province a widow of a Red Army man, having been refused land by the sowing committee, asked for help from the delegate, who demanded that the woman receive the land to which she was entitled.[111] During War Communism Smolensk delegates intervened on behalf of pregnant women, citing their right not to perform forced labor. They had learned of this right in a report at a delegates' meeting. The chairman of the village Soviet was obliged to release the women from the assigned work.[112]

At a meeting in Orel province a district organizer told of a typical day spent gathering women for a meeting. Toward evening, she reported, you are tired of talking, you have not eaten, and your head hurts. But always there is some woman who invites you home for soup and bread, saying that since you teach us for nothing, you must come to us and eat.[113]

Communist women, heartened by such signs, believed they were influencing the peasants. Some Party workers reported that when women received special attention from the Communists, they began to favor the regime more than their husbands. In certain instances, we are told, Bolshevik rural activists failed to influence the men but succeeded in organizing the women, appealing to their underprivileged position.[114]

A peasant woman who became politically active was seized upon eagerly. The middle-aged F. O. Shupurova from Siberia, in the mid-1920s a member of the All-Russian Central Executive Committee, was depicted in Soviet newspapers more than a dozen times. A poor peasant, drawn into the *Zhenotdel* orbit and intrigued by literacy and ultimately by politics, she learned to read, each night mastering two or three letters.[115] Shupurova was exceptional. Most peasant women, especially married ones, rejected socialist dreams in favor of familiar security, however miserable it appeared to the urban outsider.

Despite the aura of political ferment surrounding the Communists, much of what the Bolsheviks accomplished in rural Russia in the early years of Soviet power falls into the category, not of radical cultural innovation, but rather of increased modernization along familiar lines. More peasant women learned to read. If as late as 1930 two-thirds of the female peasant population were still illiterate, it was an advance over the pre–1914 era when in rural areas approximately nine-tenths of the women were illiterate.[116] Nurseries gained acceptance. Organizing a day nursery became by the mid–1920s a Communist ploy for "catching" the *baba*.[117] But neither literacy nor summer nurseries can be separated from a modernization process that predated the Revolution.[118]

Not even those stalwarts whom the Bolsheviks called "new women," who dotted the rural Soviet network, were types unique to Bolshevism. Independent women, coping alone for much of the year because the men of the household were away at seasonal work, had already evolved in the nineteenth century.[119] The casualties of war, even without the Revolution, would have increased their ranks.

On the other hand, women's legal equality reflected in their right to seek a divorce was uniquely Soviet. The right to a divorce appeared as a revolution of its own in villages where before 1917 a husband might obtain the priest's help in retrieving a wife who had fled to her family. One peasant recalled how at age 17 she was married to a 40-year-old man who beat her. She wanted to leave him, but her mother warned that it would be a sin.[120] Instances of village divorce during the 1920s were not widespread, compared to the number of divorces in the cities, but their social impact exceeded their actual numbers. At village meetings peasants, associating marital instability with Soviet urban life, complained that divorce was becoming frequent.[121] By the mid–1920s most of the village lawyers' cases reportedly involved alimony.[122]

The new freedom of women to divorce, together with their status as equals in the joint household, also found expression in a reported wave of household partitioning initiated by women, in many cases as part of divorce settlements.[123] Delegates working within the *Zhenotdel* network became advocates of the property rights of peasant women.[124]

Bolshevik culture presented itself to rural women as an amalgam of socialist collectivism and feminist equality—concepts that proved difficult to reconcile in a milieu of small-scale private farming. The *Zhenotdel* exhorted peasant women to build communal facilities such as nurseries and to contribute their labor without pay for the common good. Simultaneously, it supported peasant women in defense of their property rights when they separated from joint households to form smaller, less efficient economic units. Thus, the voice of female Bolshevism found itself functioning both as a reaction and a vanguard, an untenable position that no doubt contributed to that institution's political demise in 1929.

Female privatism persisted, nourished by the peasant woman's new legal equality and undaunted by Communist collectivist slogans. Its tenacity is suggested by events at the end of the decade when the regime moved to replace individual farming with the collective farm. In 1930, Kaganovich would charge that peasant women were providing much of the resistance to collectivization.[125] His belief was supported in reports of the "25,000'ers" whom the Communists sent into the countryside as *kolkhoz* organizers.[126] Female opposition to collectivization requires its own account, but we may briefly observe that peasant women fought in 1929 to preserve their poultry, livestock, and carefully wrought private economic arrangements.[127]

A final note. The popular term for these mass female outbursts against the *kolkhozy* was *babi bunt* (women's riot). In 1918 a Communist leader enthusiastically enjoined women to bury the demeaning label of *baba*.[128] But in villages women continued to refer to each other by the old term, even while participating in the new ritual of electing women to the village Soviet.[129]

Peasant women responded selectively, out of self-interest, to Bolshevik culture. They embraced equalizing features that gave them the right to initiate a household partition, to seek a divorce, or to participate in an election. Simultaneously, indifferent to incongruities, they clung to cultural symbols of the past.

Notes

1. Jonathan Lieberson, "The Silent Majority," *New York Review of Books,* October 22, 1981, p. 36.

2. Ibid. For peasant as "childlike," see Daniel Field, *Rebels in the Name of the Tsar* (Boston, 1976), pp. 213–15. For peasant as Communist, see Maxime Kovalevsky, *Modern Customs and Ancient Laws of Russia* (New York, 1970, originally 1891), pp. 61–62.

3. For criticism of Redfield's assumptions, see Oscar Lewis, *Life in a Mexican Village, Tepoztlán Restudied* (Urbana, 1951), pp. 428–29.

4. See A. I. Shingarev, *Vymiraiushchaia derevnia* (St. Petersburg, 1907), reproduced in K. M. Shuvaev, *Staraia i novaia derevnia* (Moscow, 1937), p. 173.

5. On village culture, see Sula Benet, ed. and trans., *The Village of Viriatino* (New York, 1970), pp. 67, 134, 153–54; L. A. Anokhina and M. N. Shmeleva, *Kultura i byt kolkhoznikov Kalinskoi oblasti* (Moscow, 1964), pp. 183, 246–47; *Sotsial'no-ekonomicheskie preobrazovaniia v Voronezhskoi derevne (1917–1967)* (Voronezh, 1967), p. 282.

6. Maurice Hindus, *Broken Earth* (New York, 1926), p. 283.

7. Shingarev in Shuvaev, p. 200.

8. Joshua Kunitz, ed., *Russian Literature Since the Revolution* (New York, 1948), p. 75; for details on extent of syphilis in two Russian villages in Voronezh province, 1900, see Shingarev in Shuvaev, pp. 257–75.

9. "Andron Neputevyi," in A. S. Neverov, *Izbrannye proizvedeniia* (Moscow, 1958), pp. 315–16. For reference to Lenin and Trotsky, consult original edition. See translation in Elisaveta Fen, *Modern Russian Stories* (London, 1943), pp. 121–64.

10. Hindus, p. 188, 194.

11. For statistics on Soviet village government, Moshe Lewin, *Russian Peasants and Soviet Power* (Evanston, Ill., 1975), p. 81, 26.

12. Ibid., p. 81. A bedniak was a poor peasant. A batrak was an agricultural wage laborer employed by private peasants or by their communities.

13. For such a message directed to the peasants, see K. N. Samoilova, *Krest'ianka i sovetskaia vlast'* (Moscow, 1921), p. 19.

14. On Communist language, see A. M. Selishchev, *Iazyk revoliutsionnoi epokhi: iz nabliudenii nad russkim iazykom poslednikh let, 1917–1926* (Moscow, 1928).

15. Beatrice Farnsworth, *Aleksandra Kollontai* (Stanford, 1980), p. 149.

16. See Decree on the Introduction of Divorce, December 19, 1917, in R. Schlesinger, *The Family in the U.S.S.R.* (London, 1949), pp. 30–32.

17. In 1926 the marriage age for women was raised from 16 to 18. See excerpt from "Code of Laws on Marriage and Divorce," Schlesinger, p. 155. But according to the census for 1897 only in the Transcaucasus and the Southern provinces of Central Asia was the average age of marriage below 18. For rural European Russia in 1897 the average age of marriage was 18 or over. In 1908 it remained roughly the same. See A. J. Coale et al., *Human Fertility in Russia Since the Nineteenth Century* (Princeton, 1979), pp. 152, 156.

18. See Land Code of 1922 for women's right to head a family. Schlesinger, p. 42. In 1890 the Senate ruled that women could be heads of household if this was in accord with local custom. See William T. Shinn, Jr., "The Law of the Russian Peasant Household," *Slavic Review* 20 (Dec. 1961): 605. Custom usually stipulated that the father be head.

19. On the legality of women participating in the skhod, see V. P. Danilov, "Zemel'nye otnosheniia v sovetskoi dokolkhoznoi derevne," *Istoriia SSSR* 1, no. 3 (May 1958): 98.

20. N. Rosnitskii, *Litso derevni* (Moscow-Leningrad, 1926), p. 112. Local customs varied. Prior to the Revolution, in Viriatino in Tambov province women, generally, were not allowed to take part in the council even when they became widows and heads of household. Benet, p. 45. On the other hand, Wallace describes female heads of household present at the village assemblies in northern provinces in the 1870s participating in matters relating to their own households. D. M. Wallace, *Russia* (New York, 1905), pp. 117–18.

21. V. G. Kartsova, ed., *Opyt istoriko-sotsiologicheskogo izucheniia sela "Moldino"* (Moscow, 1968), pp. 107–8. Hereafter, "Moldino."

22. See Shingarev in Shuvaev, pp. 223–24, and Anokhina and Shmeleva, p. 25.

23. Anokhina and Shmeleva, pp. 175, 181.

24. M. Ia. Fenomenov, *Sovremennaia derevnia* (Moscow-Leningrad, 1925), part II, p. 20.

25. See A. N. Anfimov, ed., *Krest'ianskoe dvizhenie v Rossii v gody pervoi mirovoi voiny* (Moscow-Leningrad, 1965), pp. 149–50, 309–10, 333–34, 385–87, 401. Women resisted consolidation during the war because they feared that with their men away, they would be taken advantage of in any reallocation of property. Examples are drawn from the provinces of Saratov, Simbirsk, Kharkov, Kazan, Perm, Orel, Tomsk.

26. M. M. Gromyko and N. A. Minenko, eds., *Iz istorii sem'i i byta sibirskogo krest'ianstva x XVII–nachale XXv* (Novosibirsk, 1975), p. 24.

27. Leo Tolstoy, *Anna Karenina* (New York, 1961), p. 605. Observations on child care written by local doctors can be used to support assumptions both of maternal neglect and devotion. On attitudes toward infants, see David L. Ransel, "Abandonment and Fosterage of Unwanted Children: The Women of the Foundling System," pp. 189–217, and Nancy M. Frieden, "Childcare: Medical Reform in a Traditionalist Culture," pp. 236–62, in D. L. Ransel, ed., *The Family in Imperial Russia* (Urbana, 1978).

28. A. A. Titov, *Iuridicheskie obychai sela Nikola-Perevoz Sulostskoi volosti, Rostovskogo uezda* (Iaroslavl, 1888), pp. 51–52, as quoted by Antonina Martynova, "Life of the Pre-Revolutionary Village as Reflected in Popular Lullabies," in Ransel, ed., p. 172.

29. F. I. Panferov, *Brusski,* trans. Z. Mitrov and J. Tabrisky (Westport, Conn., 1977, reprint of 1930 ed.), p. 20.

30. Martynova, in Ransel, ed., p. 172.

31. The Land Code abolished the Stolypin land reform that had given the head of household sole ownership of land and house. Prior to the Stolypin laws, the property of the household was owned jointly by the family. The extent to which the women were considered partners in this joint ownership is not entirely clear. In the nineteenth century women, as a rule, did not take part in the partitioning of household property. See Shinn, p. 604; Wallace, p. 85. Kubanin claims that prior to the Revolution, sisters did not receive any of the property. See M. Kubanin, *Klassovaia sushchnost' protsessa drobleniia krest'ianskikh khoziaistv*

(Moscow, 1929), p. 72. Stepniak, on the other hand, explains that sisters generally did not inherit from brothers because in marrying they went to another family and took with them a dowry. But a spinster sister or a widow who returned to live with her brothers would always receive her share from the tribunal. Stepniak (Kravchinskii, S.), *The Russian Peasantry* (New York, 1888), p. 80. According to Lewin, a woman would get something but not a full share.

32. On separate female property, see Shinn, p. 604; V. F. Mukhin', *Obychnyi poriadok' nasledovaniia u krest'ian'* (St. Petersburg, 1888), pp. 89–92; A. F. Meiendorf, *Krest'ianskii dvor* (St. Petersburg, 1909); Kovalevsky, *Modern Customs and Ancient Laws of Russia*, p. 59.

33. Benet, p. 41.

34. Kovalevsky, p. 59.

35. Benet, p. 102; Anokhina and Shmeleva, p. 175.

36. Anokhina and Shmeleva, p. 175.

37. On lack of social conscience, see Lewin, p. 22. A number of peasants did enter communes. But only a fraction of 1% ever joined. See Robert Wesson, *Soviet Communes* (New Brunswick, N.J., 1963), p. 6.

38. Samoilova, pp. 24, 29.

39. *Kommunistka*, no. 10–11 (1921): 46.

40. See *Pravda*, June 1, 1919, as cited in Wesson, p. 216.

41. Wesson, p. 216.

42. See ibid., and Sergei Tretiakov, *Vyzov* (Moscow, 1932), pp. 54, 58, 86–87, 103–4. Other sources on women in communes: P. Lezhnev-Finkovskii, *Sovkhozy i kolkhozy* (Moscow, 1928), p. 187; A. F. Chmyga, *Ocherki po istorii kolkhoznogo dvizheniia na Ukraine (1921–25)* (Moscow, 1959), p. 193; A. A. Bitsenko, *Sel'sko-khoziaistvennye kommuny* (Moscow, 1924), p. 29. Bitsenko notes the subordinate position of women communards.

43. Wesson, p. 112. See A. L. Strong, *The Soviets Conquer Wheat* (New York, 1931), pp. 121–22, on "Fortress of Communism." See Chmyga, p. 92, for widows organizing kolkhozy in early years of the Revolution.

44. Gail W. Lapidus, "Sexual Equality in Soviet Policy," in D. Atkinson et al., eds., *Women in Russia* (Stanford, 1977), p. 121.

45. See Farnsworth, pp. 284–308.

46. Thus in Gomel province out of thirty-six selected volosts systematic work was carried out only in sixteen. In Kursk province out of thirty-six volosts work was conducted in thirty-two. *Kommunistka*, no. 10 (1923): 29. And the presence of the *Zhenotdel* did not necessarily mean substantial progress. For example, a report from Penza province in 1921 indicated that after a year of work the broad mass of women in the province were affected only slightly. Still, in five volosts twenty peasant women were elected to the Soviet. *Kommunistka*, no. 8–9 (1921): 54–55.

47. *Kommunistka*, no. 10 (1923): 28. A report from Orel province pointed out that there were 45 volost organizers, nearly all serving without pay. Their work was of a low level. The women were young and fervent but ill-prepared. *Kommunistka*, no. 6 (1923): 38.

48. *Kommunistka*, nos. 10–11 (1921): 43.

49. Quoted in Samoilova, p. 6.

50. See Shingarev in Shuvaev, pp. 171–72, for illiteracy, pp. 251, 275 for illness. In Kostroma province in the late nineteenth century, a doctor reported higher rates of illness among women. D. N. Zhbankov, *Bab'ia storona* (Kostroma, 1891), p. 4.

51. Shingarev in Shuvaev, pp. 298–99.

52. For statistics on death rates, see A. G. Rashin, *Naselenie Rossii za 100 let* (Moscow, 1956), pp. 203–5. Statistics for each period show a greater death rate for infant boys. See

Zhbankov, pp. 4–5, 72, for adverse effect of migrant and factory labor on the life expectancy of peasant men.

53. Samoilova, p. 10.

54. *Kommunistka*, no. 12–13 (1921): 67.

55. Anokhina and Shmeleva, p. 266.

56. See *Krest'ianstvo i trudovaia povinnost'* (Moscow, 1920). For exemptions for women, see Farnsworth, p. 192.

57. Jessica Smith, *Women in Soviet Russia* (New York, 1928), p. 33.

58. V. Ulasevich, *Zhenshchina v kolkhoze* (Moscow, 1930), p. 58.

59. John Maynard, *The Russian Peasant* (London, 1943), p. 174.

60. Sheila Fitzpatrick, *Education and Social Mobility in the Soviet Union, 1921–34* (New York, 1979), p. 162. An example of atheism in the village: in 1924 in Voronezh "Societies of the Godless" conducted antireligious lectures and conversations utilizing village evening parties and reading huts. *Sotsial'no-ekonomicheskie preobrazovaniia v Voronezhskoi derevne (1917–67)* (Voronezh, 1967), p. 309.

61. Fitzpatrick, p. 162.

62. Rosnitskii, pp. 92–93.

63. Ibid.

64. Ibid., p. 107. Although adults were generally adverse to the idea of literacy training, in those villages where cultural work was extensive, even older women went willingly to literacy centers. Ibid., p. 106.

65. Samoilova, pp. 28–29.

66. D. P. Rozit, *Proverka raboty nizovogo apparata v derevne* (Moscow, 1926), p. 79 (examples drawn from area of Urals).

67. See *Kommunistka*, no. 3 (1924): 26, and ibid., no. 12–13 (1921): 66–67. The majority of peasant women in the Soviet were Red Army wives.

68. Ibid., no. 6 (1923): 39.

69. Ibid., p. 46. In the 1920s women without families, presumably widows, were those who participated publicly. See L. V. Ostapenko, "Vliianie novoi proizvodstvennoi roli zhenshchiny na ee polozhenie v sem'e," *Sovetskaia etnografiia*, no. 5 (1971): 101.

70. *Kommunistka*, no. 3 (1924): 26.

71. Ibid., no. 8 (1923), p. 20. For attitudes toward the Komsomol, see A. M. Bol'shakov, *Derevnia, 1917–27* (Moscow, 1927), pp. 321–36.

72. *Kommunistka*, no. 8–9 (1922): 35.

73. Rosnitskii, pp. 38–39.

74. *Kommunistka*, no. 6 (1923): 39.

75. Ibid., no. 3–4 (1923): 46.

76. Ibid., p. 47.

77. Ibid.

78. Ibid., no. 8 (1923): 29.

79. Ibid., no. 6 (1923): 39.

80. Ibid.

81. For collective purchasing organizations, see *Kommunistka*, no. 3–4 (1923): 52; no. 3 (1924): 33–36; no. 7 (1924): 33.

82. Rosnitskii, p. 54. For peasant distrust of cooperatives, ibid., pp. 52–55.

83. The number was small. By the mid-1920s, a friendly source indicated, over 500,000 women were members of consumer cooperatives, 180,000 were members of *kustarnye* (handwork) cooperatives, and "a large number" belonged to the agricultural cooperatives. Smith, p. 43. (Geographical area not indicated.)

84. *Kommunistka*, no. 3–4 (1920): 30. The presence of two horses suggests a relatively

prosperous artel. See V. A. Sidorov, *Klassovaia bor'ba v dokolkhoznoi derevne* (Moscow, 1978), p. 64.

85. See Rosnitskii, p. 81, for indication that intentions of Communist activists were not always carried out.

86. Sometimes with unhappy results. Rosnitskii, p. 113, reports a husband in Penza province beating his wife for joining a choral circle. She remained in the group.

87. Smith, p. 37.

88. *Kommunistka*, no. 10–11 (1921): 47, for description of reading material in Saratov. See p. 48 for publications aimed at peasant women.

89. *Otchet otdela TsK RKP (b) po rabote sredi zhenshchin za god raboty* (Moscow, 1921), p. 28; *Kommunistka*, no. 6–7 (1922): 6–7.

90. *Kommunistka*, no. 12–13 (1921): 55.

91. Ibid., no. 7 (1920); 34.

92. *Otchet otdela TsK RKP (b) po rabote sredi zhenshchin za god raboty* (Moscow, 1921), p. 27.

93. *Kommunistka*, no. 10 (1923): 29.

94. Ibid., no. 8 (1923): 29.

95. Ibid., no. 8–9 (1922): 35, on peasant resentment. "Patronage" (*shefstvo*) of city communists over village groups sometimes worked out badly and antagonized the peasants. For descriptions of Communist irresponsibility and insensitivity, see Rosnitskii, pp. 107–8.

96. *Kommunistka*, no. 7 (1920): 33.

97. Ibid., no. 5 (1920): 15.

98. The age of the delegate was usually between 20 and 40. *Kommunistka*, no. 10 (1923): 29. A report from Penza province is indicative, however, of the underlying mood of the peasant women toward such public work. One woman, registering herself as a delegate in the hope that she would receive some benefit, crossed her name out when she learned that the delegate did not receive any special advantages. Rosnitskii, p. 113.

99. *Kommunistka*, no. 10 (1923): 30.

100. Ibid.

101. Rozit, p. 79.

102. *Kommunistka*, no. 10–11 (1921): 46; *Otchet otdela TsK RKP (b) po rabote sredi zhenshchin za god raboty* (Moscow, 1921), p. 25 (hereafter *Otchet*).

103. *Otchet*, p. 25.

104. Ibid., p. 21. *Praktikanty* received political indoctrination from the *Zhenotdel* and they served in Soviet institutions.

105. *Kommunistka*, no. 5 (1920): 15. But see Rosnitskii, p. 112, on backward attitudes toward women in public life in other areas of Penza province.

106. *Kommunistka*, no. 8 (1923): 6. There were 50,000 village soviets in the RSFSR and 70,000 in the country as a whole. Lewin, p. 105. Few women participated politically in the first years of the revolution. In province, uezd, and volost congresses, there were never more than 4 women for every 100 men. Sometimes the proportion was as low as 0.5 women for every 100 men. Only in the city soviets was female participation higher. See tables in *Kommunistka*, no. 8–9 (1922): 5. As late as 1927 in Tver province only 32.5% of the women took part in elections to village soviets. *Sotsialisticheskoe stroitel'stvo v Tverskoi gubernii* (Moscow, 1927), p. 29, as cited in L. V. Ostapenko, "The Effect of Woman's New Production Role on Her Position in the Family," *Soviet Sociology* 12, no. 4 (1974): 94.

107. *Kommunistka*, no. 1–2 (1920): 38.

108. The provinces were: Iaroslavl, Simbirsk, Vladimir, Severnaia-Dvina, Kostroma, Pskov, Kursk, Tver, Kaluga, Gomel', Briansk, Moscow, Nizhegorod, Ivanovo-Voznesensk,

Samara. *Kommunistka*, no. 10–11 (1921): 40, 42. Female membership in the Party for the same provinces was 6,499. Ibid., pp. 40, 42. The actual numbers were probably somewhat higher since there were no returns listed for Briansk or Moscow. Only eight provinces listed any peasant women as members of the Party: Iaroslavl, Vladimir, Kostroma, Kursk, Gomel', Severnaia-Dvina, Nizhegorod, and Ivanovo-Voznesensk.

109. A. V. Chayanov, *The Theory of Peasant Economy,* ed. Daniel Thorner, Basile Kerblay, and R. E. F. Smith (Homewood, Ill., 1966, originally Moscow, 1925), p. 265.

110. Bol'shakov, pp. 352–53.

111. *Kommunistka*, no. 8–9 (1922): 35.

112. Ibid.

113. Ibid., no. 6 (1923): 38.

114. Teodor Shanin, *The Awkward Class* (Oxford, 1972), p. 176.

115. Smith, pp. 41–42.

116. On literacy, 1930, see Ulasevich, p. 58. For pre-1914, A. G. Rashin, *Naselenie Rossii za 100 let* (Moscow, 1956), p. 294.

117. Rozit, p. 80. Organization was slow. By 1924–25, Kaluga province had only fourteen nurseries. Ibid.

118. Summer nurseries inaugurated by zemstvos on a limited scale were an innovation of late-nineteenth-century Russia. In 1898 the Voronezh provincial zemstvo pioneered in the nursery movement. See Frieden, in Ransel, ed., pp. 251–53. Also see Shingarev in Shuvaev, p. 271.

119. A locale in which women predominated because as many as 60% of the men were away at wage labor (*otkhodniki*) would be called a "babii" uezd. A. G. Rashin, *Formirovanie rabochego klassa Rossii* (Moscow, 1958), p. 364. Around 1900, for example, in Viazemskii uezd in Smolensk province, 61% of the grown men and 15% of the grown women were away working. For analysis of two female-dominated areas in Kostroma province, see Zhbankov. See Smith, pp. 39, 41–42, for twentieth-century peasant new women. For fictional portrayals, see Iakov Korobov, *Katia Dolga* (Vladimir, 1958); *Mar'ia-bol'shevichka* in Aleksandr Neverov, *Izbrannye proizvedeniia* (Moscow, 1958), pp. 195–200; and *Virineia* in L. Seifullina, *Sobranie sochinenii*, vol. III (Moscow-Leningrad, 1929).

120. Smith, p. 42. Separation by mutual consent did, however, occur. Moreover, a woman who complained to the township court of serious maltreatment by her husband might, if she were lucky, and the judges well-disposed, receive permission to live apart from him. See, for example, a case in Iaroslavl province in 1869 in *Trudy Komissi po preobrazovaniiu volostnykh sudov,* vol. III (St. Petersburg, 1874), p. 158.

121. Schlesinger, pp. 147, 150. Registrar's Office statistics on divorces for one three-month period—October, November, December 1924—show that for every 10,000 inhabitants of district towns there were 7 divorces. In smaller towns for the same number of inhabitants there were 3 divorces, and for every 10,000 village inhabitants, 2 divorces. Thus in a year there would be approximately 28 divorces in district towns, 12 in smaller towns, and only 8 in villages for every 10,000 inhabitants. Ibid., p. 118.

122. Ibid., p. 151; Smith, p. 44.

123. Kubanin, pp. 71–75. For laws regulating partition of the dvor, see E. Dombrovskii, *Krest'ianskii dvor i semeino-imushchestvennye razdely* (Moscow, 1926), and N. M. Tomashevskii, *Zakony o nasledstvennosti v krest'ianskom khoziaistve* (Leningrad, 1925).

124. *Kommunistka,* no. 10 (1923): 30.

125. Farnsworth, p. 320n.; Kaganovich's speech: *XVI s"ezd vsesoiuznoi kommunisticheskoi partii (b). stenograficheskii otchet* (Moscow-Leningrad, 1931), p. 70. Also

see M. Hindus, *Red Bread* (New York, 1931), pp. 49–50, and Tret'akov, pp. 223, 307. On the other hand, widows—especially *bedniaki*—or women with husbands away for years at wage work, were more inclined to join the kolkhoz. Anokhina and Shmeleva, pp. 32, 273.

126. See reports in *Materialy po istorii SSSR,* vol. 1 (Moscow, 1955), pp. 327, 347–48, 350, 354–55, 357–58, 364, 368.

127. See M. Fainsod, *Smolensk Under Soviet Rule* (Cambridge, Mass., 1958), pp. 253–54.

128. Farnsworth, p. 149.

129. Smith, pp. 35–36.

9 / Rural Women and the Law: Divorce and Property Rights in the 1920s

BEATRICE FARNSWORTH

Beatrice Farnsworth explores the experience of peasant women in the courts of the new Soviet government by focusing on divorce law and litigation. Although only a small minority of women took advantage of their new legal rights, those who did generally found support from the state in their efforts to achieve a fair divorce settlement and property division. The new Soviet system, in the form of law, however, had rather weakly penetrated rural Soviet Russia. The practices of customary law continued to hold sway in much of the countryside. The staying power of customary law was to be expected, given the complexity of many of the new Soviet laws as well as the failure of a large part of the new legislation to adequately address the difficulties and disruption caused by divorce within the extended peasant household. According to Farnsworth, both women and men made use of the new legislation insofar as it protected them (from the particular perspective of husband or wife), while falling back on customary law when tradition better served their purposes. Farnsworth thus further develops the thesis of the previous chapter of a rational, calculating peasantry acting in its own self-interest. Although it focuses on a very specific topic, this chapter illuminates an important feature of peasant culture by highlighting the power of the peasantry to adapt and to use selectively what best serves its interest.

An editor of *Bednota*, the popular Communist Party newspaper for peasants, spoke out publicly in his journal in 1926 on behalf of women seeking divorces. He advised a peasant woman in Riazan province who wrote about her marital separation and her husband's threats: "You have to put in an application to the people's court and dissolve your marriage. Then you petition about a family-property razdel. The people's court will decide what property is coming to you. Don't pay attention to your husband when he tells you he will give you nothing."[1]

What a remarkable directive! Its implications for social change were vast in Soviet Russia, where war and revolution had dealt heavy blows to tradition. Although peasant women had been using local courts since the 1860s to protest domestic grievances and to request property, in the 1920s they did so upon government invitation with the aid and encouragement of the press, as citizens exercising new freedoms.

This chapter looks at the women for whom the *Bednota* message was

intended—women who were likely to be marginal members of the peasant household, part of a group that included not only divorced women with children but the
elderly, widows, and invalids. They also tended to be young. Divorce in rural
Russia in the 1920s was largely the province of youth.[2]

Unlike peasant women in the postemancipation era, who could use only limited
legal options, peasant women in the 1920s were free to seek divorce. They used the
law to their benefit, appealing to new Soviet legislation or to customary law,
depending on which was more immediately advantageous. Peasant men, reacting
self-protectively to women's new legal status, did the same. The arena of divorce
litigation thus provides abundant examples of peasant society interrelating with the
state, as rural Russia adapted with remarkable shrewdness to new laws and institutions.

Only a small number of women went to court in property disputes arising out of
divorces in the early 1920s—an annual figure estimated 8 divorces per 10,000
village inhabitants for 1924 (and 28 divorces for the same number of city inhabitants). By the late 1920s, divorce was perceived as a social force in the countryside,
with commentators referring to a "massive" number of rural divorces and a "wave
of partitions" initiated by women. Yet published figures remain relatively low.
Divorce statistics for 1928 in the Leningrad area indicate 15 divorces per 10,000
inhabitants in the rural areas and 98 in the city; in the Moscow area, 21 divorces
occurred per 10,000 inhabitants in the villages, and 93 in the city. According to the
1926 census for the RSFSR, 258,949 divorced women lived in rural Russia out of a
total of 402,633 divorced women. Actual numbers may have been higher, since only
registered divorces were counted in the 1926 census.[3]

For many of these women, the first decade of the Revolution was a time of
domestic upheaval, of leaving their husbands, sometimes within a year or two of
marriage, and returning to their parental homes or trying to live on their own. One
result of their separations and bitter court encounters was a degree of psychological
reorientation. Some women clung more tightly to images of a stable family; others
became independent and receptive to Soviet political messages, acting as role
models and much-publicized agents of social change in the countryside. Organizing
women's meetings and summer day care, they reminded peasant women about
doliushke zhenskoi, their sad lot.[4]

Even divorced women who did not enter the Soviet orbit might never be quite
the same. Having begun to interact with public institutions, the *baba* was on her
way to becoming a Soviet citizen. If we follow women as they left marriages and
learned to use the courts, we see how attitudes toward women and women's own
self-images began slowly to change, initiating what M. Lewin has called, "a revolutionary process in the long run."[5]

But first, before listening to women in court, we need to understand the impact
of the Land Code, the controversial and inadequate document on which peasant
women based their new property rights.

The centerpiece of rural social legislation, the Land Code of 1922, essentially
reaffirmed peasant customary law except where it equalized women's legal position
within the household. Within the first years of its promulgation, jurists and lay
people alike recognized that the Land Code's provisions for equality were ill

thought out and incomplete; its framers evidently did not anticipate the scope of family conflicts their bold innovation would generate in light of the peasant woman's new right to divorce.

To give peasant women equality meant altering married women's relationship to family property. Before the Revolution, peasant women wielded more authority in daily life than has been recognized, yet women were not considered fully equal members of the household.[6] A married woman living with her husband's family was considered a family member only as long as she was married.[7] The Land Code, in Articles 66 and 67, changed her status by decreeing that all participants in the household, regardless of age or sex, are equal members, sharing equally in its land and property. Article 73 forbade discrimination based on age or sex in household property divisions.[8]

These articles became socially disruptive when coupled with women's new freedom to leave the household. In the prerevolutionary era, a wife customarily joined her husband's family upon marriage. It was unusual for her to abandon that household during his lifetime (except for a soldier's wife or a wife whose husband worked outside the village on a seasonal basis). A couple might separate and a court might order an abusive husband to support his wife and children with a specific amount of grain, money, or food, in accord with his means, but divorce was rare.[9] When divorce became common in the 1920s and a wife could simply leave her husband without having to demonstrate cause, the question of departure took on broad significance. As an equal member of the household, a co-owner of all its property, a departing wife seemed entitled to an equal share of that property.

A wife might insist on the return of her dowry (*pridanoe*), which traditionally women kept separate from household property, part of the property acquired jointly with her husband, pay owed for her work in the household, or a portion of the property of the household with a share for her and a share for her children.[10] When a couple had minor children who remained with their mother, a woman also requested child support (*alimenta*) in addition to her property share. Child support, awarded by a people's court, was theoretically independent of what a woman received as her share, but a husband could appeal to the people's court to lower or cease child support depending on the size of his wife's portion.[11]

It was not clear whether the Land Code intended that all wives, upon divorce, press such broad demands on the household. The Land Code, precise as to a wife's property rights on entering the household, did not clarify these rights on departure. In perhaps its chief omission, the code was silent on what length of time a wife needed to live and work in the household before she might ask for an equal share were she to leave.[12] Confusion developed when some jurists assumed that the Land Code did address that question in Article 75, which stipulated that a *razdel*—a sharing of all household property, including land, in a general division—could not be requested by persons who had not reached age eighteen and who had not participated in the household with their labor or means for more than two crop rotations (usually six years). Thus a young wife who left her husband after a few years of marriage or was forced out of the household due to intolerable conditions, in many instances left with only her dowry trunk.[13] A legal ruling in 1924 exempted married women from the eighteen-year-old provision, explaining that the stipulation concerning two crop rotations had been misinterpreted and did not apply to wives in a divorce, that Article 75 did not set a minimum time for work in order for a wife to qualify for a share but the time of absence from a household after which one's rights to a share would expire. But misinterpretations continued, and women were denied property.[14] At no point did the Land Code require a minimum residency for property rights upon departure. Thus the critical problem, since peasant divorces tended to occur in the early years of marriage, remained subject to interpretation.

Other premises of the Land Code appeared so at odds with customary law when examined in the context of divorce that they were largely ignored. For example, the Land Code set forth the principle that one became a member of the household with full property rights simply at marriage. But the people's courts in the 1920s did not use the fact of marriage as a guiding principle in dividing household property anymore than did township courts in the nineteenth century. Writing in the late nineteenth century, Aleksandra Efimenko believed that one could discern the overriding principle in customary law guiding the decisions of the commune and the peasant household in handling the division of homesteads and land, economic and social conflicts, and family relationships. The principle was labor. Labor and labor alone in the nineteenth century was the source of the right to the use of property.[15] The duration of labor expended in the household continued in the 1920s to determine a wife's share, a principle fair to the long-time core members of the household but not necessarily in the interests of women and children.[16]

Courts relied on their own and local peasant judgment as to the nature of a wife's work contribution. A wife who lived in a household for only several months, for example, was unlikely to receive a full share.[17] The people's court or the Land Commission made money or in-kind substitutions depending on the length of time she lived in the household and the extent of her contribution to the general economy.[18]

Confusion over a wife's rights upon departure from her husband's or in-law's household extended to questions of what property rights, if any, she still held in her parental home if she returned. Here, too, the Land Code disappointed. It did not speak to the question of property rights upon returning to a former household in case of divorce.[19]

According to Article 66, a woman lost membership rights in her family household when she left it to enter her husband's household. She could rejoin her parents' household now like any other new member, only with the permission of all its members and the agreement of the commune as well.[20] Such situations were awkward. A parental household might be reluctant to take in an *otkhodka* (divorced daughter). If the maternal grandparents were middle peasants who could provide their daughter and grandchildren with milk, eggs, and bread, the woman was unlikely to receive any support from her husband's household. If her parents were poor, the support she received might be minimal.[21]

Jurists disagreed about whether the Land Code intended a married woman to have any claim to property in her former parental home. Article 66 of the code stated that a woman entering her husband's household acquired the right to the use of land and general property in that household and lost the right to the use of land in her former household. The ruling seemed reasonable: the young woman did not need a land share from her former home, since she would receive a land share upon the next general division as a new member of her husband's household.[22] But wasn't she, like her brother, entitled to a share of movable property in return for work? After all, "she didn't sit in her father's house with folded hands."[23] The code did not answer. The Special Committee of Highest Control for Land Disputes seemed to resolve the question negatively by stating, in 1924, that a person entering a new household through marriage or as a *primak* (a man taken into a household that had no sons) lost rights to both land and property in the former household. But the plenum of the Supreme Court of the RSFSR in 1925 altered that ruling, declaring that such a person was deprived of land only because one could not use a land share in two households.[24]

How long a married daughter held movable-property rights in her parents' household became the focus of new controversy. The logic of Article 75 suggested that a daughter, as an equal member of the household, who left home to marry might still demand a share (*vydel*) for six years. But some legal experts denied that such a right existed, arguing that Article 75, in establishing a six-year limit after which one's absence prevented one from asking for a share, did not cover daughters who left the household to marry into another household.[25]

Several arguments were used against giving a woman who left her parents' household to marry the right to ask for a share of property for six years. They ranged from fear that a peasant with several daughters would face too heavy an economic threat to protests that a woman could "get rich" if she had property rights in two households.[26] Besides, a woman often took with her a dowry, which presumably represented her share of the household. According to a finding of the plenum of the Supreme Court, the dowry represented a woman's share of the family property. If she received a dowry, she could not ask for a further share.[27] The issue was additionally complicated by the provision that if her dowry was less than what she believed her share should have been, she could appeal to court.[28]

A woman's long-term relationship to her dowry, traditionally her separate property, was also unclear. When the Land Code made a new wife an equal member of her husband's household, it raised questions in the minds of some jurists concerning a woman's relationship to her dowry. If all property were now held in common, why should a woman be deemed sole owner of the property she brought with her. Only her personal property should be considered hers alone.[29] Personal property, as defined by Article 77 of the Land Code, was that property used exclusively by separate members of the household (for example, one's clothing).[30] Property in general use by the household, even though it might have been brought into the household or acquired separately by a member, was subject to division.[31]

Questions of the dowry heightened domestic tensions, since a woman's dowry might be extensive enough—like "a whole house," in the words of a contemporary—to enable her to run a separate domestic operation within her in-law's household, milking her own cow, weaving her own cloth, and clothing her own husband and children.[32] To qualify for a property share upon departure, was a divorced woman to forgo her dowry?

It was not easy to dispense with old customs. The peasant, when he did not like Soviet legislation, sometimes ignored it.[33] So too did his wife. When it was to a woman's advantage to cling to customary law, she did so. A wife leaving a husband invariably demanded return of all her dowry: clothing, linen, utensils, cattle, and money. Article 77 added to the confusion by indicating that local custom would be taken into account in determining personal property as long as it was not in conflict with general law.[34]

Prerevolutionary practices continued with considerable regional variations.[35] In one village in Orlov province in the 1920s, a woman's cattle were returned if the marriage was not more than two years old. In Briansk province if a wife lived in a household for five or six years, the dowry usually fused with the general property and she was given a share of the household on a general basis.[36] If a wife brought in a foal, a husband could not argue that she was not entitled to take with her the grown horse it had become. The mature animal in part compensated for her loss of money and for items in the dowry that had been used up over the years.[37] Nor could a wife claim the issue from her dowry—for example, a calf born to a cow she had brought with her. The calf was the new property of the household.[38]

Money questions were also complex, since money received in a dowry rarely remained money but was converted to inventory or farmstead repairs. Frequently, a wife would accuse a husband of holding back cattle purchased with the money from her dowry or of using her dowry money for building. But just as used-up property could not be returned, neither could money used for family expenses be reimbursed.[39]

Suits involving movable property were difficult enough to resolve; cases involving a wife's request for a share of land as well created even greater problems. The Land Code obscured a woman's rights to land by its silence on whether or not a divorced woman was entitled to a share of land upon her departure—a curious omission, since the household's land increased with her entry.[40] Some guidance was provided by Article 74, which distinguished between a *vydel,* a simple sharing of property, and a *razdel,* a division that resulted in two separate households. If a departing member of the household was not planning for or was unable to establish a new farmstead, that member received a *vydel*—theoretically an equal share of the general property, excluding land.[41] A *razdel*—a full division of the property, including land—was permitted by a Land Commission only when separating members over the age of eighteen (married women could be under eighteen) planned to establish their own farms and when there was sufficient land and inventory to form a new living unit without hurting the existing household. The basic rule in a division was that each farmstead be viable. If these conditions could not be met, a land division was not permitted and a portion of general property was simply shared out.[42]

Government organs assured divorced women that if they wanted to farm independently they could receive land from either the household or the communal land fund.[43] The People's Commissariat of Agriculture, assuming a divorced woman's right to land, published sample cases which suggested that women were routinely awarded shares by land commissions.[44]

Yet candid articles in the Commissariat of Agriculture's journal indicated that whatever her intentions to farm and her legal rights to a land share, a peasant wife who left her husband was not likely to receive a share of land in his village.[45] Since most peasant divorces occurred in the early years of marriage after a wife had worked only briefly in the household, a wife's share of movable property would be considered too small and her means too meager to entitle her to establish her own farm. Meanwhile she had lost land rights in her former household. The outcome was virtual landlessness for young, divorced peasant women.

Recognizing the weakness of the Land Code, commentators suggested in the Commissariat of Agriculture's journal a revision whereby a peasant woman's land share in her parents' household be preserved for her at least until the next land redistribution in that commune.[46] Or, since most land communes reportedly violated the rules and tended to redistribute land every year rather than once every three years (each crop rotation), that a woman's land share be preserved for three years after her marriage. Then if she divorced, she could be assured of either land back home or a property share in her husband's household appropriate to her three years of labor. With that property, she could begin to develop a new household.[47]

Despite the omissions of the Land Code, and the occasional disinclination of land societies to grant women land, a certain number of divorced women did receive land—if not from communal land societies, then from Land Commissions upon appeal.[48] Once receiving land shares, divorced women faced new problems, especially if they were single mothers trying to farm alone without grown children. Before the Revolution, in areas where men were away at seasonal labor (*otkhod*), women ran the farmsteads. Their experience may not have been relevant, however, to the average woman who found herself single in the 1920s as a result of divorce. In the *otkhod* areas, the money sent by husbands or sons enabled women to hire help to plow—the farm task that even strong women seldom performed.[49]

In the 1920s, a divorced woman who received a share of land was unlikely to have other means of support to enable her to farm. She might rent out her land, returning to her parents in another village. Living with her parents, but not as a legal member of their household because she held land in another commune, a woman might circumvent the law that forbade holding land in two households by working land rented in her father's name.[50]

A divorced woman might become a *batrachka,* a member of the rural proletariat, living at a neighbor's or with a relative, perhaps a married brother or sister, and hiring out by the day. If she had children to care for, finding work might be difficult. A *batrachka* earned little: beekeeping, serving as domestic or watchwoman, market farming, shepherding, or working in the farmstead or field (gathering, reaping, and weeding). An average monthly income of less than 20 rubles in the countryside was considered low, but, by some accounts, the total monthly wage of the *batrachka* rarely exceeded 6 rubles.[51] A *batrachka* could hire out for spring and summer agricultural labor at about 60 to 75 rubles a season, which left her without income in winter. She might fill in with domestic work, perhaps in the household of a local teacher or priest. A large number of poor women joined the ranks of the seasonal workers in the sugar, peat, and fishing industries.[52]

Yet some divorced women, some 11 percent according to the 1926 census, did manage to stay on their land. A woman might arrange that her employer plow her land as part of her wages. Or she might rent out part of her land to another peasant in return for his plowing and sowing the portion remaining to her. Or she might rent all the land for half the produce or contract to cede a part of her farmstead and property to another peasant in return for his promise to work her land and pay her taxes. If she was middle-aged, she might request that he provide for her until her death. In the case of a younger woman, a son might reach the age when he could help farm.[53] In some instances, a woman's parental family worked the land share given to her.[54]

The Land Code, then, provided the legal basis on which a woman separating could demand property, but its framers, failing to foresee how broadly disruptive the rights to both household equality and divorce would be, left crucial issues unresolved. Silent on the questions of minimum residency required for a full property share, a divorced woman's rights to land on departure, and her property rights in her former parental household, the code could not facilitate the resolution of questions likely to arise during a divorce when the tension between customary law and Soviet legality would be greatest. At the local level, nineteenth-century practices, with their regional variations, tended to continue making it uncertain that women would benefit from new egalitarian principles.

According to village correspondents:

> A woman is allotted a share on a general basis if she lived in the household not less than three years. If less than three years, she gets nothing. (Vologodskii province)

> When a woman leaves alone, nothing is given. A woman without children does not appeal to the court. (Bashkiria republic)

> A woman receives the same share if she leaves alone or with children. If she worked in the household for five to eight years, she stays put—especially when she has children and her husband is obliged to build a new hut. (Viatskoi province)

> When a woman goes out from the household alone, she is given nothing. They say, "Stay. No one is banishing you." Women who leave with children are apportioned better than childless women. (Saratov province)

> If a woman alone separates, she gets some cattle, a cow or sheep, and maybe a barn or a room. When she leaves with children, she receives a proportional amount of the property. (Orlov province)[55]

Other sources claimed the following:

> Wives usually take their dowry besides a small amount given in a *vydel* (share).[56]

> A peasant woman after living for three years with her husband's family gets two or three pounds of flour and a few sacks of potatoes.[57]

> A wife being "kicked out" of a household is usually given only her own clothing.[58]

> In 50 percent of the cases, women are cheated by the household. "To women they try to allot worse."

> "To receive her share, a woman must go to court. The old people try to do her out of her share."[59]

It is to peasant women in court that we now turn. Whether appealing to the people's court for movable property or to Land Commission courts for land as well, women, unskilled in legal matters, needed help to prepare their cases. Despite Soviet protestations to the contrary, going to court was complicated. In prerevolutionary days, the process may have been easier. Under the township court system, which lasted from the emancipation of 1861 until 1912, depositions were oral. Complaints were delivered to the township elder, township scribe, or the judges themselves.[60] Although legal provision was made for permitting oral deposition by peasants in the people's courts and Land Commissions, in practice Land Commissions did not use the provision, which meant that peasant women—most of whom were illiterate—had to get legal help or at least find a literate person to bring a suit in writing. "You can scarcely find ten Land Commissions in which oral declarations are taken," one source complained.[61] Red tape, the distance of the courts, a wait of three or four months for a case to be considered, and indifferent, ill-informed workers complicated processes, particularly at the local levels.[62] While unknown numbers of women remained unaided largely because they lived in areas lacking party representation, village *sel'kory* (correspondents), contributors to the new Soviet journals, and *delegatki* (delegates to the Women's Section of the Communist Party) helped women prepare cases for Land Commissions and people's courts.[63] The Commissariat of Agriculture held public meetings at which significant and frequently occurring cases could be examined.[64]

The rural party network also acquainted peasant women with the appeals process, a legal innovation largely unavailable in the postemancipation era. Township courts in the 1860s were courts of original and final appeal whose decisions could be overturned only on procedural grounds.[65] In the 1920s, people's courts and township Land Commissions functioned as courts of first instance. Peasant women who believed that their legal rights had been violated locally could appeal to provincial courts. If still dissatisfied, they could appeal further to the Special Committee of Highest Control for Land Disputes or to the provincial procurator, in cases involving movable property. If complaints were considered well-founded, the procurator would give the case to the Supreme Court.[66] Appeals courts, closer to sources of Soviet ideology, might reverse decisions in a woman's favor.

Peasants—generally from poor households[67]—were inventive in seeking to thwart departing wives. One strategy was to deny that a woman was a legal member of the household. Wives who were not legally married—that is, whose liaisons or church marriages were not registered with the civil authorities—were particularly vulnerable. After the Marriage and Family Code of 1926 recognized de facto marriages as legal, the provision of the Land Code giving spouses equal rights to use household property was interpreted in the courts to mean unregistered (de facto) as well as registered wives.[68] But the household and the local courts sometimes interpreted the Land Code otherwise, saying that persons entering the household through an unregistered marriage acquired rights as members only after registering with the village soviet's list of homesteads. Among peasants, many de facto wives, whose marriages were unregistered, were not registered with the village soviet either. When these women sought a property share, they might learn in court that they had no property claim, that the household regarded them as working women or servants entitled only to small wages.[69] The Supreme Court in 1927 decreed that these women, often the weakest members of society, should not be deprived of rights due to failure to register. Local courts should examine a de facto wife's work contribution and compensate her accordingly.[70]

Even a de facto wife registered with the village soviet might be vulnerable. Consider Babaeva, originally a worker in the household and then a de facto wife, who sought a property share in 1926. Her husband, who left her, had been taking care of the household for an absentee owner. He received two-fifths of the property but the people's court evicted Babaeva, leaving her with nothing, on the ground that the owner had never agreed to her membership. Babaeva, who argued that she was registered with her children in the household lists as a household member, appealed successfully to the Supreme Court.[71]

K. A. Akimova found the appeals court sensitive to her right to a share of property in return for labor even when the letter of the law seemed to validate her husband's claim. Akimova had worked in her husband's household from 1921 to 1927, until she became ill and he divorced her, sending her to her brother. Akimova demanded a property share. The people's court recognized her property claim based on her work in the household, but since she could not farm because of illness, the court decreed that instead of a property share, her former husband, a middle peasant, must give her living quarters, heated and lighted, and support of 10 rubles a month. Her husband appealed, arguing that an obligation to support his former wife for life contradicted the provision of the 1926 Family and Marriage Code that a needy spouse receive support for only one year. The Supreme Court, upholding the original decision, explained that the support payments were simply in lieu of a property share to which Akimova was entitled because of her years of work in the household.[72]

Mariia Osipova appealed when her husband, Ivan Vasil'ev, tried to circumvent a court-awarded division in which the people's court awarded her and their child two-thirds of the general property of the household—198 rubles in all. A canny peasant, Ivan sold those articles which were assigned to Mariia, leaving in the household only items that, according to Article 56 of the Family and Marriage Code, could not be sold away from the household. Article 56 stipulated that when the personal means of a member of the household were insufficient to provide child support, the support was to come from that member's share of general property but only in money or products. Neither land, cattle, inventory, nor other objects of general use in the household could be forcibly taken.[73] The public prosecutor intervened on Mariia's behalf. A Supreme Court ruling found that Ivan had deliberately tried to circumvent the people's court: therefore, Mariia's share had to come from the remaining property.[74]

S. M. Urvacheva, another peasant wife who received justice upon appeal, initially received a property share for herself and her little daughter when she left her husband. But Urvacheva subsequently returned, working in the household for another year and a half. Her daughter died, and she left again. Her former husband tried to keep her property share, objecting that one of the parties to the share was no longer alive. The Supreme Court upheld the property division, explaining that as a rule a child's share must remain with the mother since it was given with the assumption that a new household was being formed.[75]

Generational conflict between fathers and sons was a familiar feature of village life. But when a daughter-in-law separated and asked for her property share, fathers and sons closed ranks. Mariia Gavrilova appealed in 1922 to the Supreme Court because her husband and her father-in-law arranged for a fictitious division between them, a common peasant device to deprive former wives of property. Mariia explained that after she requested a divorce, her husband and his father falsely claimed that they had divided the property between them and that neither now had sufficient property to divide again. Her husband contended that their marriage had been illegal. The court decided in Mariia's favor, pointing out that even if there had been no marriage, Mariia and her children still had the legal right to a property share because she had worked in the household for about twelve years.[76]

Anna Smirnova and Anna Nikiforova are examples of peasant women who, forced by in-laws to sign papers in which they gave up their property rights, launched successful court appeals. When Smirnova, the wife of a Red Army man, was pushed out of the household by her father-in-law, he had her sign a statement that she left willingly, taking all that was hers. Anna had to promise not to ask for anything more—not even grain. Smirnova subsequently appealed for a share of land and property. Both her father-in-law and her husband (who had by now divorced her) contended that Anna deserved nothing because she had worked so briefly in the household. The Land Commission, recognizing that she had worked for eight months, awarded Anna 5 rubles for each month—40 rubles in all to be paid in two installments. Anna, not satisfied, turned to the Moscow provincial Land Commission, which ruled that Anna, an equal member of the household and not a hired worker, had a right to a *razdel* (division of land and property). The court ordered an investigation to determine its scope.[77]

The appeals court upheld property rights for women exploited for their summer labor. When Anna Nikiforova, a poor working woman, married Fedor Isakov in the late winter of 1926, his family had her sign a contract in which she agreed not to be recognized as a family member until after two years. If she left before then, they had no obligation to give her a share or wages. In the autumn, the family began to force her out. Fearing a suit, they had her sign a statement that she left freely. Anna subsequently sued in the people's court for the things she brought into the household and wages for March through October 1926—100 rubles. The people's court denied the validity of the contract, recognizing her instead as an equal member of the household, not with wages owing, but with a share due her.[78] The provincial court concurred.

Not all peasant women who went to court were victims. An occasional peasant woman used the Land Code's complexities to advantage. The case of Turbabina suggests not only the resourcefulness of some peasant women, but the difficulties rural Russia had in understanding the Land Code. Turbabina, who married in 1923, left her husband that same year, subsequently suing him in people's court for the harvest from the land share he received when she entered his family household. She based her claim on Article 75 of the Land Code, which preserved for two crop rotations her right to a property share. The people's court in 1926, establishing the value of the harvest from Turbabina's land share for the years 1924 through 1926, less the cost of processing that harvest, awarded Turbabina 49 rubles, 50 kopeks. Her husband appealed. His wife, he claimed, had left him in 1923 and went to live with her father in another commune. He argued on the basis of Article 66 that Turbabina had lost her rights, having left his household. The Supreme Court pointed out that Article 66 was inapplicable because it applied only to the reverse situation—leaving the parental household to marry. The court explained that Turbabina, in leaving her husband, did not lose her right to the land given her by the commune—on the basis of Article 75 it was preserved for her for six years—but neither did she reacquire rights in her parents' household. On the other hand, the court pointed out that a significant question remained unsettled: Was Turbabina using land in the farmstead in which she now lived, and did she not therefore lose her right to land in her former husband's household, since land could not be held in two households? The case was referred back to another people's court.[79]

Winning a lawsuit, a heady victory, could be empty from a material point of view. It was by no means certain that Babaeva, Urvacheva, Akimova, Gavrilova, or any divorced woman would actually see her court-awarded share because of problems in collecting property from hard-pressed or unwilling peasant households. Reportedly, a simple court ruling in a property division that "domestic property should be divided equally" was impossible to execute, calling forth endless arguments. A household needed a detailed directive as to exactly which household and farm objects should go to whom.[80] Support was the hardest to collect. Some bailiffs estimated that 50 to 90 percent of support awards to divorced peasant women went unfulfilled.[81] In urban divorces, wages could be attached—an impossibility in the peasant household, where family members protested that there was no money and, pleading Article 56, nothing to sell to raise funds to satisfy even a court award of 5 rubles a month to a child.[82] No wonder that a peasant woman would call out in frustration at a public forum in 1926 that for a child's upkeep even a father's "cow should be sold."[83]

The value of describing peasant women's court cases is to be measured not in the uncertain relationship of court-recorded settlements to a woman's eventual property in hand, but in the contribution the case descriptions make to our understanding of the evolving psychological landscape of rural Russia. A survey of peasant divorce litigation is a study not only of family tensions but of peasant strategies encompassing both male and female protest. Unlike their nineteenth-century counterparts, aggrieved rural women in the 1920s found a support network. New Soviet periodicals, such as *Bednota* and *Krest'ianka,* eager to hear the peasant woman's voice—even in a dictated letter—encouraged correspondence, gave advice, and expressed anger at the discrepancy between the Revolution's egalitarian ideology and a divorced woman's failure to receive justice locally.[84] *Bednota,* in particular, saw itself as the voice of village society, calling on governmental organs like the Commissariat of Justice to fulfill their responsibilities toward poor women.[85]

It is impossible to determine how many women's "letters to the press" were genuine village products and how many the construct of editors concerned to further progressive political goals. But the newspaper *Bednota* described a "huge number" of bitter letters from peasant women complaining that the village soviets did not defend their rights as they were supposed to, helping to inventory possessions and making certain that a woman received child support or her court-awarded land or property share.[86] Court order in hand, women went from court officer to head of the police trying in vain to get orders filled.[87] Some found themselves destitute and forced to beg. In other instances, recently divorced peasant women who did not understand why they were without land in either their parents' or their husbands' households had scribes write letters of protest for them to Moscow, assuming that court action denying them a land share was some kind of punishment for their "profane" attitudes toward marriage.[88]

As peasant women voiced grievances to the press, unhappy households, concerned to protect their economies and resentful of a daughter-in-law's right to depart with property she may not have participated in acquiring, suggested, also to the press, that the Land Code be modified further to weaken a divorced woman's property rights. Demands came for the peasant couple to treat property as the urban couple did—dividing only what they had acquired since their marriage.[89] An irate peasant in Voronezh province questioned the equity of giving a full share to his brother's former wife who had worked in the household for seven years when his mother had worked for forty-five years and the property had been acquired by his father.[90] Another observer wondered why a peasant woman returning to her family needed any property, since both households were probably fairly equal economically.[91] Suggestions called for a minimum time before which a wife could not ask for property upon leaving the household: three to six years. Or more extreme, that Article 75 be applied to wives—that a wife not be entitled to ask for a property share until she had worked in the household for six years.[92] One angry peasant advised young village women to get to know their future husbands better before marriage so that they would not be inclined to leave them after two or three months.[93]

The bitterness of young husbands was expressed in yet another way. New forms of *chastushki*—popular peasant limericks that the historian V. P. Danilov calls a largely untapped source for rural social history in the 1920s—reflected the social impact of divorce. A husband protested:

> When we divorced in ZAGS (civil registry office)
> My wife went to court
> She wanted to take what we have
> I won't give her anything.

> My wife went mad.
> She sued me twice
> She wants half the land.
> And if I won't give her half
> She wants all the household.
> Now my father beats me
> So that I'll know better in the future.

> My wife divorced me
> She is crazy.
> She wants to destroy my family.
> She wants everything.
> She lived with me for one year
> But she wants goods for five years.[94]

Nonetheless, the late 1920s saw some movement to reinforce the property interests of peasant women. In 1927, the Commissariat of Agriculture issued a new set of instructions on family property divisions in which labor contribution was legalized as the basic principle of division. A wife's rights were, however, safeguarded. The extent of a woman's dowry would be taken into account, as well as the monetary contribution of an absent member.[95] Peasant proposals of a residence requirement before a wife could ask for a property share were rejected, as was an attempt to reduce wives' shares in comparison with that of core members of the household. Wives, children, and the elderly were given primary right to remain in the household even if the wife instigated the family separation. Before the new instructions, if a wife initiated a division the Land Commission frequently told her to construct a new household.[96]

According to a Soviet student of the Land Commissions, they were tending in the late 1920s to defend the interests of the "weaker" side of the household: the women, children, and elderly. Insofar as they did so, they abided by Soviet law that directed Land Commissions to aid the "less aware" litigants to obtain evidence on their own behalf—an interventionist stance that courts before the Revolution did not assume.[97] While Land Commissions might callously ignore Soviet directives—for example, illegally permitting a household to divide land only among its male members—in some instances they infringed on the law on women's behalf, ignoring Article 66, which stated that upon marriage women lost all rights to land in their parents' households. Instead, they permitted women to resume former rights to land in the family household, even as the Commissariat of Agriculture debated the issue.[98]

At the end of the decade, questions of a woman's right to land and property became largely moot with the onset of collectivization. The Land Commissions called into being in 1922 by wide-scale quarrels over land were abolished in 1930 as unnecessary because, as the official position explained, collectivization would sharply curtail individual household arguments.[99]

As the issue of a peasant woman's right to land and property faded, she had still not achieved real political equality. Despite the changes wrought by World War I, when women became a majority of the rural labor force (71.9 percent of the total labor force during the war was female rural labor), and despite their new legal status and greater importance after 1917, rural women in the 1920s were unlikely to head households and were kept, by tradition and public scorn, from attending communal gatherings.[100] Local authorities sometimes ignored women's equality—for example, neglecting to seek women's views in property divisions despite the rule that approval of all adult members of a dividing household was required to register a division.[101]

Village soviets, weak and backward and often not reading or understanding instructions about land divisions, kept women, the majority of the rural population, subordinate, mocking them, preventing their political participation, ignoring women's representatives (*delegatki*) whom they were supposed to include in meetings, and scaring off less aggressive women.[102] Heavy pressure from the Soviet government raised the proportion of women in the rural soviets from 1 percent in 1922 to about 10 percent in 1925, but positions of authority—chairs in soviets and officerships in the commune—remained with men. Even in areas where men worked away from home seasonally and women ran the farms in their absence, men were chosen for the soviets, although they rarely fulfilled their civic responsibilities since they were away for most of the year.[103]

If equality eluded peasant women, their numbers seeking divorce by the late 1920s caused peasant concern that familiar values and ways of life were being threatened.[104] The number of land disputes in the 1920s during the process of partitioning households—a proportion of which were divorce cases—was said to have reached "epidemic proportions."[105] One local justice estimated that a third of the claims in the area's Land Commission emanated from women who frequently referred not to local custom but to Soviet law, an indication that some rural women were beginning to identify with the new regime.[106]

That significant numbers of peasant women saw themselves in bold new ways is, however, dubious. Indeed, evidence in *chastushki* suggests that divorced peasant women tended to cling to traditional values. Although a woman could sing

> Soviet power!
> I'm not afraid of my husband
> If he beats me
> I'll divorce him

and boldly declaim

> Why are you speaking nonsense my friend
> That you won't give me my share.
> If you fool around long enough
> I'll go to court and tell them about it.

young women concluded that

> To live without a husband
> Is to grieve all the time.
> A fate no one would want.[107]

Yet the same woman who longed for a new husband might, as a result of her interaction with the Soviet legal system, be changed in subtle ways. My premise is that for young divorced women who learned to use the courts, litigation was one area that facilitated personal growth. It is true that peasant women since the 1860s had been going to court with domestic grievances; however, the experience of litigation in the 1920s appeared more conducive to developing a heightened sense of self. Soviet legislation played a role, as did the supportive milieu in which party and press aided peasant women in using their new legal rights to counter the local traditions and ad hominum practices of customary law.[108] Moreover, in the 1920s, peasant women used strategies unavailable to women in the post-1860s—most notably the elaborate appeals process.

So, too, did men. The focus of this article has been on young peasant women in the divorce process, but as wives learned to use the courts, husbands and fathers-in-law fought back using defensive strategies of their own, including appeals to Soviet law and attempts to circumvent that law to their own advantage as in bogus household divisions and coercive contracts.

The agility of the peasantry, both male and female, in responding to new institutions and laws and the persistence with which the minority of peasants involved in divorces pressed claims through the courts suggests a peasant society in the 1920s that was adaptive and inventive in pursuing self-defined interests.

Notes

I am grateful to the National Endowment for the Humanities, the International Research and Exchanges Board, and Wells College for research support, to William T. Shinn, Peter H. Solomon, and Lynne Viola for useful suggestions, and to Wendy Z. Goldman for generously sharing bibliography.

1. "Spravki chitateliam," *Bednota,* December 3, 1926, p. 3.

2. V. P. Danilov, "O russkoi chastushke kak istochnike po istorii derevni," in B. B. Piotrovskii, ed., *Sovetskaia kul'tura 70 let razvitiia* (Moscow, 1987), p. 384; *Vsesoiuznaia perepis' naseleniia 1926 goda* (Moscow, 1931), vol. 43, p. 23, for statistics on divorce age. The greatest number of divorces in the villages, for men as well as for women, occurred between ages twenty and twenty-four years. The average length of marriage ending in divorce in the countryside was 2.4 years. M. Kaplun, "Brachnost' naseleniia RSFSR," *Statisticheskoe obozrenie*, no. 7 (July 1929): 96–97.

3. *Vserossiiskii tsentral'nyi ispolnitel'nyi komitet XII sozyva. Vtoraia sessiia* (Moscow, 1925), pp. 304–5, for figure for 1924. For the late 1920s, see I. Ganeev, "V zashchitu prav krest'ianki na zemliu," *Sel'sko-khoziaistvennaia zhizn'*, no. 3 (1928): 10; *Bednota,* April 18, 1927, p. 3; and V. Nemytskii, "K voprosu o normakh nedrobimosti dvora," *Sel'sko-khoziaistvennaia zhizn'*, no. 33 (1928): 17. For partitions, see M. Kubanin, *Klassovaia sushchnost' protsessa drobleniia krest'ianskikh khoziaistv* (Moscow, 1929), p. 75, and Teodor Shanin, *The Awkward Class* (London, 1972), p. 176. For statistics for Moscow and Leningrad, see Tsentral'noe statisticheskoe upravlenie, *Statisticheskii spravochnik SSSR za 1928* (Moscow, 1929), pp. 76–79. For only registered divorces counted, see R. S. Clem, ed., *Research Guide to the Russian and Soviet Censuses* (Ithaca, N.Y., 1986), p. 144. For census figures, see *Vsesoiuznaia perepis' naseleniia 1926 goda,* vol. 26 (Moscow, 1930).

Another source gives higher divorce figures, stating that in 1927 almost 11 percent of all men and 9 percent of women entering marriage in the countryside had been previously married and divorced. W. Goldman, "Women, the Family, and the New Revolutionary Order in the Soviet Union," in S. Kruks et al., eds., *Promissory Notes* (New York, 1989), p. 65.

4. *Bednota,* June 26, 1926, p. 2; July 27, 1926, p. 2; and June 11, 1927, p. 2, for party work among rural women.

5. M. Lewin, *The Making of the Soviet System* (New York, 1985), p. 55; E. H. Carr, *Socialism in One Country, 1924–1926* (Baltimore, 1970), vol. I, p. 233, on the growing independence of peasant women in the 1920s.

6. For women's status, see Beatrice Farnsworth, "The Litigious Daughter-in-Law: Family Relations in Rural Russia in the Second Half of the Nineteenth Century," *Slavic Review* 45, no. 1 (Spring 1986): 49–64. For lack of equality in the household, see V. F. Mukhin, *Obychnyi poriadok' nasledovaniia u krest'ian* (St. Petersburg, 1888), p. 99.

7. G. Ryndziunskii, "Voprosy deistvuiushchego semeinogo prava imushchestvennyi vydel zheny," *Ezhenedel'nik Sovetskoi iustitsii,* no. 14–15 (1922): 11 (official organ of the People's Commissariat of Justice; hereafter, *ESI*).

8. *Zemel'nyi kodeks RSFSR* (Moscow, 1923), p. 14; E. Dombrovskii, *Krest'ianskii dvor i semeino-imushchestvennye razdely* (Moscow, 1926), p. 5; for women's property rights in divisions in the second half of the nineteenth century, see I. N. Milogolova, "Semeinye

razdely v russkoi poreformennoi derevne," *Vestnik Moskovskogo universiteta* no. 6 (1987): 45.

9. S. V. Pakhman, *Obychnoe grazhdanskoe pravo v Rossii,* 2 vols. (St. Petersburg, 1877–79), vol. 2, pp. 92, 97–100, 152, for court sanctioned separations. A healthy wife who left her husband in the nineteenth century and could not demonstrate cruelty might be told to support herself. Ibid., p. 99.

10. "Semeino-imushchestvennyi razdel krest'ianskogo dvora," *ESI,* no. 44–45 (1925): 1390–91.

11. *Bednota,* November 3, 1926, p. 4.

12. On the inadequacy of the Land Code, see K. M. Gazalova, "Zemel'nyi sud RSFSR i poriadok rassmotreniia spornykh del o semeino-imushchestvennykh razdelakh krest'ianskikh khoziaistv (1921–1928 g.)" in *Trudy Moskovskogo gosudarstvennogo istoriko-arkhivnogo instituta po istorii gosudarstvennykh uchrezhdenii SSSR* (Moscow, 1965), vol. 19, p. 213, and E. I. Dombrovskii, "O krest'ianskikh semeino-imushchestvennykh razdelakh," *Proletarskii Sud,* no. 8–9 (1925): 9. For silence concerning a required residency, see A. N. Granina, "Lichnyi sostav krest'ianskogo dvora," *Pravo i zhizn',* no. 10 (December 1924): 34.

13. Nezhdanov, "Bol'nye voprosy krest'ianskogo dvora," *Pravo i zhizn',* no. 7–8 (October 1924): 115–16.

14. Dombrovskii, *Krest'ianskii dvor,* pp. 20–21, 34; for Supreme Court's correct interpretation of Article 75, see V. S., "Krest'ianskii dvor v praktike Verkhsuda RSFSR," *Vlast' sovetov,* no. 30–31 (July 1928): 11. For peasant wives deprived of their rights on the basis of Article 75, see Nezhdanov, "Bol'nye voprosy," pp. 115–16; V. S., "Krest'ianskii dvor," pp. 10–11; and *Bednota,* February 28, 1923, p. 1. For more on family property divisions, see Milogolova, "Semeinye razdely," p. 42.

15. Lewin, *Making of the Soviet System,* p. 76.

16. For the work principle, see *Sudebnaia praktika RSFSR,* no. 21 (1928): 9; Dombrovskii, "O krest'ianskikh semeino-imushchestvennykh razdelakh," p. 9; and Gazalova, "Zemel'nyi sud RSFSR," p. 213. In determining household divisions, Land Commissions tended to follow the Land Code, dividing property by the number of "eaters." Gazalova, "Zemel'nyi sud RSFSR," p. 213.

17. Dombrovskii, *Krest'ianskii dvor,* pp. 20–21, 34.

18. "Stranitsa agitpropbiuro pri kollegii NKIu: Kak proizvodit' semeino-imushchestvennye razdely," *ESI,* no. 37 (1927): 1157. On money substitution, see *Sudebnaia praktika,* no. 18 (1927): 10. A wife of six months in a household whose value was estimated at 3,090 rubles received a share worth 90 rubles. A. P. Emel'ianov, *Spornye zemel'nye dela* (Moscow, 1926), pp. 52–53.

19. "Stranitsa praktika: Prava chlenov krest'ianskogo dvora, vstupivshikh po braku ili priimachestvu," *ESI,* no. 35 (1927): 1087.

20. Granina, "Lichnyi sostav krest'ianskogo dvora," p. 34; B. K. Tumskii, "V zashchitu prav krest'ianki na zemliu," *Sel'sko-khoziaistvennaia zhizn',* no. 37 (September 1927): 19.

21. On parental reluctance, see *Vserossiiskii tsentral'nyi ispolnitel'nyi komitet XII sozyva. III sessiia* (Moscow, 1926), pp. 683–84; on support, see *Vserossiiskii tsentral'nyi ispolnitel'nyi komitet XII sozyva. Vtoraia sessiia,* p. 232. One peasant woman, age twenty-two with a child, divorced her middle-peasant husband, age twenty-five, and returned to her father, a *bedniak* (poor peasant). A *bedniak*'s income in the late 1920s was estimated at 80 rubles a year. She requested child support and 5 rubles for a blanket she bought for her child. She was awarded 3 rubles for the blanket and 7 rubles a month in child support, but for only

one year. *ESI,* no. 1 (1928): 31. On *bedniak* income, see Lewin, *Making of the Soviet System,* p. 130. A peasant who was considered well-off—with at least two horses and two cows—would have to pay more. A twenty-five-year-old disabled peasant woman with one child who was divorced from a prosperous peasant after two years of marriage asked for compensation for her two years of work and 20 rubles for the child. She was awarded 10 rubles for her work and 20 rubles a month for the child. *ESI,* no. 1 (1928): 30.

22. "Spravki chitateliam," *Bednota,* December 3, 1926, p. 3, and "Nuzhno li nam pridanoe?" *Bednota,* April 8, 1927, p. 2.

23. *Bednota,* April 8, 1927, p. 2.

24. Dombrovskii, "O krest'ianskikh semeino-imushchestvennykh razdelakh," p. 9; S. Fisunov, "Prava chlenov krest'ianskogo dvora, vstupivshikh po brak ili priimachestvu," *ESI,* no. 35 (1927): 1087; *Bednota,* October 19, 1926, p. 3.

25. O. Shteger, "Esche o krest'ianskikh razdelakh," *Proletarskii sud,* no. 10–11 (December 1925): 13; I. Tumanov, "Razdel zemledel'cheskogo trudovogo dvora," *Proletarskii sud,* no. 1–2 (1925): 8.

26. Dombrovskii, "O krest'ianskikh semeino-imushchestvennykh razdelakh," p. 9; S. Fisunov, "Prava chlenov krest'ianskogo dvora vstupivshikh po braku ili priimachestvu," *ESI,* no. 35 (1927): 1087.

27. Dombrovskii, "O krest'ianskikh semeino-imushchestvennykh razdelakh," p. 9.

28. *Bednota,* October 19, 1926, p. 3.

29. G. Ryndziunskii, "Krest'ianskii dvor," *ESI,* no. 43 (1922): 4.

30. Government assurance that a woman might keep her dowry implied personal items only. See Dombrovskii, *Krest'ianskii dvor,* p. 14, for assurances.

31. *ESI,* no. 27 (1925): 951; Shteger, "Esche o krest'ianskikh razdelakh," p. 13.

32. Milogolova, "Semeinye razdely," p. 40.

33. Lewin, *Making of the Soviet System,* p. 75.

34. *ESI,* no. 27 (1925): 951.

35. In the nineteenth century, cattle and money were called *nadelok.* The money might go to her husband and the cattle might become part of the general property. Aleksandra Efimenko, "Krest'ianskaia zhenshchina," *Delo* (1873): 93; for local variations, see Mukhin, *Obychnyi poriadok,* p. 89, and Pakhman, *Obychnoe grazhdanskoe pravo v Rossii,* vol. 2, p. 132.

36. V. P. Danilov, *Sovetskaia dokolkhoznaia derevnia* (Moscow, 1977), pp. 247–48.

37. G. Ryndziunskii, "Voprosy deistvuiushchego semeinogo prava. Pridanoe zheny," *ESI,* no. 18 (1922): 4; A. Brianskii, "Vosmozhno li po delam semeino-imushchestvennykh razdelov krest'ianskogo dvora vzyskivat' skot, vyroshchennyi ukhodom otvetchika," *ESI,* no. 20 (1927): 604.

38. Ryndziunskii, "Voprosy deistvuiushchego," p. 4.

39. Ibid.

40. "Nadeliat' ili net?" *Bednota,* August 2, 1925, p. 2.

41. D. Rozenblium, "Razdel dvora," *ESI,* no. 27 (1927): 820.

42. Ibid., *ESI,* no. 37 (1927): 1156–57; Dombrovskii, *Krest'ianskii dvor,* pp. 19–20; *Bednota,* December 18, 1926, p. 1. A *razdel* did not necessarily imply equal shares to participants. The Land Commissions had the right to determine whether an equal division would give one side more than was necessary for a viable farm and the other side less. *ESI,* no. 37 (1927): 1157.

43. "Spravochnik krest'ianki," *Krest'ianka,* no. 4 (1922): 22; see Articles 82 and 83, *Zemel'nyi kodeks RSFSR,* p. 15, and B. K. Tumskii, *Kak delitsia zemlia i imushchestvo pri semeinykh razdelakh* (Moscow, 1926), pp. 27, 28, 47. If a household lacked sufficient farmstead (*usadba*) land to divide, land had to be taken from the communal land fund. Field

land would be taken from the household only if the communal land fund did not have a supply of land.

44. In one case a former wife was to receive 250 rubles to be paid out in 50-ruble installments over a five-year period and land which would be divided by "eaters" (i.e., the number of people in the household). In another example, a former wife was given land for two eaters, half of the farmstead (*usadba*), a house measuring twelve by ten, a six-year-old horse, a cow with a calf, and 100 rubles. A. P. Emel'ianov, *Spornye zemel'nye dela* (Moscow, 1926), pp. 34–35.

45. B. K. Tumskii, "V zashchitu prav krest'ianki na zemliu," *Sel'sko-khoziaistvennaia zhizn'*, no. 37 (September 1927): 19.

46. Ibid., p. 20.

47. L. Ganeev, "V zashchitu prav krest'iankina zemliu," *Sel'sko-khoziaistvennaia zhizn'*, no. 3 (1928): 10–11, and Fisunov, "Prava chlenov," 1087–88, for similar discussion.

48. S. Davidov, "Kuritsa ne ptitsa, a baba . . . bez zemli. Stat'ia 66 i otkhodki," *Bednota,* January 21, 1927, p. 2.

49. For women hiring men to plow, see information in the census described in D. N. Zhbankov, *Bab'ia storona* (Kostroma, 1891), pp. 103–10. See Rose L. Glickman, *Russian Factory Women* (Berkeley, 1984), pp. 34–35, for women plowing when necessary.

50. Davidov, "Kuritsa ne ptitsa," p. 2.

51. *ESI,* no. 44–45 (1925): 1390; I. Gromov, *Chto nado znat' batraku chtoby zashchitit' svoi prava* (Moscow, 1930); *Bednota,* August 20, 1927, p. 2; on monthly wage, see Carr, *Socialism in One Country,* vol. 1, p. 251.

52. Gromov, *Chto nado znat' batraku,* p. 36; V. U. Krupianskaia, *The Village of Viriatino,* trans. Sula Benet (New York, 1970), p. 278; on joining seasonal workers, see *Bednota,* June 4, 1927, p. 2; V. P. Danilov, "Krest'ianskii otkhod na promysly v 1920-kh godakh," *Istoricheskie zapiski,* no. 94 (1974): 87.

53. On the right to rent land for a stated period if one could not farm alone, see "Spravochnik krest'ianki," *Krest'ianka,* no. 4 (1922); on ways of coping, see Carr, *Socialism in One Country,* vol. 1, pp. 243, 251; *Bednota,* January 13, 1923, p. 4; *ESI,* no. 44–45 (1925): 1390. Statistics concerning divorced, peasant women holding land are calculated according to data in *Vsesoiuznaia perepis' naseleniia 1926 goda* (Moscow, 1930), vol. 26, pp. 39, 81–83.

54. N. V. Erokhin, *Kak poluchit' alimenty* (Moscow, 1928), p. 21.

55. Kubanin, *Klassovaia sushchnost' protsessa drobleniia krest'ianskikh khoziaistv*, pp. 74–75.

56. A. Panferov, "Obychnoe pravo v uklade krest'ianskogo dvora," *Revoliutsiia prava,* no. 2 (1927): 111.

57. *Vserossiiskii tsentral'nyi ispolnitel'nyi komitet XI sozyva. Vtoraia sessiia* (Moscow, 1925), p. 266.

58. Brianskii, "Vozmozhno li po delam semeino-imushchestvennykh razdelov," p. 604.

59. Kubanin, *Klassovaia sushchnost' protsessa drobleniia krest'ianskikh khoziaistv,* p. 75.

60. P. Czap, "Peasant Class Courts and Peasant Customary Justice in Russia, 1861–1912," *Journal of Social History* 1 (Winter 1967): 159–60.

61. "O slovesnykh zaiavleniiakh v zemel'nykh kommissiiakh," *Sel'sko-khoziaistvennaia zhizn',* no. 23 (1927): 20. On oral depositions in people's courts, see "Spravochnik krest'ianki," *Krest'ianka,* no. 8 (1922): 33. According to the 1926 census, literacy rates for ages ten and up were men, 62.4 percent literate; women, 30 percent literate. Young people were the most literate. Danilov, *Sovetskaia dokolkhoznaia derevnia,* p. 26.

62. *Bednota,* September 30, 1925, p. 2; October 22, 1925, p. 2. People's courts could

be ten to fifteen *versts* (a *verst* is about seven-tenths of a mile) from a village. *Bednota,* August 24, 1926, p. 2; August 5, 1927, p. 3, for discussion of red tape; see *Bednota,* October 6, 1928, p. 2, for peasant woman incorrectly told in court that she needed to seek child support in a distant locale where her former husband now lived. In fact, her case belonged in the local court.

63. For information on *sel'kory,* see *Bednota,* September 28, 1926, p. 2.

64. Gazalova, "Zemel'nyi sud RSFSR," p. 205.

65. Czap, "Peasant Class Courts," p. 153. After the Land Captain Act of 1889, Land Captains could appeal the decisions of Township Courts. Ibid., p. 176.

66. Tumskii, *Kak delitsa pri semeinykh razdelakh,* pp. 39–42.

67. The majority of peasants who appealed to the Land Courts appeared to be poor, although the middle peasant formed the majority of the rural population. Shanin, *Awkward Class,* p. 174. According to another source, 55.2 percent of peasants who appealed to Land Courts were poor, 43.8 percent were middle peasants, and only 1 percent were prosperous peasants. N. S. Izvekov, "K desiatiletiiu Oktiabria: zemel'nyi sud za desiat' let," *Sel'sko-khoziaistvennaia zhizn',* no. 46 (November 1927): 1–3. Gazalova, using statistics from thirty-four provinces in 1926 and 1927, states that 159,689 poor and 176,659 middle peas-ants—73.8 percent of the general number of cases—participated in quarrels over land. Gazalova, "Zemel'nyi sud RSFSR," p. 210. The poorest layer of the village population, the *batraki* (agricultural workers with little or no land), appealed in the smallest numbers. According to one report, in the first half of 1927, only 2.8 percent of all peasant complaints came from *batraki,* in the second half, 2.9 percent. *ESI,* no. 49–50 (1928): 1253.

68. Bespal'ko, "Podsudnost' del o priznanii prav chlena trudovogo krest'ianskogo dvora," *ESI,* no. 38 (1927): 1189–90.

69. Ibid.

70. V. S., "Krest'ianskii dvor," p. 10.

71. "Vstuplenie v sostav krest'ianskogo dvora po fakticheskomu braku," *Sudebnaia praktika RSFSR,* no. 23 (1927): 16.

72. "Razdel imushchestva ili alimenty?" *Sudebnaia praktika RSFSR,* no. 22 (1928): 17.

73. *Vserossiiskii tsentral'nyi ispolnitel'nyi komitet XII sozyva. III sessiia,* p. 684. For criticism of limitations based on Article 56, see *Bednota,* June 24, 1928, p. 2, and E. Sedliarov, "Bespravie vnebrachnogo rebenka po zemel'nomu kodeksu," *ESI,* no. 23 (1927): 708.

74. *Bednota,* March 2, 1928, p. 4.

75. *Sudebnaia praktika RSFSR,* no. 10 (1928): 7.

76. A rough rule not always applied was that each household should be left with at least one horse and one cow. For guidelines, see A. Afanas'ev, "K voprosy o semeinykh razdelakh," *ESI,* no. 24–25 (1922): 11, and A. Chernov, "Semeino-imushchestvennye razdely," *ESI,* no. 17 (1922): 3–4. For the court ruling in Mariia's case, see "Praktika osoboi kollegii vysshego kontrolia po zemel'nym sporam," *ESI,* no. 1 (1923): 18. On fictitious divisions to avoid support payments, see A. Monin, "Politika suda po delam o semeino-imushchestvennykh razdelakh," *Proletarskii Sud,* no. 11–12 (June 1928): 9–10, and *Bed-nota,* February 23, 1926, p. 4.

77. *Bednota,* January 4, 1928, p. 2.

78. *Sudebnaia praktika RSFSR,* no. 12 (1927): 27.

79. For Turbabina, see "Prava na zemel'nyi nadel zheny, ostavivshei dvor svoego by-vshego muzha," *Sudebnaia praktika RSFSR,* no. 22 (1927): 12; for the view that the wife or the *primak* (son-in-law or man taken into household) cannot have land rights in two house-holds, see I. Tumanov, "Razdel zemledel'cheskogo trudovogo dvora," *Proletarskii Sud,* no. 1–2 (January 1925): 8; Davidov, "Kuritsa ne ptitsa," p. 2.

80. V. Likhachev, "Napisanie do polneniei istolkovanie reshenii," *Sel'sko-khoziaistven-naia zhizn'*, no. 20 (1928): 19.

81. *Bednota*, June 24, 1928, p. 2; February 29, 1928, p. 2.

82. *Bednota*, October 20, 1926, p. 2; December 24, 1927, p. 5.

83. *Vserossiiskii tsentral'nyi ispolnitel'nyi komitet Xll sozyva. III sessiia*, p. 684. For criticism of limitations based on Article 56, see *Bednota*, June 24, 1928, p. 2, and Sedliarov, "Bespravie vnebrachnogo rebenka po zemel'nomu kodeksu," p. 708.

84. For *Bednota* wanting to hear the "voice" of peasant women, see *Bednota*, February 11, 1926, p. 3; for requests to women *sel'kory* (village correspondents) to write more letters, see *Bednota*, September 3, 1925, p. 3. *Bednota* had ninety women village correspondents. By 1927 some eighteen women's journals were being published with a reported circulation of 386,000. Gail Lapidus, *Women in Soviet Society* (Berkeley, 1978), p. 65. For failures in local justice, see *Bednota*, March 2, 1926, p. 3; June 28, 1928, p. 2.

85. *Bednota*, August 20, 1927, p. 2.

86. *Bednota*, August 9, 1928, p. 4.

87. *Bednota*, June 28, 1928, p. 2.

88. Tumskii, "V zashchitu prav krest'ianki na zemliu," p. 20.

89. *Vserossiiskii tsentral'nyi ispolnitel'nyi komitet Xll sozyva. Vtoraia sessiia*, p. 284.

90. *Bednota*, July 12, 1925, p. 3.

91. P. A. Breitburd, "Iski ob alimentakh v krest'ianskom bytu," *Vestnik sovetskoi iustitsii*, no. 20 (October 1924): 664.

92. *Vserossiiskii tsentral'nyi ispolnitel'nyi komitet Xll sozyva. III sessiia*, p. 564; Snegirov, "Vydel imushchestva zhene," *Pravo i sud* 1 (January 1925): 57–58.

93. *Bednota*, February 28, 1923, p. 1.

94. Danilov, "O russkoi chastushke kak istochnike," p. 391; I. Khrebes, *Sovremennye krest'ianskie pesni* (Moscow, 1927), p. 40.

95. Danilov, *Sovetskaia dokolkhoznaia derevnia*, pp. 253–54. The provincial land authorities reported that the new instructions of March 30, 1927, were incomprehensible and had little effect on divisions. Ibid., p. 255. On consideration of dowry, see P. S. Starkov and G. N. Kosachinskii, *Raionnyi zemel'nyi sud* (Novosibirsk, 1928), pp. 62–63.

96. Gazalova, "Zemel'nyi sud RSFSR," p. 215.

97. Beginning in 1927, the Commissariat of Agriculture, to achieve better coordination between government decrees and local court decisions, published in *Sel'sko-khoziaistvennaia zhizn'* a section entitled "To Help Volost Land Commissions," in which it explained land rights and examined cases. Reportedly, opinions of local commissions were coming closer to government directives. On Land Commissions, see Gazalova, "Zemel'nyi sud RSFSR," pp. 205, 209, 215–16. For unjust decisions toward women in some land commissions, see A. Kal'ygina, *Sovetskii sud i krest'ianka* (Moscow, 1928), p. 10, and *Bednota*, January 20, 1928, p. 4. On the interventionist stance, see N. K. Martynovskii, *Zemel'nye sudy* (Odessa, 1925), pp. 11–12.

98. Tumskii, "V zashchitu prav krest'ianki na zemliu," p. 21.

99. Gazalova, "Zemel'nyi sud RSFSR," p. 215.

100. Shanin, *Awkward Class*, p. 176. A report in 1924 indicated that 23 percent of landless families in thirty-four provinces of central Russia were headed by women. Women headed 16 percent of small-holding households and 8 percent of those with moderate allotments. V. Moirova, "Rabote sredi krest'ianok," *Kommunistka*, no. 3 (1924): 23. Few women attended communal meetings. Central Executive Committee research in 1925 showed that 2 to 3 percent attending certain gatherings were women. The Worker-Peasant Inspectorate concluded in 1926–1927 that "women play very little part in the communal gathering." D. J. Male, *Russian Peasant Organization Before Collectivisation* (Cambridge, 1971), p. 70.

101. G. Dronin, "Klassovyi podkhod pri razreshenii zemel'no-sudebnykh del," *Sel'sko-khoziaistvennaia zhizn'*, no. 33 (1928): 19; also on ignoring women, see *Bednota*, June 26, 1926, p. 2.

102. *Bednota*, September 15, 1925, p. 2; June 26, 1926, p. 2; January 14, 1927, p. 4.

103. *Bednota*, January 25, 1927, p. 2. On the low percentage of women in rural soviets, see Shanin, *Awkward Class*, p. 176. For statistics on the low participation of peasant women in the Communist Party and in political activity, see V. A. Balashov, "Obshchestvenno-politicheskaia zhizn' sovetskogo dokolkhoznogo sela," *Trudy nauchno-issledovatel'skogo instituta iazyka, literatury, istorii i ekonomiki* (Saransk, 1987), vol. 87, pp. 50–52, and G. V. Sharapov, ed., *Istoriia Sovetskogo krest'ianstva* (Moscow, 1986), vol. 1, pp. 241–42.

104. Rudolf Schlesinger, ed., *The Family in the U.S.S.R.* (London, 1949), p. 150.

105. Family property-division disputes involving land accounted for 23.2 percent of the cases before the Land Commissions in 1925–26 and 26 percent in 1926–27. Gazalova, "Zemel'nyi sud RSFSR," p. 212. In separate Land Commissions the percentages were even higher. In the Moscow provincial Land Commission in 1926, such cases accounted for a third of all disputes. Ibid.

106. Kubanin, *Klassovaia sushchnost' protsessa drobleniia krest'ianskikh khoziaistv*, p. 75; A significant number of women in the rural party network were divorced. See Ethel Dunn, "Russian Rural Women," in D. Atkinson, A. Dallin, and G. Lapidus, eds., *Women in Russia* (Stanford, Calif., 1977), p. 171. For prototype of divorced, peasant woman in party, see *Bednota*, September 19, 1926, p. 2.

108. For aid from the press, see Redaktsiia, "Krest'ianskaia Gazeta," in TsGANKh (Central State Archive of the National Economy), fond 396, opis' 2, delo 12.

10 / *Bab'i Bunty* and Peasant Women's Protest During Collectivization

LYNNE VIOLA

Lynne Viola, an associate professor of history at the University of Toronto, exam-
ines the resistance of peasant women to collectivization during the years of Stalin's
"revolution from above" (1928–1932). The Communist perception of peasant wom-
en was that of backward and ignorant babas *(a pejorative for "women"). Commu-*
nists interpreted women's resistance to be irrational, hysterical, and generally
manipulated by outside (male) forces. In this chapter, Viola suggests that peasant
women's protest belied official perceptions and was neither as irrational nor as
hysterical as it appeared to outside observers. Instead, Viola suggests that peasant
women may have manipulated official images of themselves for their own political
ends in a traditional peasant display of dissimulation. By playing the role of igno-
rant babas, *peasant women were able to get away with subversive activities more*
easily than their male counterparts, whose political actions were defined not as
irrational but as counterrevolutionary. Peasant women therefore played an impor-
tant role in the resistance to collectivization, defending their interests and demon-
strating a degree of organization and conscious political opposition rarely acknowl-
edged. By focusing on peasant women's protest, this chapter illuminates key
features of peasant culture and forms of resistance during the collectivization of
Soviet agriculture.

Bab'i bunty were an integral part of the rural landscape during the years of wholesale collectivization. The term could be translated roughly as "women's riots," yet
this translation does not begin to do justice to its specific cultural and historical
evocations. *Babii* (the adjective) is a colloquial expression for women that refers in
particular to country women with country ways. The *baba* (singular noun) is most
often perceived as illiterate, ignorant (in the broader sense of *nekul'turnaia*), superstitious, a rumor-monger, and, in general, given to irrational outbursts of hysteria.
The *baba* might best be seen as a colorful combination of the American "hag,"
"fishwife," and "woman driver" all rolled into a peasant mold. The element of
stereotype is evident. Accordingly, the modifier colors and reinforces the noun that

"Bab'i Bunty and Peasant Women's Protest during Collectivization" by Lynne Viola, *The Russian
Review,* Vol. 45, No. 1 (January 1986), is reprinted by permission. © 1986 by *The Russian Review.* All
rights reserved.

follows. A *bunt* is a spontaneous, uncontrolled, and uncontrollable explosion of peasant opposition to authority. Not quite a demonstration, it is often aimless (at least in the mind of official observers), generally unpredictable, and always dangerous. A *babii bunt,* then, is a women's riot characterized by female hysteria, irrational behavior, unorganized and inarticulate protest, and violent actions.

Such, in any case, were the denotation and connotation of the term as used by Communist Party leaders, local activists, and other observers during collectivization. Rarely, if ever, were *bab'i bunty* described or evaluated in political or ideological terms. The causes of the *bab'i bunty* were generally attributed either to the instigation of agitators, the "kulaks" [capitalist farmers] and *"podkulachniki"* (kulak henchmen), who supposedly exploited the irrational hysteria of the *baba* for their own counterrevolutionary purposes, or else blamed on the reckless and lawless actions of the cadres who implemented collectivization and had succumbed to "dizziness from success." *Bab'i bunty* appear to have been tolerated to a far greater extent than were similar protests led by peasant men. They also seem to have been dealt with less harshly in cases when criminal charges ensured, the women escaping prosecution under the RSFSR penal code article 58 for counterrevolutionary crimes. The *baba* was not perceived as the fairer sex, but as the darker sector of the already dark peasant masses; consequently, like an unruly child or a butting goat, she was often not held responsible for her actions although sometimes subject to reprimand and punishment.

Officials' perceptions of peasant actions are generally based on assumptions about peasant ways and mores. As Daniel Field has demonstrated, however, peasants appear at times to have exploited these official assumptions about themselves for their own ends. Field suggests that peasants manipulated their reputation for naive monarchism as a means of deflecting punishment and as a rationalization for confrontations with officials who, according to peasant claims, were violating the will of the tsar.[1] Although the *baba* was no longer a naive monarchist during the First Five-Year Plan period (despite some cases of a Soviet-style naive monarchism that pitted Stalin and the Central Committee of the Communist Party against local officials after the publication of Stalin's article "Dizziness from Success"), it may well be that the *bab'i bunty* belied the official perception of peasant women's protest and were neither as irrational nor as hysterical as they appeared to outside observers.

This article is an exploration of the anatomy of the *bab'i bunty* and the protest of peasant women during collectivization. It is an attempt to examine the basis of peasant women's protest, the forms that such protest assumed, and the influence of official perceptions of and government reactions to the women's actions. The article is not intended as a comprehensive treatment of peasant women during collectivization. Nor is it meant to imply that *all* peasant women were opposed to collectivization. Due to the inevitable source problems connected with a topic such as this, the article will necessarily be somewhat impressionistic and the conclusions tentative. It is based on cases of protest in (ethnically) Russian and Ukrainian villages where the *bab'i bunty* occurred; the responses of women to collectivization in Central Asia and in non-Slavic villages are not explored, due to the very different cultural styles of women there and the absence of any overt or exclusively female peasant protest in these areas.

The collectivization of Soviet agriculture gave rise to a massive wave of peasant protest and violence in the countryside during the late 1920s and early 1930s. Peasant unrest began on the eve of wholesale collectivization in 1928 during the implementation of "extraordinary measures" (i.e., forced requisitions) in state grain procurements. It continued, at varying levels of intensity, to the end of the First Five-Year Plan, by which time wholesale collectivization was basically completed.[2] The largest waves of peasant protest appear to have occurred in the second half of 1929 and in the years 1930–31. In 1929, for example, 30,000 fires were registered in the RSFSR alone and many, if not most, were attributed to arson, or the *krasnyi petukh* [red rooster].[3] The number of cases of rural mass disturbances prosecuted under article 59[2] of the RSFSR criminal code increased in 1929 from 172 in the first half of the year to 229 in the second half of the year.[4] Although similar statistical data for 1930–31 are more difficult to extract from the sources, there is little doubt that the wave of violence and unrest in those years far surpassed that of the second half of 1929.[5] Peasant violence and protest were an inevitable byproduct of forced grain requisitions, collectivization, and dekulakization and were shaped by the traditional peasant approach to radical politics.

The Communist Party was aware of the dissatisfaction of the peasantry on the eve of and during the collectivization drives of 1930–31. Party concern over the extent of peasant unrest, moreover, appears to have played a significant role in shaping policy. Olga Narkiewicz has concluded that "it was the fear of a full-scale peasant revolution (whether real or imagined)" that induced the party leadership to pursue the policy of all-out collectivization in the late autumn of 1929.[6] R. W. Davies has linked the March 1930 "retreat" from breakneck collectivization inaugurated by Stalin's 2 March article, "Dizziness from Success," and the Central Committee decree of 14 March to the widespread peasant unrest of the first months of 1930.[7] This second contention is, in fact, frankly expressed in the later editions of the official history of the Communist Party of the Soviet Union.[8] The party publicly acknowledged the extent and dangers of peasant dissatisfaction in the months following the March retreat and, in particular, at the Sixteenth Congress of the Communist Party in late June and early July of 1930. This acknowledgement was to be the most explicit admission of the extent of the threat to the state posed by peasant unrest during collectivization.

Speakers at the Sixteenth Party Congress noted the key role played by women in the protest against collectivization and the collective farm. Although the extent and intensity of the women's protest were not specified, they were serious enough for Lazar Kaganovich to make the following remark:

> We know that in connection with the excesses [*peregiby*] in the collective farm movement, women in the countryside in many cases played the most "advanced" role in the reaction against the collective farm.[9]

A. A. Andreev, the first secretary of the North Caucasus Regional Party Committee, seconded Kaganovich, claiming that women were in the vanguard in the protests and disturbances over collectivization.[10] These claims received concrete substantiation in reports written by workers and officials who served in the countryside during collectivization.[11] The reasons for the "vanguard" role of peasant women in the protest against collectivization were considered to be the low cultural and political level and backwardness of peasant women, the "incorrect approach" of rural officials, "dizzy from success," to the volatile women, and, finally, the exploitation of the women's irrational fears and potential for mass hysteria by the kulak and the omnipresent *podkulachnik.*

The party's response to women's protest against collectivization was different from its response to (male) peasant protest in general, which was usually labeled kulak opposition and dealt with by increasing the level of repression. Instead of repressive measures (although these were not always excluded), the party emphasized a more "correct approach" to peasant women—an end to the excesses—on the part of rural officials and the need to improve work among women.[12] The importance of work among women, in fact, had been a concern from at least the time of the grain procurement crisis when the potential dangers of female-led opposition to Soviet policy became clear.[13] Work among women basically had two objectives. First, it was held necessary to educate women and expand political indoctrination among them. A second task was drawing more women into active involvement in the political life of the village through participation in the women's delegate meetings, soviet elections, and membership in local soviets and the Communist Party. And, indeed, during the years of collectivization, there was a gradual, but noted improvement in such work as local officials were implored to pay more attention to women and increasing numbers of women were recruited to the party and elected to the boards of local soviets.[14] The state's response and its emphasis on the need to improve work among women were predicated upon the official conception of peasant women's protest as essentially non-political and a function of the ignorance and backwardness of the *baba.*

Nevertheless, the party's efforts were too little and too late. Moreover, and despite periodic waves of party and government expulsions and purges to offset local excesses, the party's contradictory demands of a "correct approach" to the peasantry and the timely implementation of often brutal policies made it highly unlikely that the rough, civil-war methods of rural officials would be or could be tempered or civilized. Nor could the party mitigate the effect that it perceived the kulak and *podkulachnik* had in sparking women's opposition and the *bab'i bunty.* As a consequence, the party failed to quiet the fears of many peasant women or to prevent the wave of *bab'i bunty* that erupted in the countryside as a reaction to both rumor and reality.

The Communist Party claimed that the underlying basis of women's protest during collectivization was irrational female hysteria unleashed by the "kulak *agitprop,*" or the rumor-mill, and reinforced by the women's *petit bourgeois,* small landholder instincts. It was true that the rumor-mill often played a very important role in sparking *bab'i bunty* and women's protest; it was also true that peasant women's "*petit bourgeois* instincts" played a central role in their opposition to collectivization and the transformation of the life of the village that it entailed. However, the protest engendered by the rumor-mill and by some of the policies of collectivization was not always "irrational" or the manifestation of a *petit bourgeois* class consciousness.

Rumors about collectivization and the collective farm raged through the countryside. Heated discussions took place in village squares, at the wells, in the cooperative shops, and at the market.[15] At one and the same time, there were tales of the return of the Whites and the *pomeshchiki* (landlords), the coming of Antichrist, Polish *pans,* and the Chinese, the arrival of commissars, Bolsheviks, Communists, and Soviet gendarmes, and impending famine and devastation.[16] Among the rumors were many that struck a particular resonance in the minds and hearts of peasant women. These rumors, broadly speaking, touched upon questions of religion, the family, and everyday life. Some of them assumed fantastic dimensions; others— whether fantastic or not—were sometimes based on actual occurrences.

Rumors concerning the Apocalypse were widespread at this time. During the initial stages of collectivization, there was a wholesale attack on religion and the Church, which, although largely the result of actions of local crusaders and militant atheists, was not officially condemned by Moscow until after March 1930. At this time, churches were closed down and transformed into clubs or offices, church bells were removed, village priests were hounded and imprisoned, and icons were burned. Both the onslaught on religion and the scale of the general offensive on traditional ways of life in the village served to encourage an apocalyptic mindset among the peasantry.

The collective farm became the symbol of the Antichrist on earth. In one village, old women asked, "Is it true or not?—they say that all who join the collective farm will be signed over to the Antichrist."[17] On the eve of collectivization, reports from the North Caucasus claimed that a certain personage assuming the identity of Christ was wandering through the villages proclaiming the coming of the Last Judgment. He had in his possession a document from the Virgin Mary calling for everyone to leave the collective farm prior to Judgment Day or else to face the wrath of God. The Christ of the North Caucasus also had a blacklist of collective farmers for use on Judgment Day.[18] When, in the autumn of 1929, the church was closed in the Ukrainian village of Bochkarko, it was claimed that a miraculous light issued from the church and a sign appeared on the cupola, which read: "Do not join the collective farm or I will smite thee."[19] In the village of Brusianka (Bazhenskii *raion* [district], Sverdlovskii *okrug* [county] in the Urals), tickets to the next world went on sale; they were sold in three classes and prices ranged from 50 kopeks to 2 rubles 50 kopeks.[20]

Peasant women were especially susceptible to rumors about the Apocalypse and Antichrist and to news of events like those described above. The peasant woman was the upholder of religion within the village and household, so it was natural that the attacks on religion and the Church often affected women most acutely. The peasant woman, however, was also said to be particularly responsive to tales of the supernatural. It may be that women's protest sparked by such fantastic rumors was based on a combination of devotion to the faith and superstition. It may also be that tales of the Apocalypse, which forecast an imminent cataclysm in which God destroys the ruling powers of evil and raises the righteous to life in a messianic kingdom, served as a religious justification (either perceived to be real or exploited as a pretext) for peasant resistance to the state or provided a peasant vocabulary of protest.[21] Whether a particular form of peasant protest, a pretext for resistance, or an irrational impulse, peasant women's protest raised by religious rumors and the attack on the Church derived at least in part from legitimate concerns over the fate of the Church and the believers.

There were also rumors that touched upon questions of the family and everyday life and that were especially troubling to peasant women. Some of these rumors were in the realm of the absurd, such as the rumor that spread through the countryside that four thousand young peasant women were to be sent to China to pay for the Far Eastern railroad or the variation of this rumor, which stated that only women weighing over three and one half *puds* (approximately 126 pounds) would be sent to China.[22] Mikhail Sholokhov in the novel *Virgin Soil Upturned* provides another example of rumor in the category of the absurd, most probably a variation of a rumor in actual circulation. Sholokhov writes:

> There was a nun in the village the day before yesterday. . . . She spent the night at Timofei Borshchov's and told them the fowls had been got together so we could send them to town for the townsfolk to make noodle soup with, then we would fix up little chairs for the old women, a special shape, with straw on them, and make them sit on our eggs until they hatched, and any old woman who rebelled would be tied to her chair.[23]

This rumor clearly verged on the fantastic, but it should be noted that it was based on two real grievances that women held during collectivization. These concerned the socialization of domestic livestock—the economic mainstay of a peasant woman's existence—and the introduction of incubators, opposition to which was due either to the fact that their use was predicated on the socialization of poultry or else the perhaps frightening novelty of their appearance.

In addition to these rumors, there were a series of rumors of equally fantastic dimensions, which claimed that collectivization would bring with it the socialization of children, the export of women's hair, communal wife-sharing, and the notorious common blanket under which all collective farmers, both male and female, would sleep.[24] These rumors were of obvious concern to women and, moreover, very possibly were inspired by cases when local officials either attempted to implement similar practices or told peasants that such practices were in the offing. For example, the 25,000er Gorbunevskii, working in the Crimea, announced on 1 March 1930 that his collective farm would become a commune and that all of the peasant children would be socialized. When the parents of the soon-to-be socialized children heard this, they began a massive slaughter of their also soon-to-be socialized livestock, fortunately sparing the children.[25] The RSFSR Commissar of Justice, N. M. Ianson, told of a case involving an "aesthetic deviation" that may have been the basis of tales of the export of women's hair. According to Ianson, there was a local Communist in the Urals—a former partisan and party member from 1917 or 1918—who made all the village women cut their hair short. Ianson claimed that the Communist took seriously (and literally) the propaganda centering on the need to create a new life in the village and to bring the countryside closer to the city. The Communist felt that short hair—as well as the introduction of short skirts—would give the *baba* a more urban look. One *baba*, who felt differently, wrote in a letter of complaint, "he has shamed us for all of our life, only death remains. . . ."[26] Rumors of the common blanket, which were probably the most pervasive of all, also may have derived from one or two cases when local activists discussed the promise of communism. One *Rabkrin* (Workers' and Peasants' Inspectorate) plenipotentiary told women that they would all have to sleep, along with all of the men, under one common blanket.[27] In the North Caucasus, local activists in one village actually went so far as to confiscate all blankets. They told the peasants that henceforth there would be no more individual blankets; all would sleep on a 700-meter-long bed under a 700-meter-long blanket.[28]

Many of these rumors clearly played upon the real fears of peasant women concerning issues of family and everyday life. Moreover, given the enormity of the transformation implemented by the state at this time along with the "excesses," the horrendously low level of rural officialdom, and the actual occurrence of any number of bizarre instances such as those described above, one can only say with difficulty that peasant women's protest was irrational. One could perhaps claim, as Petro Grigorenko suggests in his memoirs, that women often simply exploited the rumors of the absurd, without really believing them, as a way to attack the collective farm under the guise of irrational, nonpolitical protest and, consequently, as a way to avoid the suppression of resistance by outside forces (armed civilian forces, security troops, or the militia) as might have been the case in an overtly anti-Soviet village uprising.[29] The plausibility of this suggestion will be examined below. For now, it is sufficient to conclude that, whether pretext or actual belief, the rumor-mill struck a deep chord among peasant women who saw many of their most cherished beliefs and domestic interests under attack.

Rumors, however, were not always the spark behind the *bab'i bunty*. Quite often, protest was triggered directly by clearly articulated opposition to the implementation of radical policies. This opposition raises the issue of the "*petit bourgeois* instincts" of peasant women. Such "instincts," indeed, formed a part of the basis for resistance and figure largely in the rumor-mill, but opposition to policy deriving from so-called *petit bourgeois* concerns was often less motivated by "instinct" than by a set of rational interests, revolving around the family and the domestic economy. For example, peasant women led the protest against attempts to socialize domestic livestock because the domestic livestock was generally the basis and justification of the woman's economic position within the household. Women also protested directly and without recourse to the rumor-mill over issues concerning their children. Once again, the socialization of domestic livestock could be a threat because the loss of a milch cow could very well mean that peasant children would be without milk.[30] In later years, Stalin even admitted how important an issue the loss of a cow had been in provoking women's opposition to the collective farm when he said, "in the not too distant past, Soviet power had a little misunderstanding with the collective farm women. The issue was cows."[31] In one village, a *babii bunt* occurred over the proposed closing of a mill. The women's concern here was that, "we cannot feed our children" if the mill closes down.[32] Some women also objected to the introduction of nurseries. According to Maurice Hindus, the Ukrainian-born American reporter, this was due to the high infant mortality rate in the village. Hindus claimed that there was not a woman in the village that he visited who had not lost a child in infancy, so it was natural that these women were reluctant to entrust their children to the care of others. (This reluctance, moreover, was particularly appropriate, given the experience of caring for socialized livestock.)[33] None of these concerns derived from "instinct"; rather, they were legitimate and articulate protest against specific policies and practices associated with the initial stages of collectivization.

It is evident that official perceptions of the basis of peasant women's protest were at least in part misconceived and that the *content* of women's protest was rational and based on legitimate concerns. The question that now arises is the extent to which official perceptions about the *form* of women's protest, the *babii bunt,* were accurate?

The *bab'i bunty* were depicted as spontaneous outbursts of mass hysteria marked by indiscriminate violence, disorder, and a cacophony of high-pitched voices all shouting demands at once. Groups of women assembled at the village square became "milling crowds." And behind every *babii bunt* could be found a kulak or *podkulachnik* agitator who exploited the ignorant, irrational *babas*. Instead of calmly discussing grievances in an organized, "cultured" manner, reports describing women's protest claimed, for example, that, at soviet meetings, the women would simply vote against all measures of Soviet power regardless of content or that, at secret meetings against the collective farm in March and April 1930, the women (who formed the majority of those in attendance and were the most active participants) would all talk at once with neither chairman nor agenda, in an atmosphere of bedlam.[34] Women often physically blocked the carting away of requisitioned grain or the entrances to huts of peasants scheduled to be exiled as kulaks, forcibly took back socialized seed and livestock, and led assaults on officials. The response of officials was frequently to hide or run away and to allow the *bab'i bunty* to take their course until the women ran out of steam—for the most part without recourse to the use of force. In the first half of 1930, the end result was generally the dissolution of the collective farm. The women were seldom held responsible for their actions, thanks to official perceptions of the basis of such actions. The *bab'i bunty* thus accomplished what they set out to accomplish and the state held strong in its perceptions of peasant women's protest.

There is a most illuminating case, rare in its detail, of a *babii bunt* in the Russian village of Belovka in Chistopol canton in the Tatar ASSR in 1929 which perfectly illustrates official perceptions of and reactions to the *bab'i bunty*. The cause of the *babii bunt* in Belovka was a decision made by the local soviet in August 1929 to introduce a five-field system of crop rotation in the village and to carry out a redistribution of peasant lands. Behind the *babii bunt,* according to the description of the case, loomed the "local kulaks" and, in particular, the insidious figure of one Sergei Fomin, the "kulak" miller. The case report read:

> As a result of kulak agitation among the *dark, illiterate* [italics mine—L. V.] peasant women, a crowd of 100 people . . . firmly demanded the repeal of the decree on the introduction of the five-field system.

Despite warnings to disperse, the crowd, "supported by the general din," continued its protest, knocking to the ground and beating a member of the local soviet. At this point, other soviet activists entered the fray and, according to the report, prevented the crowd from realizing its presumed intentions of beating the activist to unconsciousness. The case was brought to the attention of the regional court, which prosecuted the ten most active *babas* and the miller Fomin, who was described as the "ideological instigator" of the disturbance. Fomin, who was also charged with setting fire to the local soviet secretary's home, was prosecuted separately, according to "special consideration." The women, prosecuted under article 59^2 of the criminal code for mass disturbances, were given sentences of imprisonment with strict isolation ranging from two to three years.

The Belovka case was reexamined by the Supreme Court in January 1930, at which time the decision of the regional court was overturned. The Supreme Court held Fomin *exclusively* responsible for the women's actions, describing him as the "ideological inspiration," the "ideological leader" and main "culprit" in the disturbance. Fomin's "counterrevolutionary organizational role" in the disturbance was the "actual root" of the *babii bunt* and, according to the Supreme Court, the regional court had failed to discern this clearly enough. In addition, the Supreme Court accused the local soviet of Belovka of insufficient preliminary preparatory work among women, something that could have mitigated the effects of Fomin's propaganda. Finally, the sentences of the women, all described as illiterate, middle and lower-middle peasants, and representative of the "most backward part of the peasantry" (i.e., women), were lessened to forced labor within the village for periods ranging from six months to one year. The purpose of the sentences was to serve as a warning and an educational measure and *not* as punishment.[35]

This case is instructive in illuminating official views of and reactions to peasant women's protest. In Belovka, the women were viewed as no more than naive dupes of the local kulaks who served as a figurative battering ram against Soviet power. The local soviet's failure to work among the women and prepare them for the new policy transformed them into ammunition, which the kulak could fire at the Soviet regime. However, the Belovka case may not tell the whole story of the *bab'i bunty*. Petro Grigorenko, in his memoirs, described the *bab'i bunty* as a kind of "tactic." The women would initiate opposition to the collective farm or other policies and the men would remain on the sidelines until the local activists attempted to quell the disorder. At that point, the more vulnerable peasant men could safely enter the fray as chivalrous defenders of wives, mothers, and daughters rather than as anti-Soviet *podkulachniki*.[36] Descriptions of *bab'i bunty* by cadres in the field offer confirmation of Grigorenko's findings and appear to belie the official image as presented in the Belovka case.

A riot that occurred in the village of Lebedevka in Kursk at the Budennyi collective farm may serve as an example. A 25,000er by the name of Dobychin, serving as a plenipotentiary for collectivization, arrived in the collective farm on 7 March. Dobychin called a meeting of the peasant women and was greeted with cries of "We do not want a collective farm" and "You want to derail the *muzhik*" [pejorative for "peasant"]. Dobychin responded, "We will not hold such types in the collective farm, good riddance. . . . [s]leep it off and you'll see that we will let the *bedniak* [poor peasant] derail him who made you drunk and sent you here." Dobychin's tactic led to a general uproar and an assault on Dobychin. The women, with one Praskov'ia Avdiushenko in the lead, approached the stage where he stood. Praskov'ia said to Dobychin, "Ah well, come nearer to us." With this, she grabbed the worker by his collar and dragged him off the stage. Dobychin somehow managed to escape, but the unrest continued and even escalated when the church watchman's wife began to ring the church bell. With this, all of the peasants entered the fray. They seized their recently socialized livestock and prepared a collective declaration requesting permission to quit the farm. This disturbance, like many others, was not suppressed, but simply ended with the collapse of the collective farm.[37]

A similar situation was described by the worker Zamiatin who was among those workers recruited from the city soviets in early 1930 to work in the local rural soviets. Zamiatin depicted the situation faced by the 25,000er V. Klinov. Zamiatin said that the approach to Klinov's village resembled an "armed camp"; on his way, he saw a sign nailed to a bridge that read: "Vas'ka [Klinov] you scum, get out. We will break your legs." When he arrived, Zamiatin found the village alive with rumors of the approach of a band of riders who were coming to kill all the Communists and collective farmers. In this village, dekulakization had already been implemented but, as happened elsewhere, the kulaks were not yet removed from the village. This omission, according to Zamiatin, had led to the crisis that existed. With Zamiatin's arrival, Klinov set about preparing for the exile of the kulaks. He began by removing the church bell, which traditionally served as tocsin to gather together the peasants in case of emergency. The heads of kulak families were exiled, and all went well until one of the exiled kulaks returned to announce that the other kulaks would soon be coming back to seek vengeance. This led to the decision to exile the families of the exiled kulak heads of households. The announcement of this decision led to an uproar. The peasant women, in an attempt to forestall this action, blocked the entrances of the huts of the kulak families. Several days later, the women also led the opposition to the attempt to cart away the village's grain by blocking the grain warehouse. This led to a *babii bunt*, followed quickly by a general free-for-all in which all the peasants participated in a pitchfork battle. The disturbance was suppressed by the militia, which was called in after all of the peasants had joined the rebellion.[38]

In both of these cases, peasant women were responsible for initiating the resistance and were soon joined by the peasant men in a general village riot. In a classic depiction of a *babii bunt* in a Cossack village in *Virgin Soil Upturned*, the Cossack men stood at the back of the crowd of women urging them on when they attacked the chairman of the local soviet. Here, the women led the attack on the grain warehouse "with the silent approval of the menfolk at the back." And while the women were dragging the chairman of the collective farm through the village, the Cossack men broke the locks of the grain warehouse and seized their grain.[39] The women served both as initiators and decoys in this disturbance.

Lev Kopelev has provided yet another description of a *babii bunt*, and one that closely conforms to Grigorenko's hypothesis. Kopelev described a disturbance in a Ukrainian village:

A "riot" also broke out in Okhochaya. A crowd of women stormed the kolkhoz [collective farm] stables and barns. They cried, screamed, wailed, demanding their cows and seed back. The men stood a way off, in clusters, sullenly silent. Some of the lads had pitchforks, stakes, axes tucked in their sashes. The terrified granary man ran away; the women tore off the bolts and together with the men began dragging out the bags of seed.[40]

Here, as elsewhere, the *babii bunt* was the first stage in a general peasant riot. Here too the women had specific aims and, whether the riots were intended to dissolve the collective farm, halt dekulakization, or retake socialized seed and livestock, they accomplished their aims.

Women tended to lead the village riots because they were less vulnerable to repression than peasant men. There were even reports of *bab'i bunty* in 1929 when the women brought their children with them into battle or laid down in front of tractors to block collectivization.[41] In the *bab'i bunty,* the men stood to the side. In non-violent protest, the situation was similar. Peasant men frequently allowed their female relatives to express opposition to policy. According to a report of a worker brigade in Tambov, in the Central Black Earth Region, the men did not go to the meetings on collectivization, but sent the women instead. When asked why they did not attend the meetings, the men replied, "They [the women] are equal now, as they decide so we will agree. . . ."[42] In this way, it was easy for a peasant to claim that he had not joined the collective farm or surrendered his grain because his wife would not let him or threatened him with divorce. The 25,000er Gruzdev was told by one peasant, "my wife does not want to socialize our cow, so I cannot do this."[43] One peasant man explained the power of the women in the following way:

> We dared not speak at meetings. If we said anything that the organizers didn't like, they abused us, called us *koolaks,* and even threatened to put us in prison. . . . We let the women do the talking. . . . If the organizer tried to stop them they made such a din that he had to call off the meeting.[44]

It is clear here that at least some peasant men recognized both their own vulnerability and the far greater leverage that peasant women had in speaking out against state policies.

Peasant women were able to get away with a great deal more than their male counterparts in resisting collectivization and the other policies of the times. Force was generally not used to suppress *bab'i bunty.* Furthermore, it would appear that women tended not to be prosecuted under article 58 of the criminal code for counterrevolutionary crimes in cases when opposition to policy led to court actions: in reports of court cases in *Sudebnaia praktika* (supplement to *Sovetskaia iustitsiia,* the organ of the RSFSR People's Commissariat of Justice) in 1930 and 1931, only men appear as defendants in cases prosecuted under article 58. This tendency, along with the infrequent use of force to suppress *bab'i bunty,* was a function of both official images of women's protest as irrational and the fear and inability of rural officials to respond effectively to the type of bedlam created by disgruntled peasant women. And, if actions reveal motives, it is likely that peasant women who rebelled against the policies of collectivization clearly understood how they were perceived and appreciated the power of their "irrational behavior."

The *bab'i bunty* that occurred during the years of collectivization were neither as irrational nor as spontaneous as the official accounts tend to conclude. The anatomy of the *bab'i bunty* and the content of peasant women's protest contained several consistent features, which belie the official images. First, the *bab'i bunty* often revealed a relatively high degree of organization and tactics. Following the initial articulation of protest, which could frequently resemble a mob scene, the peasant women would endeavor to disarm local activists or plenipotentiaries by one means or another, sound the church bell to alert the village and mobilize support, and, finally, approach directly the resolution of the problem that had given rise to the protest.[45] Moreover, the women's protest frequently had a specific goal in mind (dissolving the collective farm, seizing socialized seed or livestock, halting grain requisitions or dekulakization, etc.). Second, the women's protest was frequently based upon opposition to specific policies and, whether inspired by seemingly irrational rumors, rumors used as a pretext for resistance, or direct opposition to the implementation of policy, it derived from rational and legitimate concerns and socio-economic interests, which were under attack by the state. Third, peasant women's protest seems to have served as a *comparatively* safe outlet for peasant opposition in general and as a screen to protect the more politically vulnerable male peasants who could not oppose policy as actively or openly without serious consequence but who, nevertheless, could and did either stand silently, and threateningly, in the background or join in the disturbance once protest had escalated to a point where men might enter the fray as defenders of their female relatives. Finally, an important feature distinguished women's protest from protest (generally led by males) officially branded as "counterrevolutionary." Many of the counterrevolutionary cases prosecuted under article 58 of the criminal code in late 1929 and early 1930 occurred while the defendants were drunk. Women's protest, on the other hand, appears to have been, with few exceptions, sober and, consequently, perhaps, more rational than male protest.[46]

Several other conclusions about official perceptions of the *bab'i bunty* and women's protest supplement direct observations on the nature of peasant women's opposition during collectivization. First of all, the *bab'i bunty* were very much a part of the traditional peasant approach to political protest. Peasants rarely resisted the state through organized political action. Their resistance often assumed the aspect of a spontaneous, disorganized, irrational *bunt*. However, peasant rebellions frequently merely *appeared* irrational to outside observers, who were powerless to cope with massive explosions of discontent and who, in the case of the *bab'i bunty*, were reluctant to resort to armed force to quell riots.[47] The outside observers who wrote about the *bab'i bunty* tended, in addition, to be city people or, at the very least, of a higher cultural level than the peasants and, consequently, had a very different conception of the forms that protest and rebellion were expected to assume. The rudimentary organization behind the *bab'i bunty* and the specific grievances articulated in protest were often, in the eyes of outside observers, overshadowed or impossible to discern against the backdrop of apparent pandemonium.

Second, and of equal importance, there is a real possibility that the Communist Party was aware of the true nature and dynamics of the *bab'i bunty* and women's protest during collectivization. As Field has argued, the "myth of the tsar" was as useful to the tsarist government as it was to the peasantry. It was based on the "myth of the peasant" and provided the regime with a rationalization for any problems leading to peasant disturbances.[48] In the Soviet context, the myth of the peasant could serve several purposes. First, official images of the *bab'i bunty* and peasant women's protest could be manipulated to minimize the true nature and extent of the opposition engendered by collectivization. Second, it served a particularly useful purpose when women's protest engulfed entire villages, including poor and middle peasant women. In these cases, the party had a ready rationalization for the contradictions of the class struggle in the village, for its failure to capture the support of its poor and middle peasant allies among the peasantry. Finally, particular injustices could be attributed to officials who, it was said, were violating the essentially correct policy of the center. In this way, Moscow could, and often did, seek to divert grievances from the state to local officials, who were frequently used as scapegoats. Moreover, it is clear that, at least in the months following the March 1930 retreat, peasants also adhered or pretended to adhere to this rationalization, displaying a Soviet-style naive monarchism which pitted rural officials against Stalin and the Central Committee of the Communist Party.[49]

Peasant women played an important role in the protest that consumed many Russian and Ukrainian villages during the First Five-Year Plan, and it is important to attempt to understand the nature of this protest and the state's response to it. Yet, one cannot claim that all women were united, on the basis of similar interests, in opposition to the collective farm. Dorothy Atkinson has suggested that there were also women (widows, heads of households, wives of seasonal workers) who supported collectivization because of the difficulties of working their land alone and women, mostly young, who were genuinely enthusiastic about collectivization.[50] Furthermore, the general scale of peasant resistance to the state during collectivization should not be exaggerated. Although the exact dimensions of peasant resistance are not known, it is quite clear that the opposing sides in the rural conflicts caused by collectivization were unevenly matched. With the possible exception of the early months of 1930, the state always retained the ability to respond to peasant unrest in an organized fashion with a show of force. And—again with an exception, that of Central Asia—the confrontation between state and peasantry in no way approached the scale of a full-fledged civil war with troop formations and organized national or regional resistance. Despite these qualifications, however, the peasant unrest of these years was of sufficient scale and ferocity to force the state to take notice. And notice it did. The party admitted that the "retreat" of 1930 came about as a response to peasant unrest, and Stalin even made note of the opposition of peasant women to the attempt to socialize domestic livestock when, in 1933, he promised a cow for every collective farm household. This was clearly not a retreat from collectivization, but it was a retreat—and a retreat that proved permanent[51]—from many of the most objectionable policies and practices of those times, such as the open attack on the Church, the attempt to socialize domestic livestock, and the unsanctioned "dizziness" of local cadres who sought to impose upon the peasantry their ideas of socialist construction in the realm of everyday life. It is plausible and logical to suggest that the protest of peasant women played an important role in the amendment of policies and practices in these spheres.

The *bab'i bunty* and the outspoken protest of peasant women do not appear to have continued beyond the First Five-Year Plan. Nevertheless, during the early-years of collectivization, the *bab'i bunty* and women's protest proved the most effective form of peasant opposition to the Soviet state. Peasant women played an important role in the resistance to collectivization, defending their interests and demonstrating a degree of organization and conscious political opposition rarely acknowledged.

Notes

1. Daniel Field, *Rebels in the Name of the Tsar* (Boston, 1976), pp. 23, 209–10, 214.

2. By the end of 1931, approximately 60% of peasant households were collectivized. See I. E. Zelenin, "Kolkhoznoe stroitel'stvo v SSSR v 1931–1932 gg.," *Istoriia SSSR*, no. 6 (1960): 23.

3. V. P. Danilov, M. P. Kim, and N. V. Tropkin, eds., *Sovetskoe krest'ianstvo. Kratkii ocherk istorii (1917–1970)*, 2nd ed. (Moscow, 1973), p. 280.

4. "Doklad o rabote UKK Verkhsuda RSFSR za vtoruiu polovinu 1929 g.," *Sudebnaia praktika*, no. 8 (10 June 1930), 12.

5. For a rough indication of the scope of peasant unrest in the early part of 1930, see R. W. Davies, *The Socialist Offensive: The Collectivisation of Soviet Agriculture, 1929–1930* (Cambridge, Mass., 1980), pp. 257–58. According to one Soviet article (which, unfortunately, provides no source), there were 1,678 armed uprisings in the countryside in the period January to March 1930 alone. See B. A. Abramov and T. K. Kocharli, "Ob oshibkakh v odnoi knige. (Pis'mo v redaktsiiu)," *Voprosy istorii KPSS*, no. 5 (1975): 137. In the Lower Volga, there were 165 riots in March 1930 and 195 in April 1930 according to V. K. Medvedev, *Krutoi povorot (Iz istorii kollektivizatsii sel'skogo khoziaistva Nizhnego Povolzh'ia)* (Saratov, 1961), p. 119. In the Middle Volga, there were 319 uprisings in the first four months of 1930, as compared to 33 for the same months of 1929 according to F. A. Karevskii, "Likvidatsiia kulachestva kak klassa v Srednem Povolzh'e," *Istoricheskie zapiski*, 80 (1967): 92. And, finally, in Siberia, in the first half of 1930, there were 1,000 "registered terrorist acts" according to N. Ia. Gushchin, "Likvidatsiia kulachestva kak klassa v Sibirskoi derevne," *Sotsial'naia struktura naseleniia Sibiri* (Novosibirsk, 1970), p. 122. Data on 1931 are more scarce, but according to Zelenin, in the spring of 1931, there were open attacks (e.g., arson, destruction of livestock and agricultural equipment, etc.) in 15.8% of all collective farms; see Zelenin, "Kolkhoznoe stroitel'stvo," p. 31.

6. O. A. Narkiewicz, "Stalin, War Communism and Collectivization," *Soviet Studies* 18, no. 1 (July 1966): 37.

7. Davies, *The Socialist Offensive*, pp. 255–56. For Stalin's article and the Central Committee decree, see I. Stalin, "Golovokruzhenie ot uspekhov. K voprosam kolkhoznogo dvizheniia," *Sochineniia*, vol. 12 (Moscow, 1952), pp. 191–99; and *KPSS v rezoliutsiiakh i resheniiakh s"ezdov, konferentsii i plenumov TsK*, 7th ed., part 2 (Moscow, 1953), pp. 548–51.

8. *Istoriia KPSS*, 2nd ed. (Moscow, 1962), p. 444; and 3rd ed. (Moscow, 1969), p. 405.

9. *XVI s"ezd VKP (b). Stenograficheskii otchet* (Moscow-Leningrad, 1930), p. 70.

10. Ibid., p. 123.

11. For example, M. N. Chernomorskii, "Rol' rabochikh brigad v bor'be za sploshnuiu kollektivizatsiiu v Tambovskoi derevne," *Materialy po istorii SSSR. Dokumenty po istorii Sovetskogo obshchestva*, fasc. 1 (Moscow, 1955), pp. 347–48, 350, 354, 364–66, 369, 375; and examples cited on pp. 193–94, 197–99.

12. *XVI s"ezd VKP (b)*, pp. 70, 457. Also see similar statements in *Kollektivizatsiia*

sel'skogo khoziaistva na Severnom Kavkaze (1927–1937 gg.), (Krasnodar, 1972), pp. 262–64, 266; and *Zapadnyi oblastnoi komitet VKP (b). Vtoraia oblastnaia partkonferentsiia (5–12 iiunia 1930 g.). Stenograficheskii otchet* (Moscow-Smolensk, 1931), pp. 164–65.

13. To cite just two examples of such concern, at the Fourteenth All-Russian Congress of Soviets in May 1929, a peasant woman activist and delegate from Siberia stressed the need to improve work among women in light of a series of *bab'i bunty* during grain requisitioning. This plea then was echoed by A. V. Artiukhina, the last head of the *Zhenotdel* before its dissolution in 1930, at the Second Session of VTsIK (All-Russian Central Executive Committee of the Soviets), Fourteenth Convocation, in November 1929. Artiukhina warned that if such work was not improved, "backward" peasant women would not support collectivization and would be exploited by the kulak. See *XIV Vserossiiskii s"ezd sovetov. Stenograficheskii otchet* (Moscow, 1929), Biulleten' no. 3, pp. 11–12; and *II sessiia VTsIK XIV sozyva. Stenograficheskii otchet* (Moscow, 1929), Biulleten' no. 7, pp. 25–28.

14. See, for examples, *Chto nuzhno znat' kazhdomu rabotniku kolkhoza? (Dlia 25000 tov., edushchikh v kolkhozy)* (Moscow, 1930), p. 7; *Derevenskii kommunist*, no. 1 (12 January 1930): 32; and M. Kureiko, *25-tysiachniki na kolkhoznoi stroike* (Moscow-Leningrad, 1931), pp. 44–45. For information on the expanding role of women in political life in the countryside, see Dorothy Atkinson, *The End of the Russian Land Commune, 1905–1930* (Stanford, Calif., 1983), pp. 367–68, and Ethel Dunn, "Russian Rural Women," in Dorothy Atkinson, Alexander Dallin, and Gail Warshofsky Lapidus, eds., *Women in Russia* (Stanford, Calif., 1977), p. 173.

15. Sadovnikov, "Shefstvo nad kolkhozom 'Revoliutsii'," *Sovetskaia iustitsiia*, no. 6 (28 February 1930): 5–6.

16. These rumors were widespread and have been gleaned from many different sources. See, for examples, TsGAOR (Central State Archive of the October Revolution, Moscow), *f.* 5470, *op.* 14, *d.* 204, *l.* 54 (trade union of chemical workers, *svodka* on the work of Leningrad 25,000ers in the countryside); I. A. Ivanov, "Pomoshch' Leningradskikh rabochikh v kollektivizatsii sel'skogo khoziaistva podshefnykh raionov," *Rabochie Leningrada v bor'be za pobedu sotsializma* (Moscow-Leningrad, 1963), p. 219; N. A. Ivnitskii and D. M. Ezerskii, eds., "Dvadtsatipiatitysiachniki i ikh rol' v kollektivizatsii sel'skogo khoziaistva v 1930 g.," *Materialy po istorii SSSR. Dokumenty po istorii Sovetskogo obshchestva*, fasc. 1 (Moscow, 1955), pp. 425–26; and *Sotsialisticheskoe zemledelie*, 31 December 1930, p. 3.

17. L. Berson, *Vesna 1930 goda. Zapiska dvadtsatipiatitysiachnika* (Moscow, 1931), pp. 18–19.

18. TsGAOR, *f.* 5469, *op.* 13, *d.* 123, *ll.* 28–40 (*Dokladnye zapiski* on the activities of metal workers in the North Caucasus countryside in the fall of 1929; compiled by the metal workers' union).

19. Ibid., *ll.* 78–91 (*Dokladnye zapiski* on the activities of metal-workers in the Ukrainian countryside in the fall of 1929; compiled by the metal workers union).

20. A. Angarov, "Sel'sovet i likvidatsiia kulachestva kak klassa," *Bol'shevik*, no. 6 (31 March 1930): 25.

21. During the Schism, the Old Believers often expressed protest in similar terms. Moreover, an apocalyptic mindset among peasants seems to be a characteristic response at times of momentous upheaval and transformation. See, for example, Michael Cherniavsky, "The Old Believers and the New Religion," in Michael Cherniavsky, ed., *The Structure of Russian History* (New York, 1970), pp. 140–88.

22. Angarov, "Sel'sovet i likvidatsiia," p. 25.

23. Mikhail Sholokhov, *Virgin Soil Upturned*, trans. Robert Daglish, vol. 1 (Moscow, 1980), p. 176.

24. Berson, *Vesna 1930 goda,* pp. 18–19; *Bastiony revoliutsii. Stranitsy istorii Leningradskikh zavodov,* fasc. 3 (Leningrad, 1960), p. 241; and see note 16 above.

25. *Trud,* 28 March 1930, p. 3.

26. This local Communist was originally sentenced to six years for his "aesthetic excess" but later the term was lowered. Ianson claimed he was extremely progressive, given his social conditions. See N. M. Ianson, "O peregibakh i ikh ispravlenii," *Sovetskaia iustitsiia,* no. 11 (20 April 1930): 3, and "Rech' t. Iansona na 3-om soveshchanii sudebno-prokurorskikh rabotnikov," *Sovetskaia iustitsiia,* no. 24/25 (10–20 September 1930): 7–8.

27. *Sovetskaia iustitsiia,* no. 13 (10 May 1930): 10 (Editorial by P. I. Stuchka).

28. Angarov, "Sel'sovet i likvidatsiia," p. 21.

29. Petro G. Grigorenko, *Memoirs,* trans. Thomas P. Whitney (New York, 1982), p. 35.

30. Anna Louise Strong, *The Soviets Conquer Wheat* (New York, 1931), p. 37. It should be noted that Beatrice Farnsworth briefly mentions the rational content of the *bab'i bunty* of collectivization in an essay that appeared as this article was being revised. See her interesting "Village Women Experience the Revolution," in Abbott Gleason, Peter Kenez, and Richard Stites, eds., *Bolshevik Culture: Experiment and Order in the Russian Revolution* (Bloomington, Ind., 1985), p. 254.

31. Stalin, "Rech' na pervom vsesoiuznom s"ezde kolkhoznikov-udarnikov," *Sochineniia,* vol. 13, p. 252.

32. V. Denisov, *Odin iz dvadtsati piati tysiach* (Krasnoiarsk, 1967), pp. 19–21.

33. Maurice Hindus, *Red Bread* (New York, 1931), p. 14.

34. Berson, *Vesna 1930 goda,* p. 73; S. Leikin, "Raskulachennyi kulak i ego taktika," *Bol'shevik,* no. 13 (15 July 1930): 74; Sadovnikov, "Shefstvo nad kolkhozom 'Revoliutsii'," pp. 5–6.

35. "Nepravil'noe vydelenie dela ob ideinom vdokhnovitele massovykh bezporiadkov," *Sudebnaia praktika,* no. 3 (28 February 1930): 11–12.

36. Grigorenko, *Memoirs,* p. 35. Also see Atkinson, *The End of the Russian Land Commune,* pp. 367–68, for support of Grigorenko's conclusion.

37. G. I. Arsenov, *Lebedevka, selo kolkhoznoe* (Kursk, 1964), pp. 43–44.

38. S. Zamiatin, *Burnyi god. Opyt raboty piatitysiachnika v Rudnianskom raione na Nizhnei Volge* (Moscow, 1931), pp. 9–16.

39. Sholokhov, *Virgin Soil Upturned,* vol. 1, pp. 311, 316, 321.

40. Lev Kopelev, *Education of a True Believer* (New York, 1980), p. 188.

41. *II sessiia VTsIK XIV sozyva,* Biulleten' no. 7, p. 28.

42. Chernomorskii, "Rol' rabochikh brigad," p. 325.

43. Denisov, *Odin iz dvadtsati piati tysiach,* p. 27. It should be noted that in many cases peasant men were sincere about their wives' resistance and that there were reports of divorce and family strife over the collective farm. See Strong, *The Soviets Conquer Wheat,* pp. 114–15, and R. Belbei, *Za ili protiv. (Kak rabochii ispravliaet peregiby v derevne)* (Moscow, 1930), p. 50.

44. Hindus, *Red Bread,* pp. 169–70.

45. See the case described in Lynne Viola, "Notes on the Background of Soviet Collectivisation: Metal Worker Brigades in the Countryside, Autumn 1929," *Soviet Studies* 36, no. 2 (April 1984): 216, in which the women organizers of a rebellion called upon all women to join the protest or face a fine of three rubles.

46. "Direktiv UKK Verkhsuda RSFSR," *Sudebnaia praktika,* no. 5 (10 April 1930): 4–6.

47. Roberta Manning has analyzed peasant rebellions during the 1905 revolution and its aftermath and has concluded that, "however spontaneous and chaotic they [riots] might have appeared, they display signs of organization and prior planning and a rudimentary sense of

strategy." See her description of peasant protest in Roberta Thompson Manning, *The Crisis of the Old Order in Russia* (Princeton, 1982), pp. 148–58.

48. Field, *Rebels in the Name of the Tsar,* pp. 2, 213–14.

49. See Lynne Viola, "The Campaign of the 25,000ers. A Study of the Collectivization of Soviet Agriculture, 1929–1931" (Ph.D. dissertation, Princeton University, 1984), chaps. 4 and 5.

50. Atkinson, *The End of the Russian Land Commune,* pp. 367–69.

51. As R. W. Davies has demonstrated in *The Soviet Collective Farm* (Cambridge, 1980), the basic shape of collectivized agriculture took form in the years 1930 and 1931 as a compromise (albeit unbalanced) between the state and the peasantry, between socialist fortress-storming in the village and traditional ways. The state was forced to settle for a program minimum, in which the peasantry was allowed to maintain a private plot, domestic livestock, and limited direct access to the market. After 1930–31, the compromise would be maintained of necessity, and no longer on the basis of peasant protest, by what E. J. Hobsbawm has labeled the "normal strategy of the traditional peasantry"—passivity—which, he adds, "is not an ineffective strategy, for it exploits the major assets of the peasantry, its numbers and the impossibility of making it do some things by force for any length of time, and it also utilises a favourable tactical situation, which rests on the fact that no change is what suits a traditional peasantry best." See E. J. Hobsbawm, "Peasants and Politics," *Journal of Peasant Studies* 1, no. 1 (October 1973): 13. For further information on the shape of collective farming in the 1930s, see Roberta T. Manning, *Government in the Soviet Countryside in the Stalinist Thirties: The Case of Belyi Raion in 1937,* Carl Beck Papers in Russian and East European Studies, no. 301 (Pittsburgh, 1984).

11 / Women in the Soviet Countryside on the Eve of World War II, 1935–1940

ROBERTA T. MANNING

Roberta T. Manning, an associate professor of history at Boston College, examines the role of women in Soviet agriculture during the second half of the 1930s. This period is often known as the time of the "great retreat" because of the triumph of conservatism in many policy areas, especially those concerning women and the family. Divorce was severely restricted and abortion all but outlawed at this time. Manning, however, argues against the notion of a retreat insofar as most rural women were concerned, suggesting that the interests of production dictated otherwise in the countryside. The central government continued to encourage rural women to seek employment in nontraditional jobs and to serve in Soviet and Communist Party positions. Moreover, the new divorce and abortion laws were greeted with satisfaction by most rural women (excluding some younger and professional women) and, according to Manning, were "directed against irresponsible males rather than . . . designed to limit the options of women." The real retreat came in the form of the obstacles erected by peasant culture (represented by both men and women) and lower-level officials (many of whom were peasants by social origin) to those women who sought to work and live outside the mainstream of traditional peasant women's roles. This chapter demonstrates once again, through the experience of women, the enormous staying power of peasant culture, even in the repressive 1930s.

Like many other aspects of Soviet life in the prewar Stalin era, the role of women in the countryside remains largely unexplored. This is particularly true of the second half of the 1930s, after the upheavals of collectivization had subsided and the contours of the new agrarian order were more clearly delineated.[1] To date, our knowledge of this period is limited to the legislative decrees of June 27, 1936, to strengthen the family, make divorce more difficult, and encourage a rise in the birth rate by prohibiting abortion and providing government subsidies to women with large numbers of children. These efforts are generally viewed by scholars as a retreat on the part of the ruling Communist Party from its earlier commitment to women's liberation.[2] A recent study summed up these developments most starkly: "Thereafter, the emancipatory goal was replaced by an emphasis on the responsibilities of women to the family and the joys derived therefrom. Having been mobilized for production, women would henceforth be mobilized for reproduction."[3]

Viewed from the perspective of the countryside, where two-thirds of the Soviet populace and even more of the female population still resided, no clear-cut turn-about in government policies toward women can be discerned at the topmost levels of government in the mid- to late 1930s, although resistance to women's advancement grew at lower levels of administration, where traditional rural attitudes toward women tended to prevail. Nonetheless, the prohibition of abortion had less impact in rural localities than it did in urban areas, where the mere announcement that the government was contemplating such a move caused a rush on abortion clinics by pregnant women, fearful that their right to abortion would soon be rescinded.[4] Passage of the law resulted in a 50 to 100 percent increase in births in the major cities, overwhelming the health-care network with more births than existing medical facilities could handle.[5] Nationwide, however, the birthrate rose only 18 percent in 1937, from 24.6 per thousand in towns and cities and 32.2 per thousand in rural areas to 38.8 per thousand overall, before it declined to previous levels in 1938 and thereafter.[6] By the start of World War II, the number of fifth or higher-order births in the Soviet Union ran approximately 200,000 a year, 43 percent less than in the United States, which experienced 350,000 a year in the same period from a smaller female population.[7]

A major factor in the government's inability to raise birth rates by banning abortion was the weak development of health-care institutions outside the nation's towns and cities, which left much of rural health care in the hands of traditional village healers, wise women, and *znakhari*.[8] Even in 1939, after the June 1936 decrees substantially augmented obstetrical services for rural women, only 7,000 hospitals, 7,503 maternity homes, 14,300 clinics, and 26,700 *fel'dshers* (doctor's assistants) and *fel'dsher* stations existed to serve a rural population of 114,400,000 including 20,000,000 peasant women, ages sixteen to fifty-nine (Table 11.1). Under these conditions, freedom of abortion remained an empty right for all too many peasant women, while its repeal in 1936 was less onerous for peasants, since the state was able to monitor and control medical professionals employed in state institutions, located mainly in towns and larger villages, far more effectively than traditional healers operating out of their homes in the depths of the countryside.[9]

Moreover, traditional peasant attitudes toward the family and marriage strongly conditioned rural women's response to the June 1936 decrees. The month-long public discussion that preceded the enactment of these measures into law revealed that peasant women, with few exceptions, strongly supported the ban on abortion.[10] Indeed, some older women even suggested that criminal sanctions, including arrest, be applied to women who sought abortions as well as to abortionists and persons forcing women to undergo abortion, as the June 1936 decrees stipulated.[11] In one village near Moscow, clear-cut generational differences emerged in the course of the discussion, among older and younger collective farm women, with older women strongly supporting the government's move to ban abortion and younger women favoring the retention of the right of abortion for women with four or more children.[12] Such differences in opinion possibly explain why the ban failed to produce an increase in the number of higher-order births, as the government expected.

Table 11.1. Rural Health-Care Network, 1914–1939

Type of Medical Facilities	1914	1939
Rural hospitals	3,000	Over 7,000
Clinics staffed by doctors	4,300	14,300
Fel'dshers and *fel'dsher* stations	4,500	26,700
No. of rural district doctors		11,785[b]
No. of hospital beds (in both town and countryside)	49,000	178,900
Rural maternity homes	n.d.[a]	7,503
No. of beds in rural maternity homes	n.d.[a]	23,200
No. of rural residents		114,400,000
No. of rural women, ages 16–59		Over 20,000,000
No. of rural *raions*		4,007
No. of rural soviets		63,036
No. of collective farms		243,700

[a]Prerevolutionary Russia had 6,824 beds in maternity hospitals located chiefly in towns and cities. In 1939 the Soviet Union possessed a total of 81,500 maternity beds, including 23,200 in rural maternity homes.

[b]Data for 1938.

Sources: M. A. Vyltsan, *Zavershaiushchii etap sozdaniia kolkhoznogo stroia (1935–1937 g.g.)* (Moscow, 1978), pp. 61, 192, 224; Susan Bridger, *Women in the Soviet Countryside: Women's Roles in Rural Development in the Soviet Union* (Cambridge, 1987), p. 13; A. I. Lepeshkin, *Sovety—vlast naroda 1936–1967* (Moscow, 1967), p. 14; *Krest'ianskaia gazeta*, April 24, 1938, p. 2.

Younger, better educated rural professional women—agronomists, veterinaries, and zootechnicians—like their urban counterparts, went even further in defending freedom of choice, opposing any legal restrictions on the right of abortion.[13] N. I. Ivleva poignantly summed up the dilemmas the decrees caused rural professional women:

> I have worked four years as a senior raion zootechnician in Voronezh *oblast* [region]. I visit the farms daily and spend two months each fall and spring in the village. I can't imagine myself without work in production. I rejoice in each result of my work.
>
> When I read the law, I wondered if I will be able in the future to work this way if abortion is prohibited. I love children and have a daughter whose birth interrupted my studies. I fully understand the harm of abortion. But I am against prohibiting it, because such a law will require me to change my work or risk my health.[14]

Rural women, both peasants and professionals, tended to use the discussion to press for additional services for women and children. In one rural soviet in Belyi *raion* (district) in the Western *oblast,* the discussion centered on shortages of children's shoes and clothing in local stores, with collective-farm women arguing that the government must provide them with the ability to dress their children properly if it expected them to bear more![15] Often the discussion focused on the expansion of health- and day-care facilities and subsidies to mothers with large families promised

Table 11.2. Enforcement of the Provisions of the June 27, 1936, Decrees Concerning the Expansion of the Number of Beds for Rural Maternity Patients and the Number of Places in Day-Care Centers

	As Stipulated by the June 1936 Decrees by 1/1/39	No. Actually Possessed in 1939–1940
Rural maternity beds	41,300 (new)	23,200 (total, new and old
Year-round nurseries (*iasli*)		
Urban	800,000	n.d.
Rural	570,000	n.d.
Total	1,370,000	859,500
Year-round kindergartens		
Urban	2,100,000	n.d.
Rural	1,400,000	n.d.
Total	3,500,000	1,175,100
Seasonal nurseries[a]	9,000,000	4,049,100
Seasonal playgrounds[a]	10,700,000	1,175,100

[a]Rural, located in the main on collective farms during the height of the agricultural work season.

Sources: M. A. Vyltsan, *Zavershaiushchii etap sozdaniia kolkhoznogo stroia (1935–1937 g.g.)* (Moscow, 1978), p. 224; H. Kent Geiger, *The Family in Soviet Russia* (Cambridge, Mass., 1968), p. 194; Rudolf Schlesinger, *The Family in the U.S.S.R.* (London, 1949), pp. 273–75.

in the draft law, and many participants insisted that the government should go even further in this regard.[16] Subsequently, government spokesmen maintained that such suggestions prompted them to extend aid to mothers bearing seven or more children instead of the ten stipulated in the original draft project.[17]

The project's commitment to the expansion of the existing inadequate medical and day-care network appeared genuinely popular, although the end results, as is generally the case with Soviet welfare measures, fell far short of the government's goals (Table 11.2) because of the ubiquitous shortages of vital construction materials and the apathy of the local officials entrusted with the implementation of these measures.[18] The chairman of the Kuibyshev collective farm in Shiroko–Karamyshkin *raion,* Saratov *oblast,* told collective-farm mothers demanding a supervised playground: "You lived earlier without day nurseries [*iasli*] and playgrounds. You can live this way now too," while two collective-arm chairmen in Rodelnianskii *raion,* Odessa *oblast,* confiscated existing day-care buildings for office space.[19] Social-security administrators in Stalingrad, Ivanovo, Voronezh, and Iaroslavl *oblasts* initially denied collective-farm women the subsidies granted mothers of large families on the grounds that social-security measures did not apply to collective farmers, as was generally the case with other welfare measures. So commonplace was this interpretation of the new law that RSFSR Procurator Antonov-Ovseenko was obliged to intervene and threaten to prosecute offending officials.[20]

In rural localities, discussion of the June 1936 decrees generally focused not so much on the abortion and welfare provisions of the new law as on changes in the divorce law and in the provision of child-support payments (usually mistakingly called alimony in English-language discussions of this law). Peasant women and rural professional women alike tended to applaud the government's moves to require the presence of both spouses at divorce proceedings in government registration offices (Z.A.G.S.), to institute a progressive scale of fees for each successive divorce, to register the fact of divorce in the divorcees' passports, and to beef up child-support payments by requiring payments of one-fourth the defendants' salary for one child, one-third for two children, and one-half for three or more children. Especially popular was the institution of a two-year prison sentence for those found guilty of evading child-support payments.[21] Indeed, some collective-farm women wanted to increase the fees for divorce and the penalties for evading child-support payments beyond those stipulated in the draft decree![22]

In so acting, discussants were motivated as much by current social problems as by traditional village attitudes toward marriage. By the mid-1930s, rapid industrialization and collectivization jointly resulted in geographic and social mobility on an unprecedented scale that undermined growing numbers of Soviet families. Between 1926 and 1939, 18.5 million to 23 million persons, disproportionately able-bodied males in the prime of life, left the countryside to take up permanent residence in towns, driven by the political persecutions of the collectization period, low living standards on the new collective farms, and growing opportunities for employment, education, and advancement in the nation's expanding industries.[23] Another 5.5 million rural residents in the mid- to late 1930s, once again overwhelming able-bodied males, were temporarily absent from their native villages for lengthy periods, as a result of *otkhodnichestvo* (seasonal work outside the village), educational programs, and the military draft.[24] In 1937, 27.2 percent of rural men between the ages of sixteen and fifty-nine and 8.5 percent of rural women in the same age bracket were absent for these purposes.[25] These developments were compounded by political terror, which fell disproportionately heavily on males,[26] and demographic disasters, like World War I, the civil war, and the 1921 and 1932 famines, all of which took more male than female lives.[27] Unprecedented and growing numbers of women were consequently left to cope on their own with their children.

Fenia, the village girl in Valentin Kataev's novel *Time Forward,* who arrived in Magnitogorsk far along in her pregnancy in search of her village lover who had impregnated and deserted her,[28] was not a stock character in the Soviet fiction of the 1930s. But girls and women like her were stock characters in the real-life human dramas of the times that affected married women no less than the unmarried.[29] In 1934, 200,000 child-support cases filed in the courts of the RSFSR were filed against "fugitive fathers" (*beglye ottsy*)—men who had simply disappeared without a trace, leaving their wives, their children, and the Soviet judicial system unable to locate them. As a result, close to 40 percent of all court decisions in child-support cases remained "unrealized," since the defendant could not be located. Local law-enforcement agencies, understaffed and overburdened with political cases and a crime wave of unprecedented proportions that remains to be studied, regarded "alimony hunts" (*alimentarnye iski*) as matters of secondary importance, if not cases that were outright impossible to pursue. Moreover, even when fugitive fathers could be located, male industrial administrators, anxious to keep their workers given the high rates of labor turnover that then prevailed, often failed to cooperate with investigating authorities. Yet the male-dominated judiciary, before the adoption of the June 1936 decrees, was rarely willing to overburden fathers with high child-support payments. Indeed, 17 percent of the child-support payments awarded by the courts in the mid-1930s, before the enactment of the June 1936 decrees, amounted to less than 20 rubles a month, while in 25 percent of the cases, no payment whatsoever was imposed.[30]

But what could Soviet women expect? This, after all, was an era in which fugitive fathers from the Western *oblast* could be found as far away as Siberia or even Kamchatka.[31] Local party committees in the mid- and late 1930s were often overwhelmed by petitions from former wives of local officials begging the party to collect child-support payments due them from their husbands' salaries![32] Even as high an official as Ivan Petrovich Rumantsev, long-time *obkom* (regional party committee) secretary in the Western *oblast,* refused to pay—in October 1936, after all the fanfare over the new family legislation—his former wife the full amount of child support awarded by the courts under the old procedures. Yet the payments came to a much smaller proportion of his salary than the new legislation stipulated![33] No wonder village women strongly welcomed the new, stricter policies on child support and divorce, rightfully regarding these initiatives as measures directed against irresponsible males rather than policies designed to limit the options of women.[34]

The contemporary Soviet press reinforced such perceptions of the legislation. In 1936, *Pravda* published more photographs of fathers with young children and of children in day-care centers than pictures of mothers of large families, while photographs of women involved in nontraditional pursuits far outnumbered those of women portrayed primarily as wives and mothers (Table 11.3). If these photographic images tell us anything, they indicate the continuing stress that the Communist Party and Soviet government placed on women's roles in production. Half the women who appeared in *Pravda* photos in 1936 were featured for their work achievements, and virtually all were identified in the captions by occupation.

Official encouragement of women's roles in production was especially strong in the countryside, where females came to provide 59.5 percent of the available rural labor force by the end of the 1930s[35] and an even larger proportion of those involved in actual agricultural work, like raising crops and caring for livestock. High rates of male out-migration from the countryside in the wake of the collectivization of agriculture were compounded by the tendency of the remaining rural males to move into the better paid positions, like administrative posts on the new collective farms and mechanical work as tractor and combine drivers and Machine Tractor Station (MTS) mechanics and administrators (Table 11.4). In 1940, administrative work on the nation's 243,000 collective farms, as chairmen, assistant chairmen, managers of livestock farms, brigade leaders, bookkeepers, and accountants, occupied 1.8 million persons, while 2.4 million were employed by the MTSs.[36] Such positions

Table 11.3. Photographic Images of Women Published in *Pravda*, 1936 (photographs of individual women and women in mixed groups)

No. of Photographs Published		**No. of Photographs of or with Women**	
Total	On Page 1	Total	On Page 1
1,970	246	478 (24.3%)	82 (33.3%)
Women portrayed as mothers and wives			
Mothers of large families (7–15 children)		8[a]	0
Mothers with newborns or about to give birth		7[b]	0
Participants in various conferences of wives (of executives in heavy industry, of military commanders, etc.)		37[c]	14
Photos of fathers with young children (without mothers)		11[d]	0
Photos of children in day care		12	0
Working women			
Industrial workers		21	2
Industrial Stakhanovites		51	10
Agricultural Stakhanovites		99[e]	23
Rank-and-file collective farmwomen		26	5
Professionals		30[f]	3
Other workers		3[g]	3
Women in politics or official positions			
Women politicians		33	4
Women attending political meetings		24[h]	7
Low-level rural officials		29[i]	1
Other pursuits			
Entertainers		23	1
Students		31[j]	2
Athletes		28	2
Race-car drivers		6	2
Aviators		13[k]	3[l]
Parachutists		8	0
Spanish women soldiers		8	0
Sharpshooters		8[k]	0
Vorshilov calvaryists		2	0
Civil-defense first aid		2	0
Glider pilots		2	0

[a]Two of whom are shown with their husbands, including an award-winning Uzbek woman cotton farmer.

[b]Two of whom are shown with their husbands.

[c]Includes one women identified as a sharpshooter, one as a glider pilot, and one as an aviator. The last—Polina Osipenko—subsequently overturned Amelia Earhart's world record for a long-distance flight and vowed to do this at the military commanders wives' conference!

[d]Includes four record-setting aviators.

[e]Those portrayed were livestock workers, involved in raising technical crops such as cotton, sugar beets, and flax, or mechanical workers such as tractor, flaxpuller, and combine drivers.

[f]Included three engineers, two agronomists, two zootechnicians, one professor, one artist, one mining technician, seven scientific researchers, and twelve teachers.

[g]Includes one fisherwoman and two workers in the timber industry.

Table 11.3. (*Continued*)

[h]In the main, meetings or activities in support of the Spanish Republic or to condemn the defendents in the Kamenev–Zinoviev trial.

[i]Includes ten collective-farm chairwomen, one assistant collective-farm chairwoman, five rural soviet chairwomen, seven collective-farm brigade leaders, two managers of collective-farm dairy farms, and two postmen.

[j]Almost all were either outstanding secondary-school students or enrolled in higher education.

[k]Includes one woman pictured in military uniform said to be an auditor at a military academy training army officers.

[l]One of these, Tamara Aleksandrovna Kazarinova, who was shown in military uniform and identified as the commander of an aviation detachment (*aviiachasti*), was given the Order of Lenin; another, Marina Nesterenko, was identified as both the commander of aviation health care in the Kiev Military District and a delegate to the conference of wives of Red Army commanders.

Source: *Pravda*, January 1, 1936, to December 31, 1936.

Table 11.4. Representation of Males and Females in Leading Posts in Agriculture, 1936

Position	% Men	% Women	Of the Women, % Under Age 25
MTS cadres			
MTS directors	99.6	0.4	0
Assistant MTS directors	91.8	8.2	0
Agronomists	90.3	9.7	60.6
Traveling mechanics	99.2	0.8	75
Combine drivers and helpers	93.7	6.3	80.6
Tractor brigade leaders and assistant leaders	99.3	0.7	66.7
Tractor drivers	96.0	4.0	79.0
Collective-farm cadres			
Collective-farm chairmen and assistant chairmen	97.3	2.7	10.6
Members of collective-farm boards	81.9	18.1	12.3
Chairmen of collective-farm revision commissions	84.9	15.1	20.7
Accountants (*chetovody*), bookkeepers, and their assistants	95.5	4.5	63
Managers of livestock farms	83.9	16.1	19.3
Livestock brigade leaders	78.5	21.5	38.3
Cattle tenders (*skotniki*)	49.3	50.7	22.4
Stable hands (*koniukhi*)	96.8	3.2	18.8
Field brigade leaders	97.3	2.7	18.7
Link leaders	33.2	66.8	37.6
Chauffeurs	99.3	0.7	14.3
Managers of clubs	89.4	10.6	62.4

Source: A. Malukhina, "Zhenshchiny v kolkhozakh—bol'shaia sila," *Sotsialisticheskaia rekonstruktsiia sel'skogo khoziaistva*, no. 3 (March 1938): 32

Table 11.5. Contributions of Men and Women to Basic Agricultural Work on the Collective Farms, 1935 (numbers of men, women, and adolescents in each 100 collective-farm brigades)

Form of Work	Men		Women		Youths (12–15)[a]	
	No.	%	No.	%	No.	%
Field brigade	240	44.4	300	55.5	0	0
Cattle brigade	350	41.3	435	51.4	62	7.3
Pig brigade	151	40.5	202	54.1	20	5.4
Sheep brigade	245	61.6	122	30.6	31	2.5

[a]Unlike the collective-farm population age sixteen and over, which suffered from an acute and growing surplus of females over males, younger collective farmers were rather evenly divided between the sexes, with males enjoying a slight edge. In 1939, 51.5% of collective farmers between the ages of fifteen and sixteen were male, and 48.5% were female. Warren Eason, *The Agricultural Labor Force and Population of the USSR, 1926–41* (Santa Monica, Calif., 1954, p. 31.

Source: M. A. Vyltsan, *Zavershaiushchii etap sozdaniia kolkhoznogo stroia (1935–1937 g.g.)* (Moscow, 1978), pp. 104–6.

engaged close to a quarter of the 16.6 million rural males over the age of sixteen,[37] while another quarter (27.2%) were temporarily absent from the countryside for reasons of work, education, and military service.[38]

Women therefore accounted for at least two-thirds of the 31.3 million persons employed in manual work on the collective farms in 1940.[39] Even in 1935, when women's involvement in work on the collective farms was significantly less substantial, women provided the majority of members of collective-farm brigades in all major areas of the economy, save sheep raising (Table 11.5). The situation was particularly critical in the non–Black Soil Region, the area of traditional peasant *otkhodnichestvo*, where up to 90 percent of the field work on some collective farms was performed by women.[40] A British visitor described one such collective farm near Leningrad, ten miles east of the town of Luga: "most of the work was done by women, the men having drifted into the towns and gone away to lumbering camps. The fields were badly tilled and a goodly proportion of the land neglected."[41]

Hard-pressed collective-farm chairmen, under government pressures to produce more and meet hefty levels of procurements, sought to stem the male exodus. Some chairmen resisted the efforts of state enterprises to recruit workers in the countryside. Others unilaterally expelled or denied *trudoden* (labor-day)* payments to families whose male *otkhodniki* failed to return regularly to participate in the harvest.[42] Such initiatives were repeatedly condemned by higher authorities, who intervened periodically to halt these practices,[43] aggravating existing labor shortages in industry.[44] Yet men actually present in the countryside contributed more working time than women to the collective farm, including administrative work (Tables 11.6 and 11.7). This, plus the fact that men tended to concentrate in the better-paying, year-round positions, allowed males to earn two-thirds of the trudoden earned by collective farmers in 1937.[45]

*Unit of payment on collective farms, calculated according to the type of labor performed.

Table 11.6. Seasonality of Women's Work on Collective Farms in the Western *Oblast*, 1933–1934

Month	% of Collective Farmers Working on the Collective Farm		No. of Days Worked for Each Working Collective Farmer	
	Men Age 16–59	Women Age 16–59	Men Age 16–59	Women Age 16–59
January	69.6	39.3	15.6	10.7
February	76.4	26.8	13.9	9.3
March	83.1	38.8	16.9	9.4
April	77.7	39.0	18.5	11.9
May	88.0	72.1	21.9	13.7
June	93.0	83.1	21.5	14.3
July	89.9	88.1	26.4	22.8
August	93.0	88.1	26.5	22.3
September	97.3	87.4	23.3	18.6
October	98.0	84.7	21.4	16.6
November	91.0	78.1	18.9	13.5
December	83.8	65.0	19.0	11.2

Source: *Kollektivizatsiia sel'skogo khoziaistva v zapadnom raione RSFSR (1927–1937 g.g.)* (Smolensk, 1968), p. 471.

Women's work on the collective farms was more seasonal. Women were also responsible for the "private" or household garden plot and the familial livestock. These tasks were traditionally considered women's work under the sexual division of labor that prevailed before the collectivization of agriculture.[46] Both the household plot and livestock were generally situated near the home so that this sort of work could be more easily coordinated with housekeeping and child rearing than work on the collective farm, at least as long as the chronic short supply of day-care institutions, particularly year-round facilities, continued to exist in the coun-

Table 11.7. The Work of Able-Bodied Collective Farmers (age 16–59), 1937 (based on time budget studies of selected collective-farm households)

Where Worked	% Males	% Females
Worked on collective farm	58.9	35.3
Worked at MTS	2.5	0.2
Away for *otkhodnichestvo*, military service, and studies	27.2	8.5
All other, include work on household	11.4	56.0
garden plot	5.7	24.1
No. of hours per worker per year devoted to work on household garden plot	153.3	619.5

Source: Nancy Nimitz, *Farm Employment in the Soviet Union, 1928–1963* (Santa Monica, Calif., 1965), p. 76.

tryside.[47] Women consequently provided more than 80 percent of the labor expended on household plots, which supplied collective-farm families in the 1930s with the bulk of their food other than grain products and a large portion of their cash income as well.[48] Some accounts of life in the Soviet countryside in the 1930s maintain that collective-farm women, like all collective farmers, worked less than individual peasants did before collectivization.[49] Women, too, could avail themselves of the right of a two-month paid maternity leave granted by the model collective-farm charter of 1935.[50] To be sure, this leave was only half as long as the maternity leaves accorded urban workers and employees.[51] Women on these leaves received only half the average monthly *trudoden* payments they normally earned.[52] Nonetheless, the leaves were highly popular among collective-farm women, although some chairmen, short of labor at critical periods of the crop cycle, denied women such leaves, especially initially, in 1935 and 1936.[53]

Rather than penalize families of *otkhodniki* or deny women their maternity leaves, national authorities preferred to deal with the harvesttime labor shortages on the collective farms by raising the minimum number of *trudoden* required of collective-farm members[54] and recognizing outstanding work achievements. Outstanding workers were awarded Stakhanovite or shockworker status, along with consumer goods in short supply, opportunities for upward mobility, and attention from the mass media, like that normally accorded entertainers and celebrities in other lands. Not surprisingly, given the demographic structure of the agricultural labor force, the bulk of agricultural Stakhanovites—perhaps as many as 80 percent[55] and an even larger proportion of those involved in field work—appear to have been females.[56] This stands in marked contrast to industrial Stakhanovites, among whom women not only were far less prominent but were actually underrepresented.[57]

In agriculture at least, the most renown women Stakhanovites, who enjoyed the most attention from the press and led major emulation movements as Stakhanov did in coal mining, appear to have been young (under the age of twenty-five) and uncommonly physically attractive. Other women, older and less attractive, whose achievements matched or exceeded that of these leaders tended to receive far less press attention.[58] Women Stakhanovites in agriculture tended to concentrate in three areas of production: mechanical work, livestock tending, and the cultivation of technical crops requiring processing by industry, like flax, cotton, and sugar beets.[59] Much of this work was unusually arduous and little was mechanized, which may explain why most agricultural Stakhanovites, like their counterparts in industry, were under the age of twenty-five.[60] Significantly, almost all the agricultural work for which women received recognition in the 1930s, save mechanical work, had been considered primarily women's work before the collectivization of agriculture.[61]

The cultivation of cotton, flax, and sugar beets, unlike Russia's traditional grain crops, was exceedingly labor intensive, required much time-consuming, backbreaking physical labor, and resisted mechanization due to its complexity. Even when harvesting machines were available, as in the case of flax, they often malfunctioned or worked so poorly as to require a second harvesting by hand. Nonetheless, the amount of land planted in these crops more than doubled in the 1930s, giving the government ample reason to encourage women involved in such work.[62]

Livestock rearing, especially the position of milkmaid, was the best paid of the occupations for which collective-farm women were likely to be given recognition in the 1930s, other than mechanical work, because of its year-round rather than seasonal character. Between 750,000 and 1 million Soviet women were employed as milkmaids in the late 1930s,[63] although this may have been the most taxing female agricultural occupation of all. If the press is any indication, only a single male "milkmaid" then existed—Makar Semenovich Ivaniun of the Stalin collective farm, Shtepovskii *raion,* Khar'kov *oblast,* who was attracted to this work by the high pay and honors accorded the women employed as milkmaids on his collective farm.[64] Men were apparently reluctant to become "milkmaids," given the rigid sexual division of labor that prevailed in the countryside, both before and after collectivization. Work as a milkmaid also entailed long hours of exhausting physical toil. The standard workday for milkmaids extended from 3:00 to 5:50 A.M. until 9:00 to 10:00 P.M., punctuated by several two- to three-hour breaks, during which these women had to cope with housework, cooking, laundry, and child care as well as care of their familial livestock and garden plots.[65] The average workload for milkmaids was ten to twelve cows, although some serviced as many as eighteen cows. Award-winning milkmaids who milked *rekordistki* (record-setting cows) of necessity milked fewer cows, since more time had to be spent milking highly productive animals.[66]

Milkmaids not only milked their cows but also were obliged to feed, water, and clean them and to care for any calves born to their cows through the first several weeks of life. To water a single cow, a milkmaid had to haul 80 to 100 pails of water a day. Some spent as many as four to five hours daily hauling water alone, for virtually no collective farms were then supplied with running water.[67] Hauling feed and manure, taking milk to the butter factory, and grinding up fodder could easily consume another two hours, while milking appears to have taken at least four to five hours a day.[68] Milking was a repetitive process involving 140 to 300 squeezes of a cow's udders a minute and up to 50,000 a day, cramping the hands and joints, if not the entire body.[69] No wonder that prize-winning milkmaids often used their access to the press to agitate for a reduction in their workloads[70] and that the turnover rates for this occupation remained among the highest in agriculture. Nationwide, 27.1 percent of all milkmaids transferred to other work each year,[71] and only 9.1 percent remained in this occupation for more than five years.[72] In some regions, like Novosibirsk, Sverdlovsk, and Kuibyshev *oblasts,* the annual turnover rate ran as high as 43 percent.[73]

One factor in these high turnover rates was the frequency of occupational illnesses among milkmaids. The most common of these ailments was an affliction known as *neiromagleiia,* often developing after three to five years of work and entailing severe aches and pains in a milkmaid's fingers and joints, which could leave a woman incapable not only of milking properly but also of tending to basic household chores, such as doing the laundry. In extreme cases, a woman could find herself unable to do any housework or even to leave her home. Boils, pustules, and abscesses also frequently developed on milkmaids' fingers near the fingernails, due to the improper cleaning of the hands, the lack of days off, and the cold and moisture present in the cattle barns, particularly during the long Russian winters.[74]

Scientists studying these complaints tended to attribute them to the often excessive division of labor that prevailed on the collective farms, unlike the individual peasant economy in which a variety of tasks were performed in the course of a day.[75] Another common occupational disease, brucellosis, threatened all categories of livestock workers, not just milkmaids. This highly infectious ailment, which killed 55,200 cattle in the Soviet Union in 1935, 88,900 in 1936, and 36,900 in the first five months of 1937,[76] was spread from animals to humans through personal contact or consumption of the unpasteurized milk of infected beasts.[77]

The third major area of agricultural work for which women were given considerable recognition was mechanical work, as tractor, combine, and flax-puller drivers and MTS mechanics. Such work in many ways was every bit as onerous as the work of a milkmaid. Women mechanical workers had to endure the same problems as their male colleagues—long hours, irregular pay,[78] and excessively poor living conditions in the fields during the growing season, when drivers were often obliged to live away from home for weeks on end, sleeping under the open skies or in cramped, dirty, dark, ill-equipped trailers without heating or bathing facilities, dependent on the mercies of the local collective farmers for food and even water.[79] Drivers rode exposed to the elements and to field dust and noxious exhaust fumes, and accidents and breakdowns were commonplace.[80]

Women drivers, however, also suffered a series of additional problems unique to their sex, as the first rural women working in an area of the economy claimed and dominated by men. Existing tractors and combines were Soviet-manufactured copies of common American machines, designed to conform to the bodily proportions of males, not females. Women drivers found the iron seats highly uncomfortable and sometimes had problems reaching the pedals or steering wheel.[81] Peoples' Commissar of Agriculture Chernov responded to such complaints in August 1936 by ordering the seats on all wheeled tractors to be redesigned to make them more suitable for women drivers. But like many other decrees from the center, these orders were often ignored by local officials.[82] MTS leaders tended to resist central pressures to attract or retain female drivers. They discouraged women who wished to enter training programs for drivers, failed to hire all the women drivers trained, provided women drivers with the worse equipment available, failed to service their machines adequately in the field, and seemed eager to rid themselves of the services of even the most successful and experienced women drivers.[83] A senior mechanic in the Osinskii MTS in Sverdlovsk *oblast* dismissed twenty-three-year-old Mariia Litvinova, who had worked successfully as a tractor driver for three years, telling her that "women are too weak to drive tractors and we have enough men."[84] After Pasha Angelina astonished local MTS officials in the Donbas at age seventeen by plowing more than any other driver in her MTS in her first season of work, she was offered a promotion as a storekeeper in the oil depot to remove her from tractor work. When Pasha resisted this move, she was told, "We don't need women [baby] in the MTS!"[85] Yet a study undertaken by the Central Committee *orgburo* (organizational bureau) in Iaroslavl *oblast* concluded that women made better machine drivers than men, since they were more disciplined and careful and tended to work more land than the average male driver.[86]

Collective-farm leaders and ordinary peasants, both men and women, resisted women's intrusion into this unorthodox line of work. Collective-farm chairmen refused to provide women tractor brigades with the support workers they needed, such as water carriers, cooks, and fuel carriers, leaving both drivers and machines without water or food, while brigade leaders often failed to prepare the fields adequately for machine work.[87] Pasha Angelina, one of the nation's first women tractor drivers, was greeted by a hostile crowd of collective farmers on her first day of work in the fields in the summer of 1930, shouting, "You have lost all shame," while her family and fiancé, a fellow tractor driver, begged her to give up tractor work.[88] When Pasha appeared several years later in the fields at the head of the Soviet Union's first women's tractor brigade, collective-farm women turned out en masse to prevent the women's brigade from entering the field for fear they would spoil the plowing. However, after the women's brigade finished the plowing in record time, the same women who had protested earlier brought them food in gratitude for their good work.[89]

Mechanical work nonetheless remained a corrosive factor in the personal life of the girls and women who engaged in this occupation, long after women drivers ceased to be a novelty in the Soviet countryside. Women drivers acquired a disreputable reputation among their fellow villagers, since they worked late hours with male drivers and mechanics at the MTS during the repair season and frequently spent nights during the growing season in the fields in the company of men with time on their hands and few recreational outlets, save drinking.[90] When pregnancy resulted from such experiences, the women were mercilessly teased by the men among whom they worked as well as the rural population at large, prompting at least one girl in 1937 to commit suicide.[91] Rape, too, must have figured among the problems of women drivers, since it was not uncommon in the underpoliced countryside, although reports of rapes rarely surfaced in the press.[92]

The morality of married women employed in mechanical occupations was no less suspect than that of the unmarried. Pasha Angelina's mother-in-law wondered aloud why her granddaughter resembled Pasha so closely but failed to look at all like her son. Stung by such remarks, Pasha's husband, the *raion* Komsomol secretary, demanded that Pasha give up tractor driving and spend more time with her baby, as did other mothers.[93] Pasha's marriage, like her earlier "understanding" with her childhood sweetheart, eventually broke up over her refusal to abandon her tractor.[94] All this occurred at a time when Pasha Angelina was a national heroine who had been invited to the Kremlin to meet with Stalin and Kalinin and receive the Order of Lenin, then the nation's topmost honor, becoming a celebrity pursued by crowds of admirers, journalists, and filmmakers to the point that she often found it difficult to work.[95] One wonders how less well-known women must have fared under these circumstances.

Even without provoking such "family crises," machine driving was not easy to combine with motherhood, given the long hours and time spent away from home in the fields. Pasha Angelina used her access to the press to demand mobile day-care centers for the children of women drivers so that they could accompany their mothers into the fields.[96] Few, if any, MTSs, however, responded to this call; thus few women with children ever took up this occupation, and 80 percent of women tractor and combine drivers remained under the age of twenty-five, since most left

Table 11.8. Representation of Women Among Tractor Drivers, 1930–1948

Year	No. of Tractor Drivers of Both Sexes	No. of Women Tractor Drivers	% Women
1930	36,000	2,000–3,000	5.5–8.3
1935	495,500	19,000	3.8
1937	588,900[a]	43,900[a]	6.4
1938	685,000[a]	57,500[b]	8.3
1939	690,000	24,000	3.5
1940	812,000	64,000[a]	7.9
1943	n.d.	n.d.	54–57
1948	612,475	36,136	5.9

[a]As of January 1 of the given year; otherwise, as of the end of the year unless noted.
[b]As of March 1938.

Source: Iu. V. Arutiunian, *Mekhanizatory sel'skogo khoziaistva SSSR v 1929–1957 g.g. (Formirovanie kadrov massovykh kvalifikatsii)* (Moscow, 1960), pp. 16, 38, 46, 59–60, 68–69, 296; A. Malukhina, "Zhenshchiny v kolkhozakh—bol'shaia sila," *Sotsialisticheskaia rekonstruktsiia sel'skogo khoziaistva*, No. 3 (March, 1938): 32.

this work after marrying or having children.[97] After World War II, when central authorities apparently ceased to encourage women to enter this profession, the number of women drivers declined significantly (Table 11.8). By the 1950s, the withdrawal of women from mechanical work had proceeded so far that Pasha Angelina, organizer of the first women's tractor brigade and one of the few Soviet women to remain in this occupation until the end of her life, had little choice but to become the leader of a men's brigade.[98] Long before then, however, the representation of women in this occupation tended to fluctuate enormously (Table 11.8), shaped by periodic campaigns from the center to increase the number of female mechanical workers and resistance from below, from local society and officialdom alike.[99]

The central authorities' efforts to recognize and reward the labor contributions of female agricultural Stakhanovites also experienced resistance from below. The Soviet press and archives of the time are filled with reports of attacks on Stakhanovites by their fellow villagers. Almost inevitably, with few exceptions, the Stakhanovites singled out for such treatment were women.[100] Most of these incidents were quite minor, involving little more than taunts, threats, insults, and harassment, or minor property damage, such as breaking windows in a Stakhanovite's home or allowing livestock to graze or trample on a Stakhanovite's garden plot. In more extreme cases, a Stakhanovite's home or shed might be set on fire or her work destroyed by letting livestock into her link's flax field[101] or feeding needles or poison to her best record-setting dairy cow.[102] Such incidents commonly occurred in Russian villages, both before and after the 1917 Revolution, and apparently served as the means by which the village community and its members expressed feelings of jealousy or resentment toward the good fortune of others and sought to control the behavior of deviant villagers. Such acts essentially functioned much like the traditional European charivari and should probably be regarded as its Russian counterpart.[103] The Soviet press portrayed such incidents most sensationally in the politically charged climate of the 1930s as manifestations of class struggle or the work of "hostile" and "class alien elements." But local officials tended to ignore or play down the importance of such events, realizing that such incidents were an integral part of traditional rural culture.[104]

Occasionally, beatings and even murders of Stakhanovites transpired and left the authorities with little choice but to intervene.[105] Sometimes male collective-farm officials joined in the persecution of women Stakhanovites or even encouraged such behavior on the part of other collective farmers, especially when the women concerned had been singled out for special treatment, such as expense-paid trips to the *oblast* capital or even Moscow, gifts of highly desirable consumer goods in short supply (such as bicycles and phonographs), and the award of state orders (*ordeny*), the nation's highest decorations, which inevitably involved meetings with Stalin and Kalinin and other state and party leaders in the Kremlin and a good deal of publicity in the press. Such farm officials could fail to record a Stakhanovite's *trudoden* earnings or her milk yield accurately, reduce the rations of her record-setting livestock, or even sell her group of cows or pigs to a neighboring collective farm out of the conviction that many of the achievements ascribed to her actually should have been attributed to them as farm leaders.[106]

Such jealousy was enhanced by the fact that such awards not infrequently resulted in promotion to administrative positions or opportunities for higher education. By 1937 and 1938, many of the nation's best known women Stakhanovites, including Mariia Demchenko, Pasha Angelina, Pasha Kovardak, E. Drobiagina, and M. Globa, along with well-known male Stakhanovites like the legendary combine driver Konstantin Bovin, were enrolled in the nation's top agricultural colleges.[107]

Even when Stakhanovites did not receive such spectacular opportunities, their work achievements often resulted in increased work norms for other peasants, while the attention accorded Stakhanovite women ran counter to the traditional patriarchal culture of the Soviet countryside. Recognition of individual work achievements of women was a novelty in rural localities. Before the collectivization of agriculture, women's work took place in the context of the male-dominated individual peasant household and resounded to the credit of the male *khoziain*, or household head, usually a woman's father, brother, or husband. But the new collective-farm system rewarded the individual work of males and females alike after the establishment of the *trudoden* payment system. Under this system, males were no longer *khoziain* to the same degree that they had been earlier, and women became more acutely aware of their own contributions to the family economy. In the process, some also became more assertive in their relations with their husbands. One woman who grew up on a collective farm in Kalinin *oblast* remembered the impact of the trudoden system on her parents' marriage:

> Mother won her card as a member of the collective farm, and on the card her work days were entered. She had as many work days as Father had. She used to take her membership card and wave it in Father's face.
> "You always said you supported me. Now you see I am earning as much as

you," she declared. "So I have as much to say as you have, don't I? You had better not say anything more to me." Then Father had nothing to say. He would mumble and keep the peace for the time being.[108]

Perhaps the loss of status experienced by men within the household and vis-à-vis the administration of the new collective farms accounts for masculine propensities to leave agriculture altogether in the 1930s or move into administrative positions that would allow them to remain *khoziain*.

At any rate, rural officials at the *raion* and rural soviet levels of government tended to promote women to administrative positions in the collective farms and rural soviets only under pressure from higher authorities at the national and *oblast* levels of the party and state. Throughout the 1930s, central soviet authorities launched repeated campaigns to increase the representation of women in nontraditional occupations and administrative posts in the countryside. Higher authorities were motivated in part by the increasingly female composition of the rural working-age population and the continued outflow of rural males, especially those with administrative and mechanical skills. As Stalin pointed out in justifying such policies: "Women are a great force on the collective farms. To suppress this force would be criminal. Our obligation is to promote women in the collective farms and allow this force to become a reality."[109] Subsequently, as international tensions rose and a new world war loomed on the horizon, Soviet leaders sought to increase the pool of women officeholders and mechanical workers so that the countryside would not be depleted of such essential cadres in the event of war.[110]

In 1933 and 1934, national authorities went so far in pursuit of these goals as to resurrect the *zhenotdel* in the countryside in the form of the *zhenorg* or *zhenpolit*, a female official appointed deputy head of the MTS political section and given the task of creating a female collective-farm *aktiv* and of training and promoting women mechanical and political cadres. Although the *zhenorgi* did not survive long after the abolition of the MTS political sections at the end of 1934,[111] by 1934 and 1935, the representation of women nationwide among Communist Party members, tractor drivers, and women rural soviet chairmen and deputies was noticeably larger than it had been in the early 1930s (Tables 11.8–11.10).

Table 11.9. Representation of Women in the Rural Soviets, 1926–1937 (% of women chairmen and deputies)

Year	Rural Soviet Chairmen (%)	Rural Soviet Members (%)
1926	0.6	9.9
1931	5.0	21.0
1934	7.7	26.3
1936	6.7	26.4
mid-1937	4.1[a]	n.d.

[a]In mid-1937 there were 2,500 rural soviet chairwomen in the 60,791 rural soviets with elected governments.

Sources: A. I. Lepeshkin, *Mestnye organy vlasti sovetskogo gosudarstva (1921–1936 g.g.)* (Moscow, 1959), pp. 206, 399; *Vlast sovetov*, no. 4 (February 28, 1937): 5; M. Lorish, "O vovlechenii zhenshchiny v rabotu sovetov," *Sovetskoe stroitel'stva*, no. 11 (November 1937):83; *Pravda*, July 24, 1937, p. 2.

Table 11.10. Representation of Women in CPSU

Year	% Women Members CPSU
1927	12.1
1929	13.7
1932	15.9
1934	16.4
1937	14.8
1939	14.5
1941 (Jan.)	14.9

Source: T. H. Rigby, *Communist Party Membership in the USSR, 1917–1967* (Princeton, 1968), p. 361.

In 1935 the *zhenorgi* were replaced by decrees and exhortations from above for the promotion of women, such as the campaign from 1935 to 1937 to promote women to offices on the collective farms and increase the number of women mechanical workers in the non–Black Soil Region, the area of traditionally heavy peasant *otkhodnichestvo*.[112] Representation of women in mechanical work and administrative positions on the collective farms did rise (Tables 11.8 and 11.11) but for only the duration of the campaign, stagnating or even declining thereafter.[113] At the end of the campaign, the post of link leader alone was held predominantly by women, for links were used mainly in cultivating technical crops, considered traditionally to be "women's work." Women made their strongest gains in the mid-1930s among managers of dairy farms and livestock brigade leaders, again in

Table 11.11. Women Collective-Farm Cadres (% of women holding such offices and positions), 1935–1939.

	1935	1936	1937	1938
Collective-farm chairmen	1.7	2.6	2.6	2.6
Assistant chairmen	3.5	n.d.	4.4	3.7
Heads of revision commissions	2.2	1.8	3.0	3.0
Members of revision commissions	n.d.	15.1	15.1	n.d.
Heads of livestock farms	14.4	16.1	23.0	18.3
Livestock brigade leaders	8.9	21.5	23.4	22.0
Zootechnicians and *vetfel'dshers*	2.0	2.5	11.7	n.d.
Agronomists	3.5	n.d.	4.8	10.0
Field brigade leaders	2.4	2.7	4.2	4.7
Bookkeepers/accountants	3.5	4.5	6.2	6.2
Link (team) leaders	n.d.	66.8	66.0	67.0
Stablehands/horsetenders	n.d.	3.2	n.d.	n.d.
Milkmaids	n.d.	100	n.d.	n.d.

Sources: M. A. Vyltsan, *Zavershaiushchii etap sozdaniia kolkhoznogo stroia (1935–1937 g.g.)* (Moscow, 1978), p. 113; A. Malukhina, "Zhenshchiny v kolkhozakh—bol'shaia sila," *Sotsialisticheskaia rekonstruktsiia sel'skogo khoziaistva*, no. 3 (March 1938): 32; N. Krupskaia, "Zhenshchina-aktivnyi borets za dela mira, za sotsializma," *Vlast sovetov*, no. 4 (February 1938): 25; *Kolkhozy v vtoroi piatiletke* (Moscow, 1938), pp. 60–80.

an area of the economy traditionally dominated by women. The number of women agricultural professionals, like bookkeepers, accountants, agronomists, zootechnicians, and *vetfel'dshers,* also rose noticeably, since those who held such positions required some specialized training, which was still in chronically short supply in the countryside. The representation of women in such posts was likely to grow more in the future, because women accounted for 30.2 percent of the students enrolled in higher agricultural education in the mid- to late 1930s.[114] Although overall gains were modest, the large number of collective farms that then existed—close to 250,000—meant that tens of thousands, if not hundreds of thousands, of women came to occupy leadership, professional, and managerial positions in a rural society that had hitherto excluded them entirely from positions of leadership and authority.[115] Nonetheless, a disproportionate number of these women officials were concentrated in the non–Black Soil Region, the area of the country on which the campaign had focused.[116]

But after the campaign to strengthen non–Black Soil collective farms subsided, the number of women in administrative posts on collective farms ceased to grow or even declined somewhat in 1938 (Table 11.11). Representation of women among tractor drivers fell precipitously in 1939 (Table 11.8), prompting yet another campaign by the center. At the Eighteenth Congress of the Communist Party in March 1939, well-known women tractor drivers, such as Pasha Angelina, Pasha Kovardak, and M. Mukhortova, issued an appeal at the behest of party leaders for the training of 100,000 women drivers in 1939. More women responded to this appeal than was anticipated, and between 130,000 and 150,000 women drivers were trained, but the MTSs employed only 64,000 in 1940—still substantially more than the 24,000 women tractor drivers employed the previous year.[117]

In the mid-1930s, women also failed to hold on to earlier gains in the rural soviets and at higher levels of administration in town and *raion* soviets. The representation of women in the rural soviets grew substantially from 1926 to 1934 (Table 11.9) because of the activities of the MTS *zhenorgi* and a campaign by local party *obkoms* to increase the representation of women in these posts during the 1934 elections to the local soviets.[118] But subsequently, the number of rural soviet chairwomen and women deputies fell substantially (Table 11.9), with women simply being removed by their superiors on the grounds of "passivity" or failure to cope with their work. Some chairwomen were given no reasons for their dismissal.[119] In Semiozersk rural soviet, Kazan *raion,* one such woman was told, "You women are not necessary as members of the rural soviet."[120]

Paradoxically the decline of women's representation in the soviets coincided with an upsurge in interest on the part of rural women in public officeholding. Public discussion in the countryside of the new 1936 constitution invariably tended to focus on the constitutional provision granting women equal rights. Collective-farm women used the discussion to demand more leadership positions for rural women[121] or to assert their rights vis-à-vis their husbands. In Mishinskii rural soviet, Gzhatsk *raion,* Western *oblast,* the introduction of the constitution was followed by a dramatic upsurge in legal complaints filed by wives against husbands who beat them, on the grounds that wife beating was unconstitutional![122] When the All-Union Central Executive Committee met in July 1937 to implement the constitution by adopting a new election law, speakers noted with dismay the insufficient representation of women in the soviets at all levels of government.[123]

Under the impetus of such developments and the spread of the Great Purges among male officeholders in the summer and fall of 1937, the national press launched yet another campaign to promote women to responsible positions.[124] In the course of this campaign, the press began to discuss the problems confronting women officeholders, noting continuing educational disparities between rural women and men and the chronic shortage of year-round day-care institutions in the countryside.[125] But all participants in this discussion agreed that the main obstacle to women's promotion was the attitude of male officials, who, as one woman reporter put it, "look on Soviet women through the eyes of the old accursed *Domostroi.*"*[126] The Soviet press in 1936 and 1937 contained numerous reports that newly appointed women officials in the countryside found it difficult to establish their authority vis-à-vis local male officials, even their nominal subordinates. Women rural soviet deputies frequently were not informed of soviet meetings, while new rural soviet chairwomen found they could not attract a quorum of deputies to soviet meetings.[127] New collective-farm chairwomen, appointed as a result of campaigns, often found their orders ignored or subverted by male brigade leaders, storekeepers, and chairmen of the farm revision committees. In extreme cases, chairwomen were beaten by their subordinates, denied grain for their *trudoden* payments, or threatened with bodily harm. One collective-farm chairwoman in Mokokhov *raion,* Kalinin *oblast,* found herself unable to dislodge her predecessor. The poor woman, in despair, wrote to *oblast* authorities, "He often threatens me that he'll burn out my eyes or do me some other sort of harm and I have begun to fear even to go out of my apartment in the evening."[128] Not surprisingly, women officials encountered the most fierce opposition in the Moslem societies of Central Asia. In Tadzhikistan alone in 1937, nine women "activists"—collective officials and Stakhanovites—were murdered, while one collective-farm chairwoman was subjected to two unsuccessful attempts on her life and the burning of her home. Other activists were beaten or put in chains by their husbands, often acting under social pressure.[129]

Given such resistance, it is surprising that thousands of women in the countryside in the mid- to late 1930s, including 2,500 rural soviet chairwomen and 7,000 to 10,000 collective-farm chairwomen—not only managed to continue to hold responsible offices but worked, in the words of *Pravda,* "no worse but better than men."[130] In the wake of the Great Purges, successful women officials and agricultural Stakhanovites, who had begun their careers as rank-and-file collective farmers, were appointed to responsible positions, at the *raion* level or above. For example, in 1938, Karitina Moliakova, creator of the Moliakov flax links, became the head of the Kalinin *oblast* agricultural department, the local affiliate of the Commissariat of Agriculture, after a brief stint as a collective-farm chairwoman.[131] Award-winning milkmaid Evdokiia Egorevna Borisova became director of the Lenin stock-breeding state farm (Staro-Iurevskii *raion,* Riazan), where she had worked as a milkmaid for eight years,[132] while the prize-winning woman tractor

---

*Sixteenth-century guide to management of home and family.

brigade leader M. F. Timashov assumed the directorship of her own Shishovskii MTS (Voronezh *oblast*).[133] By 1939, twenty former collective-farm women in Moscow *oblast* worked as heads and assistant heads of *raion* land departments, positions that virtually no women had held.[134]

In these years, too, a woman who had begun life as a rank-and-file collective farmer, Polina Osipenko, galvanized the nation by setting seven world aviation records, including the record for distance formerly held by the renowned American aviatrice Amelia Earhart. Osipenko's feats—the daring rescue of her all-woman crew when they ran out of fuel in a remote area of Siberia on one of their record-setting flights and her triumphant tours around the country, including visits to her native village—and her tragic death in a plane crash "while performing her military duty" as a first lieutenant in the Red Army, like much about the 1930s, appear larger than life. Certainly, Osipenko's example was used by the Soviet press to stress the opportunities that "victorious socialism" had opened for Soviet women, in contrast to the curtailment of their opportunities under fascism.[135]

Osipenko's achievements and the continued campaigns from the center to promote women to official positions in the countryside indicate that no "Great Retreat" from emancipatory goals can be discerned in the Soviet government's policies toward rural women in the mid- to late 1930s. Indeed, in these years peasant women enjoyed more opportunities to engage in nontraditional activities than ever before. But these opportunities depended on the patronage and support of the Soviet state, whose own low-level rural officials continued to oppose nontraditional roles for women. As the Great Purges swept many low-level rural officials to positions of authority at higher levels of government,[136] such resistance could only become more effective. Moreover, central authorities increasingly intervened to promote new roles for women as a means to prepare for the coming world war. Once the war had come and gone, the impetus for state intervention on women's behalf no longer existed.

Notes

1. Most existing studies of women during the prewar Soviet period focus on the 1920s and early 1930s and neglect the second half of the 1930s: Fannina W. Halle, *Women in Soviet Russia* (New York, 1933); Jessica Smith, *Women in Soviet Russia* (New York, 1928); Rudolf Schlesinger, ed., *The Family in the USSR: Documents and Readings* (London, 1949), pp. 30–234; Gail Warshofsky Lapidus, *Women in Soviet Society: Equality, Development and Social Change* (Berkeley, 1978); William Mandel, *Soviet Women* (New York, 1975), pp. 64–75; G. N. Serebrennikov, *The Position of Women in the USSR* (London, 1937), pp. 87–116.

2. Sheila Rowbotham, *Women, Resistance and Revolution* (New York, 1974), pp. 134–69; Nicholas S. Timasheff, *The Great Retreat: The Growth and Decline of Communism in Russia* (New York, 1946), pp. 192–203; Schlesinger, *The Family in the USSR*, pp. 235–347; H. Kent Geiger, *The Family in Soviet Russia* (Cambridge, Mass. 1968), pp. 76–106.

3. Lewis H. Siegelbaum, *Stakanovism and the Politics of Productivity in the USSR, 1935–1941* (Cambridge, 1988), p. 236.

4. *Rabochii put* (Smolensk), May 30, 1936, p. 2.

5. Within a year of the repeal of legal abortion, the birth rate in Moscow and Leningrad doubled, and births increased by 50 percent in Kiev, Minsk, Baku, Tashkent, Tbilisi, and Frunze, and 85 percent in Khar'kov. *Pravda*, March 3, 1937, p. 1; April 8, 1938, p. 3; August 2, 1937, p. 3, and *Sotsialisticheskoe zemledelie*, June 27, 1937, p. 2.

6. M. A. Vyltsan, *Zavershaiushchii etap sozdaniia kolkhoznogo stroia (1935–1937 g.g.)* (Moscow, 1978), p. 193.

7. Geiger, *Family in Soviet Russia*, pp. 189, 363.

8. For the role of these healers in prerevolutionary times, see Samuel C. Ramer, "Traditional Healers and Peasant Culture, 1861–1917," in Esther Kingston-Mann and Timothy Mixter, eds., *Peasant Economy, Culture and Politics, 1800–1921* (Princeton, 1990). For the persistence of such practices well into the 1930s, see a very interesting press account about a professionally trained midwife's struggle against the fifteen traditional healers operating in her rural soviet, after she accepted a position in a collective-farm maternity home in Kiev *oblast*. *Pravda*, August 6, 1936, p. 3.

9. In the public debate over the June 27 decrees, it was recognized that the enforcement of the ban on abortions was more problematic in the countryside. See, for example, *Sotsialisticheskoe zemledelie*, June 5, 1936, p. 4, and Geiger, *Family in Soviet Russia*, p. 195. Only in the 1950s did nonprofessional midwives disappear in the village of Viriatino (Tambov *oblast*). *The Village of Viriatino* (Garden City, N.Y., 1970), p. 263. However, even in Moscow and Leningrad, illegal abortions increased by only 2 to 3 percent after passage of the new law. The 1938 trial of a Leningrad abortionist, who had operated "several years" before the death of one of her clients called her operations to the attention of the authorities, suggests that traditional nonprofessional healers operated in town as well as in the countryside even before the legal abortions were banned, as does the large number of "incomplete abortions" handled by urban abortion clinics in the 1920s and 1930s. *Pravda*, December 14, 1938, p. 6; Schlesinger, *Family in the USSR*, pp. 174–75, 180–81. Some doctors in town found a way to get around the new law, by taking advantage of the provision of the June 1936 decrees that allowed women to have abortions if the pregnancy threatened their health. Some doctors even justified such abortions on grounds of a threat to a woman's mental health, thus provoking an angry article in *Pravda*. *Pravda*, September 15, 1936, p. 4.

10. See, for example, *Sotsialisticheskoe zemledelie*, June 1, 1936, p. 4; June 5, 1936, p. 4; June 6, 1936, p. 4; June 10, 1936, p. 4; *Pravda*, May 28, 1936, p. 2; May 29, 1936, p. 4; May 30, 1936, p. 4; May 31, 1936, p. 3; June 1, 1936, p. 4; June 2, 1936, p. 3; June 3, 1936, p. 4; June 4, 1936, p. 3; June 5, 1936, p. 4; June 6, 1936, p. 4; June 8, 1936, p. 2; June 11, 1936, p. 3; June 12, 1936, p. 3; and *Krest'ianskaia gazeta*, June 8, 1936, p. 2.

11. See, for example, *Sotsialisticheskoe zemledelie*, June 1, 1936, p. 5; June 5, 1936, p. 4.

12. *Sotsialisticheskoe zemledelie*, June 2, 1936, p. 4.

13. See, for example, *Sotsialisticheskoe zemledelie*, June 4, 1936, p. 4; June 11, 1936, p. 4; and Schlesinger, *Family in the USSR*, pp. 255–58.

14. *Sotsialisticheskoe zemledelie*, June 4, 1935, p. 4.

15. Smolensk Archive, WKP 239, pp. 4–5.

16. See, for example, *Sotsialisticheskoe zemledelie*, June 1, 1936, p. 4; June 5, 1936, p. 4.

17. G. Vainstein, "Zabota o zhenshchine-materi i vospitanie detei," *Sovetskoe stroitel'stvo*, no. 7 (July 1936): 47.

18. Ibid.; *Pravda*, December 21, 1936, p. 3; February 18, 1937, p. 4; March 3, 1937, p. 1; April 8, 1938, p. 3. *Pravda* on June 29, 1937 (p. 4), attributed the shortfall to "Bukharinist enemy spies" in key positions in the social insurance program.

228

Peasant Women After the Revolution

19. *Sotsialisticheskoe zemledelie,* June 24, 1937, p. 1.

20. *Krest'ianskaia gazeta,* July 20, 1936, p. 1; July 22, 1936, p. 1.

21. See, for example, *Rabochii put* (Smolensk), June 10, 1936, p. 1; June 11, 1936, p. 2; and *Sotsialisticheskoe zemledelie,* June 6, 1936, p. 4; June 8, 1936, p. 4; June 10, 1936, p. 4; June 11, 1936, p. 4. For the provisions of the June 1936 decrees on divorce, see Schlesinger, *Family in the USSR,* pp. 278–79. Earlier under the provisions of the existing 1926 marriage law, only one party to a divorce needed to be present at the registry, with the other being notified by mail of the proceedings; no sliding scale of registration fees for more than one divorce existed, and those who failed to pay child support were sentenced to six months of forced labor at their place of work, which amounted to merely docking some of their salary. For this, see Schlesinger, *Family in the USSR,* pp. 154–68, and Vainstein, "Zabota o zhenshchine-materi i vospitanii detei," pp. 44–45.

22. See, for example, *Sotsialisticheskoe zemledelie,* June 1, 1936, p. 4; June 9, 1936, p. 4; June 10, 1936, p. 4; and *Krest'ianskaia gazeta,* June 8, 1936, p. 2.

23. V. P. Danilov, M. P. Kim, and N. B. Tropkin, *Sovetskoe krest'ianstvo: kratkii ocherk istorii (1917–1970)* (Moscow, 1973), p. 324; V. M. Selunskaia, *Sotsial'naia struktura sovetskogo obshchestva: istoriia i sovremennost'* (Moscow, 1987), p. 82. The higher figure comes from the more recently published work.

24. Iu. B. Arutiunian, "Kollektivizatsiia sel'skogo khoziaistva i vysvobozhdenie rabochei sily dlia promyshlennosti," *Formirovanie i razvitie sovetskogo rabochego klassa (1917–1961 g.g.)* (Moscow, 1964), p. 102. Of these, 2 to 3 million annually between 1935 and 1940 worked in industry or construction on *ognabor,* while the draft took increasing numbers of young peasant men as the Soviet armed forces increased close to tenfold between 1934 and the start of World War II—from 562,000 to approximately 5 million troops. A. I. Vdovin and V. Z. Drobizhev, *Rost rabochego klassa SSSR 1917–1940 g.g.* (Moscow 1976), p. 120; Abram Bergson, *The Real National Income of Soviet Russia Since 1928* (Cambridge, Mass., 1961), p. 365.

25. Nancy Nimitz, *Farm Employment in the Soviet Union, 1928–1963* (Santa Monica, Calif., 1965), p. 76.

26. Geiger, *Family in Soviet Russia,* pp. 120–27, 241. See also Robert Conquest, *The Great Terror: Stalin's Purge of the Thirties* (New York, 1968), p. 711, and J. Arch Getty and William J. Chase, "The Moscow Party Elite of 1917 in the Great Purges," *Russian History* 5, pt. 1 (1978): 108.

27. The 1926 census showed 4,462,000 more rural women than men, with the sex gap heavily concentrated among the able-bodied population, ages fifteen to thirty-nine as a result of World War I, the Civil War, and the 1921 famine. V. P. Danilov, *Sovetskaia dokolkhoznaia derevnia: naselenie, zemlepol'zovanie, khoziaistvo* (Moscow, 1977), p. 24.

28. Valentin Kataev, *Time Forward* (Bloomington, Ind., 1976), pp. 13–14, 42–54.

29. For some poignant examples of this, see *Krest'ianskaia gazeta,* September 18, 1936, p. 4; July 4, 1936, p. 3.

30. Vainstein, "Zabota o zhenshchine-materi i vospitanii detei," pp. 44–45.

31. See, for example, *Rabochii put* (Smolensk), April 3, 1936, p. 3, and *Krest'ianskaia gazeta,* June 8, 1936, p. 2.

32. See, for example, Smolensk Archive, WKP 234, pp. 288–91, and WKP 362, pp. 249–50.

33. Smolensk Archive, WKP 239, p. 126.

34. The *Pravda* editorial "Father" (*Otets*) supports such an interpretation. *Pravda,* June 9, 1936, p. 1. For a translation of this editorial, see Schlesinger, *Family in the USSR,* pp. 266–69.

35. Susan Bridger, *Women in the Soviet Countryside: Women's Roles in Rural Development in the Soviet Union* (Cambridge, 1987), p. 13.

36. Selunskaia, *Sotsial'naia struktura sovetskogo obshchestva*, p. 118.

37. For the sexual breakdown of the rural labor force at the end of the 1930s, see Warren Eason, "The Agricultural Labor Force and Population of the USSR: 1926–41," Rand Corporation Research Memorandum, Santa Monica, Calif., 1954, p. 105.

38. Nimitz, *Farm Employment in the Soviet Union*, p. 76.

39. Selunskaia, *Sotsial'naia struktura sovetskogo obshchestva*, p. 118.

40. *Sovetskoe stroitel'stvo*, no. 1 (January 1936): 29. For a discussion of the impact of prerevolutionary *otkhod* in one province in this region, see Barbara Alpern Engel, "The Woman's Side: Male Out-Migration and the Family Economy in Kostroma Province," *Slavic Review* 45, no. 2 (Summer 1986): 257–71.

41. *British Foreign Office Russia Correspondence*, 1937, Reel 6, vol. 21106, p. 126.

42. See, for example, Smolensk Archive, WKP 239, 1936, p. 215.

43. See, for example, the investigation of the Western *oblast* control commission of how local collective farms were fulfilling the agricultural charter (*ustav*) and the 1938 SNK/CC resolution forbidding illegal expulsions from the collective farms, including those of the families of *otkhodniki*. WKP 390, pp. 107, 109, 114, 120, 126, 142; *Sobranie postanovlenii i rasporiazhenii pravitel'stva SSSR*, no. 18 (April 29, 1938): 289–91; *Sotsialisticheskoe zemledelie*, February 13, 1936, p. 3; Vyltsan, *Zavershaiushchii etap sozdaniia kolkhoznogo stroia*, pp. 247–52.

44. The labor shortage was so acute in the mining and peat industries that the government moved in February 1938 to exempt the families of workers in these industries from agricultural taxes and to grant them the right to purchase grain and fodder at state prices from the collective farms. Collective-farm chairmen who resisted this decree were threatened with arrest. *Pravda*, February 14, 1938, p. 3.

45. *Sotsialisticheskoe zemledelie*, April 8, 1937, p. 1.

46. *Village of Viriatino*, pp. 95–96.

47. Vyltsan, *Zavershaiushchii etap sozdaniia kolkhoznogo stroia*, p. 100.

48. Women devoted, on the average, 619.5 hours per year to the household garden plot, compared with 153.3 hours a year for men. Nimitz, *Farm Employment in the Soviet Union*, p. 76. At this time, 79 percent of the cash income of collective farm families came from the sales of produce from household garden plots and earning outside of agriculture, given the low procurement payments to the collective farms for the produce purchased by the government. Ibid., p. 91; Vyltsan, *Zavershaiushchii etap sozdaniia kolkhoznogo stroia*, pp. 158–81.

49. See, for example, Pearl S. Buck, *Talk About Russia with Masha Scott* (New York, 1945), pp. 36–39, and A. Malukhina, "Zhenshchiny v kolkhozakh—bol'shaia sila," *Sotsialisticheskaia rekonstruktsiia sel'skogo khoziaistva*, no. 3 (March 1938): 33.

50. Vyltsan, *Zavershaiushchii etap sozdaniia kolkhoznogo stroia*, p. 34.

51. However, urban maternity leaves were cut back by half in 1939, a move which would indicate that there were limits to efforts to mobilize urban women for reproduction rather than production, as the war approached. *Pravda*, December 15, 1938, p. 3.

52. The costs of such leaves amounted to 100 million rubles in money and 10 million puds of grain annually and were borne by the collective farms. *Pravda*, October 4, 1937, p. 6.

53. See, for example, WKP 390, p. 252; *Kollektivizatsiia sel'skogo khoziaistva v zapadnom raione RSFSR (1927–1937 g.g.)* (Smolensk, 1968), p. 594; *Vlast sovetov*, no. 11 (June 1937): 20.

54. Alexander Baykov, *The Development of the Soviet Economic System* (Cambridge, 1946), p. 314.

55. For example, fifty-five out of the sixty-six agricultural Stakhanovites in Belyi *raion* in 1937 were female. Smolensk Archive, WKP 321, pp. 35–38. The eleven males here were all mechanical workers.

56. By 1938, more than half (757) of the 1,500 women awarded *ordeny*—state orders like the prestigious Order of Lenin, Order of the Red Banner, Order of the Toiling Red Banner, and the Red Star, which were among the nation's highest awards—received such awards for achievements in agriculture. Malukhina, "Zhenshchiny v kolkhozakh" p. 35.

57. Siegelbaum, *Stakanovism and the Politics of Productivity in the USSR*, pp. 170–71.

58. See, for example, *Pravda*, March 12, 1936, p. 1; September 1, 1936, p. 1; September 17, 1936, p. 1; November 14, 1936, p. 1; November 19, 1936, p. 1; November 22, 1936, p. 1; *Sotsialisticheskoe zemledelie*, December 5, 1935, p. 3; April 27, 1938, p. 3.

59. All the female agricultural Stakhanovites whose photographs were published in *Pravda* in 1936 worked in one of these three areas of the agrarian economy. *Pravda*, January 1, 1936, to December 31, 1936.

60. Siegelbaum, *Stakanovism and the Politics of Productivity in the USSR*, p. 172; Vyltsan, *Zavershaiushchii etap sozdaniia kolkhoznogo stroia*, pp. 94–95, 126–29.

61. Cotton, a crop strongly promoted by the Soviets after collectivization, was an exception to this general rule. Vyltsan, *Zavershaiushchii etap sozdaniia kolkhoznogo stroia*, pp. 126–29.

62. Cotton, a crop that was not grown to any significant degree before the collectivization of agriculture, was an exception to this general rule. Ibid., p. 148.

63. *Sotsialisticheskoe zemledelie*, August 16, 1935, p. 3.

64. *Sotsialisticheskoe zemledelie*, January 27, 1938, p. 3.

65. *Krest'ianskaia gazeta*, December 18, 1936, p. 2; *Sotsialisticheskoe zemledelie*, August 16, 1935, p. 3; December 11, 1935, p. 1; P. Shkobin, "Organizatsiia truda v MTF," *Sotsialisticheskaia rekonstruktsiia sel'skogo khoziaistva*, no. 9 (September 1938): 49; S. Kobalenchuk, "Organizatsiia pastshchnogo soderzhaniia skota v molochnozhivot-novodcheskikh sovkhozakh," *Sotsialisticheskaia rekonstruktsiia sel'skogo khoziaistva*, nos. 4–5 (April–May 1933): 175; F. Trizno, "Zhivotnovodstvo krasnoznamennogo plemennogo sovkhoza 'Karavaevo,' " *Sotsialisticheskaia rekonstruktsiia sel'skogo khoziaistva*, no. 10 (October 1938): 105.

66. *Sotsialisticheskoe zemledelie*, October 11, 1936, p. 1; October 30, 1936, p. 1; August 30, 1936, p. 2.

67. *Sotsialisticheskoe zemledelie*, October 4, 1937, p. 2; November 10, 1937, p. 1.

68. Shkobin, "Organizatsiia truda v MTF," pp. 46–50.

69. *Sotsialisticheskoe zemledelie*, August 11, 1935, p. 3; August 22, 1935, p. 2.

70. See, for example, *Sotsialisticheskoe zemledelie*, December 5, 1935, p. 3; and A. Kuznetsov, "Geroini kolkhoznogo zhivotnovodstva," *Sotsialisticheskaia rekonstruktsiia sel'skogo khoziaistva*, no. 3 (March 1936): 148–68.

71. *Sotsialisticheskoe zemledelie*, July 24, 1938, p. 3.

72. *Kolkhozy v vtoroi piatiletke* (Moscow, 1938), pp. 60–80.

73. *Sotsialisticheskoe zemledelie*, February 24, 1939, p. 1.

74. *Sotsialisticheskoe zemledelie*, August 11, 1935, p. 3; August 16, 1935, p. 3; August 20, 1935, p. 3; August 18, 1935, p. 3; August 22, 1935, p. 3; August 23, 1935, p. 3; July 20, 1937, p. 3; August 12, 1937, p. 3; A. Kazakov, "Rabota otdela truda vsesoiuznogo nauchno-issledovatel'skogo sovkhoznogo instituta v 1935 g.," *Sotsialisticheskaia rekonstruktsiia sel'skogo khoziaistva*, no. 11 (November 1935): 236–37.

75. *Sotsialisticheskoe zemledelie*, August 21, 1935, p. 2; June 23, 1937, p. 1; A.

Kuznetsov, "Dvukhsmennaia organizatsiia truda doiarok," *Sotsialisticheskaia re-konstruktsiia sel'skogo khoziaistva*, no. 9 (September 1939): 39–46. Professor Kharchenko of the Timiriazevskii Agricultural Academy, however, denied that illnesses of a milkmaid's hands were a common complaint, insisting that he had encountered only three such cases in his entire career. When pressed, he claimed that such ailments were caused by improper movements of the hands during milking and that the solution to this problem was to replace female milkmaids with men, who presumably would know how to milk correctly! *Sotsialisticheskoe zemledelie*, August 22, 1935, p. 3.

76. Vyltsan, *Zavershaiushchii etap sozdaniia kolkhoznogo stroia*, p. 155.

77. "Brucellosis. Undulant Fever. Malta or Mediterranean Fever," in A. B. Christie, *Infectious Diseases: Epidemiology and Clinical Practice* (London, 1980), pp. 832–37; A. Larbrisseau, E. Maravi, F. Aguilera, and J. M. Marinez-Lage, "The Neurological Complications of Brucellosis," *Le Journal canadien des sciences neurologigues* 5, no. 4 (November 1978): 369–76; "Brutsellez (Brucellosis)," *Selkhoziaistvennaia entsiklopediia* (Moscow, 1969), vol. 1, pp. 596–97.

78. As late as the spring of 1938, *Pravda* noted that "many" drivers still had not been paid for 1937 or even 1936. *Pravda*, April 1, 1938, p. 3; *Krest'ianskaia gazeta*, March 20, 1938, p. 1. Moreover, drivers were paid not by the day but by the amount of land worked. Breakdowns, which were frequent since the average Soviet tractor was expected to work four times as much land a year as its American counterpart, were costly to drivers, as were the chronic shortages of fuel and spare parts, which increased the periods of "down time" and prompted the hard-pressed MTSs to impose hefty fines on drivers who wasted fuel. *Sotsialisticheskoe zemledelie*, June 30, 1936, p. 1; June 14, 1937, p. 1; *Krest'ianskaia gazeta*, May 10, 1936, p. 3; June 8, 1936, p. 3; June 10, 1936, p. 3; June 26, 1936, p. 3; June 30, 1936, p. 1; *Pravda*, November 11, 1936, p. 2.

79. *Krest'ianskaia gazeta*, June 8, 1936, p. 3; July 8, 1936, p. 3; July 10, 1936, p. 3; *Sovetskoe stroitel'stvo*, no. 7 (July 1936): 50.

80. *Sotsialisticheskoe zemledelie*, July 17, 1936, p. 1; August 1, 1936, p. 2; *Krest'ianskaia gazeta*, July 24, 1937, p. 2.

81. See, for example, *Sotsialisticheskoe zemledelie*, July 17, 1936, p. 1. Women drivers also complained, as did their male associates, of the difficulties experienced in gaining access to the motors when repairs were necessary.

82. *Sotsialisticheskoe zemledelie*, August 8, 1936, p. 1.

83. See, for example, *Sotsialisticheskoe zemledelie*, August 8, 1938, p. 3; March 24, 1938, p. 2; Arkadii Slavutskii, *Praskov'ia Angelina* (Moscow, 1960), pp. 24–32; and Smolensk Archive, WKP 390, pp. 109, 97, 115, 119, 130, 190–91, and WKP 538, pp. 179, 444, 493.

84. *Krest'ianskaia gazeta*, April 26, 1936, p. 2.

85. Slavutskii, *Praskov'ia Angelina*, pp. 32–37.

86. Vyltsan, *Zavershaiushchii etap sozdaniia kolkhoznogo stroia*, p. 114. The best women drivers, like the 20,000 members of the 1,250 women's tractor brigades participating in the 1937 competition of women tractor brigades—who accounted for half the women tractor drivers currently employed by the MTSs—plowed an average of twice the existing MTSs averages. *Pravda*, February 12, 1937, p. 2. The topmost women drivers, like Pasha Angelina, worked 1,200 hectares in 1935, when the average MTS tractor worked only 372.1 hectares. *Sovetskoe stroitel'stvo*, no. 1 (January 1936): 38.

87. *Sotsialisticheskoe zemledelie*, March 24, 1938, p. 2.

88. Slavutskii, *Praskov'ia Angelina*, pp. 29–30.

89. Ibid., pp. 37–42.

90. Soviet authorities sought to combat this reputation by organizing separate women's

brigades and recruiting women drivers from the wives of current tractor and combine drivers. See, for example, *Pravda*, March 6, 1937, p. 4, and March 26, 1937, p. 3.

91. See, for example, one such case in the Kozel'sk MTS (Western *oblast*). Smolensk Archive, WKP 238, p. 347. The national press, however, does not seem to have aired such incidents, although this one was discussed in the oblast press. *Rabochii put*, April 21, 1937.

92. For example, see Smolensk Archive, WKP 321, p. 241; WKP 111, pp. 154, 159; WKP 538, pp. 35, 61; WKP 415, p. 46; *Krest'ianskaia gazeta*, June 24, 1936, p. 3. The first two cases entailed the rape of three collective farm women by two MTS drivers in Belyi *raion* in 1937.

93. Slavutskii, *Praskov'ia Angelina*, pp. 60–67.

94. Ibid., pp. 20–30, 178–79. Pasha seems to have been an unusually committed feminist. She was originally attracted to tractor driving by a desire to convince her older brother and boyfriend that she was as good as they were (ibid.). She often used her public appearances to push for additional services or opportunities for women. For example, at the Tenth Komsomol Congress in April 1936, Pasha insisted that too few of the delegates were female and demanded that the majority be women at the next congress, a dream that has yet to be achieved fifty years later. She also demanded more responsible positions for girls, maintaining that "in individual localities women are still weakly promoted. Somehow they fear to promote more girls. Often even the girls themselves fear promotion. But when they are placed in responsible positions they begin to feel themselves responsible for the business at hand and work no worse than others. We have girls who have already begun to work and begun to understand this. (applause)

"It is necessary to help them only at first. If they are helped at first, they themselves will begin to work outstandingly [*otlichno*]." *Pravda*, April 15, 1936, p. 2.

95. Slavutskii, *Praskov'ia Angelina*, pp. 47–52; *Pravda*, April 15, 1936, p. 2.

96. *Krest'ianskaia gazeta*, November 28, 1938, p. 1.

97. In one MTS, only three of the twenty-eight women enrolled in a tractor-driving course were mothers, and this was reported as an unusual case. *Sotsialisticheskoe zemledelie*, October 17, 1937, p. 2. See also *Krest'ianskaia gazeta*, May 18, 1936, p. 1, and Malukhina, "Zhenshchiny v kolkhozakh," p. 32.

98. Slavutskii, *Praskov'ia Angelina*, pp. 160–210.

99. For the campaigns to increase the number of women drivers, see pp. 224–25.

100. For example, all the victims on a list of nineteen attacks on Stakhanovites in Sychevka *raion* (Western *oblast*) between May and September 1937 were female. Smolensk Archive, WKP 202, pp. 195–96.

101. Ibid.

102. Autopsies found needles in the stomachs of three prize dairy cows that died in three widely scattered areas of the country in the spring of 1936 alone—Kirov *krai* and Iaroslavl and Kursk *oblasts*. *Krest'ianskaia gazeta*, March 18, 1936, p. 3; March 20, 1936, p. 3; March 28, 1936, p. 4; March 30, 1936, p. 1; April 2, 1936, p. 3; April 16, 1936, p. 2; April 24, 1936, p. 3; April 26, 1936, p. 3; May 8, 1936, p. 3; October 14, 1936, p. 3. Vera Shaposhnikova, *Zhemchuzhina v ozherel'e* (Moscow, 1972), pp. 113–14.

103. For the role of the charivari in enforcing sexual mores in preindustrial European villages, see Louise A. Tilly and Joan W. Scott, *Women, Work and Family* (New York, 1978), pp. 39–40, and Edward Shorter, *The Making of the Modern Family* (New York, 1975), pp. 46, 64–65, 218–27.

104. Smolensk Archive, WKP 202, pp. 195–96. Most of the cases on the Sychevka list of attacks on Stakhanovites were of this nature and remained uninvestigated six months later.

105. For examples of such cases, see *Sotsialisticheskoe zemledelie*, April 20, 1937, p. 4, and Smolensk Archive, WKP 202, p. 195. Even then far from all of these incidents were

politically inspired. See, for example, press accounts of the murder of a Stakhanovite by her former husband, an ex-convict sentenced for embezzlement, which seems to be little more than a violent family quarrel. *Krest'ianskaia gazeta,* November 4, 1936, pp. 2–3.

106. See, for example, *Krest'ianskaia gazeta,* March 20, 1936, pp. 1, 3; April 16, 1936, p. 3; April 24, 1936, p. 3; October 14, 1936, p. 3.

107. For this, see *Pravda,* April 16, 1936, p. 3; October 20, 1937, p. 4; March 23, 1938, p. 4; *Sotsialisticheskoe zemledelie,* October 10, 1937, p. 4; October 22, 1938, p. 1; March, 8, 1938, p. 1; April 12, 1938, p. 4; April 26, 1938, p. 3; July 20, 1938, p. 3. However, the attrition rate was rather high. Only nineteen of the twenty-six recipients of state orders (*ordeny*) for work in agriculture who enrolled in the Timiriazev Agricultural Academy in the fall of 1937 were still there in the spring of 1939. *Sotsialisticheskoe zemledelie,* October 20, 1937, p. 4; *Pravda,* June 2, 1939, p. 4. Women were more likely than men to drop out, given the enduring educational disparities between rural men and women. At any rate, Mariia Demchenko described herself as "completely illiterate" at the time she enrolled in the Voronezh Agricultural Institute. Although remedial education was arranged for her, she was distracted by constant public appearances and lecture tours arranged for her by the party and Komsomol. Testimony in the Harvard Interview Project indicates that she never achieved her "dream" of becoming an agronomist. *Pravda,* April 16, 1936, p. 3; *Project on the Soviet Social System Schedule B Interviews,* no. 67. Pasha Angelina withdrew from the Timiriazev Academy in her third year of study upon the birth of a second child. Slavutskii, *Praskov'ia Angelina,* pp. 79–81. Konstantin Bovin, who was equally famous and whose education was interrupted by his election to the Supreme Soviet in 1937 and the onset of the war, managed to return to the Timiriazev Academy after the war and to become a faculty member there. *Moscow News,* March 27–April 3, 1988, p. 16.

108. Buck, *Talk About Russia,* p. 37. Both Stalin and the Soviet feature film *The Rich Bride* (*Bogataia nevesta*) portrayed the impact of the *trudoden* system on the position of women in the countryside in much the same way. For this, see *Sotsialisticheskoe zemledelie,* March 26, 1938, p. 4, and Stalin's speech to the Second Congress of Collective Farm Stormworkers on November 10, 1935. I. V. Stalin, *Sochineniia* (Stanford, Calif., 1967), vol. 1, pp. 75–76. Rasputin's perceptive short story, "Vasilii and Vasilisa" indicates that some peasant men were "desexed" by their loss of *khoziain* status and the recognition of women's individual labor contributions by the collective farms. Certainly, this development figured in the life-long feud of the main characters in this story, which begins in the 1930s. Valentin Rasputin, "Vasilii i Vasilisa," *Vek zhivi—vek liubi rasskazy* (Moscow, 1982), pp. 151–77.

109. *Krest'ianskaia gazeta,* March 6, 1936, p. 1.

110. See, for example, *Pravda,* August 26, 1938, p. 2, and Slavutskii, *Praskov'ia Angelina,* pp. 72–73.

111. Robert F. Miller, *One Hundred Thousand Tractors: The MTS and the Development of Controls in Soviet Agriculture* (Cambridge, Mass., 1970), pp. 245–46. Data from the Western *oblast* indicate that the *zhenorgi* continued to operate in the early months of 1935.

112. *Sotsialisticheskoe zemledelie,* December 21, 1935, p. 1; *Sovetskoe stroitel'stvo,* no. 1 (January 1936): 26–29.

113. In the Western *oblast,* only the repeated intervention of the party *obkom* could ensure even the partial implementation of this decree. *Ocherki istorii Smolenskoi organizatsii KPSS* (Smolensk, 1985), p. 220.

114. At this time, this was true of only 13 percent of the students in higher agricultural education in England, 1.5 percent in Germany, and 1.3 percent in Italy. However, women were less well represented in Soviet agricultural *vuzy* in the Soviet Union than in other kinds of higher educational programs for 39.5 percent of the students in higher education were then female. *Pravda,* October 10, 1937, p. 2.

115. For example, at the start of 1936, 7,000 women served as collective-farm chairmen, 170,000 as members of collective-farm boards, 200,000 as field brigade leaders, 19,000 as managers of dairy farms, and 25,000 as tractor, combine, and truck drivers, while 329,726 women were members of rural soviets. *Pravda,* December 22, 1936, p. 1; *Sotsialisticheskoe zemledelie,* February 13, 1935, p. 4; *Sovetskoe stroitel'stvo,* no. 3 (March 1937): 27; A. I. Lepeshkin, *Mestnye organy vlasti sovetskogo gosudarstva (1921–1936 g.g.)* (Moscow, 1959), p. 399.

116. For example, in Melitopol *raion,* a model *raion* outside the non–Black Soil Zone that was the subject of a contemporary Soviet study to illustrate the achievements of the collective-farm system, not a single one of the *raion*'s thirty-six collective farms had a woman chairman in 1936, while only two collective farms had female assistant chairmen. Only 1.4 percent of the brigade leaders were women, along with 5.9 percent of the managers of dairy farms, 6.8 percent of the bookkeepers and accountants, 4 out of the 508 tractor drivers, 6 of 164 combine drivers, and 1 of 164 MTS chauffeurs. A. E. Arina, G. G. Kotov, and K. V. Loseva, *Sotsial'no-ekonomicheskie izmeneniia v derevne: Melitopol'skii raion (1885–1938 gg.)* (Moscow, 1939), p. 359.

117. Arutiunian, "Kollektivizatsiia sel'skogo khoziaistva," pp. 59–60; *Sotsialisticheskoe zemledelie,* July 21, 1939, p. 4.

118. The Western *obkom,* for example, ordered that 50 percent of the rural soviet deputies overall in the *oblast* be female after the 1934 soviet elections, with female majorities in the areas of high *otkhod* and with at least 35 to 40 percent of the deputies elsewhere being women. The *obkom*'s instructions to local party *raikoms* on the elections also stipulated that they not allow women candidates to be voted down or to withdraw their candidacies, as had occurred in earlier elections. Although the results fell short of the *obkom*'s goals, women accounted for 34.5 percent of the rural soviet deputies elected here in 1934. Smolensk Archive, WKP 176, p. 159, and WKP 263, p. 88.

119. M. Lorich, "O vovlechnii zhenshchin v rabotu sovetov," *Sovetskoe stroitel'stvo,* no. 11 (November 1937): 83; no. 5 (May 1937): 101; *Vlast sovetov,* no. 4 (February 28, 1938): 26; no. 4 (February 1937): 5; *Pravda,* July 24, 1937, p. 2.

120. *Pravda,* July 24, 1937, p. 2.

121. Vyltsan, *Zavershaiushchii etap sozdaniia kolkhoznogo stroia,* p. 239.

122. *Vlast sovetov,* no. 11 (June 1937): 38.

123. *Krest'ianskaia gazeta,* July 8, 1937, p. 5.

124. For example, see *Pravda,* July 24, 1937, p. 2; July 9, 1937, p. 2; July 10, 1937, p. 3; September 11, 1937, p. 1; *Vlast sovetov,* no. 18 (September 1937): 14; and Lorich "O vovlechenii zhenshchin v rabotu sovetov," pp. 80–86.

125. *Pravda,* July 9, 1937, p. 2.

126. *Pravda,* July 24, 1937, p. 2.

127. See, for example, ibid., and *Vlast sovetov,* 1937, no. 4 (February 28, 1937): 13–15.

128. *Krest'ianskaia gazeta,* April 26, 1936, p. 3.

129. *Pravda,* September 15, 1937, p. 2.

130. *Pravda,* October 23, 1938, p. 2.

131. *Sotsialisticheskoe zemledelie,* September 9, 1938, p. 3.

132. *Pravda,* February 15, 1938, p. 6.

133. *Sotsialisticheskoe zemledelie,* October 27, 1937, p. 1; October 30, 1937, p. 3.

134. *Partiinoe stroitel'stvo,* no. 5 (March 1939): 41.

135. *Pravda,* July 3, 1938, pp. 1–2; July 6, 1938, pp. 3, 6; July 7, 1938, p. 1; September 25, 1938, p. 3; October 4, 1938, p. 3; October 5, 1938, pp. 1–4; October 13, 1938, pp. 1–2; *Sotsialisticheskoe zemledelie,* May 12, 1939, p. 1; May 14, 1939, p. 1; May 15, 1939, p. 1. Osipenko decided to become an aviator in 1929, after the first aircraft she ever saw landed

near her collective farm, which her family had joined in 1927. In pursuit of this dream, which one might think was impossible for a poor peasant girl with only two years of schooling, Osipenko traveled to Sevastopol, where she took a job in the cafeteria of a local army flying academy. Having joined the party and convinced the local party organization to support her ambitions, she was admitted to the academy as a student and trained to become a military pilot. In 1935, determined to be the best in the world, she began to train to break world records for altitude and soon accomplished what she promised Stalin she would do at the conference of wives of Red Army commanders—"to fly higher than any other girl in the world." *Pravda,* July 6, 1938, p. 2.

136. Roberta T. Manning, "The Great Purges in a Rural District: Belyi Raion Revisited," *Russian History* 16 (1989): 418.

12 / The Role of Women in Soviet Agriculture

NORTON D. DODGE AND MURRAY FESHBACH

Historical work on peasant women during World War II and the Khrushchev period is almost nonexistent. In this chapter, Norton D. Dodge, professor emeritus of economics at the University of Maryland, and Murray Feshbach, professor of demography at Georgetown University, made an early attempt to explore the role of women in the agricultural labor force, basing their research largely on the Soviet census of 1959. Focusing on the 1950s, but also highlighting several key prewar and wartime developments, Dodge and Feshbach show the extent to which agriculture had become dependent on female labor in the course of a demographic revolution (spurred on by industrialization and collectivization) characterized by massive population movement, mostly of youth and males, from the rural to the urban sectors. Women remained behind to perform most of the backbreaking physical labor in agriculture and, except during the war years, held few managerial positions and were infrequently employed in skilled or mechanized work in the collective-farming system. Although some rural women, mostly younger ones, benefited from educational opportunities, most continued to live as their mothers and grandmothers before them, albeit within the new system of Soviet collectivized agriculture. Rural women also constituted the main labor in the private agriculture sector—that is, the traditional domestic economy of the peasant household. This chapter illuminates the extent to which state-initiated modernization in the Soviet Union failed to affect the basic nature of women's labor in agriculture.

Soviet industry has expanded at a record pace during the past four decades and today ranks second only to the United States. Nonetheless, at the time of the 1959 census the majority (53 percent) of the 56.6 million women who worked in the Soviet Union were still in agriculture, and the bulk (84 percent) of these were engaged in unskilled, nonspecialized work. Thus, a woman working in a field brigade on a state or collective farm or selling her hard-earned produce at collective-farm markets is still more representative than the woman factory worker or the highly trained and more enlightened professional woman who is so often publicized in Soviet literature and the press. The pattern and rhythm of the lives of Soviet farm women,

"The Role of Women in Soviet Agriculture" by Norton D. Dodge and Murray Feshbach in Jerzy F. Karcz, ed., *Soviet and East European Agriculture* (Berkeley and Los Angeles: University of California Press, 1967), pages 265–302. Copyright © 1967 The Regents of the University of California. Reprinted by permission.

trapped in the backwaters of the agricultural economy, have been little touched by the twentieth century. Their fictional counterparts are vividly portrayed in Abramov's *Vokrug da okolo*, Solzhenitsyn's *Matrenin dvor*, and Iashin's *Vologodskaia Svadba*, and the isolation and archaic cultural patterns of their villages have been strikingly described in recent sociological studies such as *Selo Viriatino v proshlom i nastoiashchem*.

Our fundamental objective here is to set forth the facts of female participation in the agricultural labor force and from these to deduce Soviet policy on the utilization of women in agriculture. Although we shall focus on the present, some speculations regarding the future will be ventured. Our approach will be primarily statistical and economic since the space at our disposal forces us largely to neglect the sociological.[1]

Employment of Women in Soviet Agriculture

Major Trends

In prerevolutionary Russia when all but a very small proportion of the working population were engaged in agricultural pursuits, the work of planting, cultivating, and harvesting were as much a part of a woman's life as a man's. However, the industrialization drive in the late 1920s induced important changes in the pattern of male and female employment. Owing to the long agricultural heritage of Russia, the share of women in the agricultural labor force (49.7 percent) was already high in 1926 and had increased by a dozen percentage points to 61.5 by 1959 (see Table 12.1). In 1926, approximately nine-tenths of the women in the labor force were in agriculture, which then meant private agriculture. Men, also, were primarily employed in agriculture although the proportion (80 percent) was somewhat smaller. By 1939, as a result of the demands of industry, the proportion of working women employed in agriculture had declined to 73.1 percent while the proportion for men was only a little more than half. Further industrialization and the effects of World War II reinforced these trends. By 1959, only 55.3 percent of employed women were in the agricultural labor force and 42.7 of employed men. The shift from a concentration of women workers in agricultural employment to a rough balance between agricultural and nonagricultural employment reflects, of course, the vast economic transformation in the Soviet Union which has converted from a largely backward and agrarian society into a comparatively highly developed and complex one, possessing an advanced industrial sector along with a large agricultural sector still relatively backward and insulated in many ways from modern industrial civilization.

Women in the Population–Employment Balance in 1959

Data from the 1959 census are used to describe the structure of population and employment because they provide detailed socioeconomic characteristics not obtainable in regular employment statistics based on establishment reports or sample surveys.

Table 12.1. Trends in the Agricultural and Nonagricultural Labor Force, by Sectors, Socioeconomic Category, and Sex, U.S.S.R., Censuses 1926, 1939, 1959

Sector of the Economy and Socioeconomic Category	1926				1939				1959			
	Thousand Persons			Percent Females	Thousand Persons			Percent Females	Thousand Persons			Percent Females
	Both Sexes	Males	Females		Both Sexes	Males	Females		Both Sexes	Males	Females	
Total labor force	84,500	45,300	39,200	46.4	89,800	49,300	40,500	45.1	108,995	52,440	56,556	51.9
Nonagricultural labor force (including Armed Forces)	12,800	9,200	3,600	28.1	34,800	23,700	10,900	31.2	60,704	33,864	26,841	44.2
Agricultural labor force	71,700	36,100	35,600	49.7	55,000	25,400	27,600	53.8	48,291	18,576	29,715	61.5
Private farmers[a]	70,500	35,300	35,200	49.2	12,600	4,400	8,200	65.1	9,957	946	9,011	90.5
Collective farmers	—	—	—	—	36,300	16,600	19,700	54.3	31,723	13,731	17,992	56.7
Agricultural workers and employees	1,200	800	400	33.3	6,100	4,400	1,700	27.9	6,611	3,898	2,713	41.0
					(percent)							
Total labor force	100.0	100.0	100.0	—	100.0	100.0	100.0	—	100.0	100.0	100.0	—
Nonagricultural labor force (including Armed Forces)	15.1	20.3	9.2	—	38.8	48.5	26.9	—	55.7	64.6	47.5	—
Agricultural labor force	84.9	79.7	90.8	—	61.2	51.5	73.1	—	44.3	35.4	52.5	—
Private farmers	83.4	77.9	89.8	—	14.0	8.9	20.2	—	9.1	1.8	15.9	—
Collective farmers	—	—	—	—	40.4	33.7	48.6	—	29.1	26.2	31.8	—
Agricultural workers and employees	1.4	1.8	1.0	—	6.8	8.9	4.2	—	6.1	7.4	4.8	—

[a]Includes individual farmers and persons occupied solely in subsidiary agriculture.

Sources: 1926 and 1939: Warren W. Eason, "Labor Force," in Abram Bergson and Simon Kuznets, eds., Economic Trends in the Soviet Union (Cambridge, Mass.: Harvard University Press, 1963), p. 84. Itogi-1959-SSSR, Tables 30 and 33, pp. 96–97 and 104–5.

Females made up 49 percent of the underaged, 54 percent of the able-bodied, and 74 percent of the overaged population. Among those employed in the labor force, women made up 52 percent of the total, 50 percent of the able-bodied group, and 68 percent of the overaged group.[2]

The large proportion of agricultural workers in the civilian labor force (46 percent), the high ratio of women in the agricultural labor force (54 percent in the socialized and private independent sector and 91 percent in the private subsidiary sector), and the high proportion of employed women who are in agriculture (53 percent) are some of the most striking characteristics of the Soviet economy shown in Table 12.2.

Four categories of workers are employed in agriculture. In 1959, the largest category (31.7 million) was made up of those who are members of, and contribute most of their labor to, collective farms. A second group, 6.6 million in 1959, are the workers and employees engaged in agriculture primarily on state farms.[3] A third group are those engaged primarily in private subsidiary farming. Numbering more than 9.8 million in 1959 they are mostly members of collective-farm families. In addition, this last figure includes members of families of workers and employees in the state-farm sector who raise livestock and work private garden plots producing vegetables and fruit for their own use and the local market. The fourth category of agricultural workers—individual peasants—has almost passed out of existence, for only 92,000 were left in 1959. Of the three significant categories of agricultural workers, women made up 57 percent of the collective farmers, 91 percent of the

Table 12.2. Civilian Labor Force, by Sector, Socioeconomic Category, and Sex, U.S.S.R., January 15,1959

Category	Total (in thousands)	Males (in thousands)	Percentage Distribution	Females (thousands)	Percentage Distribution	Percent Females
Total civilian labor force	105,372	48,817	100.0	56,555	100.0	53.7
Agriculture	48,291	18,576	38.1	29,715	52.5	61.5
Collective farmers	31,723	13,731	28.1	17,992	31.8	56.7
Workers and employees	6,611	3,898	8.0	2,713	4.8	41.0
Individual peasants	92	32	0.1	60	0.1	65.2
Private subsidiary sector	9,865	914	1.9	8,951	15.8	90.7
Industry, construction, transportation, and communications	36,575	22,423	45.9	14,152	25.0	38.7
Trade, public dining, etc.	5,171	1,993	4.1	3,178	5.6	61.5
Education, science, and public health	9,793	2,864	5.9	6,928	12.3	70.7
Housing, communal economy, administration, financial system	4,660	2,385	4.9	2,275	4.0	48.8
Other branches	882	575	1.2	306	0.5	34.7

Sources: Itogi-1959-SSSR, Tables 30 and 33, pp. 96–97 and 104–105.

workers in private subsidiary agriculture, and 41 percent of the workers and employees in the agricultural sector.

Women in Nonprofessional Agricultural Employment

Women still perform most of the "physical" work in agriculture. A comparison of the proportion of women engaged in primarily physical occupations in agriculture (excluding those in the private subsidiary economy) for the years 1926, 1939, and 1959 reveals a deterioration in the position of women over the years.[4] In 1926 the proportion was 50 percent, and in both 1939 and 1959 it stood at 58 percent. By 1959, however, the absolute number of women had declined to almost half the 1926 level, corresponding, of course, to the overall decline in the number of persons employed in agriculture. Many younger rural women have entered industry, construction, trade, and the professions, while older women lacking mobility have remained behind.

Older persons remaining in agriculture, and the younger shifting into industry and other expanding sectors of the economy, is a phenomenon often observed in economic development. Figure 12.1 shows the age distribution of males and females employed in "physical" occupations in agriculture (excluding the private subsidiary sector). Here the proportion of men and women in the older age groups is higher than in other sectors.[5] Furthermore, women engaged in agriculture tend to be older than men; approximately 42 percent were 40 years of age or older versus 35 percent of the men.

Fig. 12.1. Age distribution of males and females employed in "physical" occupations in agriculture, January 15, 1959 (excluding private subsidiary agriculture).

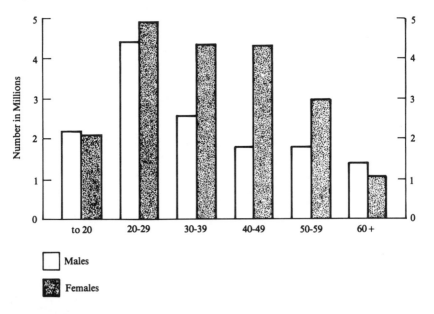

□ Males

▓ Females

Source: Table 12.A1.

Women on Collective Farms

Before World War II the proportion of female able-bodied collective farmers showed an upward trend. According to Table 12.3, women made up 46 percent of the total number in 1936 and 53 percent in 1938. During the war, owing to the draft and the transfer of men into industry and youths into labor-reserve schools, the proportion of women among able-bodied collective farmers climbed to a record high of 76 percent. The postwar high of 63 to 65 percent was reached in 1950–1953, when, as a consequence of the Korean conflict, the government was drafting men into the army or shifting them to industry. In 1963, the date of the last available information, the proportion had declined to 56 percent.

The contribution of women to collective-farm labor can be measured in several ways: in terms of absolute numbers; the proportion of the total which are women; the proportion of labor-days (*trudodni*) earned by women, and the proportion of man-days worked by women. We find that the female contribution in absolute numbers over the past decade (Table 12.3, col. 1) shows a substantial decline from 1938 when the number of women collective farmers was almost 4 million higher than in 1959. The percentage of women among able-bodied farmers working on collective farms still remains several points higher than in the late 1930s, despite the steady decline since the peak of 76 percent during the war. The decline since 1950 in both the number of collective-farm women working and their proportion of the total reflects, of course, the increased efficiency of labor on collective farms in the decade of the 1950s.

In applying the third measure, we must remember that the labor-day is not a measure of time worked by a composite yardstick that reflects the type and quality of work performed. A tractor or combine driver, for example, earns more labor-days per shift than a worker in a field brigade. Local rates are based upon national minimums for certain occupations but still vary from region to region. The situation in the Ukraine in 1957 can be considered fairly typical: able-bodied males received on the average 1.91 "labor-days" for every "man-day" while women received only 1.68. As a rule, the coefficient for men is higher because they do more complicated and harder work.[6]

The different expectations for the two sexes are reflected in the minimum number of labor-days or man-days required. Typically, the number of days which must be worked by women is considerably smaller than the number required of men. For example, in 1957, at the "Kirov" collective farm in Kharkov *oblast'* [region], the minimum for males 18 to 50 years of age was 300 labor-days and for males 50 to 60 years of age, 250. For women 18 to 40 years of age the minimum was 200 days, and for women 40 to 50 years of age and for nursing mothers the minimum was 150.[7] An indication of the smaller contribution of women also is given in Table 12.4. The situation had not improved in 1959: 4.1 percent of the women collective farmers who were required to earn the minimum number of days did not work even one day, while 14.1 percent did not earn the obligatory minimum.[8] Further increases in the proportion of nonparticipants occurred in 1961 and 1962 when 5 and 5.3 percent, respectively, did not participate in the socialized economy.[9] Women fail to fulfill the norm principally because they devote their energies to private garden plots and the home. Both the smaller labor-day versus

Table 12.3. Contribution of Able-bodied Women to Collective-farm Labor, U.S.S.R., Selected Years

Year	Number (thousand)	Index (1940 = 100)	Percent of all Able-bodied Workers on Collective Farms	Percent of Total Labor Days Earned by Women	Index of Average Number of Labor Days Earned by Women (1940 = 100)
1936	17,896.2[a]	104	46.2[a]	n.a.	n.a.
1938	18,705.8[a]	108	52.7[a]	n.a.	n.a.
1940	17,275.0[b]	100	54[c]	42[c]	100[c]
1941	8,485.1[d]	49	52[g]	40[d]	n.a.
1942	8,913.7[d]	46	60[d]	n.a.	n.a.
1943	9,191.6[d]	53	72[d]	n.a.	n.a.
1944	8,575.9[d]	50	76[d]	70[d]	n.a.
1945	8,216.0[d]	48	76[d]	n.a.	n.a.
1950	(18,306)[e]	106	64[f]	n.a.	n.a.
1953	(16,859)[e]	98	63[c]	52[c]	122[c]
1955	(17,336)[e]	100	61[c]	50[c]	139[c]
1957	(16,342)[e]	95	59[c]	48[c]	138[c]
1958	(15,950)[e]	92	58[c]	47[c]	140[c]
1959	(14,916)[e]	86	57[c]	49[c]	n.a.
1961	(12,264)[e]	71	56[g]	48[h]	n.a.
1962	(11,872)[e]	69	56[i]	49[h]	n.a.
1963	n.a.	n.a.	56[j]	n.a.	n.a.
1964	n.a.	n.a.	55[k]	n.a.	n.a.

Note: By census definition, able-bodied women are 16 to 54 years of age, and able-bodied men are 16 to 59. This is also used for employment statistics. Figures in parentheses are derived.

Sources:

[a]*Prob. ek.,* no. 7 (1940): 119

[b]*Istor. arkhiv,* no. 6 (1962): 30.

[c]*Zhen. i deti-1961,* p. 129. The figure for 1959 in column 3 is in terms of man-days.

[d]Iu. V. Arutiunian, *Sovetskoe krest'ianstvo v gody Velikoi Otechestvennoi voiny* (Moscow, 1963), pp. 66–67.

[e]Estimated by multiplying the percentage of women able-bodied participants in column 3 times the total number of able-bodied participants in corresponding years. For 1950 (28,603,000), 1953 (26,761,000), and 1957 (27,699,000) from Iu. V. Arutiunian, *Mekhanizatory sel'skogo khoziaistva v 1929–1957 gg.* (Moscow, 1960), p. 271, excluding able-bodied farmers working in state industry, transport, etc.; for 1955 (28,419,000) and 1956 (29,382,000) estimated by multiplying the average number of able-bodied collective farmers from V. G. Venzher, *Voprosy ispol'zovaniia zakona stoimosti v kolkhoznom proizvodstve* (Moscow, 1960), p. 73, by the number of agricultural collective farms from *Narkhoz-1956,* p. 140, and *Narkhoz-1959,* p. 423; for 1958 a total of 27,500,000 was reported in Iu G. Feigin et al., eds., *Osobennosti i faktory razmeshcheniia otraslei narodnogo khoziaistva SSSR* (Moscow, 1960) p. 404, excluding members working in state establishments and institutions and full-time students; for 1959 (26,168,000) the total number was estimated by multiplying the total number of collective farmer participants by the percentage of able-bodied collective farmers (35,411,100 × 0.739)—N. I. Shishkin, ed., *Trudovye resursy SSSR* (Moscow, 1961), pp. 98–99; for 1961 and 1962, total number of able-bodied participants of 30,400,000 and 29,559,000, respectively, are given in E. S. Karnaukhova and M. I. Kozlov eds., *Puti povysheniia proizvoditel'nosti truda v sel'skhom khoziaistve SSSR* (Moscow, 1964), p. 56.

[f]*Zhen.-SSSR-1960,* p. 42.

[g]*Zhen. i deti-1963,* p. 109.

[h]Estimated as follows: Ibid. gives 171 and 173 man-days worked by able-bodied women in 1961 and 1962, which when multiplied by the number of able-bodied women (col. 1) yields 2,097 and 2,054 million man-days worked by able-bodied women. Total number of man-days worked by all able-bodied collective farmers was obtained by multiplying the average number of able-bodied participants (21,900,000 and 21,200,000 in 1961 and 1962, Karnaukhova, op. cit.) and the average number of man-days worked by each (198 and 199, ibid., p. 63). Thus, in 1961, 2,097 million man-days divided by 4,336 million man-days equals 48 percent and in 1962, 2,054 million man-days divided by 4,219 million man-days equals 49 percent.

[i]G. I. Shmelev, *Raspredelenie i ispol'zovanie truda v kolkhozakh* (Moscow, 1964), p. 113.

[j]*Vest. stat.,* no. 2 (1965): 93.

[k]Ibid., no. 1 (1966): 92.

243

Table 12.4. Utilization of Collective-farm Labor Resources, by Sex, U.S.S.R., 1953

Number of Labor-days Earned	Percent		
	Total	Men	Women
None	2.6	1.4	3.3
Up to 50	5.8	2.5	7.6
51 to 100	7.0	3.0	9.3
101 to 200	26.4	15.9	32.3
201 to 300	21.8	20.7	22.3
301 to 400	15.7	20.9	12.8
More than 400	20.7	35.6	12.4
Total	100.0	100.0	100.0

Source: N. I. Shishkin, ed., *Trudovye resursy SSSR* (Moscow, 1961), p. 109

man-day coefficient and the fewer man-days worked have the result that women, on the average, contribute less work measured in labor-days than men and as a result of this smaller number of labor-days, the series showing the percent of labor-days earned by women collective farmers (Table 12.3) is, on the average, about ten percentage points or approximately a fifth below the percentage of women collective farmers.[10] The importance to the economy of female participation in the agricultural labor force is, therefore, exaggerated unless allowance is made for the difference between the number of available women laborers and the work they actually perform.

National data available for 1959 show that able-bodied females required to earn the minimum number of days averaged sixty-seven man-days less work than males.[11] The 1956–1958 data for Krasnodar *krai* [region][12] a fairly typical agricultural region, are similar in their internal distribution to the 1959 national data. Although women constituted 57 percent of the able-bodied collective farmers in the U.S.S.R. in 1959 (see Table 12.3), in Krasnodar *krai* they contributed only 46.4 percent of the total man-hours expended in all types of activity—on the collective farms, in the state sector, for other individuals, and on their own garden plots.[13] By far the largest share of their time was contributed to the collective farms where for the four-year period 1956 to 1959 they devoted approximately 58 percent of their work time.[14] The next largest claim on their time was work in the private subsidiary economy—on private plots, in wood-cutting, fishing, hunting, and as independent artisans. In no year for which data are given did women work less than a third of their time in private activity.[15]

Because female collective farmers devote substantially more of their time to private plots than do men, women accounted for 80.6 percent of the labor time spent in the private subsidiary agricultural economy. Men, on the other hand, devoted over more than a third again as much of their time as women to work on collective farms. Women's share in the work of state and cooperative organizations was slightly smaller. However, when all agricultural activities are taken together, including work on private plots, women accounted for 55.5 percent of the total labor inputs, measured in man-hours, of able-bodied men and women in 1959.[16] This total is close to the share of able-bodied women on collective farms (57 percent).

In appraising the contribution of women to collective farm work, we must consider not only the quantitative but also the qualitative aspects of their contribution. Among women collective farmers, 17.4 million, or 97 percent, are engaged in "physical" labor.[17] Of these, 14.5 million, or 83 percent, are employed in non-specialized and unskilled work compared with 66 percent of the male collective farmers engaged in physical labor (see Table 12.5).

Of the two major branches of collective farm activity—crop-growing and animal husbandry—the former is highly seasonal whereas the latter requires constant attendance throughout the year. According to the 1959 census, women comprised 51 percent (2,221,000) of the 4.4 million animal-husbandry workers. Most of them, and especially the milkmaids and poultry workers, are girls and young women with children of preschool age.[18] However, the proportion of collective-farm women employed in animal husbandry in 1959 was small (12.8 percent).[19] The overwhelming proportion of collective-farm women (87.2 percent) were employed in seasonal field work—the planting, cultivating, and harvesting of crops—where they made up 66 percent of the workers.[20] Data from Rostov *oblast'* show wide monthly variations in the rates of female participation in collective-farm work—in 1960, fewer than 57 percent of the women employed in July worked during January—February and November–December.[21] Therefore, many women are able to devote much time during slack periods to their private plots, the care of their children, and other household duties. Such irregular participation has tended to keep women from developing the knowledge and skills required for the more attractive kinds of work in agriculture. Furthermore, it is young men rather than girls who are encouraged or sent by collective farms to obtain specialized training. For example, in 1960 only 1.7 percent of all students entering agricultural mechanization schools were girls.[22] As a result, most collective-farm women spend their lives doing the least interesting and least challenging work.

After the abolition of the machine tractor stations in 1958, the bulk of the MTS [Machine Tractor Station] workers were transferred to the collective farms, and by the time of the 1959 census were classified as collective farmers. The jobs performed by the MTS workers—who numbered 3 million in 1954—were usually among the more highly skilled and better paying jobs in agriculture. As Table 12.6 indicates, the proportion of women in these occupations was very small. Despite the ubiquitous sturdy girl tractor driver in Soviet fiction, she remains largely a creature of the propaganda mill. Only during World War II did women make up a significant percentage of those employed in the machine tractor stations as drivers or mechanics. For example, in Rostov *oblast'* in 1943, 41 percent of the tractor drivers and 50 percent of the combine operators were women.[23] However, the important role women played in the machine tractor stations diminished drastically with the passing of wartime exigencies.

Women in the Private Subsidiary Economy

The second group of agricultural workers are those engaged in the private subsidiary sector. In 1959 almost 10 million persons reported work in the private subsidiary economy as their principal occupation. It consists almost entirely of work on private

Table 12.5. Number and Percent of Women Among Collective and State Farmers Engaged in Predominantly Physical Labor by Occupation, U.S.S.R., January 15, 1959

	Collective Farmers			State-Farm and Other Workers		
	Number		Percent Female	Number		Percent Female
Occupation	Total	Female		Total	Female	
Total employed in physical labor	28,728,425	17,420,143	60.1	5,071,233	2,261,473	44.6
Administrative and supervisory personnel						
Heads of livestock and poultry subfarms	134,983	20,227	15.0	8,114	2,046	25.2
Brigadiers of field brigades	232,772	19,295	8.3	26,364	3,396	12.9
Brigadiers of livestock brigades	31,697	4,043	12.8	42,790	7,718	18.0
Other brigadiers	195,940	10,256	5.2	66,948	6,243	9.3
Skilled workers and junior supervisory personnel						
Bookkeepers	23,443	4,363	18.6	6,671	1,835	27.5
Tractor and combine drivers	1,259,261	9,571	0.8	1,130,031	7,669	0.7

Implement handlers and workers on agricultural machinery	124,751	1,774	1.4	25,481	1,296	5.1
Field-team leaders	149,666	130,664	87.3	6,839	5,845	85.5
Specialized agricultural workers						
Workers in plant breeding and feed production	524,606	374,167	71.3	86,661	58,297	67.3
Cattle farm workers	701,449	423,786	60.4	260,014	122,178	47.0
Milking personnel	1,150,363	1,136,923	98.8	281,126	278,686	99.1
Stablemen and grooms	716,017	50,708	7.1	299,274	34,852	11.6
Swineherds	420,541	381,145	90.6	142,601	132,682	93.0
Herdsmen, drovers, shepherds	550,657	96,356	17.5	202,958	44,655	22.0
Other livestock workers	113,874	23,920	21.0	74,681	38,812	52.0
Poultry workers	116,557	108,886	93.4	45,596	42,996	94.3
Beekeepers	62,603	9,497	15.2	17,383	4,085	23.5
Orchard and vineyard workers	50,854	20,887	41.1	55,541	34,441	62.0
Vegetable and melon growers	56,539	45,546	80.6	28,290	22,118	78.2
Irrigators	7,975	861	10.8	11,635	2,154	18.5
Nonspecialized agricultural workers	21,991,868	14,523,178	66.0	2,130,267	1,350,240	63.4

Source: *Itogi-1959-SSSR*, pp. 159–60.

Table 12.6. Share of Women in MTS Personnel, by Occupation,
U.S.S.R., 1948, 1954 (percent of total personnel)

	May 1, 1948	May 5, 1954
Personnel servicing tractors and agricultural machinery	7.5	3.9
Drivers	1.1	0.7
Repair workers	4.4	3.3
Workers employed on construction	n.a.	35.7
Wage workers of subsidiary units, dining halls, kindergartens, and others	44.5	34.6

Source: Iu. V. Arutiunian, *Mekhanizatory sel'skogo khoziaisva SSSR v 1929–1957 gg.* (Moscow, 1960), pp. 296–297, 299, 303.

garden plots[24] with only a negligible amount of handicraft work included.[25] These activities constitute a major remnant of private enterprise in the Soviet Union which continues for very practical reasons. As a result of intensive cultivation, private plots, which occupied only 3.7 percent of the sown area in 1959, accounted for a substantial share of total farm output, particularly of certain key products such as potatoes (64 percent), meat (41 percent), milk (47 percent), and eggs (81 percent).[26] By 1961, the sown area of the plots had shrunk to 3.3 percent but the production continued to be very nearly as important as previously.[27]

The plots are cultivated by members of families of collective farmers, of state-farm workers, and of other workers and employees. The first is the largest group, accounting for 58 percent of the total number reported employed in this sector by the 1959 census. The allocation of the remaining 42 percent between families of state-farm workers and of other workers and employees may be estimated at 30 and 12 percent, respectively.[28] When employment is converted to man-year equivalents, so that labor inputs from all sources are taken into account, the share of families of collective farmers (including the labor of persons classified as collective farmers but who work on the plots in their spare time) is estimated to have been 71 percent of total labor inputs in the subsidiary economy.[29] No further breakdown of the remainder has been attempted.

Women account for the great majority of the workers in the private subsidiary economy: in 1959 almost 9 million women made up 91 percent of the workers of both sexes (Table 12.1). Among the able-bodied age groups, their share was even larger (96 percent) since men in this age group were usually engaged full-time in the socialized sector. Their share among over- and underage workers was slightly smaller (86 percent). A very high proportion of the persons employed in the private subsidiary sector is in the overage group (60 and more for men and 55 and over for women). Among women of all ages employed in this sector, the majority are more than 45 years of age,[30] and 46 percent are in the overage group.[31] Typical would be the grandmother who leaves the socialized labor force to take care of grandchildren and the garden plot because the daughter or daughter-in-law is likely to be a better earner in the socialized sector.

Women on State Farms and in Other State Agricultural Enterprises

The third group of agricultural workers are those on state farms and in other state agricultural enterprises such as repair-technical stations. These workers and employees, numbering 6.6 million in 1959, have the same employment status as those in industry and other nonagricultural branches of the economy.[32]

The proportion of women among state-farm and related workers is smaller than among collective farmers, only 41 percent.[33] Like women collective farmers, women working on state farms are primarily assigned to the less skilled jobs. Of the 2.7 million women employed in this sector, almost 2.3 million, or 92 percent, were reported by the 1959 census as engaged in "primarily physical" labor. Approximately three-fifths of these were nonspecialized workers who made up 63.4 percent of total employment in this category.

The percentage of women differs widely among the different agricultural occupations, but the pattern shown for workers and employees in Table 12.5 is similar to that for collective farmers. If we combine the collective-farm and state-farm sectors, we find that 80.7 percent, or 15.9 million of the 19.7 million women wage workers and collective farmers, are unskilled. These women represent 66 percent of the total of unskilled farmers of both sexes. Of those engaged in administrative work of the limited type shown in Table 12.5, women number only about 20 percent of the total. Only among field-team leaders do they have the majority (87.3 percent), and this job is basically a foreman-type position where the workers supervised are predominantly women. The remaining areas of employment of women in specialized categories are not necessarily those of highly skilled occupations.

Since the three categories of agriculture which we have discussed utilize well over half of the women in the Soviet labor force, it is evident that the majority of women who work are still engaged in heavy, physical labor. We should not forget that for every woman pursuing a challenging or stimulating career, there is a brigade of farm women bent to their tasks in the fields.

Women Administrators and Specialists in Agriculture

In the economy as a whole, women have made up an increasing proportion of the administrative, managerial, and specialized personnel. In 1941, 31 percent of these personnel were women and in 1957, 50 percent. Gains were made in every field for which information is available, but the role of women varies widely from one branch of the economy to another. The highest percentages are found in public-health institutions (88 percent) and educational-cultural services (66 percent). In trade and distribution, women comprise 46 percent and in government administration 44 percent. Much lower are the proportions in industry (31 percent), transportation and communications (28 percent), and construction (22 percent). Our particular concern, agriculture, has the lowest proportion of the major branches of the economy—21 percent.[34]

At the highest managerial level—chairmen of collective farms and directors of state farms and other state agricultural enterprises—women are rare (see Table 12.7).

Table 12.7. Administrators and Specialists on Collective and State Farms, by Occupation and Sex, December 1, 1956

	Men and Women		Women		
	Number (thousands)	Percentage Distribution	Number (thousands)	Percentage Distribution	Percent Women
Total	566.7	100.0	119.0	100.0	21
Collective farm chairmen and directors of state farms	89.9	15.8	[1.7]	[1.4]	[1.9]
Agronomists	106.2	18.7	42.5	35.7	40
Animal-husbandry technicians	69.1	12.2	30.4	24.5	44
Veterinarians, veterinary *feldshers*, veterinary technicians	73.9	13.0	13.3	11.1	18
Unspecified	227.5	40.1	[31.1]	26.3	[10]

Sources: Zhen.-SSSR—1960. p. 49. N. I. Shishkin, ed., *Trudovye resursy SSSR* (Moscow, 1961), p. 140, reports that about 1,000 of the more than 52,000 chairmen and directors of collective and state farms at the beginning of 1960 were women. This percentage (1.9 percent) is applied to the number of collective and state farms at the end of 1956 (89,000) to derive the estimate of 1,700 women chairmen and directors at the end of 1956. See *Narkhoz-1958*, pp. 494, 514.

Only during World War II did the proportion of women in these posts become significant, rising from 2.6 percent at the end of 1940 to 14.2 percent at the end of 1943. At the close of 1944, however, their share had declined to 11.8 percent and a year later to 8.1 percent.[35] With demobilization, government policy encouraged experienced officers to return to their home villages to serve as chairmen. The drive to consolidate farms launched in 1950 also caused a further shrinkage of opportunities for women since a man was more likely to emerge as chairman of combined farms. At the end of 1956 less than 2 percent of the chairmen and directors were women, and at the present time 2 percent of the chairmen and 1 percent of the directors are reported to be women.

Khrushchev has remarked on the absence of women in executive posts. On December 26, 1961, he is reported to have said at a regional farm conference in Kiev: "We all know what an enormous role women play in all the sectors in the building of communism. But for some reason there are few women in this hall. Just take a pair of binoculars and have a look around. What is the reason for this? It will be said that it is mainly administrative workers who are present here. It turns out that it is the men who do the administrating and the women who do the work."[36]

Despite official concern for the small role of women among administrators, little progress appears to have been made in increasing their importance. Women do, however, make up a large percentage of the agricultural specialists on state and collective farms (see Table 12.7), and the growth in the number of women professionals with a secondary specialized or higher education in agriculture has been rapid (see Table 12.8). Among agronomists they account for 40 percent of the total; among livestock specialists, 44 percent; and among veterinary doctors and techni-

Table 12.8. Women Specialists Employed in Agriculture, U.S.S.R., Selected Years[a]

| Year | With a Specialized Secondary Education | | With a Higher Education | |
	Number (thousands)	Percent	Number (thousands)	Percent
1941	n.a.	n.a.	18	25
1954	n.a.	n.a.	55	41
1955	116	46	65	41
1956	117	40	70	39
1957	123	40	74	38
1959	147	41	87	39
1960	155	41	94	39
1961	166[b]	43	100	41
1962	180[b]	44	107	42
1963	176[b]	43	109	41

[a]Only specialists with a specialized secondary or higher education in the fields of agronomy, animal husbandry, veterinary science, and forestry are included; "practicals" are excluded.

[b]Excludes forestry specialists whose number is insignificant.

Sources: Zhen. SSSR-1960, pp. 58–59; *Zhen. i deti-1961*, pp. 138–39; *Zhen. i deti-1963*, pp. 118 and 1920; *Sred. spets. obraz.-1962*, p. 42; *Narkhoz-1956*, pp. 210–11; *Narkhoz-1959*, pp. 615–16; *Narkhoz-1962*, p. 472; *Vyssh. obraz.-1961*, pp. 52, 66.

cians, 18 percent. These three occupational groups account for almost 75 percent of the women employed as agricultural managerial and specialized personnel.

How does the productivity of male and female agricultural specialists compare? Have women contributed as much to agricultural technology as their male counterparts? Although data which would permit definite answers to these questions are almost entirely lacking, some inferences from one kind of measure regarding the relative productivity of male and female agricultural scientists can be made from an examination of the contributions of men and women to the scholarly literature. Clearly, the contribution of women to scholarly journals is much less than would be expected from their numbers (see Table 12.9). This disparity may be largely, perhaps wholly, explained by the fact that professional women are not exempt from burdensome and time-consuming home responsibilities and are often less strongly motivated in pursuing their professional careers than men because of their dual commitment.

Factors Affecting the Employment of Women

Of primary importance in encouraging female participation in the agricultural economy is the shortage of males in the rural population. Although a shortage existed before World War II, the problem became acute during the war and has continued to be a serious problem. Of primary importance in discouraging women from participating in the labor force, in agriculture as in other branches of the economy, is

Table 12.9. Comparison of the Share of Women in Various Agricultural Occupations with Their Share in Authorship of Articles in Related Professional Journals, U.S.S.R., 1940, 1960

Speciality	Percent of Women in Specialty		Percent of Articles by Women Authors		Ratio		Sample Size	
	1940	1960	1940	1960	1940	1960	1940	1960
Agronomists, animal husbandry technicians, veterinarians, and foresters	25	39	15	24	.60	.62	430	676
Agronomists	n.a.	41	16	25	—	.61	156	345
Veterinarians	16	31	6	16	.38	.52	274	331

Sources: The method followed has been to count the number, based on surname suffixes, of male and female contributors to leading professional journals in agricultural fields for which information on the percentage of women professionals is known. The percentage of contributions by women has then been compared with the proportion of women in a given field. Only articles of a substantial nature were included in the sample. In instances where two, three, four, or more authors were listed, fractional credit was given to each author. The journals sampled included Sovetskaia agronomiia, Sovetskaia veterinariia, Zemledelie, and Vestnik Akademii sel'skokhoziaistvennykh nauk (in 1940, Doklady Vsesoiuznoi Akademii sel'skokhoziaistvennykh nauk). The few articles by women animal husbandry technicians or foresters have been allocated under agronomists or veterinarians.

the conflict between responsibilities to a husband and children and to a job. Attempts to reduce this conflict have resulted in a number of measures such as the enactment of protective legislation and the provision of child-care facilities. Still a third factor affecting female participation is educational attainment. Agronomy, veterinary medicine, and other specialized fields, require much training while agricultural field work demands a minimum. Therefore, availability of education to women and the extent of their motivation to obtain this training largely determine the extent and nature of their participation in the agricultural labor force.

The Male Deficit in the Rural Population

The acute shortage of males in the rural population at the time of the 1959 census, particularly in the age groups over 35 years, is dramatically shown by the population pyramid in Figure 12.2. The shortage will remain a problem for at least another two decades at the end of which time the imbalance in the sexes will be largely righted in the able-bodied age group. This shortage of males in the rural population is primarily the cause of the high proportion of women in the major branches of agriculture shown in Figure 12.1.[37] This proportion reaches a peak of 70 percent in the 40–49-year age group and exceeds the proportion of males in all other age groups, with the exception of the under-20 and over-60 age groups.

Fig. 12.2. Age distribution of males and females employed in "physical" occupations in agriculture, January 15, 1959 (excluding private subsidiary agriculture).

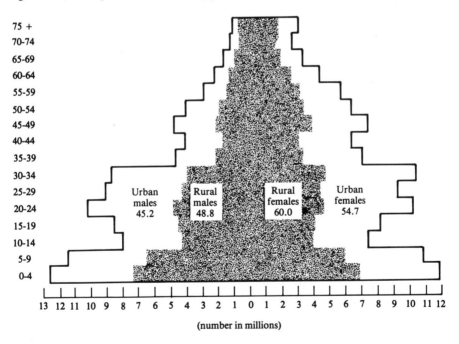

(number in millions)

Source: Table 12.A1.

The imbalance of the sexes in rural areas has had other important effects. Although according to 1959 data a higher proportion of rural men than urban men are married, there are simply not enough men to go around. In fact, if all rural males in the most depleted age groups married, no more than 50 to 60 percent of the females in that age range could marry. The significance to agricultural employment of the low proportion married among rural women is that about 12 million women in the age range 20 through 59 years (more than one-third the number of women in the rural labor force) do not have husbands upon whom they may depend for their livelihood. The implications of this for female employment cannot be over-emphasized for it is reasonable to assume that virtually all these women must work for a living. As the numbers of men and women become more balanced, the proportion of unmarried women will probably decline, and, although marriage does not afford the Soviet woman immunity from employment, married women are not as likely to be in the labor force as their unmarried counterparts.

Family Versus Work

Family demands play an important role in determining the extent and nature of the participation of women in the labor force. The burden of domestic duties may deter a woman from entering or remaining in the labor force especially while her children are young. According to the 1959 census, 45 percent of women in the able-bodied ages outside the Soviet labor force had children under 7 years of age, and 59 percent had children under 14 years of age.[38] Although we do not know the exact corresponding proportions for women in the able-bodied ages who work, it is expected that these would be smaller. Not unexpectedly, sample data for Siberia show that there is a negative correlation between family size and desire to work.[39] However, circumstances force many women with large families in both urban and rural areas to work, a fact reflected in the high participation rate of women in the Soviet labor force.

The second effect of the heavy burden of housework is its debilitating influence upon the energies, and, consequently, upon the productivity of many women workers. According to figures cited by Shishkin, a working woman with a family will be busy three more hours a day than the full-time housewife. The woman worker–housewife typically has two hours less time for self-education, reading, entertainment, and rest and gets one and one-half hours less sleep.[40] Men share little of the burden as sample data for four collective farms show (Table 12.10).

The time spent by women in household work on work days is characteristically between 35 and 40 minutes less on advanced collective farms than on backward farms, due to the existence on the former of more facilities such as electricity, child-care centers, dining halls, and bakeries, which lighten the women's burden.[41] Thus, any significant reduction in the burden of housework for Soviet farm women will depend primarily upon three developments: (1) a marked improvement in public utilities, such as running water and electricity; (2) the more widespread provision of labor-saving household devices on both a private and communal basis; and (3) the provision of more child-care facilities. To the present, progress in all these areas has been remarkably slow. In 1956, two-thirds of the urban families had to carry their

Table 12.10. Time Spent by Collective-farm Members in Housework, by Sex and Type of Day, U.S.S.R. (percent of total housework done)

Length of Time	Workdays		Days Off	
	Men	Women	Men	Women
Up to 1 hour	77	3	85	10
1 to 2 hours	12	11		23
2 to 4 hours	8	20	9	26
4 hours or more	3	66	6	41
Total	100	100	100	100

Source: L. Bibik, *Biull. nauch. inf.*, no. 6 (1961): 49.

water in buckets from a communal tap or pump. In rural areas, where conditions are even more primitive, a household with running water is a rare exception. Hot water is practically unavailable even in the cities, where it is estimated that less than 3 percent of the population has hot water.[42] Thus, for a working woman the family washing alone can take the equivalent of two strenuous days a week which must be fitted into the evenings and days off.[43] Public facilities for laundry and dry cleaning exist only in the cities and even there they are entirely inadequate.

Rural Child-Care Facilities

Only 40 percent of the collective farms are equipped with nurseries or kindergartens and half of these are of a seasonal character—inadequacies which restrict the participation of many women in the labor force and which the government naturally hopes eventually to eliminate.[44] From the meager data available for the postwar years, we can estimate that only 6 percent of rural nursery-age children (2 months to 3 years) can be accommodated in permanent nursery facilities (the percentage is double for the cities). However, when the largely rural seasonal nurseries are taken into account, the situation is improved, and in the periods of peak labor demand in agriculture a substantial proportion of nursery-age children can be accommodated in some sort of facility.

Kindergartens admit children aged 3 to 6, and, like nurseries, their capacity is insufficient to accommodate more than a small percentage of kindergarten-age children. Reported enrollment of 3,800,000 children in 1962 represents 20 percent of an estimated 19.3 million children in the 3- to 7-year age group.[45] Because of the unequal distribution of facilities in urban and rural areas, however, an estimated 37 percent of urban, but only 7 percent of rural children of kindergarten age can be accommodated in kindergarten facilities.[46] Collective farmers in particular have to rely on summer playgrounds for the care of their children. In 1955, only 30,400 children were accommodated in collective-farm kindergartens, while 523,700 children of kindergarten age were cared for at collective-farm playgrounds.[47] Although the precise number of seasonal kindergartens and summer playgrounds in 1962 is not known, their capacity was probably sufficient for more than a million children.[48] If so, they provided facilities, admittedly often makeshift, for an additional 10 to 12 percent of the rural children of kindergarten age. Nonetheless, most rural children of kindergarten age are of necessity cared for at home.[49] The capacity of rural child-care facilities of all types still falls far short of the number needed to permit women with young children to rely upon them rather than upon other arrangements to free themselves for participation in the labor force. The day when the Soviet farm woman is freed from domestic responsibilities appears to lie many decades in the future. In the interim, these responsibilities will continue to conflict with the full participation of women in the labor force.

Education of Women in Agriculture

The third major factor affecting the character and extent of female participation in the agricultural labor force is education. Although males and females theoretically have equal access to education in the Soviet Union, in practice there are some significant differences in the proportion of male and female enrollments at different educational levels and in different fields, reflecting primarily the divergent motivations and interests of each sex. There are also important differences between the proportions of both sexes enrolled in urban and rural areas.

Through the first seven grades the proportion of boys and girls is approximately equal in urban and rural areas. In grades eight to ten, however, the proportion of girls in rural areas is six percentage points below that of urban girls, although the rural girls in these grades outnumber the boys.[50] In the republics with a Moslem tradition, many girls, particularly the rural, marry young and leave school. In the Uzbek Republic in 1955, for example, girls made up 48 percent of the urban enrollment in grades 8 to 10 but only 26 percent of the rural.[51]

Training in agriculture is carried out at four types of institutions: state vocational-technical schools and trade schools for the mechanization of agriculture; specialized secondary educational institutions; higher educational institutions; and graduate programs at research institutes (and at higher educational institutions).

Vocational-technical schools train youths aged 14 to 17 in a variety of skills, including tractor-driving and repair work. The proportion of girls in all vocational-technical programs has declined since the war, when it was 25 percent, to less than 15 percent in recent years.[52] The percentage of girls in specifically agricultural training programs probably has been much smaller since few women are engaged in repair work and tractor-driving.

Specialized secondary educational institutions in the agricultural field train assistant agronomists, breeding technicians, mechanics, veterinary aides, bookkeepers, and so on. These are not among the most popular occupations for girls as Table 12.11 indicates. Nevertheless, in 1959, more than 100,000 girls are estimated to have been enrolled in agricultural technicums.[53] The distribution of women among the broad fields of specialization in specialized secondary educational institutions has remained essentially the same since the 1920s. Women have predominated in health and medicine (83 to 90 percent of the total); the proportion enrolled in education, art, cinematography, economics, and law has also been high (more

Table 12.11. Share of Women in Student Enrollment in Specialized Secondary and Higher Educational Institutions, U.S.S.R., Selected Years[a] (percent)

Year	Specialized Secondary Educational Institutions		Higher Educational Institutions	
	Total Enrollment	Enrollment in Agricultural Fields	Total Enrollment	Enrollment in Agricultural Fields
1926	n.a.	n.a.	30.9	16.3
1927	37.6	15.4	28.5	17.4
1928	n.a.	n.a.	29.1	18.4
1929	n.a.	n.a.	29.2	20.4
1930	38.8	31.0	28.3	25.4
1931	n.a.	n.a.	30.8	28.1
1932	44.7	33.5	33.3	30.6
1933	43.9	30.1	36.5	32.1
1934	44.1	31.6	38.0	31.8
1935	43.0	30.2	39.5	30.2
1936	46.7	29.3	41.0	29.3
1937	51.6	28.7	43.3	30.2
1940	54.6	37.0	58.0	46.1
1945	67.1	66.0	77.0	79.0
1950	43.6	41.0	53.1	39.3
1955	54.8	43.0	52.3	39.3
1956	52.0	44.0	51.0	39.0
1957	48.0	38.0	47.0	31.0
1959	46.0	36.0	45.0	28.0
1960	47.0	38.0	43.0	27.0
1961	48.0	38.0	42.0	26.0
1962	49.0	38.0	42.0	25.0
1963	49.0	38.0	43.0	25.0
1964	49.0	37.0	43.0	25.0

[a]Day as well as evening students are included in enrollment figures on which the calculations are based.

Sources: Specialized secondary educational institutions: Data for 1927, 1940, 1945, 1950, 1955, and 1958–61: *Sred. spets. obraz.-1962,* p. 92; for 1930, 1932–37, and 1956–57: Nicholas DeWitt, *Education and Professional Employment in the U.S.S.R.* (Washington, D.C.: National Science Foundation, 1961), p. 613; for 1962: *Narkhoz-1962,* p. 573; for 1963: *Narkhoz-1963,* pp. 566 and 578; for 1964: derived from *Vest. stat.,* no. 2 (1965): 95.

Higher educational institutions: Data for 1945 are inconsistent with those in the rest of the table. Data through 1956, except 1945: DeWitt, op. cit., p. 654; for 1945: *Vyssh. obraz.-1961,* p. 86; for 1956–58: *Narkhoz-1959,* p. 751; for 1959–61: *Narkhoz-1961,* p. 699; for 1963: *Narkhoz-1963,* pp. 566 and 578; for 1964: derived from *Vest. stat.,* no. 2 (1965): 95.

than 75 percent). In industry, construction, transportation, and communications the proportion of women students, initially less than one-tenth, has remained relatively low, averaging about a third of the enrollment. Agriculture has been slightly more popular, the percentage of women ranging between 29 and 44 percent except during the war when the proportion of women was dramatically higher.

The percentage of women enrolled in higher educational institutions before the revolution was severely limited. Since then, however, Soviet higher educational institutions have become genuinely coeducational. Health and education have been the fields most favored by women. In the mid-1920s women accounted for only 16 percent of the enrollment in agriculture and 7 percent in engineering. Apart from a doubling of the percentage of women in engineering and smaller increases in the agricultural and socioeconomic fields, the situation changed little during the remainder of the 1920s. However, as the drive to industrialize gained momentum in the early 1930s, special efforts were made to expand the enrollment of women in higher educational institutions, primarily in institutions in the agricultural, engineering, and socioeconomic fields where female enrollments were low.

By 1935 the proportion enrolled in agriculture had risen to 30 percent while the overall proportion of women in higher education approached 40 percent, owing to the large numbers of women in health and education. The proportion of women continued to increase in the late 1930s up to 58 percent of the total in 1941 when the proportion in agriculture was 46 percent. As a result of the war, women accounted for 77 percent of total enrollment in 1945 and 79 percent of those enrolled in agriculture. However, by 1950, the proportion of women in higher education was well below the 1940 level, and beginning in 1955, when the proportion was 52 percent, a rather sharp decline set in. Each year the proportion dropped one or two percentage points until it reached 42 percent in 1961 where it appears to have stabilized. Women continue to predominate in health and education, but in the health field they dropped from 69 percent in 1955 to 52 percent in 1964 and in the educational-cultural field from 72 to 64 percent. In engineering the decline was from 35 to 29 percent. In agriculture, which now had the lowest percentage of women of any major field, the decline was from 39 to 25 percent.

Whether these downward trends have stopped cannot be definitely determined since the reasons for the change are not clear. Undoubtedly changes in the admission regulations for higher education which followed the school reforms in 1958 have had an effect on the enrollment of women since they gave preference to ex-servicemen and persons with two or more years of work experience. Further changes made in the spring of 1965, however, would seem to have largely restored the earlier situation of equal access.

An extensive sampling of candidate degrees (roughly comparable to a Ph.D. degree) in selected years (see Table 12.12) shows that at the graduate level the proportion of women in agriculture and veterinary medicine has been close to the

Table 12.12. Estimated Percentage of Women Recipients of Candidate and Doctoral Degrees, Agricultural and Veterinary Fields, U.S.S.R., Selected Years

Degree and Field of Study	1936–37	1941–45	1956–58	1959–61	1962–64
Candidate degrees, all fields	20.5	n.a.	32.8	30.0	27.9
Agricultural and veterinary fields	19.5	n.a.	36.1	33.1	28.6
Doctoral degrees, all fields	9.6	5.5	14.8	17.7	21.2
Agricultural and veterinary fields	n.a.	2.7	12.5	11.1	13.0

Source: Norton T. Dodge, *Women in the Soviet Economy* (Baltimore: Johns Hopkins University Press, 1966).

average for all fields and also close to the proportion of female undergraduates enrolled in agriculture.

The percentage of women earning Soviet doctoral degrees in agriculture is much smaller, however, both in comparison with other fields and with the percentage receiving candidate degrees. The declining proportion of women at higher levels of education accounts in part for the smaller proportion of women occupying the more responsible and highly specialized jobs in agriculture.

Levels of Educational Attainment

Reflecting the history of enrollments and the smaller number of jobs in agriculture which require advanced educational training, the educational attainment of rural women is not only substantially below that of rural men but also is below that of urban women.[54]

Before World War II these male–female and urban–rural disparities were particularly marked, but since then the gaps have been significantly narrowed. For example, in 1939 two and one-half times as many rural men as women in the able-bodied age group had a higher education, whereas in 1959 men outnumbered women by only 50 percent. The proportion of all persons with a higher or secondary education, including incomplete secondary education, increased 3.5-fold between 1939 and 1959 (see Table 12.13). The greatest improvement (19.8 times) was achieved by women collective farmers in the rural population. But in spite of the educational gains made by collective-farm women, they remain educationally the most backward of the major socioeconomic groups in the Soviet Union. In 1959, nearly half of these women had less than a four-year education (see Table 12.A3). The level of their education varied greatly with age. Among women over 40 years of age, from 70 to nearly 100 percent have less than a four-year education. This is indeed a lost generation so far as education is concerned. It is evident that the government has concentrated its educational efforts elsewhere, where expected returns were higher. In the lower age groups, where real effort has been made, substantially more women have achieved higher levels of education.

Further information on the level of male and female educational attainment in the various major agricultural sectors and branches is given in Table 12.14. It is interesting to note that the select group of women engaged in the technical or administrative side of agriculture is, for the most part, as well educated as the men. At the administrative level, 17.7 percent of the women have a higher education and 21.6 percent a secondary specialized education. The proportion of women with a higher (14.5 percent) or secondary (24 percent) specialized education employed in veterinary and other establishments serving agriculture also is high and exceeds that of men. The educational level of women exceeds that of men in repair-technical and related stations as well.

Many more years will be required before the average educational level of women in agriculture is appreciably raised. Until that time, lack of education will continue to reduce the contribution of women and inhibit the role which they play. The older women, in particular, will continue to perform the least skilled and least attractive tasks while men will dominate the more responsible and skilled occupa-

Table 12.13. Workers, Employees, and Collective Farmers with Higher and Secondary Education, by Type of Residence, U.S.S.R., 1939, 1959[a] (number per thousand of total population in a given group)

Residence Group and Sex	Total		Workers		Employees		Collective Farmers	
	1939	1959	1939	1959	1939	1959	1939	1959
Total population	123	433	82	386	519	893	18	226
Male	136	434	100	393	455	859	26	261
Female	104	431	44	377	639	921	11	198
Urban population	242	564	96	424	555	898	50	241
Male	235	537	122	430	496	872	63	287
Female	255	597	54	413	641	918	26	193
Rural Population	63	316	60	311	454	879	17	226
Male	81	337	73	320	394	828	24	260
Female	42	294	27	296	632	927	10	198

[a]Including those with incomplete secondary education for all groups and both years.

Source: Itogi-1959-SSSR, p. 116.

Table 12.14. Educational Levels of Persons Employed in Agriculture, by Branch and Sex, U.S.S.R., January 15, 1959 (per thousand employed)

Branch	Completed Higher Education		Specialized Secondary and Incomplete Higher Education		General Secondary and Incomplete Secondary Education		Elementary and Incomplete Seven-Year Education		Less than a Four-Year Education	
	Male	Female	Male	Female	Male	Female	Male	Female	Male	Female
All agriculture	5	2	20	9	258	198	415	310	302	481
State farms	10	5	29	16	265	233	436	332	260	414
Collective farms	2	1	14	6	249	192	411	308	324	493
Repair technical stations (RTS), machine-tractor stations (MTS), machine-livestock stations (MZhS), drainage stations (LMS)	17	32	50	110	417	406	435	228	81	224
Other agricultural enterprises and establishments	15	14	46	43	210	247	425	317	304	379
Organizations servicing agriculture and veterinary institutions	140	145	235	240	260	299	233	163	132	153
Administration of agriculture (trusts, offices, etc.)	148	177	171	216	311	361	282	123	88	123
Individual peasant farming	0.4	0.2	3	2	95	65	278	188	624	745

Source: Itogi-1959-SSSR, pp. 125, 127.

tions in spite of the exhortations of Soviet leaders to recruit more women for such posts.

Conclusions

A number of conclusions regarding Soviet manpower policies in agriculture can now be ventured. The past three censuses show that agriculture has become increasingly dependent upon female labor. The number of women as a proportion of the agricultural labor force increased from 50 percent in 1926 to 62 percent in 1959. During the same period, as a result of the growth of industry, the proportion of the female labor force engaged in agriculture has declined from 91 percent to 53 percent. Thus, although agriculture remains the major occupation of Soviet women, and the bulk of the women in agriculture are still engaged in unskilled, backbreaking work, many women have shifted into more attractive occupations in other sectors of the economy or have entered careers in agriculture which require specialized training and offer substantial satisfactions.

The policy of the government has clearly been to let the older generation of women continue working at unskilled, low-productivity jobs in agriculture, and little effort has been made to educate or train this group. On the other hand, men and younger women were drawn into industry in large numbers up to the outbreak of World War II. Since 1939, the number of men employed in agriculture has shrunk further—by 7 million—largely due to war losses. The 18.6 million men (versus 29.7 million women) who remained in agriculture in 1959 were for the most part employed in the more productive and skilled occupations. Thus, the government "placed its wager on the strong"—on men and younger women—providing them with the education and specialized training required for the more appealing and remunerative jobs.

From a purely economic standpoint, the neglect of the older generation of women would seem logical. The seasonality of much of their work, the shorter period during which investment in their training could be recouped, and the smaller learning capacity of older women prevents as high a return as from effort devoted to men or young women. Similarly, the difference in the proportions of women employed in the three major sectors of agriculture—41 percent of state-farm workers, 56 percent of collective farmers, and 91 percent of those working the private plots— would seem to reflect differences in the productivity of men and women in the varying kinds of work required by these sectors.

The relative share and importance of women with a secondary specialized or higher education in agriculture has increased significantly since 1926, although little relative improvement has been shown in recent years, and the share of women remains below that of men. The smaller proportion of women enrolled in secondary specialized and higher educational institutions also has its economic justification. The distractions of family responsibilities and related factors result in the productivity of women professionals being less, on the average, than that of men. However, since agriculture has not been so attractive a field for women as medicine or education, a process of self-selection has kept the proportion of women receiving specialized training in agriculture relatively low, and Soviet manpower planners have never felt the necessity to restrict the proportion of women enrolled in agricultural fields. Indeed, during the 1930s they successfully increased the proportion. But should a higher proportion of women be engaged in the more responsible agricultural occupations? If discrimination against hiring women in these jobs exists, and it undoubtedly does to some extent, a higher proportion would seem desirable on economic grounds. Nevertheless, the conflict between job and family mentioned above, which becomes more acute as the burden of professional responsibilities increases, can be expected to continue to restrict quite legitimately the role of women in administrative work.

In favoring the extensive utilization of women in agriculture—witness their paeans to champion tractor drivers and pig raisers—Soviet leaders seem to be attempting to make a virtue of necessity. However, as the older generation of farm women dies off, as mechanization and modernization in farming methods advance, and as the shortage of males in the Soviet working age population diminishes, we can expect a decreased reliance on women as the "work horses" of agriculture. A slow shift of women out of the marginal and archaic types of work in which so many are now occupied—gleaning after the combine, tending loose cattle, hand-hoeing corn—can also be expected. Past experience has shown, however, that evolution in Soviet agriculture is a slow and uncertain process. Like the horse, women are likely to coexist with the tractor, yielding useful service to Soviet agriculture for many decades to come.

APPENDIX

Table 12.A. Age Distribution of Males and Females Employed in "Physical" Occupations in Agriculture, U.S.S.R., January 15, 1959[a]

Age Group	Number (in thousands)		Percentage Distribution		Percentage	
	Males	Females	Males	Females	Males	Females
All ages	14,150	19,743	100.0	100.0	41.8	58.2
To 20	2,206	2,132	15.6	10.8	50.9	49.1
20–29	4,391	4,896	31.0	24.8	47.3	52.7
30–39	2,585	4,363	18.3	22.1	37.2	62.8
40–49	1,796	4,304	12.7	21.8	29.4	70.6
50–59	1,778	3,001	12.6	15.2	37.2	62.8
60 plus	1,394	1,046	9.8	5.3	67.1	42.9

[a]Excluding private subsidiary agriculture.

Source: Calculated from *Itogi-1959-SSSR*, pp. 136, 143, 162–63, 168.

Table 12.A2. Distribution of Population by Residence, Age, and Sex, U.S.S.R., January 15, 1959

(Thousands)[a]

Age	Total			Urban			Rural			Percent Females	
	Total	Males	Females	Total	Males	Females	Total	Males	Females	Urban	Rural
All ages	208,827	94,050	114,776	99,978	45,208	54,769	108,849	48,842	60,007	54.8	55.1
0 to 4 years	24,328	12,388	11,940	10,158	5,176	4,982	14,170	7,212	6,958	49.0	49.1
5 to 9 years	22,034	11,220	10,814	9,538	4,860	4,678	12,496	6,360	6,136	49.0	49.1
10 to 14 years	15,309	7,770	7,539	6,996	3,554	3,452	8,313	4,226	4,087	49.3	49.2
15 to 19 years	16,499	8,296	8,203	8,062	3,975	4,087	8,437	4,321	4,116	50.7	47.5
20 to 24 years	20,343	10,056	10,287	10,892	5,295	5,597	9,451	4,761	4,690	51.4	49.6
25 to 29 years	18,190	8,917	9,273	9,505	4,694	4,811	8,685	4,223	4,462	50.6	51.4
30 to 34 years	18,999	8,611	10,388	10,269	4,702	5,568	8,730	3,909	4,820	54.2	55.2
35 to 39 years	11,591	4,528	7,062	6,039	2,352	3,687	5,551	2,176	3,375	61.1	60.8
40 to 44 years	10,408	3,998	6,410	5,514	2,219	3,295	4,894	1,779	3,115	59.8	63.6
45 to 49 years	12,263	4,706	7,558	6,221	2,518	3,703	6,042	2,187	3,855	59.5	63.8
50 to 54 years	10,447	4,010	6,437	5,094	2,004	3,091	5,352	2,006	3,346	60.7	62.5
55 to 59 years	8,699	2,905	5,793	3,896	1,359	2,537	4,803	1,547	3,256	65.1	67.8
60 to 64 years	6,697	2,348	4,349	2,781	953	1,828	3,916	1,395	2,521	65.7	64.4
65 to 69 years	5,039	1,751	3,288	2,092	717	1,376	2,947	1,034	1,913	65.8	64.9
70 to 74 years	3,805	1,273	2,532	1,392	401	991	2,413	812	1,601	71.2	66.3
More than 75 years	4,167	1,268	2,899	1,525	438	1,086	2,642	889	1,752	71.2	66.3
Age unknown (error of closure and rounding)	8	4	4	[5]	[2]	[0]	[5]	[3]	[3]		

[a]Minor discrepancies are due to rounding.

Sources: Total population: U.S. Bureau of the Census, *Projections of the Population of the U.S.S.R., by Age and Sex*, International Population Reports, Series P-91, no. 13 (Washington, D.C.: Government Printing Office, 1964), p. 21. Urban and rural population: *Itogi-1959-SSSR*, pp. 50–51; P. G. Pod'iachikh, *Naselenie SSSR* (Moscow, 1961), p. 34.

Table 12.A3. Employment in Agriculture by Residence, Socioeconomic Category, and Sex, U.S.S.R., January 15, 1959

Residence and Sex	Total	Workers	Employees	Collective Farmers	Individual Peasants, Independent Artisans	Private Subsidiary Agriculture
Total employment	48,290,768	5,918,418	693,004	31,722,835	91,671	9,864,801
Males	18,575,560	3,458,342	439,938	13,731,230	32,147	913,903
Percentage male	38.5	58.4	63.5	43.3	35.1	9.3
Females	29,715,208	2,460,076	253,106	17,991,604	59,524	8,950,898
Percentage female	61.5	41.6	36.5	56.7	64.9	90.7
Total urban employment	3,263,435	810,197	200,138	1,169,552	11,055	1,072,493
Urban males	1,264,674	509,500	121,454	571,436	3,912	58,372
Percentage male	38.8	62.9	60.7	48.9	35.4	5.4
Urban females	1,998,761	300,697	78,684	598,116	7,143	1,014,121
Percentage female	61.2	37.1	39.3	51.1	64.6	94.6
Total rural employment	45,027,333	5,108,221	492,916	30,553,282	80,616	8,792,308
Rural males	17,310,886	2,948,842	318,484	13,159,794	28,235	855,531
Percentage male	38.4	57.7	64.6	43.1	35.0	9.7
Rural females	27,176,447	2,159,379	174,422	17,393,488	52,381	7,936,777
Percentage female	61.6	42.3	35.4	56.9	65.0	90.3

Source: Itogi-1959-SSSR, p. 104.

Table 12.A4. Educational Level of the Employed Population, by Residence, Socioeconomic Category, and Sex, U.S.S.R., January 15, 1959 (persons per thousand in a given group)

Residence and Socioeconomic Category	Higher, Incomplete Higher, Specialized Secondary Education		General Secondary Education		Seven-Year and Incomplete Secondary Education		Primary and Incomplete Seven-Year Education		Less than a Four-Year Education	
	Male	Female	Male	Female	Male	Female	Male	Female	Male	Female
Total population										
Total	103	116	60	68	271	247	386	272	180	297
Workers	23	16	56	63	314	298	459	353	148	270
Employees	508	476	124	161	227	284	121	69	20	10
Collective farmers	14	6	29	18	218	174	413	308	326	494
Urban population										
Total	153	184	82	109	302	304	362	243	101	160
Workers	27	19	67	76	336	318	449	350	121	237
Employees	533	459	129	169	210	290	110	71	18	11
Collective farmers	28	10	38	23	221	160	420	292	293	515
Rural population										
Total	56	60	40	34	241	200	408	295	255	411
Workers	14	9	36	34	270	253	480	361	200	343
Employees	450	523	113	139	265	265	146	64	26	8
Collective farmers	13	6	29	18	218	174	412	309	328	493

Source: Itogi-1959-SSSR, p. 115.

Table 12.A5. Educational Level of the Collective-Farm Population by Socioeconomic Category, Age, and Sex, U.S.S.R., January 15, 1959 (persons per thousand in a given group)

Socioeconomic Category and Age	Higher, Incomplete Higher, and Specialized Secondary Education		General Secondary Education		Seven-Year and Incomplete Secondary Education		Elementary and Incomplete Seven-Year Education		Less than a Four-Year Education	
	Male	Female	Male	Female	Male	Female	Male	Female	Male	Female
Total population	10	4	24	14	148	112	285	209	533	661
10 years and older	13	5	33	18	203	139	390	260	361	588
10 to 19 years	1	2	42	43	312	335	402	375	243	245
20 to 24 years	30	26	118	76	386	367	398	372	68	159
25 to 29 years	20	11	22	12	201	171	598	515	159	291
30 to 34 years	25	10	18	13	266	232	530	497	161	248
35 to 39 years	32	9	28	14	252	160	465	424	223	393
40 to 44 years	28	5	17	4	131	43	465	245	359	703
45 to 49 years	15	2	8	1	49	10	347	118	581	869
50 to 54 years	8	1	5	1	27	6	291	104	669	888
55 to 59 years	5	—	5	1	20	5	271	82	699	912
60 to 64 years	3	—	4	1	14	4	234	61	745	944
65 to 69 years	2	—	3	—	11	3	202	49	782	948
70 years and older	1	—	2	—	7	2	134	29	856	969

Source: Itogi-1959-SSSR, pp. 113–114.

Notes

1. For an interesting sociological background and for earlier estimates based on prelimi-nary results of the census, see Demitri Shimkin, "Current Characteristics and Problems of the Soviet Rural Population," in Roy D. Laird, ed., *Soviet Agricultural and Peasant Affairs* (Lawrence: University of Kansas Press, 1963), pp. 79–127. Our study is based on final census results which were not available to Shimkin in 1962.

2. U.S. Congress, Joint Economic Committee, *Annual Economic Indicators for the U.S.S.R.* (Washington, D.C.: Government Printing Office, 1964), Table V-A-1, pp. 44–45.

3. The combined term "worker and employee" has a very special meaning in Soviet terminology. Persons so designated are paid wages or a salary by the state or by (state-owned) enterprises and are entitled to a specified set of fringe benefits, including pension rights and rights to an annual vacation.

4. *Itogi-1959-SSSR*, p. 168; *Zhen. i deti-1961*, pp. 114–19; *Zhen. i deti-1963*, pp. 94–99.

5. See Norton T. Dodge, *Women in the Soviet Economy* (Baltimore: Johns Hopkins University Press, 1966).

6. I. Paskhaver, *Balans trudovykh resursov kolkhozov* (Kiev, 1961), p. 74.

7. Ibid., p. 264.

8. N. I. Shishkin, ed., *Trudovye resursy SSSR* (Moscow, 1961), p. 109. A collective farmer's income from the collective farm is typically reduced by 10 percent for failure to work the required minimum number of labor-days per year. Cf. O. D. Dubinskaia, *Prava i obiazannosti chlenov kolkhoza* (Moscow, 1957), p. 34.

9. U.S. Congress, Joint Economic Committee, *Current Economic Indicators for the U.S.S.R.* (Washington, D.C.: Government Printing Office, 1965), Table VI-8, p. 83.

10. However, the 1959 figure of 49 percent applies to man-days worked. A shift to this form of reporting collective-farm labor inputs was made in this year.

11. M. P. Vasilenko, *Puti preodeleniia sezonnosti truda v kolkhozakh* (Moscow, 1962), p. 53.

12. B. I. Braginskii, *Proizvoditel'nost' truda v sel'skom khoziaistve: Metodika ucheta i planirovaniia* (Moscow, 1962), p. 194.

13. Vasilenko, pp. 23–24.

14. Ibid., and Braginskii.

15. The closer a collective farm is situated to an urban center, the fewer the number of labor-days worked in the socialized sector, especially by female labor. This is the result of higher returns from work on private plots. See V. Komarovskaia, V. Luzgina, and V. Shatskii in I. A. Borodin, ed., *Ispol'zovanie trudovykh resursov v sel'skom khoziaistve SSSR* (Moscow, 1964), p. 211.

16. Calculated from data in Vasilenko.

17. *Itogi-1959-SSSR*, Tables 23, 46, pp. 104–5, 160.

18. G. Shmelev and V. Ladenkov, *Ek. sel'. khoz.*, no. 10 (1962): 30.

19. Ibid. According to Shishkin, p. 99, the corresponding percentages for both sexes from collective farm annual reports are: 1956—11.7; 1958—12.1, 1959—12.6 percent.

20. For both sexes, Shishkin, p. 99, gives the following percentages: 1956—79.8; 1958—78.8; 1959—78.2 percent.

21. Shmelev and Lazenkov, p. 29. For earlier and similar figures, see B. Babynin, *Prob. ek.*, no. 2 (1940): 71.

22. Only 1 percent of all students entering such schools in the R.S.F.S.R. were girls. The corresponding percentages for other major republics were: Ukraine—0.7; Belorussia—0.5;

Kazakhstan—4.3 percent. Cf. G. I. Shmelev, *Raspredelenie i ispol'zovanie truda v kolkhozakh* (Moscow, 1964), pp. 121–122.

23. *Izvestiia,* August 18, 1943.

24. The 1959 census data on employment in the private subsidiary economy are considered to be the least reliable data in the census by Soviet as well as non-Soviet demographers. The reason is that it was the respondent who determined himself whether this was his principal occupation.

25. Evidence on the distribution of labor inputs (for men and women) among the various aspects of the private subsidiary economy is available for the Rostov *oblast'* during 1957–1960. In this period, 75 to 82 percent of the total number of man-hours were spent in animal husbandry, 16–23 percent in crop production, and only 1–3 percent in other activities. The latter include procurement and collection of forest products, fishing, hunting, independent artisan and handicraft work. Cf. Shmelev, p. 131.

26. These figures are for the years 1959 and are calculated from data in *Sel'khoz-1960,* pp. 235–38, 240–43, 348, 350–51, 354–56, 359.

27. Calculated from *Narkhoz-1961,* pp. 300, 319, 321, 376, 391.

28. In making this estimate, it is assumed that the proportion of workers not in state farms and employees in the private subsidiary sector is fairly accurately reflected by the percentage of urban element employed in this sector. The presumption is that the number of members of families of collective- or state-farm workers who live in urban areas is more or less exactly offset by the number of members of families of other workers and employees who live in rural areas and who are engaged in private subsidiary agriculture. The relevant data are not provided by the 1959 census. Even if such a breakdown were available, reservations about the validity of the data would be in order. It may be presumed that many collective farmers, who devote much of their time to their plots, are listed by census takers as working on the collective farm, although they earn only a small number of labor-days. The importance of cultivation of urban or suburban garden plots by families of workers and employees is provided by data on the city of Saratov (1959 population: 581,000): more than 2,000 acres were reported as cultivated by 13,339 families. Cf. S. A. Osipov, "Flowering Gardens," *Soviet Women,* no. 4 (1960): 11. See also data on the share of the private nonagricultural plot in per capita consumption in the nonagricultural sector as a whole in 1956, quoted by Jerzy F. Karcz, "Quantitative Analysis of the Collective Farm Market," *American Economic Review* S4:4, part I (June 1964): 332.

29. M. Weitzman, M. Feshbach, and L. Kulchycka, "Employment in the U.S.S.R.," in U.S. Congress, Joint Economic Committee, *Dimensions of Soviet Economic Power* (Washington, D.C.: Government Printing Office, 1962), p. 662.

30. M. Ia. Sonin, *Aktual'nye problemy ispol'zovaniia rabochei sily v SSSR* (Moscow, 1965), p. 195.

31. The number of underage workers in the private subsidiary sector is small and is consequently ignored in our discussion. It should be remembered that the census would not classify a pupil, working on the family plot during the summer months, as employed in private subsidiary agriculture. This is a major reason why census data are not very helpful in analyzing labor inputs into the subsidiary sector.

32. *Itogi-1959-SSSR,* Tables 30, 33, pp. 96–97, 104–5.

33. Ibid.

34. The exceptions are public health where women make up 85 percent of the workers and employees and 88 percent of the managerial personnel and specialists; and educational and cultural services where the respective percentages are 69 and 66.

35. Iu. V. Arutiunian, *Sovetskoe krest'ianstvo v gody Velikoi Otechestvennoi voiny* (Moscow, 1963), p. 289. The proportion of women chairmen of collective farms and women

directors of state farms has varied considerably among the different republics. It is usually much lower in more backward areas, such as Transcaucasia and Central Asia, than in the R.S.F.S.R. and Belorussia, where at the end of 1944 women made up almost 15 percent of the total.

36. *Izvestiia,* December 26, 1961.

37. The rural population does not, of course, include all those who are employed in agriculture. Nor is that portion of the rural population which is employed engaged exclusively in agricultural pursuits. The basic relationships between urban, rural, and total agricultural employment are shown in Table 12.A2.

38. *Itogi-1959-SSSR,* p. 251.

39. A. N. Gladyshchev, *Izv. Sib. otd. Ak. nauk,* no. 11 (1962): 16–17.

40. Shishkin, p. 146.

41. L. Bibik, *Biull. nauch. inf.,* no. 6 (1961): 50. More than 80 percent of the collective farms are reported to have been electrified at the beginning of 1963. See G. Sarkisian, *Ek. sel.' khoz.,* no. 12 (1964): 15. On many of these farms, however, electricity was available only for lighting.

42. Even in Moscow, only 10 percent of the apartments had hot water in 1956. See Timothy Sosnovy, "The Soviet City," in U.S. Congress, Joint Economic Committee, p. 337.

43. Elena Whiteside, "For Soviet Women: A 13-Hour Day," *New York Times Magazine,* November 17, 1963, p. 28.

44. V. F. Maier and P. N. Krylov, eds., *Planirovanie narodnogo potrebleniia SSSR* (Moscow, 1964), p. 64. The number of places in Soviet nurseries during 1913–1962 will be found in Dodge.

45. The number of children from 3 to 7 years old is based on estimates of the Soviet population by year of age for each year from 1950 to 1981, prepared by the Foreign Demographic Analysis Division of the U.S. Bureau of the Census in June 1962. Statistical data on the number, enrollment, and staff of urban and rural kindergartens during 1913–1962 are given in Dodge.

46. The estimate of the number of urban and rural children of kindergarten age was made by dividing the total for this age group into the proportions of urban and rural population of children in the new-born to 9-year age group given in the 1959 census. Cf. *Itogi-1959-SSSR,* pp. 60–66.

47. *Cultural Progress in the U.S.S.R.* (Moscow, 1958), p. 198.

48. In 1955, a total of 971,000 children were cared for in summer playgrounds. See ibid., p. 199. Of these, 815,000 were in rural areas; 771,000 of the latter were at playgrounds of the collective farms. Of these, 524,000 (68 percent) were 3 to 7 years old. Accordingly, we may assume that some 550,000 of the 815,000 children in rural areas were of kindergarten age. By 1959 the total number of children accommodated had increased by more than 50 percent (or to 1,155,000; cf. *Narkhoz-1959,* pp. 738–39). It is not unreasonable to assume that further expansion has occurred since then, given the expansion of other child-care facilities.

49. The cost of kindergarten care is given in Decree No. 1314 of the Ministry of Higher Education of the U.S.S.R., dated September 10, 1948, as quoted in *Vysshaia shkola: Osnovnye postanovleniia, prikazy i instruktsii* (Moscow, 1957), p. 487.

50. *Kul't. stroi.-1956,* pp. 176–77.

51. Ibid.

52. See Nicholas DeWitt, *Education and Professional Employment in the U.S.S.R.* (Washington, D. C.: National Science Foundation, 1961), pp. 157–61.

53. Ibid., p. 179. DeWitt estimates that total enrollment in agricultural technicums in 1959 was 300,000.

54. *Itogi-1959-SSSR,* p. 81.

13 / Soviet Rural Women: Employment and Family Life

SUSAN BRIDGER

In this 1983 article, Susan Bridger, a researcher at the University of Bradford in England and author of Women in the Soviet Countryside *(Cambridge, 1987), describes the continuing sexual inequality of rural women in the family and at work. The patterns of occupational segregation by gender, first noted by Manning for the 1930s and then discussed in detail by Dodge and Feshbach for the immediate post-Stalin years, continued in full force during the Brezhnev period (1964–1982). Rural women remained the central figures in unskilled agricultural labor. In addition, rural women, even more than their relatively better-off urban counterparts, suffered from the rigors of the "double shift"—that is, the second shift of household labor following work outside the home. Traditional sex-role stereotyping, reinforced by a central government anxious to halt the fall in birth rates and by the state-controlled press, served to reinforce rural women's heavy burden of labor. Bridger suggests, however, that rural women did not suffer in silence. Instead, they expressed their dissatisfaction over unsatisfactory work and domestic conditions by migration in record numbers to the cities, low productivity, high turnover, and an increasing rate of divorce. This chapter again illustrates the minimal impact that Soviet modernization had on the labor of rural women and further concludes that many contemporary rural women are unwilling to tolerate existing conditions.*

Since 1917 the Soviet countryside has been seen by successive generations of Soviet policy-makers as a problem area. From the first days of the revolution the Bolsheviks were obliged to come to terms with the essential paradox of their position: having seized power with the support of the relatively tiny urban working class, they were obliged to consolidate their gains in a country where four people in every five lived on the land.[1] Armed with an ideology which made the proletariat the focus of social progress and faced with international hostility, the Soviet government was from the first committed to urban development and industrial growth. Alternate attempts at appeasement and coercion of the peasantry throughout the 1920s to ensure a supply of grain for the cities led ultimately to a massive use of force in 1930 when the campaign for rapid collectivisation of agriculture was begun. Since the 1930s, government attitudes towards the rural population have been fundamentally

271

exploitative: its role has been to feed the cities and to provide a pool of surplus labour to facilitate industrial development. The women of the countryside have invariably been seen as the most backward and conservative sector of society with the lowest levels of education and training and the highest resistance to the aims and appeals of the Communist Party. Yet, as the problems of agriculture continue to provide a major headache for Soviet planners, it has become clear that rural women today are no longer a dormant and uncomplaining mass. Soviet observers of rural life are becoming increasingly aware that the fulfilment of women's demands is a crucial element in the success or failure of agriculture in many regions of the USSR.

Until as late as 1960 the majority of the Soviet population lived in the rural areas. Today the rural share of the population has fallen to 37 percent, a considerably larger proportion than in other developed industrial countries.[2] Yet despite the relatively large numbers of people who live on the land, Soviet agriculture is in many areas faced with an acute shortage of skilled labour. Where industrial development has been most intense, in European areas of the USSR and in Siberia, the demands of the factories for labour and the attractions of city life have drawn millions of young people away from their native villages during the past two decades. Since 1970 the rural population of the Non Black Earth Zone, the northern half of the European USSR and a major area of mixed farming, has fallen by more than a fifth, most of the migrants to the cities being young people. As this trend is expected to continue, farming in this region is faced with the problem of an ageing and low-skilled workforce.[3] Although the government has invested heavily in agriculture since the mid-1950s, and levels of mechanisation have increased dramatically, productivity has remained low. Without a skilled and stable workforce, economists warn, capital investment will remain ineffective.

In recent years the state has increasingly come to look to women to help solve its economic problems. As the birthrate has fallen, the need for labour has prompted the state to urge both urban and rural women to have larger families. At the same time the immediate demands of the economy have led to appeals to rural women to operate agricultural machinery and staff livestock farms. Many of the demands of national government have met with local resistance, either from women themselves, or from men who are unwilling to admit women to traditionally male occupations. As young women increasingly reject the few occupations which are effectively open to them in the countryside in favour of more satisfying work and better conditions in the towns, economic planners and farm managers are being obliged to take notice of women's response in their efforts to solve agriculture's problems.

Female Employment in Rural Areas

Machine Operators

A chronic shortage of skilled workers in arable farming has, since 1969, prompted the Soviet government to introduce a series of measures to encourage women to train and work as agricultural machine operators. In the 1930s a number of patriotic appeals led to the training of thousands of peasant women to drive tractors, at that time a symbol of technological progress on the new collective farms. The few women who in this way became heroines of the early five-year plans were joined by an army of former trainees when war broke out in 1941. As skilled men left the farms for the front, women came to dominate tractor and combine driving in the USSR.[4] Yet immediately after the war the proportion of women in these jobs fell dramatically: men were returning from the war and workers were urgently needed in the traditional female sphere of dairying. Most important of all, women themselves were tired of work which, under the agricultural organisation of the day, obliged them to accept difficult living and working conditions and took them away from their homes and children for prolonged periods. In the postwar years this work, which was once a symbol of emancipated womanhood, has become an almost exclusively male domain. By 1970 the number of women employed as machine operators had dwindled to such a low level that it was no longer recorded in the Soviet census. At the same time, the high turnover of men in these jobs and the migration of many to the cities caused sufficient concern for the government to attempt a new campaign of female recruitment.

New legislation has provided for the development of vocational training for women to become machine operators. Once at work, women in these jobs receive additional holidays and retirement at 50 after 15 years' service. Farm managements are obliged by law to provide women with the newest machines and full technical support, and to set work quotas for women 10 percent lower than for men. At the same time the press has tried to attract women into this work by focusing attention on those few who have become highly successful machine operators. Yet after 13 years the results of the campaign have been meagre: less than 1 percent of agricultural machine operators are women.[5]

The reasons for this lack of success are debated regularly in the national press. It has become clear that many aspects of the work which women dislike are unattractive to men also; design faults in tractors and combines lead to excessive amounts of time spent on repairs, whilst the vibration, fumes and dust experienced by drivers are all much higher than approved safety levels.[6] Yet the extremely long hours worked by most machine operators in distant fields during peak periods are especially difficult for women who bear prime responsibility for childcare and domestic tasks. These factors are, in themselves, enough to dissuade most women from seeking training, yet they are reinforced by the common practice in rural schools of providing technical education for boys only and by the reactions of parents, husbands and teachers who regard the work as unsuitable for women.

Yet for many women who are undeterred by traditional notions of 'women's work', and who receive training as machine operators, the battles are only just beginning. The principal difficulties encountered by women who attempt to take up the work are created by the attitudes of male managers and workmates. 'It's extremely important', remarked one leading woman tractor driver, 'how women are received by men who see the machine operator's profession as practically their monopoly. It has to be said that the reception can be none too friendly.'[7] Farm managers who are unwilling to employ women in this work but are reluctant to be seen as openly obstructive often resort to the ploy of providing women with an ancient wreck in the hope that they will give up the work in despair. As complaints to the press make plain, this stratagem is often successful. 'It's misery, not work!

All I did were endless repairs', is a typical grievance.[8] Managements regularly flout the law by assigning new machines to men, the usual excuse being, 'It's a heavy tractor; you won't be able to work on it. You'll just spoil it.'[9] Likewise, the technical back-up for women stipulated in the new laws often fails to materialise, sometimes deliberately: 'You go to the mechanic and he curses you. He hasn't got time to mess about with your tractor: in working hours he either reads a book or mends his own motorbike.'[10] In the worst examples of discrimination, farm managers simply refuse to employ women in the job for which they have trained. A not untypical story which found its way into the press involved a girl who came top of her class in the final qualifying exams for tractor drivers. She was promised a new tractor but later told there were none available, though all the boys who studied with her were assigned machines at once. She was finally employed washing out milk churns and became the object of ridicule of her former classmates who would greet her with, 'It's your own fault. You should have been born a boy and you'd have been driving a tractor long ago.'[11]

The intervention of the press and Communist Party occasionally rights the wrongs suffered by aspiring women tractor drivers. Yet it is clear that in far more cases women simply give up the unequal struggle and find other work in the village or seek skilled work in the towns. The only areas of the country in which the campaign has been a success are those in which local party secretaries have taken government measures seriously and have adhered to the letter of the law. In a tiny minority of cases local officials have looked beyond the legislation and considered the needs of women in agricultural employment. In the most outstanding example, Millerovo district in the Rostov Region, over a quarter of tractor brigades are staffed solely by women. All the women in these brigades enjoy full technical support, priority access to childcare facilities and mobile shops with goods in high demand, the use of field stations with showers and rest rooms and the provision of transport to and from work. Most important of all, the large numbers involved make possible the establishment of a two-shift system for women which cuts working hours and permits regular days off.[12]

Without efforts of this type, which attempt a genuine response to the needs of women in the countryside, there is little likelihood that sufficient numbers of women will ever be found to solve staff shortages in this field. Women are clearly no longer prepared to be self-sacrificing in response to patriotic appeals. In the absence of a national emergency they expect more sensitivity to their needs and attention to their demands if they are to fulfil the role the government has in mind.

Dairying

Unlike tractor driving, dairying has always been regarded as an appropriate occupation for women. In peasant households before collectivisation, the care of dairy cows was considered to be women's work and, since 1930, women have dominated dairy farming on both collective and state farms so totally that in most regions of the USSR over 96 percent of staff involved in milking are women.[13] Yet dairying is far from being an easy option in the conditions of the Soviet countryside. Cows in the USSR have traditionally been milked three times a day, making unsocial hours a permanent feature of the dairy woman's working week. A typical day in dairying stretches from four or five in the morning until six or seven in the evening, whilst on a significant proportion of farms women are on call from the first milking session at 3 A.M. to the end of the third milking session at ten or eleven at night. Under this single-shift system women are free to return home between milking times in both morning and afternoon, yet the effect of such a work schedule, as one writer has put it, is that 'women do not in fact feel free from their work at any time of the day or night'.[14]

Not only are the hours worked in dairying extremely awkward but, for many women, holidays are rare. On collective farms dairy women receive an average of no more than one day off per week throughout the year, giving them less free time than any other group of workers in industry or agriculture. Add to this the fact that on a high proportion of farms feeding and mucking out are still done by hand and that machinery in dairy units often breaks down and is left unrepaired, and a picture emerges of a job which makes extremely high demands of women's time and energy.[15] The rewards for all this effort are high by the standards of agricultural wages, with women often receiving higher basic pay than agricultural machine operators. As the work not only pays well but, unlike work in arable farming, provides a constant income throughout the year, dairying attracts women who are single parents or married with large families.[16] Women with heavy family responsibilities are clearly prepared to endure the rigours of the job for the sake of the financial security that it brings.

In recent years investment in dairy farming has greatly improved levels of mechanisation. Over 40 percent of dairy farms are now fully mechanised which has greatly reduced the physical strain of the work and has diminished the risk of premature arthritis in the hands, the major occupational health hazard of milking staff.[17] Yet mechanisation alone has proved insufficient to attract young women into dairying and many farms have suffered from labour shortages over the past decade. The problem of staffing has prompted farm managements to take a fresh look at traditional work schedules and the resulting innovations have now been adopted as recommended practice by the USSR Ministry of Agriculture. The favoured system of the ministry, already in use on the more progressive farms in the USSR, involves milking twice a day rather than three times and splitting the long working period into two shifts. Each woman works either the morning or evening shift, alternating each week, and, as extra staff can be attracted by the shorter hours, deputising dairy women ensure that everyone works a five-day week. A survey of farms using the two-shift system found that, since its introduction, the number of women under 30 employed on their dairy units had doubled.[18] The publicity which this system has received in the national press has provoked increasing complaints from women who feel that they have put up with arduous working conditions for too long, and has led many to voice demands for regular days off. For many, however, the most common response to poor conditions is to look for work elsewhere. Farm managers are increasingly coming to realise that without reasonable hours of work and adequate levels of mechanisation they are faced with the constant problem of high staff turnover and low productivity.

In some regions, however, staff shortages have become so severe that the problem cannot easily be solved by a rearrangement of work schedules. In Pskov Province, for example, in the north-west of the European USSR, dairy units are so short of labour that it is literally impossible to introduce a two-shift system, and without such a system young women refuse to work on the farms.[19] Thus a vicious circle is created in which the old-style dairy farms become dominated by elderly women and the problem becomes ever more acute. In recent years the Komsomol has attempted to alleviate situations of this type by directing nearly 400,000 of its members into dairying and by urging whole classes of school-leavers to remain on the farms for at least a year before going on to further education or work elsewhere.[20] It remains to be seen, however, whether campaigns of this type will have any long-term effect on staff turnover or working conditions.

In recent years it has become evident that the mechanisation of dairying does not always provide better jobs for women but may provide increased opportunities for men. There is a clear tendency amongst farm managers to employ men in the most highly mechanised units both in dairying and in other areas of animal husbandry. In many cases, women are employed exclusively in machine-milking, whilst back-up staff serving dairy units are men with technical skills. Very few women are trained in technical colleges as machine operators for livestock farms and cases have been reported where farms have been fully mechanised but no attempt has been made to retrain experienced women livestock workers as technicians or operators. It is significant that, as young women are refusing to work on old-fashioned dairy farms, young men from the new, highly mechanised units are increasingly to be found amongst the prizewinners in national competitions for milking machine operators. With the advent of machinery, men clearly feel that this work is no longer beneath their dignity; as two recent prizewinners remarked, 'It's a machine operator's profession now.'[21]

Agricultural Labourers

For women who are not prepared to tolerate prevailing working conditions in livestock units and are unwilling to make the attempt to become machine operators, opportunities for congenial skilled work in the villages are very few indeed. The largest group of women employed in the countryside are agricultural labourers whose work in arable farming is seasonal, low-skilled and often backbreaking. More than two-thirds of all female agricultural workers are employed in this manner, the content of their work changing with the demands of the farming year.[22] As most of the work involved in tillage and harvesting has now been mechanised, women labourers are involved principally in work which is seen as subordinate to the main agricultural campaigns: sorting seed in winter, weeding root crops in spring, stacking hay in summer, lifting potatoes and beet in the autumn. Female manual labour is also extensively employed in the cultivation of cotton, rice and fruits of all kinds. In practice, the sharply seasonal pattern of arable farming over much of the USSR means that, whilst machine operators can be transferred to a wide variety of driving jobs during the winter, manual workers are often temporarily unemployed, or are recruited on a casual basis for work during the winter months.

As manual agricultural labour is therefore both seasonal and unskilled, the income which these women receive is considerably less than they could earn in dairying. The work is typically the province of middle-aged and elderly married women who are poorly educated and lack any sort of professional training. Women with young children are also often attracted to the work precisely because of the seasonal idleness and less stringent work schedule. Though these women frequently express dissatisfaction with the nature of the work itself, it often appears to be the only way of earning money where childcare facilities are inadequate or nonexistent.[23] Manual fieldwork is by nature arduous and repetitive, demanding constant exertion. A women sugarbeet grower gives an example of what is involved in thinning out the beet seedlings after sowing:

> The main thing is not to make a mistake when, straining your eyes and summoning all your patience, you try to leave the strongest seedlings in the rows, not to litter them with sickly shoots. Up to thirty sprout in every metre but you only keep six or seven. You have to leave enough room for the root to grow between each seedling that you keep. Altogether up to 400,000 seedlings are pulled up from each hectare. And you have to bend over every one of them, have a long look at some of them; you don't choose immediately as if one were as good as another. And from the very first the weeds have to be pulled up. Your back aches and your feet get heavy. That's what it's like, farming the crop.[24]

Despite high levels of mechanisation in certain processes, sugarbeet still demands a great deal of manual labour. The manner in which the production of this crop has changed as mechanisation has increased provides probably the most graphic illustration of the rigid division of labour between the sexes in agriculture. As the operation of agricultural machinery is so thoroughly dominated by men, the leading teams of workers in sugarbeet production are now male or led by men. There have been few attempts to train women, who have been long involved in beet production, to drive the new machinery. Instead, an extraordinary split has developed in which, as one journalist put it, 'the men have the machines, the women have years of experience, natural patience and the knack of dealing with this capricious crop'.[25]

There is evidence that women feel upset at this turn of events, and particularly at the way in which their work has been devalued with the coming of machines. There have been complaints that, whilst the men get honours and rewards the women are still toiling unnoticed as their grandmothers did. Certainly, it is a state of affairs which holds little appeal for young women, as one team leader in the Ukraine remarked,

> Those of us who are used to manual work are getting older. When we finish work who will grow the beet? Young girls today have secondary education so of course it's hard on them to become labourers. Unskilled work scares them off. There's no way out of this. We need 100 per cent mechanisation in beet production. There's no question about it. But until the technology is developed it's essential to raise the status of manual work in operations which decide the fate of the harvest.[26]

To ease the problem several areas have experimented with various types of bonus system for manual workers which have proved popular with the women involved. Some farm managements have tried to introduce two-shift working at peak periods to cut working hours, or to use greater quantities of herbicides to avoid much of the heavy work involved in weeding fields sown with vegetables.[27] Alongside these initiatives there have been occasional attempts in the press to paint glowing portraits of leading women farm labourers. Yet the job performed by the largest single group of women in the Soviet countryside remains in the eyes of the world at large, and of the women themselves, an extremely unglamorous profession.

Between 1959 and 1970 the number of women employed in rural areas fell by a sixth to just under 22 million. In the same period, patterns of rural employment altered considerably as the industrial and service sectors of the rural economy expanded. In 1959 more than three-quarters of working women in the countryside were employed directly in agriculture. By 1970 one woman in three was working in the service sector, rural industry or education and welfare.[28]

Industry and the Service Sector

The expansion of the service sector and rural industry has begun to provide an alternative for women to manual labour in agriculture. Though rural industry in particular still employs very few women in Central Asia and the Caucasus, in the more developed European areas of the country this aspect of the rural economy is becoming increasingly important. In the most highly developed regions of the Baltic republics, one in five rural women is now employed in industry and construction, transport or communications.[29] The industries in which women are employed are, in the main, connected with local agricultural production, for example, food processing, the production of animal feed or textiles. Additionally, women are employed in factory farming units which may be independent of state or collective farms and produce primarily eggs, chicken and pork. A survey of rural industry in Belorussia in the early 1970s found that the majority of its employees were men. The women employed in factories were generally less well-educated than the men and concentrated in the least skilled work. Young people did, however, make up a far higher proportion of the workforce in industry than on the farms; one in five as against one in ten; in the youngest age-groups the women had higher levels of education than their male peers.[30] For young women who have no wish to leave the countryside, the development of industry offers some the chance of skilled work, though conditions in rural factories have been found to fall short of approved standards of health and safety. The rigid division of labour characteristic of agriculture is, however, perpetuated in factory farming, where women look after the animals and men operate the machines. Although little information is available about this aspect of women's employment, limited evidence suggests both that the hours are reasonable and that the work is particularly well paid by comparison with equivalent work on the farms.[31]

The service sector, though expanding, cannot as yet provide sufficient job opportunities for girls leaving school who would like to take up skilled work in their native village. The provision of services is, however, seen as a fundamentally female sphere of work with employees from health workers to cooks seeing themselves as members of the 'caring professions'. Unskilled women workers in the service sector appear to have on average higher levels of education than unskilled workers in agriculture. It would appear that women are content to undertake jobs which make few demands of their abilities in exchange for better working conditions than can be found in farming.[32]

Specialists and Managers

At specialist level in health and education, women predominate in both town and country. In the countryside, teaching is slightly less feminised than in the towns but, even so, more than three-quarters of rural teachers are women. Despite their numerical predominance, women are disproportionately concentrated in class teaching, whilst the majority of head teachers are men. Though rural teachers are overall less highly trained than their urban counterparts, they nevertheless represent the largest group of workers in the countryside with higher or specialised secondary education.[33] Though Soviet law provides for a range of benefits to rural teachers in order to attract a stable workforce into education in the countryside, it is clear that many women experience problems in obtaining housing and find the usually unavoidable necessity of keeping an allotment difficult to combine with the demands of their work in the schools and in the cultural life of the village. As a result, teachers who remain in the countryside are usually of rural origin. Both teaching and medicine are extremely popular choices of profession with rural girls, yet the lower standards of rural education have meant that school-leavers often experience great difficulty in gaining a place in a medical or pedagogical institute. As a result, rural schools suffer from a high turnover of young staff from urban backgrounds who work their compulsory three-year period in the countryside and then return to the town at the first opportunity.[34]

Whilst specialists in health and education are predominantly female, men form the majority of agricultural specialists in the USSR. Women make up approximately two-fifths of agronomists and veterinary surgeons or technicians, their proportion having risen slowly over the last ten years. Amongst other specialists employed by the farms, women form a majority of accountants and economists. It is significant that the rural bias against women working with machines extends to specialist level; just over 5 percent of engineers and technicians on the farms are women, despite the fact that women make up almost half the engineers employed across the country as a whole.[35]

Farm managers are increasingly recruited from the ranks of agricultural specialists, yet very few of them, less than 1 in 50, are women. Women remain a minority at the lower level of brigade leader or head of a livestock unit. Although women form the overwhelming majority of livestock workers, no more than 40 percent of management posts in this area are held by women.[36] Surveys have indicated that the dearth of women in management persists despite the fact that women are often more highly trained than men. This has been found to stem on the one hand from a reluctance to promote women to posts of responsibility due to an underestimation of their abilities and, on the other hand, from a tendency amongst women themselves to refuse these jobs due to family responsibilities. Women are often unwilling to take on work which is very demanding and time-consuming when they are at the same time expected to cope almost single-handed with the demands of their families. Commenting on this situation recently, a district party secretary in the Ukraine remarked:

> It is evident that a woman on whose shoulders lies the main burden of concern for the running of the home and the children's upbringing at times finds herself faced with an unhappy dilemma: work or home? And so we lose high-class specialists and good, competent managers.[37]

Nikita Khrushchev, at a farm conference in Kiev in 1961, commented on the workforce in agriculture that, 'It turns out that it is the men who do the administrating and the women who do the work.'[38] Twenty years on, Khrushchev's crude but telling observation is echoed in the interview with the Ukrainian district party secretary, 'The strong and healthy man is to be found sitting behind an office desk, whilst out in the fields where there is mud, dust and heavy physical work, there is the woman.'[39]

Although the participation of women in the rural workforce is slowly changing, the overwhelming majority remain firmly at the bottom of the chain of command, their chances of promotion strictly limited by the burdens of the 'double shift' and discriminatory attitudes in the workplace. The findings of rural sociologists and complaints to the press make it clear that many women feel their powerlessness acutely. Complaints by women to party officials are principally about rudeness, indifference and high-handed attitudes towards them on the part of their male superiors. The press provides numerous examples of women who are upset at finding themselves not only expected to work in deplorable conditions but also the target of obscenities and condescension.[40] Employment in the countryside remains firmly divided by sex both in areas of work and on the ladder of promotion, and women are clearly resentful of those who add insult to injury by taking advantage of this state of affairs.

The Changing Rural Family

In recent years, concern over labour shortages in both urban and rural areas has increased as the birthrate has fallen. In the past, increased industrial output in the Soviet Union has been largely dependent on an expanding labour force; labour productivity has remained considerably lower than in other developed countries. In recent years government attention has turned to the family to secure the workforce of the future. The birthrate in rural areas of the Soviet Union has always been higher than in the towns, yet the sharp decline in births which took place in the towns during the 1960s was experienced in the villages also. Outside the predominantly Moslem areas of Central Asia and the Caucasus, the small family characterised town and country alike: more than three-quarters of rural families in the Russian Republic now have no more than two children. Nevertheless, the birthrate amongst rural women is today higher in all age-groups than it is in the towns, and this is especially marked amongst older women; births to women over 30 in the countryside are more than double the number in the towns.[41] The higher rural birthrate is not merely a continuation of traditional practices but reflects living and working conditions in the countryside. The seasonal nature of much agricultural work has in effect always served as a form of part-time employment for women with young children, housing is considerably less cramped than in the cities whilst relatives and neighbours are more readily available to assist with child-minding. In addition, the countryside provides a less hazardous environment for children and one in which they are encouraged to participate in their parents' concerns from an early age by helping on the family's allotment. Yet the development of the small family in the last 20 years provides an indicator of changing attitudes towards marriage and family life in the countryside. For centuries peasant tradition placed an enormous burden on women in the home and on the family's land, at the same time as it continually reinforced their subordination to men at every level of society. The poverty of the Russian peasantry made marriage a matter of economic calculation: romantic attachments were a luxury few could afford. 'Let a wife be like a cow so long as she is strong', ran the proverb which succinctly summarised this state of affairs.[42] Rural attitudes towards marriage slowly began to change between the wars under the impact of social upheaval caused by the revolution, changing legislation and the propaganda of the Communist Party's Women's Department. Yet the calamitous losses of the Second World War left a generation of rural women with little hope of marriage and a tendency to accept gratefully any husband who came their way. The following account from a woman who married in the early 1950s provides a graphic example of the prevailing attitudes of the post-war years:

> He came from a neighbouring village for another girl but she refused to marry him. His friend suggested me. They called me out of the club into the street. It was a dark night. They made the proposal and I, just imagine, knowing about his character and good qualities only from what I'd heard, accepted at once.[43]

Over the past two decades, the spread of secondary education and increasing geographical mobility have led to a considerable modification in rural attitudes towards the family. A more favourable demographic balance, together with the impact of the mass media, have had a profound effect on women's views of marriage. Young women especially have come to see emotional fulfilment as a primary function of family life. Although the choice of a marriage partner remains more restricted in the countryside than in the towns, women appear to have abandoned the prosaic attitudes of the past in favour of a search for personal happiness.

Romance

Letters to the press indicate that rural women are increasingly preoccupied with romance, 'Love with a capital L', as one writer recently put it: 'What if it's my destiny to marry him and because of my parents I've let it pass me by?' 'I know that love comes once in a lifetime and I have fallen in love for good. But the one I love has married someone else. What am I to do now?'[44] These anguished questions in letters from teenage girls are not unusual in portraying the act of falling in love as a dramatic and unrepeatable event. Older married women recounting their experiences and expressing their opinions on personal relationships characteristically place a high value on romantic love as an uplifting and enriching experience: 'Not everyone experiences a great love, it's a gift.' 'I can't forget that time when I felt as if I had wings', are typical of the sentiments expressed by rural women in letters to the magazine *Krest'yanka* ('The Peasant Women').[45] The content of many of these letters makes it clear that this yearning for love is often likened to a fleeting romance in later life or associated with an unhappy personal experience. Many women letter-writers explain that they did not marry for love in the strict sense but for a whole range of reasons, from the need for companionship or to numb disappointment to a sense of pity or, in some cases, revenge. Other correspondents starkly express the feeling that love is something which they have missed in life and which they would dearly like to experience:

> I envy those letter writers; they have all loved someone. It doesn't matter if it was unrequited or if they were married, it doesn't matter what their relationship was with the one they loved. The main thing is that they know what it is to love. But I feel hurt; am I any worse than other people, or am I just unfeeling?[46]

Love is seen by many older correspondents as unobtainable and beyond one's normal expectations of married life. As such it is to be treasured and worth suffering for: 'My dear', wrote the elderly aunt of a woman involved in an extra-marital affair, 'if you feel a love like that and he returns it, cherish it, don't insult it, don't break down. Hold your head high and go on through everything, only don't re-nounce love.'[47] This unexpected reaction is indicative of how far women have travelled from the pragmatic and utilitarian attitudes they were constrained to adopt in the past.

Domestic Labour and Childcare

The appearance of romance as an element in rural life has undoubtedly led women in the countryside to entertain far higher expectations of marriage than did their mothers or grandmothers. Yet although the old-established male despotism in the family has all but disappeared from the countryside, marital relationships remain far from egalitarian. As in the towns it is usual in the countryside for men to abnegate all responsibility in domestic labour and childcare, leaving their wives to face the double shift of full-time employment plus almost sole responsibility for the home. In rural conditions, domestic labour is particularly arduous and time-consuming. Though electricity is supplied to nine out of every ten rural homes, and the majority now receive gas, around two-thirds of the housing stock of collective and state farms and almost all housing privately built by rural inhabitants was, in the mid-1970s, without running water, mains sanitation or central heating. In regions where villages are scattered over vast areas or where capital investment has tradi-tionally been very low, these amenities become rarer still.[48] The heavy work in-volved in carrying fuel and water is unavoidable in many Soviet villages today. A survey of the Novgorod Region in north-west Russia found that the average family spent between 12 and 14 hours each week fetching water and that almost all the family's free time for two months was absorbed by preparing firewood in time for the winter.[49]

Where homes are equipped with modern amenities, rural dwellers are still handicapped by comparison with their urban counterparts through the lack of shops and consumer services. Complaints to the press by women on the subject paint a picture of sparsely filled shops with erratic opening hours, interminable delays over repairs, and shoddy workmanship on finished goods. As a result, women are obliged to make regular trips to town to obtain essential items for the home. Both men and women in the countryside work far longer hours in the domestic economy than do city-dwellers and this is due chiefly to the tending of private allotments and the keeping of livestock. In rural conditions this small-scale private agriculture remains essential for the provision of basic vegetables, meat and dairy products; estimates suggest that around half the average rural family's food is produced on these allotments.[50] The nature of domestic labour in the villages is therefore far broader than in the cities and involves men in a good deal of work on the allotments in particular. It must be said, however, that jobs which form the major components of housework in the cities—washing, shopping, cooking, childcare, cleaning—are regarded as women's work in the villages. Time-budget surveys provide a rough guide to the amount and type of domestic labour performed by men and women in rural areas. On an average working day, men spend around half an hour on domestic tasks whilst women spend between three and five hours, mostly on cooking and clearing up. The greatest amounts of time are spent by older women and by those who have least access to shopping facilities, especially where all bread has to be home-baked.[51] In addition to these traditionally 'female' tasks within the home, women supply most of the labour on the private allotments. Men's contribution is often restricted to the repair or construction of shelters for livestock and preparing the soil for the vegetables. Women generally have the major responsibility for the care of livestock and for the day-to-day upkeep of the vegetable garden. A recent survey in Western Siberia found that in areas where well-stocked shops were rare, women put in nearly 23 hours a week on their allotments, compared with a maximum of 12 hours a week worked by the men.[52] A large-scale survey in the Russian Republic found that rural women had only eleven hours free time each week, less than half that of women in the towns.[53]

In village and town alike, the overwhelming responsibility for childcare falls to women. Though places in rural creches and nursery schools have more than doubled since the mid-1960s they in no way meet the very high demand of rural women. Over the country as a whole, one in four rural children of nursery age has a place in some form of pre-school institution, though many of these are seasonal facilities intended to free women for work in the peak agricultural season.[54] Letters to the press indicate the growing demand for nursery facilities by women who cannot find relatives to take care of their children whilst they are at work, and are no longer content to sit at home or to leave their children unattended during the day. Whether children have nursery places or not, their care in the evenings and on days off rests primarily with women. Sociologists have in recent years noted with concern that a large proportion of rural women experience difficulty in bringing up their children, and that this is often a direct result of the lack of help or understanding received from their husbands. Many women complain that their husbands show no interest in childcare; a recent survey found that in 40 percent of families the wife had sole responsibility for the children's upbringing.[55] Though sociologists are beginning to stress the need for greater participation by fathers, there is little evidence of action being taken. The head teacher of a nursery school in the north of the European USSR described her approach to the subject:

> Not long ago we held a fathers' evening. . . . I suggested that before beginning the discussion we should listen to the children; what do they think of you, how do they see you? And I switched on the tape recorder. . . . Everyone grew quiet and pricked up their ears. 'My daddy never plays with me or takes me for walks' came a voice from the tape. 'When daddy's drunk I'm frightened of him.' 'On his day off daddy takes me for walks; he tells me all sorts about the trees, about the street, about birds.' 'My daddy gets tired after dinner, lies on the couch and watches television, but mummy washes up and does the washing. Mummy says, "clear the table", but he replies, "clear it yourself." ' That night quite a few left the nursery school shamefaced. We're not in the town here, everyone knows everyone else and could easily recognise the children by their voices. Some of them were indignant— what a thing to do, playing a tape! It's outrageous!—But I thought, if it's hit home then it's been some use.[56]

Sadly, initiatives such as this remain no more than isolated incidents, and it is still a rare household in which the parents share childcare and domestic chores. As one rural sociologist has observed, 'There still remains a considerable gulf between the proclamation of political equality and legal regulation of equal rights and actual equality in practice between men and women in family and personal relationships.'[57]

The Soviet Media and the Rural Family

The gross inequalities within the family which are characterised by the present distribution of domestic labour cannot, however, simply be dismissed as 'survivals' of the old peasant mentality which will disappear in time. Although rural conservatism certainly has a role to play in dissuading young couples from attempting an egalitarian approach to housework,[58] this cannot explain the universality of female oppression within the home. Leonid Brezhnev, for example, was himself on record as noting that 'We are still far from having done everything possible to ease the double burden which [women] bear at home and at work.'[59] Yet the response to the problem by politicians and sociologists alike is to speak in terms of improved consumer services, communal facilities and childcare institutions. Despite the existence of a whole body of information on male inactivity in the home and the knowledge that improved services cost money and are most unlikely to materialise in the near future, the press remains extremely unwilling to attack sexist attitudes in anything other than the most perfunctory manner. It is significant that the most trenchant comments on the subject by sociologists who are concerned either with the family or with women's role in the workforce appear in dissertations which are unavailable to the general public. In the popular press the advocacy of male participation in domestic labour is, with rare exceptions, confined to a cursory, 'my husband helps me with everything', in interviews with leading women workers.[60]

If the media are reticent on the subject of the husband's role in the home they are, however, far from reserved on the question of the ideal wife and mother. In line with government priorities the press emphasises motherhood as a woman's most important function and devotes a good deal of attention to the encouragement of large families. Throughout the 1970s articles with titles such as 'The Village of Heroines' and 'The Greatest Happiness' have portrayed women who have received the title of 'Heroine Mother'—for giving birth to more than ten children—as models for emulation by their rural readership.[61] Yet no doubt conscious that the lifestyles of Heroine Mothers are so far removed from those of most women as to be almost meaningless, and in line with official promotion of the three-child family, the press has recently adopted a more subtle approach. The image of motherhood as the highest expression of femininity is conveyed to rural women through interviews with leading film and stage actresses. In a typical example, Ada Rogovtseva, People's Artist of the USSR, in response to the question, 'what does being modern mean to you?', replies:

> Being first and foremost an ordinary mum! Being a good wife, a loving daughter. . . . Our emancipation never liberated us from this great female duty and never took away these great joys. In my opinion, the fear of having children and the neglect of family responsibilities are signs of social laziness.[62]

The growing emphasis on femininity, as it is defined by the state's propagandists, whilst cushioning the government's pro-natalist stance, makes extraordinarily complex demands of women who are at the same time expected to be exemplary members of the workforce.

In interview after interview with women who have highly successful careers it is made plain to the reader that, for a woman, achievements at work are not enough. 'A woman remains a woman,' as one female journalist put it, 'and her great strength is probably that, whilst on par with men at work, she reserves for herself that area of women's affairs which make her the custodian of the family hearth.' The subjects of these interviews themselves echo the theme: 'Happiness in a home depends on the woman', declares a woman machine operator and we are told that her husband and sons are better workers than those who do not have such a loving and caring woman to look after them.[63] This emphasis on the woman as homemaker is at its most explicit in occasional articles offering advice to young couples on avoiding marital discord. One such piece in a magazine aimed at rural readership warns wives not to be jealous or possessive and, above all, not to nag: 'Men really value women's indulgence . . . their talent for forgiveness'. The writer urges the young wife to take an interest in her husband's work—'Ask him about the new tractors or how the meeting of the collective farm management committee went'—and never to neglect her appearance or forget a man's love for his stomach; 'There is of course no need to make a cult of cooking, but to say you hate it is unnatural.' Husbands meanwhile are informed that, although they are the head of the family, they should take care to include their wives in decision-making. They are advised of the importance of paying their wives compliments, buying them presents and expressing gratitude for their help: 'When she gives you a clean shirt say "Thank you, Lenochka". When she notices an article in a magazine to do with your work say "Clever girl, Tamara, thank you!" '[64] Such a prescription for marital bliss—pretending that women have no concerns outside the home and relying so heavily on male condescension and female deference—cannot but reinforce the traditional village view of 'a women's place'. In the absence of an autonomous women's movement, there is no one to point out how demeaning and patronising to women such articles can be. Nor is there anyone to warn how the new emphasis on femininity is likely to increase the already prodigious levels of male egocentricity.

Surveys of rural attitudes make it clear that women, especially those who are young and fairly well educated, are increasingly unwilling to tolerate their husbands' lack of consideration, rudeness, heavy drinking and indifference towards the care of their children. Only a tiny minority of rural women now believe that housework and childcare is the woman's sole responsibility, yet surveys indicate that the overwhelming majority of men help their wives either irregularly or not at all.[65] Women's resentment at what they clearly see as parasitic behaviour by many men occasionally appears in letters to the press. A typical outburst runs:

> Nowadays all the work and all the worry about the family lie in the main on women. Men have no sense of responsibility either towards their family, or towards their children or towards their work. And so they start to 'play around', first they like one woman, then another. . . .[66]

The logical outcome of an ideology which makes women the source of harmony in the home is to place the burden of guilt on women's shoulders should discord arise. Women are warned to take care when voicing their grievances:

> The demands of modern young women are as a rule justified, but the manner in which they are expressed is not always appropriate. Many wives do not understand that they should spare their husbands' self-esteem, that they should not be too categorical or express their demands abruptly. Otherwise a husband may develop an inferiority or guilt complex towards his family and the whole thing may boil over from time to time in drunkenness and rows.[67]

In a similar vein, women are deemed to hold the key to men's attitudes towards their children. A letter from a young woman, Nadya, written to *Krest'yanka* magazine to express her feelings after she and her young baby have been deserted by her husband, receives the following commentary:

> A man who has a child is still not a father. To become one he must take upon himself a father's functions. And in this a great deal depends upon the woman. . . . Nadya didn't succeed in teaching her husband to be a father.[68]

Thus women are at fault for being too insistent or not insistent enough; they have, it seems, no one but themselves to blame if they fail to walk the tightrope between their own self-respect and the demands of the male ego. In this mass of exhortations to women men are, by implication, portrayed as extraordinarily passive recipients of female care. The suggestion is clearly made that the woman, as 'the custodian of the family hearth', is responsible for her husband's sobriety, for his becoming a good father, even for his being an industrious worker. She is urged to show diplomacy in the face of provocation and indulgence to what are portrayed as the inevitable masculine failings; in short, she is to be a mother to her husband as well as to her children.

Conflict and Divorce

The pressure on women to combine their many roles smoothly and efficiently inevitably produces unwanted physical and psychological effects. A survey of women agricultural workers in the Ukraine found that the overwhelming majority complained of fatigue at the end of the working day before beginning the second half of their 'double shift'. Nearly 80 percent of these women said that they found it difficult, and at times very difficult, to cope with their workload at home and in their jobs, a finding supported by surveys of women in other sectors of the economy. In an unpublished dissertation one prominent writer on the role of women in the economy has blamed overwork as a cause of increasing psychological strain on women which has contributed to the falling birthrate, marital breakdown and child neglect. A writer on divorce has noted that, 'discord between spouses often results from placing on a woman full responsibilities at work and at the same time expecting her to be a good housewife', an opinion supported by letters to the press on the subject.[69] The rising divorce rate has become a source of concern to those in government who see a stable family as essential if the birthrate is to rise.

The divorce rate in rural areas is far lower than in the towns; although well over a third of the Soviet population lives in the countryside, only one divorce in six is granted to a rural couple. During the 1970s, however, the rate of increase in divorce has been significantly higher in the countryside than in the cities.[70] Social pressure in small rural communities does much to militate against divorce and, for women especially, chances of remarriage are considerably lower than in the towns. It is significant, therefore, that the majority of divorce petitions are brought by women and, of these, over 40 percent state the husband's alcoholism as the reason for requesting dissolution of the marriage. One survey of rural divorce has indicated that in the majority of cases marital breakdown was in some way connected with heavy drinking by men.[71]

Though bouts of drunkenness are by no means a new phenomenon in the countryside, the pattern of drinking appears to have changed a great deal. Orgies of universal drunkenness were a feature of traditional Russian peasant festivals, especially those which marked the end of periods of heavy agricultural work. Today heavy drinking is no longer confined to occasions of mass celebration but takes place steadily throughout the year and forms for many men a principal leisure activity. It is not difficult to imagine the effect on relationships within the family of such an attitude to alcohol. Though domestic violence receives very little publicity in the Soviet press, it is clear from the occasional report and from the importance attached by women activists to combating drunkenness that it is by no means unknown in Soviet villages.[72]

The sale of alcohol is strictly controlled by law in the USSR yet it is evident that supply is rarely a problem in rural areas. Not only is home-distilling a frequent practice, but wines and spirits are often sold in state shops in a manner which contravenes the law. Over the last decade complaints by rural women to the press about illegal alcohol sales have become a regular feature. Women complain that, whilst local shops are empty of essential household items, they often carry plentiful supplies of alcohol which can be bought on credit at any hour of the day or night.

This seemingly puzzling state of affairs stems from the fact that targets in the five-year plans for shop trading are set by monetary value and it is thus considerably easier to fulfil the plan by selling expensive items such as alcohol rather than the more mundane products required in the running of a home. The immediate results of this practice are the accumulation of large debts by many men and the consequent family rows on pay day.[73] Women's complaints to local officials often fall on deaf ears and are only answered following the intervention of the press. It seems clear that women are becoming increasingly aggrieved at what they see as official insensitivity to the misery which the drink problem causes. A recent letter to *Krest'yanka* about the effects of the opening of a new public bar in a rural community in Belorussia is typical:

> Until this drinking establishment appeared it was a bit quieter in our village. What did they build it for? Was it to make drunkards of our husbands? If that was it, then it has successfully achieved its mission. . . . The bar is flourishing but the money can't be found to build a nursery school, and many women who would like to go to work are obliged to sit at home with the children.[74]

When the failure to take the problem seriously is coupled with indifference to women's own needs, a complaint to a national magazine is often seen as the only way to combat local inertia.

The traditional conservatism of country-dwellers on the question of divorce makes itself felt in cases involving marital infidelity. It is a commonly held belief in the countryside that a marriage should not be broken up because one of the partners has fallen in love with someone else. In letters to the press many women express the view that responsibility toward's one's children should take precedence over a search for personal happiness. The writers often make it clear that their opinion results from personal experience and is adhered to despite their evident distress:

> We met in the fields. A middle-aged man got down from a tractor and asked me for a drink of water. That was all. But he fell in love with me and started to follow me around. We both have families. The whole village began to talk about it. I won't pretend that I love my husband. It probably wasn't love at all but just pity when we decided to unite our lives. But now there's no escape for me. I have to live for the children. My friends tell me, 'you'll live, you'll get used to it, you'll love.' No! My heart aches and loves someone else. How can this have happened? Who's to blame? Can it really be that hot July day and that glass of water?[75]

Surveys of rural opinion have shown that, in circumstances such as these, rural inhabitants are far less likely to condone the break-up of a marriage than are city-dwellers, with women more frequently opposed to divorce than men. It is clear, however, that younger people in the villages are less inclined to adopt hard and fast moral rules than their parents' generation and display sympathy for those who face difficult personal decisions.[76] Yet for people who live in small villages fear of public censure remains a major deterrent to anyone contemplating an extramarital affair, as this account by a woman school teacher who left her husband for another man demonstrates:

> He and I have had to put up with a lot of unpleasantness. People look askance at us, there's no way to avoid it in our village—this is where you really envy townspeo-

ple! His wife is ready to pounce on me like a tigress, after all, we work together. My husband calls me obscene names and of course my children and pupils are all around. . . . How do you endure this sort of thing! . . . I know that there are sure to be readers who will write about family duty, moral rules and so on. I too am all for a strong, healthy family where mutual understanding, respect and love reign, where joy and hardships come equally, where there are no lies or betrayals. But if for years on end there has been none of this and there is only an outward show of real relationships—then, there is no family![77]

In marked contrast to the peasant family of the past, research has shown that young women in the countryside today are often better educated than their husbands. As a result they are no longer prepared to accept the standards of family life experienced by their mothers and grandmothers.[78] As women's expectations of marriage increase, there is every indication that the rate of divorce in rural areas will continue to rise.

In its anxiety to raise the birthrate, the state is putting pressure on women with heavy commitments at work and in the home to have more children. At the same time, little effort is being made to challenge the apathy and inertia of men within the family. Inevitably, many women clearly resent the burdens placed upon them and see the restriction of their family size as the only way to obtain a manageable workload. For rural women, the growing readiness to air their grievances marks a decisive break with the past. It seems improbable that women who are demanding nursery schools and consumer services and expressing their concern at the quality of personal relationships will respond positively to the current wave of pro-natalist propaganda. Without a radical change in men's attitudes towards their wives and children, the aims of the state and the behaviour of women in family life seem likely to remain at loggerheads.

Migration to the Cities

In many areas of the USSR the characteristic response of the young to rural conditions is a move to the town. Men and women alike are seeking a higher standard of living and a different lifestyle from that of their parents. Until relatively recently, migrants from the villages to the towns across the Soviet Union have been predominantly men. Now, however, in the most developed areas of the country migration is higher amongst young women.[79] A major reason for this change lies in the pattern of employment which has developed in agriculture.

As educational standards in the countryside have risen, opportunities for women to find skilled work have remained small. Indeed, as mechanisation has increased in agriculture, the demand for female labour has actually declined. The traditional rural view that machines are not for women has led to a paradoxical situation in which the most prosperous and highly automated farms are often those which offer women the worst conditions of work. Where nothing but manual labour is open to them, women's rate of migration from the countryside is at its highest. As one rural sociologist has concluded, 'The prevailing division of labour between men and women in agriculture limits the productive activity of women collective farmers, fosters dissatisfaction with their work, lowers their productivity and opposes the interests of society.'[80]

Surveys of the plans of school-leavers have shown that girls consider work with agricultural machinery to be closed to them and regard work outside agriculture as highly attractive. Girls are encouraged in their wish to study for such occupations by their mothers. Far from wishing to see their daughters settle nearby them in the village, it is clear that many mothers have high aspirations for their children which reflect their own dissatisfaction with agricultural work:

> Her father and I have spent our whole lives in muck and filth, let Zina do some
> other work. There's nothing for her to do in the country. . . . But if she wants to,
> then we're not against it. She can sit in an office, she can learn book-keeping by all
> means.

Such a comment is said to be characteristic of many older unskilled women in the countryside.[81]

The rigid division of labour in agriculture has, in many regions, led to a severe demographic imbalance in the working population under the age of 30. Where unmarried young men far outnumber eligible women, it is proving difficult to retain a stable workforce of trained machine operators on the farms. The 'bride problem', as it has become known, is obliging farm managers and local party officials to listen seriously to women's demands for better conditions and the provision of skilled work. As one state farm director put it, 'This is now the number one problem . . . and we won't get it off the agenda until we create good working and living conditions for women.'[82] The effect of high rates of female migration has been to bring issues affecting rural women to the forefront of debates on the future of agriculture. Where there is a lack of childcare facilities, adequate consumer services and, above all, skilled work in acceptable conditions, women in ever larger numbers are refusing to remain on the land.

In recent years planners have attempted to keep young women in the countryside by opening subsidiary industrial units on the farms and expanding services as a means of providing attractive employment. Some farms have diversified, for example by introducing fur-farming or bee-keeping, in an effort to provide women with productive work. Others have revived traditional peasant crafts on a commercial basis to supply souvenirs for the tourist trade. Yet, as at least one economist has pointed out, subsidiary industries would become considerably less profitable if every farm were to see them as the answer to the problem of female employment. Other warning voices have observed that, to see the development of the service sector as the answer, as many do, is to forget the Marxian tenet that only the active involvement of women in production can ensure economic and social equality between the sexes.[83]

The many local approaches to the provision of skilled work for rural women are at one in their assumption that men are the central figures in agriculture. Rural attitudes towards women and technology have proved to be so entrenched that farm managers rarely consider the recruitment of women into work on machines as a serious option. Government campaigns to tackle this pronounced bias against women machine operators had a marked lack of success during the 1970s. One reason for their failure lies no doubt in the ambivalence of official images of women presented in the popular press. As journalists have attempted to combat the prejudices which keep women off machines, they have simultaneously released a stream of pronatalist propaganda which has reinforced traditional notions of femininity. It seems unlikely, therefore, that great strides will be made in promoting equal opportunities on the land as long as boosting the birthrate remains the government's top priority.

For most rural women, sexual inequality remains a fact of life both within the family and in employment. Until widespread efforts are made to tackle discrimination in the workplace and to lighten the workload in the rural home, thousands of young women will continue to see a move to the city as the only means of obtaining the lifestyle they desire.

Notes

1. B. S. Khorev and V. N. Chapek, *Problemy izucheniya migratsii naseleniya* (Moscow, 1978), p. 173.

2. *Narodnoe khozyaistvo SSSR v 1980 g* (Moscow, 1981), p. 7; The rural population stood at 23 percent in the United Kingdom in 1971, 25 percent in Canada in 1976, 27 percent in the United States in 1970 and 30 percent in France in 1968. See United Nations Department of International Economic and Social Affairs, *Demographic Yearbook, Historical Supplement* (New York 1979), pp. 193–202.

3. *Sovetskaya Rossiya* (24 August 1982), p. 2.

4. Yu. V. Arutyunyan, *Mekhanizatory sel'skogo khozyaistva SSSR v 1929–1957 gg.* (Moscow, 1960), p. 59.

5. *Sel'skaya nov'*, no. 8. (1981): 7.

6. M. Fedorova, 'Ispol'zovanie zhenskogo truda v sel'skom khozyaistve', *Voprosy ekonomiki*, no. 12 (1975): 58.

7. *Sel'skaya nov'*, no. 8 (1979): 7.

8. *Krest'yanka*, no. 9 (1978): 5.

9. *Krest'yanka*, no. 4 (1977): 16.

10. Ibid.

11. *Krest'yanka*, no. 1 (1977): 28.

12. *Krest'yanka*, no. 5 (1981): 7.

13. *Itogi vsesoyuznoi perepisi naseleniya 1970 goda*, vol. 6 (Moscow, 1973), pp. 166–242,

14. V. I. Staroverov, *Sotsial'naya struktura sel'skogo naseleniya SSSR na etape razvitogo sotsializma* (Moscow, 1978), p. 235; L. P. Lyashenko, 'Otnoshenie molodezhi k sel'skokhozyaistvennomu trudu', in T. I. Zaslavskaya and V. A. Kalmyk, *Sotsial'no-ekonomicheskoe razvitie sela i migratsiya naseleniya* (Novosibirsk, 1972), p. 146.

15. Fedorova, 'Ispol'zovanie zhenskogo truda', p. 62; *Narodnoe khozyaistvo 1980*, p. 112.

16. L. A. Erem'yan and V. N. Martynova, 'Analiz sostava zhenshchin, zanyatykh v zhivotnovodstve sovkozov', in I. N. Lushchitskii, ed., *Proizvodstvennaya deyatel'nost' zhenshchin i sem'ya* (Minsk, 1972), p. 192.

17. *Narodnoe khozyaistve 1980*, p. 112.

18. *Krest'yanka*, no. 1 (1981): 11; Fedorova, 'Ispol'zovanie zhenskogo truda', p. 15.

19. *Sovetskaya Rossiya* (24 August 1982), p. 2.

20. *Krest'yanka*, no. 10 (1981): 7.

21. *Krest'yanka*, no. 9 (1978): 5; *Krest'yanka*, no. 12 (1978): 4.

22. *Itogi . . . 1970*, vol. 6, p. 166.

23. V. P. Zagrebel'nyi, 'Formirovanie otnoshenii sotsial'nogo ravenstva zhenshchin i muzhchin-kolkhoznikov v usloviyakh razvitogo sotsializma' (Candidate Degree dissertation, Kiev, 1977), p. 61; Lyashenko, 'Otnoshenie molodezhi', pp. 149–51.

24. *Krest'yanka*, no. 3 (1980): 11.

25. *Krest'yanka*, no. 4 (1980): 15; *Krest'yanka*, no. 4 (1981): 14.

26. *Krest'yanka*, no. 8 (1978): 11.

27. *Krest'yanka*, no. 10 (1980): 13–14; *Sel'skaya zhizn'* (15 January 1980), p. 3.

28. *Itogi . . . 1970*, vol. 5, p. 202; *Itogi vsesoyuznoi perepisi naseleniya 1959 goda. SSSR (svodnyi tom)* (Moscow, 1962), p. 108.

29. *Itogi . . . 1970*, vol. 5, pp. 202–94.

30. Z. I. Monich, V. G. Izokh and I. V. Prudnik, *Rabochii klass v strukture sel'skogo naseleniya* (Minsk, 1975), pp. 44–53.

31. L. M. Volynkina, 'Ispol'zovanie zhenskogo truda v kolkhozakh Kostromskoi oblasti' (Candidate Degree dissertation, Moscow, 1976), pp. 126–33.

32. *Nauchno-tekhnicheskii progress i sotsial'nye izmeneniya na sele* (Minsk, 1972), p. 60; *Krest'yanka*, no. 8 (1979): 3.

33. P. A. Zhil'tsov, *Vospitatel'naya rabota v sel'skoi shkole* (Moscow, 1980), pp. 52–56; R. K. Ivanova, *Sblizhenie sotsial'no-ekonomicheskikh uslovii zhizni trudyashchikhsya goroda i sela* (Moscow, 1980), p. 76.

34. *Krest'yanka*, no. 6 (1980): 26; L. G. Borisova, 'Ustoichivost' uchitel'skikh kadrov sela', in Zaslavskaya and Kalmyk, *Sotsial' no-ekonomicheskoe*, pp. 183–85; N. A. Shlapak, 'Zhiznennye plany sel'skoi molodezhi i ikh realizatsiya' (Candidate Degree dissertation abstract, Sverdlovsk, 1967), p. 15.

35. *Narodnoe khozyaistvo 1980*, pp. 285–87; Staroverov, *Sotsial'naya struktura*, pp. 265–66.

36. *Narodnoe khozyaistvo 1980*, pp. 285–87.

37. *Krest'yanka*, no. 11 (1981): 25; Monich et al., *Rabochii klass*, p. 86.

38. *Izvestiya* (26 December 1961), p. 4.

39. *Krest'yanka*, no. 11 (1981): 25.

40. Zagrebel'nyi, 'Formirovanie otnoshenii', p. 100. See also, for example, *Krest'yanka*, no. 8 (1979): 20–21; *Sel'skaya zhizn'* (15 February 1980), p. 1.

41. *Narodnoe khozyaistvo 1980*, p. 31; *Zhenshchiny v SSSR* (Moscow, 1975), p. 92; V. Perevedentsev, *270 millionov* (Moscow, 1982), p. 15.

42. Elaine Elnett, *Historic Origin and Social Development of Family Life in Russia* (New York, 1926), p. 105.

43. *Krest'yanka*, no. 10 (1981): 26.

44. *Krest'yanka*, no. 8 (1981): 32; *Krest'yanka*, no. 2 (1980): 11.

45. *Krest'yanka*, no. 9 (1981): 29; *Krest'yanka*, no. 1 (1982): 28.

46. *Krest'yanka*, no. 10 (1982): 27.

47. *Krest'yanka*, no. 1 (1981): 29.

48. Ivanova, *Sblizhenie*, p. 70; N. A. Medvedev, *Razvitie obshchestvennykh otnoshenii v sovetskoi derevne na sovremennom etape* (Moscow, 1976), p. 129.

49. R. V. Ryvkina, *Obraz zhizni sel'skogo naseleniya* (Novosibirsk, 1979), p. 198.

50. *Literaturnaya gazeta* (24 August 1977), p. 11

51. V. D. Patrushev, ed., *Byudzhet vremeni sel'skogo naseleniya* (Moscow, 1979), pp. 125, 134; G. G. Markova, 'Svobodnoe vremya i razvitie lichnosti zhenshchin-kolkhoznits na sovremennom etape stroitel'stva kommunizma' (Candidate Degree dissertation, Rostov on Don, 1977), pp. 52–62.

52. *Problemy derevni i goroda,* vol. 2 (Tallin, 1979), p. 105.

53. *Literaturnaya gazeta* (17 January 1979), p. 12.

54. *Sel'skaya zhizn'* (28 May 1980), p. 3.

55. Z. A. Yankova and V. D. Shapiro, eds., *Vzaimootnoshenie pokolenii v sem'e* (Moscow, 1977), p. 59.

56. *Krest'yanka,* no. 3 (1980): 23.

57. Yu. G. Serebryakov, *Kul'tura i byt sovremennoi derevni* (Cheboksary, 1977), p. 68.

58. *Literaturnoe obozrenie,* no. 5 (May 1977): 51.

59. *Krest'yanka,* no. 10 (1980): 6.

60. See, for example, *Sel'skaya zhizn'* (18 August 1979), p. 4.

61. *Sel'skaya zhzn'* (14 September 1979), p. 4; *Sel'skaya zhizn'* (19 August 1979), p. 4.

62. *Krest'yanka,* no. 6 (1982): 26.

63. *Zhenshchiny-mekhanizatory* (Moscow, 1979), p. 60; *Sel'skaya zhizn'* (21 October 1979), p. 4.

64. *Sel'skaya nov',* no. 10 (1979): 33

65. M. G. Pankratova, *Sel'skaya sem'ya v SSSR i nekotorye problemy planirovaniya* (Moscow, 1970), p. 4; Zagrebel'nyi, 'Formirovanie otnoshenii', pp. 135, 167; T. D. Ermolenkova, 'Izmenenie sotsial'nogo polozheniya zhenshchiny-krest'yanki v protsesse stroitel'stva sotsializma', *Vestnik Belorusskogo Gosudarstvennogo universiteta imeni V.I. Lenina,* series 3, no. 1 (1973): 56.

66. *Krest'yanka,* no. 1 (1982): 28.

67. *Krest'yanka,* no. 6 (1982): 25.

68. *Krest'yanka,* no. 3 (1982): 27.

69. N. P. Rusanov, ed., *Okhrana truda zhenshchin v sel'skom khozyaistve* (Orel, 1979), p. 73; N. M. Shishkan, 'Sotsial'no-ekonomicheskie problemy zhenskogo truda v usloviyakh razvitogo sotsializma' (Doctoral Degree dissertation abstract, Moscow, 1978), p. 19; Yu. A. Korolev, *Brak i razvod; sovremennye tendentsii* (Moscow, 1978), p. 121; Perevedentsev, *270 millionov,* p. 32.

70. A. G. Volkov, 'Sem'ya kak faktor izmeneniya demograficheskoi situatsii', *Sotsiologicheskie issledovaniya,* no. 1 (1981): 38.

71. *Sotsiologicheskie issledovaniya,* no. 3 (1976): 78; Zagrebel'nyi, 'Formirovanie otnoshenii', p. 171; V. N. Kolbanovskii, ed., *Kollektiv kolkhoznikov* (Moscow, 1970), pp. 215–16.

72. See, for example, *Krest'yanka,* no. 11 (1981): 11; *Krest'yanka,* no. 12 (1979): 20; Yu. Arutyunyan and Yu. Kakhk, *Sotsiologicheskie ocherki o Sovetskoi Estonii* (Tallin, 1979), p. 56.

73. *Krest'yanka,* no. 10 (1979): 27; *Krest'yanka,* no. 7 (1975): 28.

74. *Krest'yanka,* no. 5 (1980): 29.

75. *Krest'yanka,* no. 1 (1982): 28–29.

76. Arutyunyan and Kakhk, *Sotsiologicheskie ocherki,* p. 51.

77. *Krest'yanka,* no. 1 (1982): 29.

78. M. G. Pankratova, *Sel'skaya sem'ya v SSSR—problemy i perspektivy* (Moscow, 1974), p. 10.

79. T. I. Zaslavskaya and I. B. Muchnik, *Sotsial'no-demograficheskoe razvitie sela. Regional'nyi analiz* (Moscow, 1980), p. 109.

80. Zagrebel'nyi, 'Formirovanie otnoshenii', p. 81.

81. *Molodoi Kommunist,* no. 9 (1977): 86.

82. *Krest'yanka,* no. 12 (1978): 5.

83. *Sovetskaya Rossiya* (24 August 1982), p. 2; Volynkina, 'Ispol'zovanie zhenskogo truda', p. 34.

14 / Rural Women and *Glasnost*

SUSAN BRIDGER

Glasnost, *or "openness," is an integral part of Gorbachev's policy of* perestroika
*(restructuring). It is intended to allow for open discussion of all previously censored
aspects of the past and present. In this 1988 article, Susan Bridger takes an early
look at the effects of* glasnost *on the treatment of rural women's problems in the
press. Although the problems of labor and family remained the same—perestroika
had not altered the basic contours of sexual inequality in the rural home or farm—*
glasnost *at least opened up discussion of the plight of farm women. While journalists and scholars debated problems and solutions, ordinary women took advantage of the new policy by airing their grievances in letters to the press. In doing so,
they risked the wrath of local officials who could easily apply pressure and harassment for negative exposure. Many more women, however, expressed their dissatisfaction "with their feet," by continuing to move to the cities. This resolution, as
Bridger suggests, is not a happy one for Soviet agriculture, and until the problems
of rural women are addressed, agriculture will continue to suffer from low productivity and high out-migration among its central labor constituency.*

Some of the most difficult working and living conditions in the USSR are experienced by rural women. Heavy manual labour characterises not only their working
day but much of their domestic life as well. Women predominate in under-mechanised livestock units and in unskilled gang labour on the farms. At home, manual
agricultural work continues on the private plots which are essential in keeping rural
families fed. The lack of mains water supplies and the inadequacy of rural shops and
services further complicate housework and vastly increase women's overall workload.

Yet, if rural women were portrayed as a downtrodden and uncomplaining mass
by commentators on the village in the 1920s, they can no longer be viewed in this
light today. The rural press has not waited for the spur of Gorbachev's policy of
glasnost to act upon rural women's increasingly voluble complaints. Pieces of
investigative journalism prompted by women's letters to the editor have been regular features for many years. Their public exposure of high-handed management and
bureaucratic indifference has undoubtedly encouraged rural women to see the press
as a fruitful avenue for securing improvements in local conditions.

"Rural Women and Glasnost" by Susan Bridger, *Bradford Occasional Papers: Essays in Language,
Literature and Area Studies,* No. 9 (1988), pages 103–116. Copyright © 1988 University of Bradford.
Reprinted by permission.

Nevertheless, the dissatisfaction of rural women with the nature of work on the land is nowhere more graphically displayed than over the migration of young people to the cities. In response to the jobs on offer across much of the European USSR and Siberia, young women rather than men are today the first to reject the countryside in favour of education and work in the city. They are supported in this by mothers who actively encourage them to seize their opportunity to escape the toil of rural life. 'Do you think I've educated her, fed her, clothed her for so many years for nothing? . . . There's no need for her to mess about in muck and filth', runs a typical mother's comment.[1] In their attitudes towards the departure of their daughters from the village, older women regularly betray their distaste for the conditions they have been constrained to endure and make it clear that they expect something better for their children.

The Rural Press and the Policy of *Glasnost*

The changing political climate in the USSR since Mikhail Gorbachev's accession to power has allowed the depth of women's dissatisfaction with rural conditions to emerge more clearly. In line with the rest of the Soviet media the effect of the policy of *glasnost* in the rural press has been striking. Though critical investigative articles are no strangers to magazines such as *Krest'yanka* (Peasant Woman) and *Sel'skaya nov'* (New Countryside), they have frequently appeared in the past in awkward juxtaposition against the standard reporting of successes in production. Now, much of the character of these magazines is changing.

Thoughtful articles from specific rural areas analyse economic and social problems and describe, often with brutal honesty, the conditions faced by women working in livestock and arable farming. Round-table discussions draw together experienced women workers, agriculture ministry officials, sociologists and farm managers. Explanations and pledges are sought from local and national figures in response to women's complaints.

With a proposal to base its first issue of 1988 entirely on readers' requests, *Krest'yanka*'s editors promised a closer dialogue with its readership on issues as diverse as working practices, child psychology and sex—'do you think no-one's interested in the intimate side of family life?' a correspondent demanded. Increasingly forthright consumer articles and published letters attack the lack of basic goods in rural shops and the 'insurmountable problem' of acquiring essential items such as boots and school uniforms.[2] Editors besiege their readers with requests for comments, criticisms and suggestions to open up debate on the pressing problems which face the countryside.

As the new openness unlocks the sealed vaults of the country's Stalinist past, the rural press has begun to make its own contribution to the re-examination of recent history. The December 1987 issue of *Sel'skaya nov'* presented a lengthy interview with three eminent historians whose work on the history of collectivisation had been suppressed during the Brezhnev years and who had themselves been condemned as 'slanderers of collectivisation'. The article, with its discussion of Stalin's role in forced collectivisation, the fate of the dispossessed peasants and the famine of

1932–1933, was promised as the first of a series on the history of the Soviet countryside, for 'a society embarking on an enormous, revolutionary transformation needs the whole truth about its past'.[3]

The extent of the transformation required to establish conditions acceptable to young, educated rural women today can be gauged from the content and tone of recent articles. In the sphere of work, discussion of change is no longer confined to a consideration of economic and organisational questions involving increased automation or the application of new working practices. The acknowledged need for a radical improvement in women's working conditions has begun to focus attention upon a far wider range of social and political issues. Sex discrimination in the workplace, the role of the trade unions and the enforcement of Soviet law have become inescapable questions for those seeking genuine reform.

Women's Work on the Land

The major area of skilled work for women on Soviet farms is animal husbandry, especially dairying. Milking cows was traditionally regarded as a female task in pre-revolutionary Russia. As late as the 1950s, Soviet researchers found that men commonly refused to milk cows even if they required the milk for their own use, on the grounds that this was 'women's work'. Today, men form a small but growing proportion of workers in dairying, concentrated in the most highly mechanised dairy units. Where automation remains rudimentary the old prejudices persist. A report from Tomsk Region in 1986 described how demobilised conscripts were persuaded to staff a dairy unit on their native farm which suffered from low yields and a high turnover of workers. Far from becoming the farm's hope for the future, they all rapidly gave up the work because of the low level of mechanisation, commenting, 'It's obvious that this really isn't a man's job'.[4]

The predominance of manual labour and extremely unsocial hours which characterise dairying on many Soviet farms has led increasing numbers of young women to adopt the view that it is not a woman's job either. Nevertheless, this very heavy and demanding work continues to be seen as the archetypal female occupation on the farms. The three-times-a-day milking routine traditionally employed in dairying leads to an extremely prolonged working day with short breaks between milking sessions where women trail to and fro between home and work: 'In the evenings your house stands unheated. In the day time you've just started the washing when it's time to go back to work. You have to count the minutes'. Even where a two-cycle milking system is in operation, a low level of mechanisation can still prolong the working day in a way which young women find unacceptable. As one experienced dairy woman explained, 'Young dairy women have kept leaving the unit and they'll go on leaving. Who wants to get up at three and four in the morning every day and still be in the unit at midnight?' The high turnover of employees in under-mechanised units compounds existing problems. Where units become permanently short-staffed, the remaining dairy women lose days off and holidays, whilst shift systems which offer a shorter working day cannot be established. Despite the steady automation of dairy units and the gradual introduction of shift systems, dairy women continue to work on average the greatest number of hours per year of any group of employees in Soviet agriculture or industry.[5]

Glasnost has allowed frank descriptions to emerge of exactly what women are expected to endure on dairy units. Some 200,000 dairy women in the USSR still milk exclusively by hand. Reporting from one such unit a journalist recently recorded the explanation of the unit's only young worker of her reasons for staying in such a place. She described her intense love of animals, the talent she had discovered for getting the cows to give higher yields and then added, almost as an afterthought:

> We drag the hay ourselves in winter . . . and we have to wash everything by hand, in cold water. Our hands are all split and cracked and they stink because they get clogged up with manure. There's nothing you can do to stop it. In the mornings your fingers won't move—my husband has to dress me while I just cry. When you're coming back from milking you can't button your coat. It's alright in summer, but in winter the cracks get twice as wide. It brings tears to your eyes!

Small wonder that local schoolgirls responded to the journalist's questions with, 'Be a dairy woman? No, we're not crazy'.[6]

Unlike dairying, driving agricultural machines has never been regarded as women's work in the USSR. Only in wartime did women form a substantial proportion of tractor and combine drivers on the farms; immediately after the war their numbers dropped dramatically and have consistently remained less than 1 percent of the total employed since the 1950s. A campaign to recruit women into this sphere of work, particularly in labour-shortage areas, has been in operation since 1969. It has met with a resounding lack of success. Changes in the law allowing women preferential access to new machines and a range of fringe benefits, together with encouraging articles in the press, have not been enough to combat either unattractive working conditions or the prejudice of those who view the work as a male prerogative. Through the 1980s the numbers of women employed in this work have fallen steadily to a mere 17,000 by 1987.[7]

The rural press chose this same year to replace the familiar success stories from the few women who have made this work their career with an in-depth investigation of the reasons why the job remains out-of-bounds to the mass of rural women. The picture which emerged was not new to readers of Soviet sociological surveys or literature on occupational health. Indeed, much of the information presented had appeared piecemeal in the occasional critical press articles since the mid-1970s. Nevertheless, the lengthy round-table discussions and investigative articles which appeared in 1987 provided a catalogue of woe unprecedented in the popular press. The poor quality design and production of agricultural machinery, related occupational disease, the appalling work organisation leading to excessive overtime and a lack of holidays were chronicled in detail.

Commenting on the state of agricultural machinery during one of these discussions, the trainer of the Soviet ploughing team commented that it was 'simply amazing' that there were still 17,000 women employed in the work. In response, an experienced woman tractor driver remarked, 'No-one makes us choose a "man's job". But just where are the "women's jobs" in the village? I think being a dairy woman is harder than being a machine operator'.[8]

The added ingredient in working on machines, however, which makes the job untenable for most women is overt sex discrimination, taking the form of obstruction and hostility from colleagues and superiors. Women's complaints about male attitudes have surfaced in the press at regular intervals since the mid-1970s. In August 1987, *Sel'skaya nov'* based a particularly detailed piece on an extremely long and pitiful letter from a recently retired woman who had responded in 1973 to the campaign to recruit women tractor drivers. Her story was one of constant harassment from male colleagues, managers and officials. Resentment at her receipt of a new tractor, as provided for under the 1969 law, led to regular acts of sabotage of the machine by the men she worked with, a rising tide of hostility in which the farm management and trade union officials colluded, depriving her of sick pay, bonuses and, ultimately, of half her pension. In conclusion she wrote:

> I often wonder now whether I should have responded to the slogan, 'Women—to the tractors!' It doesn't take much to come out with a slogan, but creating proper conditions is a different matter. I often used to be invited to speak in schools, to talk about how interesting it was to work on a tractor. We've got to carry out propaganda, they'd say, get the young people, especially the girls, to stay on the collective farm. But I used to refuse: I don't want to deceive young people but to tell them the truth—but that was no good. That's not what's expected of people who go into schools to carry out propaganda.[9]

Since the 1930s, women have habitually been seen as a reserve army to be pulled in and out of work driving agricultural machinery as demand dictated. As a result, there has never been any shortage of commentators to take the view that, as conditions for women in this area are difficult, it would be better to avoid employing them altogether. In this, another form of chauvinism comes into play, as a round-table discussion in *Krest'yanka* revealed with this comment from an official of the agricultural machine production ministry: 'Carrying out our chivalrous duty towards women means working so that they don't have to sit at the wheel of a tractor'. The eminent rural sociologist, Vladimir Staroverov, was quick to respond.

> If we're going to talk about 'chivalrous duty', I regard that as being about providing women with good machines, not exploiting women's enthusiasm by asking them to work on tractors which are hard work for a man, knight that he is. . . . In republics with a high level of mechanisation, the proportion of women working in agriculture is considerably lower than where the level of mechanisation is low because manual work is 'women's work'. Is it really easier to work manually than on a machine? We've just completed a survey in Moldavia. There it's mostly vegetables and orchards, women's jobs—because it's hard to mechanise them. Who smokes tobacco? The men. But it's the women in white headscarves who grow it. Along come your machines and it's 'Move up, girls, here I am, your knight, come to replace you. Don't ask me what you're going to do or what you'll earn. That's your problem. Machines are a man's business'.[10]

As Staroverov indicates, agricultural modernisation has little to offer women as long as technology is viewed as a male sphere in the countryside. Where machines replace traditionally female manual labour in arable farming and horticulture, women are rarely trained to operate them and are relegated to subsidiary manual tasks. In

consequence, the status of women's work in agriculture is increasingly depressed as women are concentrated in unskilled, low-paid jobs. It is a situation which is scarcely calculated to encourage young women to stay on the farms.

Today, 98 percent of manual workers in arable farming, market gardening and fruit farming are women. Women also form the vast majority of labourers in other areas of farming such as animal husbandry. Their work is monotonous, exhausting and highly seasonal, resulting in lengthy periods of unemployment through the winter months. At the National Women's Conference held in Moscow in early 1987, Valentina Tereshkova, the former cosmonaut and long-time head of the Committee for Soviet Women spoke at length about women's working conditions in the USSR. Her speech included an example of problems faced by agricultural labourers:

> This is what women workers from the village of Osipovka, Buryat Autonomous Republic, wrote to the Committee for Soviet Women. 'Our work is backbreaking. We have to move sacks of mixed feed weighing 50 to 60 kilos each. We carry out the manure from the dairy unit manually.' Letters like this come from other regions of the country. How long will women have to work in these conditions?[11]

It is a significant symbol of political change that the head of the Committee whose title has for so long seemed an unfortunate misnomer should at last speak out on behalf of those she purports to represent. Nevertheless, what she failed to say about the case quoted above is illustrative both of the limits of *glasnost* and of the fundamental nature of the problems to be tackled if the 'revolutionary transformation' of Soviet society is to be achieved. For the work undertaken by the women who wrote to Tereshkova is almost certainly in contravention of Soviet legislation on health and safety at work. The law of December 1981 states that women must not be required to lift a weight of more than 15 kilos. If weights are carried throughout a working shift the maximum load at any one time must not exceed 10 kilos. In the same way, the excessive compulsory overtime and the lack of holidays complained of both by dairy women and women machine operators represent a habitual disregard for Soviet employment legislation in the interests of production. As one prizewinning woman tractor driver described her far from atypical working life: 'You work in the field from 6 in the morning until 10 at night, you can't even go to the cinema, relax on a Sunday, get out on the river or in the woods. I haven't known what a day off is in 15 years of work. I've never once had a summer holiday'.[12]

Soviet Law and the Role of the Trade Unions

The exploitation of women workers by farms seeking to meet economic targets relies both on women's ignorance of their rights and on the difficulties involved in the enforcement of legal provisions. The former question, though not discussed in Tereshkova's speech, was taken up by a delegate to this same conference, a regional judge from the Ukraine at another of *Krest'yanka*'s round-table discussions:

> At meetings with women or with managers of factories and farms I sometimes ask, 'Whose consent do you have to get before you can dismiss a pregnant woman from work?' People start to guess, come out with the most varied suggestions. But they

shouldn't have to guess, they should know: no-one has the right to dismiss a pregnant woman, not on anyone's orders. What does this example show us? Legal illiteracy. I'm not talking about knowing articles of the Criminal Code, but about a familiarity with the law in areas which affect us all. People who know their rights feel more socially significant, more confident in life. They are aware that the state is behind them, protecting their interests. . . . Women bring their problems to me, not in my capacity as a judge, but as chairperson of the women's soviet. It often turns out that they need legal advice. Tears and despair stem from this ignorance of their rights in conflicts at work, over housing, divorce, division of property, establishment of paternity and so on.[13]

Not all members of the Soviet legal profession share this woman's enthusiasm. As described above, positive discrimination enshrined in the 1969 law on women machine operators meets with far from universal approval in the countryside. Women's right to be assigned new machines as they become available is a particular bone of contention. A lawyer working for the local agricultural organisation in a district of Saratov Region expressed his horror at the possible consequence of such a law being put into practice: 'Can you imagine what it would be like if women knew about their right to the best machines?!' Yet it is difficult to imagine that many women machine operators in the USSR can still be ignorant of this particular provision of the law when so much publicity has been given to it in the press over the years. It seems more likely that the women in this lawyer's district who complained to the press about the quality of the machines they were assigned, amongst a range of other common problems, simply saw no other way to achieve the desired result.[14]

The question of informing people of their rights and enforcing employment legislation goes far beyond the thorny problem of sex discrimination touched on in this particular example. For it reopens the debate on the role of the trade unions in a socialist society and almost inevitably raises the spectre of workers organising to secure their entitlements under law. Its implications for farms managers and local officials must make many share the preference of the Saratov lawyer for a statute book which remains a work of fiction.

In any society, individuals who take on their employers to remedy injustice or malpractice at work may find themselves in an extremely vulnerable position. In the Soviet countryside, farm managers, trade union representatives and local Party officials are almost certain to be at one in viewing the demands of the plan as paramount. An individual who complains therefore runs the risk of being seen as a nuisance whose actions obstruct the smooth running of the farm's affairs. Press articles prompted by readers' letters make it plain that management, in its efforts to maintain the status quo, is able to make life extremely uncomfortable for individuals seeking change. Employees who find that local Party and trade union officials have closed ranks with management may ultimately discover that a plea for press intervention is their only effective form of defence.

Articles investigating the complaints of farm employees not infrequently paint a depressing picture of authoritarian management stifling criticism by victimising the workers concerned. This no doubt explains why letters to the press are often anonymous. Though journalists regularly express their disapproval of such a practice, the situations described in their articles make the choice of anonymity understandable.[15] The overriding demands of plan fulfilment which make local officials reluctant to act against oppressive and illegal management practices serves to concentrate considerable power in the hands of farm managers. The shared concern over production which may lead to an uncritical support of management by trade unions and the local Party apparatus is not, of course, an exclusively rural phenomenon. Yet the atmosphere conveyed by press stories suggests that its results may seem particularly oppressive in the countryside where employees effectively live at their place of work and where changing one's job may also involve leaving one's native village. Taken to its logical extreme, the abuse of managerial authority and its tacit approval by local officials in the interests of plan fulfilment is able to produce a phenomenon as spectacular as the Adilov case, publicised in the Soviet press.[16]

At a far more mundane and commonplace level, journalists' stories regularly reveal why an appeal to the national press is such an important channel for individual grievances where power is abused. An example which illustrates the point particularly well appeared in *Sel'skaya molodezh'* (Rural Youth) in August 1987. The article reported the positive responses of local Party and Komsomol committees in Kalinin Region to an earlier investigative piece prompted by young dairy women's complaints about their working conditions. As the second article was being prepared for publication, however, the editors received a letter from a young man on the same farm describing both the consequences of their intervention and the treatment he himself had received for criticising the farm's management. The original article, the writer of the letter explained, had created enormous interest on the farm and received the support of all its employees. Many had been able to give further examples of the problems described when talking amongst themselves. Instead of conducting an open discussion of the article and meeting the employees' criticisms, however, the farm's management condemned the magazine outright for producing a farrago of lies and half-truths. Subsequently, pressure was brought to bear on workers who had been interviewed by the magazine until they retracted what they had said. The writer of the letter then described how his own criticisms of conditions on the farm had provoked strenuous efforts on the management's part to get rid of him. Each time he complained to local Party officials the farm's director dismissed him from work; each time the dismissal was found to be unfair by the courts and he was reinstated. Finally, the state farm director triumphed after dismissing the writer for the seventh time:

> Using his connections, Mel'nikov put pressure . . . on the People's Court which considered my complaint of unfair dismissal . . . and the final dismissal was found to be fair. Many of the documents had been rewritten, orders had been changed, essential witnesses were 'worked on'. . . . Under the personal supervision of the director, all the documentation supporting (my complaints) was destroyed. . . . Nothing has changed for the better since your correspondent came. There is no *perestroika*, no *glasnost* here[17]

As this article demonstrates, press intervention does not always work miracles. The power of an appeal to the national press—effectively an agent of the Party centre—has its limits, as editors tacitly admit when follow-up stories describe a lack of action on the problems which gave rise to a complaint. During 1987, journalists began more frequently to issue warnings that recalcitrant managements would be kept under observation until improvements were secured.[18]

For the individuals concerned, however, the use of the press in this way remains an extremely unwieldy method of seeking redress: the consideration of their initial complaint by the newspaper or magazine concerned, the dispatch of a journalist to their district, the publication of an article holding oppressive management up to public opprobrium, a response to press intervention by local officialdom and, hopefully, the ultimate righting of wrongs all takes time and, in the interim, may expose the complainant to a good deal of unpleasantness. The fact that such a method is employed so regularly testifies to the difficulty of finding a solution on the spot.

It would be misleading to suggest that despotic management is the rule in Soviet agriculture. Yet it cannot be denied that a system which makes the fulfilment of production targets the prime interest of both management and unions is open to abuse and may leave individuals without an effective local channel for resolving grievances. The inability or unwillingness of the trade unions to protect their members' interests is most clearly demonstrated by the habitual disregard of employment legislation on the farms, especially on the question of overtime and holidays.

The problems involved in improving rural working conditions have led to a growing questioning in the press of the dual role of the trade unions in the Soviet workplace. The journalist reporting on the harassment of the woman tractor driver described above, for example, concluded her article with an attack on the 'total identity' of trade union officials with the management line, commenting, 'For decades the trade unions have in fact patterned their behaviour on an unconditional support of managers. They have seen everything, including conflicts with ordinary workers, through the managers' eyes'.[19] In a similar vein, the head of the national body concerned with women's employment protection observed:

> Rural trade unions are heavily in the workers' debt—for the fact that they work from dawn till dusk, that two-shift working is not introduced, that flexible shifts have been forgotten and that days off and holidays are frequently compensated for in cash rather than giving people necessary rest. In my opinion, occupational disease amongst rural women is caused above all by the shortcomings of the local trade unions. The law provides every possibility for organising proper working conditions. They only have to make use of it.[20]

It would appear that on many Soviet farms, the trade unions' prescribed role of assisting management to meet economic targets effectively incapacitates them as defenders of the workers they represent.

Migration and *Glasnost*

As long as rural women continued to tolerate bad conditions and management riding roughshod over their rights, this challenge to the established role of the trade unions in agriculture could always be put off to another day. In the words of a recent article, 'We all love heroes. . . . There is a breed of people who are devoted. It's they who have probably propped up agriculture until now.' Though older women struggle on in prevailing conditions, they have made it plain that they do not see the needless self-sacrifice imposed on the farms as a fit road for their daughters to travel: 'Better to sweep the streets in town or sew on buttons in a factory than to stay here. You can't work, you can't earn, you can't feel like a human being'.[21]

Women's discouragement of their children from repeating their experience and the mass abandonment of the village by girls leaving school across much of the European USSR and Siberia has created severe and increasingly urgent problems for the farms as their workforce ages and dwindles. As young women leave, dairy units become chronically under-staffed and the turnover of male machine operators becomes abnormally high: where eligible women are scarce, young men cannot be prevented from taking their skills elsewhere. Men who remain on the farms often find themselves unmarried well into their late twenties, an undesirable phenomenon in a country anxious to raise its birthrate.

Attempts at solving the problem of keeping young people on the land range from the introduction of subsidiary industries on the farms specifically for the employment of women to the operation of a form of marriage bureau for single rural people through the columns of the national press. None of this, however, resolves the major problem of providing skilled agricultural work in acceptable conditions for young women leaving rural schools. For this to be achieved, the fruits of *glasnost* will need to be seen far beyond the pages of the press, out in the dairy units and trade union committees of Soviet farms. Until they are, the loudest noise that rural women make will continue to come from their departing feet.

Notes

1. *Molodoi kommunist,* 9 (1977): 86.

2. *Krest'yanka,* 8 (1987): 27 and 10 (1987): 5; *Sel'skaya nov',* 9 (1987): 16–17.

3. *Sel'skaya nov',* 12 (1987): 14–17.

4. *Komsomol'skaya pravda,* 23 December 1986, p. 1. See also Susan Bridger, *Women in the Soviet Countryside* (Cambridge, 1987), pp. 58–59.

5. *Sel'skaya molodezh',* 9 (1987): 26; *Krest'yanka,* 1 (1987): 17; *Lyudi v gorode i na sele* (Moscow, 1978), p. 64.

6. *Sel'skaya molodezh',* 9 (1987): 26.

7. *Krest'yanka,* 8 (1987): 15; Bridger, 30–39.

8. *Krest'yanka,* 8 (1987): 16.

9. *Sel'skaya nov',* 8 (1987): 9–11.

10. *Krest'yanka,* 8 (1987): 16–17.

11. *Izvestiya,* 1 February 1987, p. 3.

12. E. B. Gruzdeva and E. S. Chertikhina, *Trud i byt sovetskikh zhenshchin* (Moscow, 1983), p. 66; *Krest'yanka,* 8 (1987): 17.

13. *Krest'yanka,* 4 (1987): 4–5.

14. *Krest'yanka,* 3 (1987): 22–23.

15. *Krest'yanka,* 9 (1987): 4 and 1 (1988): 4. See also *Sel'skaya zhizn',* 2 (August 1979): 3.

16. *The Guardian,* 21 January 1988, p. 1. Akhmadjan Adilov, former director of a prosperous farm complex in Uzbekistan, was arrested in 1985. It is alleged that his abuse of power culminated in the physical ill-treatment, imprisonment and murder of employees.

17. *Sel'skaya molodezh'*, 8 (1987): 16–17.
18. Ibid.; *Krest'yanka*, 9 (1987): 4.
19. *Sel'skaya nov'*, 8 (1987): 11.
20. *Krest'yanka*, 8 (1987): 18.
21. *Sel'skaya nov'*, 9 (1987): 26 and 8 (1987): 9.